Third Edition

COMMUNITY POLICING
AND
PROBLEM SOLVING
Strategies and Practices

KENNETH J. PEAK
University of Nevada, Reno

RONALD W. GLENSOR
Reno, Nevada, Police Department

Upper Saddle River, New Jersey 07458

Library of Congress Cataloging-in-Publication Data

Peak, Kenneth J., 1947–
    Community policing and problem solving: strategies and practices / Kenneth J. Peak,
Ronald W. Glensor.—3rd ed.
        p. cm.
    Includes bibliographical references and index.
    ISBN 0-13-091270-0
        1. Community policing. 2. Crime prevention—United States—Citizen participation. 3.
Police administration. 4. Police-community relations. 5. Community policing—United
States. 6. Police administration—United States. I. Glensor, Ronald W. II. Title.

HV7936.C83 P43 2002
363.2′3—dc21   2001021682

Publisher: Jeff Johnston
Executive Editor: Kim Davies
Production Editor: Linda B. Pawelchak
Production Liaison: Barbara Marttine Cappuccio
Director of Production and Manufacturing: Bruce Johnson
Managing Editor: Mary Carnis
Manufacturing Manager: Cathleen Petersen
Art Director: Cheryl Asherman
Cover Design Coordinator: Miguel Ortiz
Cover Designer: Scott Garrison
Cover Image: © Tracey L. Williams / Courtesy of Somerset County Police
    Academy, North Branch, NJ, Dr. Richard Celeste, Deputy Chief, Executive Director
Marketing Manager: Ramona Sherman
Editorial Assistant: Sarah Holle
Composition: Lithokraft II
Printing and Binding: R.R. Donnelley & Sons

Pearson Education LTD., *London*
Pearson Education Australia PTY. Limited, *Sydney*
Pearson Education Singapore, Pte. Ltd.
Pearson Education North Asia Ltd., *Hong Kong*
Pearson Education Canada Ltd., *Toronto*
Pearson Educación de Mexico, S.A. de C.V.
Pearson Education—Japan, *Tokyo*
Pearson Education Malaysia, Pte. Ltd.

10 9 8 7 6 5 4 3 2 1
ISBN 0-13-091270-0

To the next generation:
Chelsea, Taylor, Madison,
Charli Jo, and Haley.

K. J. P.

To my wife, Kristy, and children,
Breanne and Ronnie, for their
continuing love, support,
and patience.

R. W. G.

CONTENTS

PREFACE   **xv**

ABOUT THE AUTHORS   **xx**

FOREWORD   **xxiii**

THE EVOLUTION OF POLICING: PAST WISDOM AND FUTURE DIRECTIONS   **1**

Introduction   1

British Contributions   2

Policing Comes to America   3
*Early beginnings 3 ◇ Movement toward reform 9 ◇
The professional crime fighter 12*

The Changing Wisdom of Policing   17
*More recent studies of police work 17 ◇ Viewing "sacred cow"
methods with caution 18 ◇ Time for a new approach 20
◇ The community problem solving Era 21*

Rewriting Police Agency History   24

SUMMARY ◇ NOTES

◇2◇

A Nation in Flux: Changing People, Crime, and Policing　　**29**

Introduction   29

The Changing Face of America   30

Demographics and jobs: A bifurcated society 30 ◇ Coming to America: Immigration trends 31 ◇ The graying of America: Implications and concerns 32 ◇ A generational divide 33 ◇ Haves and have-nots 34

The Changing Nature of Crime   34

Crime in America: Reasons for its decline 34 ◇ The juvenile crime debate 38 ◇ Crime accelerators: Guns, drugs, and alcohol 41 ◇ The new challenge: Computer crime 43 ◇ The impact of prison and jail populations 43

Fear of Crime   44

Effects of crime and disorder 44

Significance for the Police   47

Keeping neighborhoods safe 47

Summary ◇ Notes

◇3◇

Attending to the "Customer": Community Oriented Government　　**51**

Introduction   51

Citizens as Clients and Customers   52

Individualism versus clienthood 52

Communitarianism and Volunteerism   53

Citizens fulfilling responsibilities 53 ◇ Volunteerism in action 54

Building Partnerships   55

Improving Customer Service: Total Quality Management   59

Definition and rationalization 59 ◇ Principal elements 64

Use of Surveys   66

Criminal Justice: Organizations in Need of Attention   66

Wanted: A different "MO" 67 ◇ Rewarding failure 68 ◇ Borrowing ideas from business 69

Partners in Community Justice   69

Prosecution 70 ◇ Defense 71 ◇ Courts 71 ◇ Corrections 72

Some Illustrations of Community Oriented Government   73

Mason, Ohio: Reinventing government and customer service 74 ◇ Lawrence, Massachusetts: TQM and focusing on customer needs 75

Other Examples   75

Closure   77

Summary ◇ Notes

4

COMMUNITY ORIENTED POLICING AND PROBLEM SOLVING: "COPPS"   **80**

Introduction   80
Community Policing   81
  Basic principles 81 ◇ *Differences in community policing
  and traditional policing 82*
Problem Oriented Policing   84
  Early beginnings 84 ◇ *Basic principles 86*
  A broader role for the street officer 88 ◇ *Testing problem
  oriented policing 89* ◇ *"S.A.R.A.": The problem solving
  process 90*
A Collaborative Approach: "COPPS"   97
  Basic principles 97 ◇ *A definition and illustration 99*
Crime Analysis Tools   103
  Analyzing crime: Definition, functions, and types 103
  ◇ Crime mapping 107 ◇ *Police reports 110* ◇ *Call for
  service analysis 110* ◇ *Surveys 116* ◇ *Software for COPPS 117*
  *◇ Contemporary community policing activities of
  local agencies 118*
SUMMARY ◇ NOTES

5

CRIME PREVENTION: FOR SAFE COMMUNITIES   **122**

Introduction   122
A Brief History   123
Today's Shifting Emphasis   126
Needed: Community Involvement   128
Crime Prevention and COPPS   130
Crime Prevention through Environmental Design   133
Situational Crime Prevention   136
Issues and Problems   143
  Implementation 143 ◇ *Displacement of crime 144*
  ◇ Evaluation of results 146
What Works and Does Not Work in Crime Prevention   146
  What prevents or reduces crime 146 ◇ *What does not
  appear to be successful 147* ◇ *What holds promise 148*
Six Safer Cities and Their Pathbreaking Work   149
SUMMARY ◇ NOTES

6

PLANNING AND IMPLEMENTATION: TRANSLATING IDEAS INTO ACTION   **157**

Introduction   157
Strategic Thinking   158
Strategic Planning   158
    Basic elements 158 ◇ The planning cycle 160
    ◇ Environmental scanning: A needs assessment 161
The Planning Document: A Guide for Implementation   162
    Elements and issues 162
Implementing COPPS   165
    Departmentwide versus experimental district 165 ◇ Principal
    components of successful implementation 167
Tying It All Together   175
    An example: Montgomery County, Maryland 175
General Obstacles   182
Ten Ways to Undermine COPPS   184
SUMMARY ◇ NOTES

7

FROM RECRUIT TO CHIEF: CHANGING THE AGENCY CULTURE   **189**

Introduction   189
Change in Organizations: A Formula   190
Requirements for Planned Change   191
    Radical versus gradual change 191 ◇ Avoiding the
    "bombshell" technique 193 ◇ Changing organizational
    values 193
The Prevailing Police Culture   194
    Debilitating beliefs 194
Ye Olde Management Style   196
    The bureaucracy of policing 196
Changing to COPPS   197
    Potential for resistance and conflict 197 ◇ "We're too busy
    to change" 198
Roles of Key Leaders   199
    The chief executive as change agent 199 ◇ Middle
    managers 200 ◇ First-line supervisors 201
    ◇ "Recapturing officers' time" for problem solving 204
Role of the Rank-and-File Officers   208
    Change begins with recruitment 208 ◇ Ownership:
    A "prescription for change" 209

Case Studies   210
  Camden, New Jersey: Build a blueprint 211 ◇ Hayward,
  California: Hiring, training, and evaluating personnel 211
  ◇ Broken Arrow, Oklahoma: Beat a path toward change 212
SUMMARY ◇ NOTES

◇ 8 ◇

TRAINING FOR COPPS: APPROACHES AND CHALLENGES   216

Introduction   216
COPPS Training Nationally   217
Training Police Officers, Generally   217
Determining Training Needs   219
Imparting New Knowledge and Retaining Learned Skills   220
  The recruit academy 221 ◇ Field training officers 222
  ◇ In-service 222 ◇ Roll call 223 ◇ Specialized training 225
Training Technologies   227
The Training Program   228
  Purpose, objectives, components 228 ◇ Other training
  considerations 240
A Sample Training Program   245
SUMMARY ◇ NOTES

◇ 9 ◇

POLICE IN A DIVERSE SOCIETY   249

Introduction   249
Police and Minorities: A History of Conflict   250
  Changing laws and civil unrest 250 ◇ Police–public views
  toward each other 252
Minorities and the Criminal Justice System   253
  Sources of tension: Racial profiling and other field tactics 253
  ◇ Is there systematic discrimination against minorities? 257
Improving Police–Minority Relations   258
  Complicating factors, possible solutions 258
What COPPS Can Do   259
  Confronting the issues 259 ◇ Understanding cultural
  customs, differences, problems 260
Employing a Diverse Police Department   264

What Works: Successful Initiatives 265
  Chelsea, Massachusetts, and conflict intervention 265
  ◇ *Serving immigrant victims: Philadelphia and Jackson
  Heights 266* ◇ *Other approaches: A museum tour,
  a unique citizens' academy, a helping hand with
  naturalization 267*
Responding to Hate Crimes 268
On the Street: Some Perplexing Scenarios 268
SUMMARY ◇ NOTES

NEW STRATEGIES FOR OLD PROBLEMS: COPPS ON THE BEAT   276

Introduction 276
Drug Violations 277
Gangs 279
Special Populations and Problems 282
  The mentally ill 283 ◇ *The homeless 284*
  ◇ *Alcohol-related crimes 286*
Domestic Violence 288
School Violence 290
Rental Properties and Neighborhood Disorder 292
Prostitution 296
Other Selected Problems 297
  Cruising 297 ◇ *False alarms 299* ◇ *Teen hangouts
  in video arcades 299*
SUMMARY ◇ NOTES

THE "DEVIL'S ADVOCATE": ADDRESSING CONCERNS WITH COPPS   306

Introduction 306
The Issues 307
  Concern and response 1: Is there a true "community"? 307
  ◇ *Concern and response 2: Is this a proper role for
  the police? 309* ◇ *Concern and response 3: Does the concept
  violate the political neutrality of police? 311* ◇ *Concern and
  response 4: Can COPPS work when it cannot cure the
  underlying societal problems of crime and disorder? 312*
  ◇ *Concern and response 5: Does the concept require*

too much officer discretion? 313 ◇ *Concern and response 6: Is this simply a faddish, costly gimmick? 314* ◇ *Concern and response 7: Do officers possess the intellectual capacity and temperament to sustain the concept? 315* ◇ *Concern and response 8: Can police departments change from within? 317* ◇ *Concern and response 9: Will adequate evaluations be done of COPPS? 318* ◇ *Other concerns: Zero tolerance and existing without federal funds 319*

SUMMARY ◇ NOTES

EVALUATING COPPS INITIATIVES **324**

Introduction   324
Before Assessing COPPS: Rationale and Preliminary Questions   326
Doing the Job Right: Selecting an Outside Evaluator   327
Using the Proper Criteria   328
The old versus the new 328 ◇ *Three general criteria 329* ◇ *Evaluation measures 331*
Officer Performance Evaluations   331
COPPS skills, knowledge, and abilities 333 ◇ *The rating scale 335*
Use of Surveys   336
Polling the community 338 ◇ *Neighborhood surveys 340* ◇ *Surveying officers 341* ◇ *Analyzing the data 343*
Case Studies   343
Chicago, Illinois 344 ◇ *Lawrence, Massachusetts 344*
SUMMARY ◇ NOTES

SELECTED AMERICAN APPROACHES **348**

Introduction   348
Large Communities   348
Austin, Texas 348 ◇ *Chicago, Illinois 349* ◇ *Fort Lauderdale, Florida 352* ◇ *Fresno, California 352* ◇ *St. Louis, Missouri 353* ◇ *St. Petersburg, Florida 355* ◇ *San Diego, California 356*
Medium-Size Counties and Cities   357
Arlington County, Virginia 357 ◇ *Eugene, Oregon 357* ◇ *Grand Rapids, Michigan 359* ◇ *Hayward, California 359* ◇ *Lincoln, Nebraska 360* ◇ *Reno, Nevada 361* ◇ *Savannah, Georgia 362* ◇ *Spokane, Washington 363* ◇ *Tempe, Arizona 364*

Small Communities   365
> *Abington, Virginia 365* ◇ *Arroyo Grande, California 366*
> ◇ *Elmhurst, Illinois 367* ◇ *Gresham, Oregon 368*
> ◇ *Orange County, Florida 368*

Federal and State Agencies   369
> *A federal approach 369* ◇ *State police and universities 369*

SUMMARY ◇ NOTES

14

IN FOREIGN VENUES: COPPS ABROAD   **374**

Introduction   374

Canada   375
> *Victory in Vancouver 376* ◇ *The Royal Canadian
> Mounted Police 378*

Community Policing in Japan   379
> *The earliest community-based approach 379* ◇ *The koban 380*

Australia's Policing Strategy   382
> *"Stopbreak" in Queensland 382* ◇ *A pilot project
> in Toowoomba 384*

COPPS in Great Britain   390
> *A guiding philosophy 390* ◇ *Early initiatives 390* ◇ *The role
> of constables 392* ◇ *Contemporary approaches 393*
> ◇ *Cleveland police and problem youth 395*

COPPS in Other Venues   395
> *Scotland 395* ◇ *Isle of Man 396* ◇ *Israel 398*
> ◇ *Hong Kong 398* ◇ *New Zealand 400* ◇ *Scandinavian
> countries 402*

SUMMARY ◇ NOTES

15

LOOKING FORWARD WHILE LOOKING BACK: THE FUTURE   **407**

Introduction   407

Crime and Federal Largesse with COPPS   408

The Good, Bad, and Ugly   408
> *Possibly good . . . 409* ◇ *Conceivably bad . . . 411*
> ◇ *The ugly . . . 415*

Rebellion of the Rank-and-File, Or, "Revenge of the Grunts"   416

Questions for the Future   417

SUMMARY ◇ NOTES

APPENDICES

A

PROBLEM SOLVING CASE STUDIES **421**

B

A COMMUNITY SURVEY IN FORT COLLINS, COLORADO **427**

C

A STRATEGIC PLAN SURVEY IN PORTLAND, OREGON **436**

INDEX **439**

PREFACE

This book is about policing at its most important and challenging levels—in neighborhoods and in communities across the nation and abroad. It is about a new policing, one that encourages collaboration with the community and other agencies and organizations that are responsible for community safety. It is a style of policing that requires officers to obtain new knowledge and tools such as problem solving, and it is grounded in strategic thinking and planning to enable agencies to keep up with the rapid changes occurring in our society. This policing style also allows agencies to make the necessary organizational and administrative adjustments to maintain a capable and motivated workforce.

ASSUMPTIONS AND KEY TERMS

This book is grounded on the assumption that the reader is most likely an undergraduate or graduate student studying criminal justice or policing. Or, the reader is a police practitioner, with a fundamental knowledge of police history and operations, or is working in a government agency outside policing and needs to know about community policing and problem solving. Citizens who are involved with the police in solving neighborhood problems and are curious about community oriented policing and problem solving (COPPS), and the innovative and collaborative strategies that can be employed with this initiative, can also be served well by reading this book.

This book alone cannot transform the reader into an expert on COPPS. It will, however, impart some of the major underpinnings and prominent names, theories, practices (with myriad examples), and processes that are being implemented to control and prevent crime, disorder, and fear.

A considerable number of textbooks have already been written about community policing. Most of them, however, emphasize its philosophy and provide little information about its *practical* aspects—putting the philosophy into daily practice. This practice of community policing is the primary focus of this book, as indicated in its title. In addition to familiarizing the reader with strategies and practices, this book also challenges the reader to be open minded and to consider traditional policing methods and why innovation should occur.

While some fundamental components of COPPS contribute to its success, no one single form of COPPS exists or can be copied onto a compact disk or downloaded via the Internet. COPPS is an individualized, long-term process that involves fundamental institutional change, going beyond such simple tactics as foot and bicycle patrols or neighborhood police stations. It redefines the role of the officer on the street, from crime fighter to problem solver and neighborhood intermediary. It forces a cultural transformation of the entire police agency, involving changes in recruiting, training, awards systems, evaluations, and promotions.

It has been said that problem solving is not new in policing, that police officers have always tried to solve problems in their daily work. As is demonstrated throughout this text, however, problem solving is not the same as solving problems. Problem solving in the context of COPPS is very different and considerably more complex. It requires that officers identify and examine the underlying causes of recurring incidents of crime and disorder. Such policing also seeks to make thinking "street criminologists" of our police officers, empowering them to focus on the settings for crimes, rather than on the persons committing them. Such an approach presents great challenges for those patrol officers who are engaged in analytical, creative work.

Given the extent to which COPPS has evolved since the publication of our second edition, the authors understand the challenges involved with writing this text. Like its two predecessors, this third edition might still be viewed as a work in progress; today's "snapshot" of what is occurring nationally with respect to COPPS may need to be drastically revised in the future.

We also emphasize that this book is not a call for a complete discarding of policing's past methods, nor do we espouse an altogether new philosophy of policing in its place. Rather, we recommend that the police borrow from the wisdom of the past and adopt a holistic approach to the way police organizations address crime and disorder.

We are quite pleased with the work that has been done by many police practitioners and academicians here and abroad who have made substantive contributions to the COPPS approach. But the traditional, reactive, "cops-as-pinballs" philosophy is still very much alive in many agencies. We discuss in later chapters how, sadly, merely creating a "crime prevention specialist" position, putting an officer on foot or bicycle patrol, or anticipating the receipt of federal dollars can cause many agencies to claim to have implemented COPPS when in fact they have not. Innovations such as these not only misrepresent the true potential and functions of COPPS, they also set unrealistically simplistic goals and expectations for its work.

Thus, as this book explains, much work remains to be done. It is through these ongoing efforts that new directions for policing will evolve.

ORGANIZATION OF THE BOOK

To understand the methods and challenges of COPPS, we first need to look at the big picture. Thus, in the first three chapters we discuss (1) the history of policing and the major transformations over time that led to the present community policing era, (2) some of the many changes occurring in America and what the police must do to confront them, and (3) how governments and the police should turn to and involve their "customers," the public, in making neighborhoods safer places in which to live and work. These initial three chapters help to set the stage for Chapter 4, which is the "heart and soul" of the book, and for the later discussions of COPPS. Following is a chapter-by-chapter breakdown of the book's 15 chapters.

Chapter 1 begins with a brief discussion of Britain's and Sir Robert Peel's influence and the Metropolitan Police Act in England. Next we review the evolution of policing in America, followed by a look at police and change. Then we examine the community problem solving era, including its principal components, why it emerged, and how it evolved.

Chapter 2 opens with an examination of the many rapid changes that are occurring in the United States. Next is a consideration of the changing nature of criminality in this country. Then we examine fear of crime and its effects on neighborhoods. The chapter concludes with a view of what all of these changes mean for the police.

Chapter 3 explores how governments and the police should and do conduct business with respect to their customers' needs. This reinvention of government empowers citizens to reclaim their neighborhoods and to improve their overall quality of life. Some local governments refer to this "community oriented government" movement as the next step in community policing.

The foundation of the book is presented in Chapter 4. Included are discussions of the separate concepts of community policing and problem oriented policing. We maintain throughout the book that these are complementary core components. Included are in-depth discussions of collaborative partnerships and problem solving. The problem solving process is introduced as the officers' primary tool for understanding crime and disorder. Crime analysis and mapping tools used to support problem solving are also discussed.

Crime prevention involves much more than developing programs and distributing brochures. Chapter 5 looks at two important and contemporary components of crime prevention: crime prevention through environmental design (CPTED) and situational crime prevention. These methods help officers understand how opportunities for crime can be blocked and how environments can be designed or changed to lessen a person's or location's vulnerability to crime.

Chapter 6 examines the need for police organizations to engage in strategic thinking in order to be prepared for future challenges. This chapter also discusses the strategic planning process and how to assess local needs and develop a planning document as a roadmap. Then it shifts to the implementation of COPPS per se, considering some vital components: leadership and administration, human resources, field operations, and external relations. Included are several general obstacles to implementation.

In Chapter 7 we recognize that police agencies have a life and culture of their own and address how police agencies must modify their culture from top to bottom in order to fully embrace COPPS. The separate roles and responsibilities of chief executives, middle managers, and rank-and-file officers are included, as are some case studies of agencies that have modified their culture for adopting the COPPS approach.

Another difficult challenge for those agencies involved in COPPS is the training and education of police officers and others. After looking in Chapter 8 at why police officers comprise a challenging learning audience, we consider means and approaches for training, including a training needs assessment. Then we discuss some methods and review some available technologies for conducting training. Included are some ideas for the curriculum of a COPPS training program.

Chapter 9 examines the history of relations between the minorities and the police, and how COPPS can enhance those relations. Included are discussions of cultural differences, customs, and problems; diversity in police organizations; police responses to hate crimes; and some scenarios.

Today's police struggle with an almost overwhelming array of social problems. Chapter 10 describes the application of COPPS to several of those problems, including drug trafficking, gangs, special populations (the mentally ill, the homeless, and those addicted to alcohol), domestic violence, school violence, rental-property and neighborhood disorder, prostitution, and others. Exhibits and case studies are included throughout this chapter and demonstrate the power of collaborative partnerships and problem solving.

Several writers have raised concerns and criticisms with the COPPS concept. The literature reveals more resistance to community policing than to problem solving. This is largely due to academics and practitioners who have incorrectly associated community policing with community relations. Chapter 11 examines these concerns—what we have termed the "devil's advocate" position toward COPPS. We believe that it is important for these concerns to be aired and given a response. Nine issues or problems that have been raised are addressed.

Athough COPPS has been implemented and praised across our nation as well as in foreign venues, what has remained in question is the degree to which the success of these programs has been measured. Chapter 12 confronts the issue of evaluation, beginning with the rationale for evaluating COPPS and social interventions generally, and then reviewing the criticisms of past evaluative efforts. Included are the different methods for evaluation and criteria that can be employed to assess agencies' efforts. Case studies of agencies and research are presented.

Chapter 13 highlights agencies' efforts to implement COPPS in the United States. Featured are case studies in 21 jurisdictions: seven large (categorized as having more than 250,000 population), nine medium-sized (between 50,000 and 250,000 population), and five small (less than 50,000). In addition, brief descriptions of such initiatives appear in several exhibits throughout the chapter.

COPPS has indeed gone international, and much can be learned from looking at the activities and approaches undertaken in foreign venues. In Chapter 14 we travel to Canada, Japan, Australia, Great Britain, Scotland, Israel, Hong Kong, New Zealand, the Scandinavian countries, and the Isle of Man. Other venues are also discussed in five exhibits in the chapter.

Chapter 15 explores the future, beginning with the recent good news of lower overall crime rates and federal assistance for COPPS efforts and what each means for the future. Then we look at those forces that may influence COPPS in years to come: some indicators that are *good*, some that could conceivably be *bad*, those that are *ugly*. Included are a review of the rank-and-file officer and some relevant questions for COPPS in the future.

We believe that this book comprehensively lays out how COPPS is being embraced around the world. Perhaps one of the book's major strengths lies with its many case studies (more than 60 exhibits are scattered throughout the book, in addition to a large number of other examples), showing how the concept is planned and implemented, operationalized, and evaluated.

We are grateful for the helpful suggestions made by the followig reviewers of this chapter: James Albrecht, John Jay College of Criminal Justice; Francis Schreiner, Mansfield University; and Quint Thurman, Wichita State University.

Ken Peak
Ron Glensor

ABOUT THE AUTHORS

Kenneth J. Peak, Ph.D., is professor and former chairman of the criminal justice department at the University of Nevada, Reno (UNR), where he was named "Teacher of the Year" by the UNR Honor Society for 1984–85 and served as acting director of public safety in 1989. He recently authored *Policing America: Methods, Issues, and Challenges* (3d ed., 2000) and *Justice Administration: Police, Courts, and Corrections Management* (3d ed., 2001) and has published 50 journal articles and additional book chapters on a wide range of justice-related subjects. He has served as chairman of the Police Section, Academy of Criminal Justice Sciences, and is deputy editor of *Police Quarterly,* and is past president of the Western and Pacific Association of Criminal Justice Educators. Dr. Peak entered municipal policing in Kansas in 1970 and subsequently held positions as criminal justice planner for southeast Kansas; director of the Four-State Technical Assistance Institute, Law Enforcement Assistance Administration; director of university police, Pittsburg State University; and assistant professor at Wichita State University. He received two gubernatorial appointments to statewide criminal justice committees while in Kansas and holds a doctorate from the University of Kansas.

Ronald W. Glensor, Ph.D., is a deputy chief of the Reno, Nevada, Police Department (RPD). He has more than 25 years of police experience and has commanded the department's patrol, administration, and detective divisions. In addition to being active in the development of and training for the RPD's community oriented policing and problem solving (COPPS) initiative since 1987, he has provided COPPS training for more than 250 police agencies throughout the United States and in Canada, Australia, and the United Kingdom. Dr. Glensor was the 1997 recipient of the prestigious Gary P. Hayes Award conferred by the Police Executive Research Forum, recognizing his contributions and leadership in the policing field. He has also spoken at numerous national conferences on the implementation of COPPS and the utilization of citizen surveys. He served a six-month fellowship as problem oriented policing coordinator with the Police Executive Research Forum in Washington, D.C., and received an Atlantic Fellowship in public policy, studying repeat vicitimization at the Home Office in London. He is co-author of *Police Supervision* (with K. Peak and L. K. Gaines) and is co-editor of *Policing Communities: Understanding Crime and Solving Problems* (with M. Correia and K. Peak); he has also published in several journals and trade magazines. He is an adjunct professor at the University of Nevada, Reno (in the CJ department's bachelor of arts degree in COPPS) and instructs at area police academies and criminal justice programs. His education includes a doctorate in political science and a master's of public administration from the University of Nevada, Reno.

Foreword

In the 1960s and early 1970s, the police struggled to sort out their role in addressing significant increases in crime, violence, and drug abuse. The police found themselves squarely in the middle of the civil rights movement as African Americans sought to break the bonds of racism in all aspects of our society. The police were also on the front line in dealing with the dramatic changes in society as young Americans questioned the wisdom of the war in Vietnam and challenged the status quo. Activism was also present in the ranks of the police. It was during this time that the police began to seriously seek the answers to fundamental questions about how they could best serve the needs of the community.

It had always been accepted that random preventive patrol, rapid response to calls for service, and criminal investigations were the best way for the police to address crime problems. The police saw themselves as "law enforcers" and were comfortable with the idea that their primary purpose was to arrest those who broke the law and bring them before the court. This, they believed, was the most effective way to deter crime. Research findings, however, suggested that these tactics did not have the impact that the police had always assumed they did. Moreover, the research suggested that police might enhance their contribution to addressing crime with different approaches.

Research on random patrol and rapid response implied that the police might be able to manage their time better and direct their energies toward activities with greater benefits. Criminal investigation research helped police understand the importance of the work of the officer who conducts the initial investigation and the value of forensic science in solving crime. Examinations of repeat call locations, repeat victims, and repeat offenders indicated that a more direct focus on these areas would yield better outcomes than the traditional focus on incidents.

Some police departments began to experiment with Herman Goldstein's problem-oriented policing idea. Other departments focused on initiatives aimed at putting the police in closer touch with the community. These efforts fell under the general heading of "community policing" and consisted of programs such as foot and bicycle patrol and neighborhood-based store front offices. There was an enormous sense of urgency in the effort to improve the effectiveness of the police when crime, violence, and drug abuse spiraled out of control in the late 1980s when crack cocaine ravaged the nation's urban centers. Both problem-oriented and community policing received considerable attention though the late 1980s as the National Institute of Justice Harvard Executive Sessions published the Perspective Series that was widely distributed, read, and discussed by both practitioners and academics throughout America.

These ideas were very much a part of the political landscape in the 1992 national elections. Broad-based national support existed for the idea of community policing, and it became the corner stone of President Bill Clinton's proposal to hire 100,000 police officers. Community policing was given an enormous boost with the creation of the Office of Community Oriented Policing Services in the U.S. Department of Justice in 1994 with considerable resources to increase the number of police officers engaged in community and problem oriented policing by 100,000. For the first time in U.S. history, both the president and the majority of the U.S. Congress agreed on approaches to policing that deserved the support of the federal government. It was not entirely clear at the time what community policing and problem-oriented policing were and how to go about putting them in place. Nevertheless, the anecdotal evidence was persuasive enough for the government to allocate immense resources to local governments to add 100,000 police officers and provide training, technical assistance, technology, and evaluation to implement these ideas.

Following several years of observation and practice of community and problem-oriented policing, Ken Peak and Ron Glensor published the first edition of *Community Policing and Problem Solving: Strategies and Practices* in 1996. That volume attempted to provide greater clarity to the ideas of community policing and problem solving. Peak and Glensor set forth the foundation of the concepts and addressed implementation challenges and issues. They provided examples of how police agencies tackled these challenges along with case studies of specific problem solving successes. They talked about evaluation as well.

In 1999 they published the second edition of *Community Policing and Problem Solving: Strategies and Practices*. This edition looked at these strategies from the perspective of the development of a considerable amount of experience with trying these ideas out throughout America with the support of the U.S. Department of Justice Office of Community Oriented Policing. Peak and Glensor were able to build on the first edition with many examples of how police agencies faced the trials and tribulations of changing cultures within their departments.

Now Peak and Glensor bring forth the third edition of *Community Policing and Problem Solving: Strategies and Practices*. Like the first two editions, this volume makes an enormous contribution to our understanding of the application of these concepts in policing. This volume reflects several more years of experience and knowledge about community policing and problem solving. It adds tremendous insight into the complexity of policing.

The third edition contains 15 chapters that put community policing and problem solving into the real world of policing. The book begins with an examination of how these concepts mesh with the evolution of policing. In the next two chapters, Peak and Glensor look at the impact of crime on America and how local government has had to change to meet the needs of an emerging neighborhood power base.

With this foundation, they carefully frame and examine the concepts of community policing and problem solving. Following is a chapter that puts situational crime prevention and crime prevention through environmental design—ideas that fit very comfortably with problem solving and community policing. They move on to a discussion of strategic thinking and the culture of policing. Both areas are critical to the ability of a police department to make the kind of changes required for community policing and problem solving to thrive.

The book contains chapters on minority cultures and the social issues that police must confront in developing and sustaining meaningful community relationships. They also provide a number of case studies that help provide a complete understanding of problem solving and community policing in today's world. The final chapter in the book helps the reader look to the future and the direction in which Peak and Glensor think policing might be moving.

Although the police have made tremendous progress over the past 30 years, daunting challenges remain. We saw huge declines in reported crime through the decade of the 1990s—in some cities, crime is at its lowest level in more than 25 years. In a decade of broad-based change, including the implementation of community policing, one would think that the relationship between the police and the minority community would be at its best. Though it is very difficult to gauge, press accounts of concern over so-called "racial profiling" suggest that police face significant hurdles in strengthening the confidence of the minority community. Moreover, for the first time since the late 1960s crime and/or drug abuse was not a part of the national election debate in the year 2000. How that will affect the police remains to be seen, but it could certainly mean an end to, or at least a significant reduction in, the federal investment in policing.

The change in the political environment makes *Community Policing and Problem Solving: Strategies and Practices* an even more important contribution. Ken Peak and Ron Glensor have balanced their considerable talents as an academic and practitioner to produce a book that will help police confront an uncertain future: a future with waning political support, continuing (perhaps increasing) concerns from minority communities, perhaps an end to the decreases in reported crime and no conclusive evidence of the most effective policing approaches. Peak and Glensor help students of policing and practitioners think through these issues with greater insight. They do indeed make a contribution and a difference.

Darrel W. Stephens

Biographical Sketch

Darrel W. Stephens was appointed Charlotte police chief in September 1999. He was the city administrator for the City of St. Petersburg for just over two years after accepting the position in June 1997. He was responsible for day-to-day oversight and management of all city operations and a workforce of more than 3,000 employees. He also served as police chief in the St. Petersburg Police Department from December 1992 to June 1997. He spent most of his career in policing, including $6\frac{1}{2}$ years as the executive director of the Washington, D.C.–based Police Executive Research Forum (PERF).

He began his career in 1968 as a police officer with the Kansas City, Missouri, Police Department, which included a 10-month visiting fellowship at the National Institute of Justice in 1972. He became the assistant police chief in Lawrence, Kansas, in 1976. In 1979, he accepted the position of police chief in Largo, Florida. In 1983, he became the police chief in Newport News, Virginia, and that department became nationally recognized for its work with problem oriented policing and provided much of the foundation for community policing. He has coauthored several books and published many articles on policing issues. He holds a BS degree in the administration of justice from the University of Missouri–Kansas City and a MS degree in public administration from Central Missouri State University.

THE EVOLUTION OF POLICING
Past Wisdom
and Future Directions

To understand what is, we must know what has been, and what it tends to become.

—Oliver Wendell Holmes

Slaying sacred cows makes great steaks.

—Dick Nicolosi

INTRODUCTION

It is difficult to accurately establish the beginning of community oriented policing in America. Perhaps, because of its burgeoning popularity, the term *community policing* has been used to describe a wide array of reform efforts, few of which have been subjected to rigorous evaluation. The notion of community policing is not altogether new; parts of it are as old as policing, emanating (as we discuss later) from concerns about policing from the early nineteenth century.

1

We also must mention at the outset of this book that community policing and problem solving is not a unitary concept but a collection of related ideas. Several prominent individuals, movements, studies, and experiments have brought policing to where it is today. In this chapter we examine the principal activities involving the police for more than a century and a half—activities that led to the development of community policing and problem solving.

Our historical examination of policing begins with a brief discussion of Britain's and Sir Robert Peel's influence and the Metropolitan Police Act in England. Next we review the evolution of policing in America, including the emergence of the political era and attempts at reform through the professional crimefighter model. Then we consider police and change, including how research has debunked "sacred cow" policing methods, demonstrated the actual nature of police work, and shown the need for a new approach. Next, we examine the community problem solving era, including the principles of this new model, why it emerged, and how it evolved. Finally, we briefly discuss how many city police departments and county sheriff's offices are, in effect, rewriting their agency's history, even posting them on their organization's Internet Web pages, including their conversion to the community oriented policing and problem solving (COPPS) initiative. In a sense, these agencies are explaining to the public—and their own employees—how they have evolved at the local level.

BRITISH CONTRIBUTIONS

The population of England doubled between 1700 and 1800. Parliament, however, took no measures to help solve the problems that arose from the accompanying social change.[1] London, awash in crime, had whole districts become criminal haunts with very bold thieves. In the face of this situation, Henry Fielding began to experiment with possible solutions. Fielding, appointed in 1748 as London's chief magistrate of Bow Street, argued against the severity of the English penal code, which provided for the death penalty for a large number of offenses. He believed the country should reform the criminal code in order to deal more with the origins of crime. In 1750, Fielding made the pursuit of criminals more systematic by creating a small group of "thief-takers."[2] When Fielding died in 1754, his half-brother John Fielding succeeded him as Bow Street magistrate. By 1785, his thief-takers had evolved into the Bow Street Runners—some of the most famous police officers in English history.

Later, Robert Peel, a wealthy member of Parliament, believed strongly that London's population and crime merited a full-time, professional police force. But many English people and other politicians objected to the idea, fearing possible restraint of their liberty. They also feared a strong police organization, because the criminal law was already quite harsh (by the early nineteenth century there were 223 crimes in England for which a person could be hanged). Indeed, Peel's efforts to gain support for full-time, paid police officers failed for seven years.[3]

Peel finally succeeded in 1829. His bill to Parliament—entitled "An Act for Improving the Police in and near the Metropolis"—became known as the

Metropolitan Police Act of 1829. The General Instructions of the new force stressed its preventive nature, saying that "The principal object to be attained is 'the prevention of crime.' The security of persons and property will thus be better effected, than by the detection and punishment of the offender after he has succeeded in committing the crime."[4] It was decided that constables would don a uniform (blue coat, blue pants, and a black top hat) and be armed with a short baton (known as a truncheon) and a rattle (for raising an alarm). And each constable was to wear his individual number on his collar where it could be easily seen.[5]

Peel proved very farsighted and keenly aware of the needs of a community oriented police force, as well as the needs of the public, who would be asked to maintain it. Indeed, Peel perceived that the poor quality of policing was a contributing factor to the social disorder. Accordingly, he drafted several guidelines for the force, many of which focused on improving the relationship between the police and the public. He wrote that the power of the police to fulfill their duties depended on public approval of their actions; that as public cooperation increased, the need for physical force by the police decreased; that the officers needed to display absolutely impartial service to law; that force should be used by the police only when the attempts at persuasion and warning had failed, and then only the minimal degree of force possible should be used. Peel's statement that "The police are the public, and the public are the police" emphasized his belief that the police are first and foremost members of the larger society.[6]

Peel's attempts to appease the public were well grounded; during the first three years of his reform effort, he encountered strong opposition. Peel was denounced as a potential dictator; the *London Times* urged revolt, and *Blackwood's Magazine* referred to the bobbies as "general spies" and "finished tools of corruption." A national secret body was organized to combat the police, who were nicknamed the "Blue Devils" and the "Raw Lobsters." Also during this initial five-year period, Peel endured one of the largest police turnover rates in history. Estimates range widely, but it is probably accurate to accept the figure of 1,341 constables resigning from London's Metropolitan Police between 1829 and 1834.[7]

Peel drafted what have become known as "Peel's Principles" of policing, most if not all of which still apply to today's police community. They are presented in Figure 1.1.

POLICING COMES TO AMERICA

Early Beginnings

The New York Model

Americans, meanwhile, were observing Peel's overall successful experiment with the bobbies on the patrol beat. Industrialization and social upheaval had not reached the proportions that they had in England, however, so there was not the urgency for full-time policing that had been experienced in England. Yet by the

1. The basic mission for which the police exist is to prevent crime and disorder as an alternative to the repression of crime and disorder by military force and severity of legal punishment.
2. The ability of the police to perform their duties is dependent upon public approval of police existence, actions, behavior, and the ability of the police to secure and maintain public respect.
3. The police must secure the willing cooperation of the public in voluntary observance of the law to be able to secure and maintain public respect.
4. The degree of cooperation of the public that can be secured diminishes, proportionately, the necessity for the use of physical force and compulsion in achieving police objectives.
5. The police seek and preserve public favor, not by catering to public opinion, but by constantly demonstrating absolutely impartial service to the law, in complete independence of policy, and without regard to the justice or injustice of the substance of individual laws; by ready offering of individual service and friendship to all members of the society without regard to their race or social standing; by ready exercise of courtesy and friendly good humor; and by ready offering of individual sacrifice in protecting and preserving life.
6. The police should use physical force to the extent necessary to secure observance of the law or to restore order only when the exercise of persuasion, advice, and warning is found to be insufficient to achieve police objectives; and police should use only the minimum degree of physical force which is necessary on any particular occasion for achieving a police objective.
7. The police at all times should maintain a relationship with the public that gives reality to the historic tradition that the police are the public and that the public are the police; the police are the only members of the public who are paid to give full-time attention to duties which are incumbent on every citizen in the interest of the community welfare.
8. The police should always direct their actions toward their functions and never appear to usurp the powers of the judiciary by avenging individuals or the state, or authoritatively judging guilt or punishing the guilty.
9. The test of police efficiency is the absence of crime and disorder, not the visible evidence of police action in dealing with them.

FIGURE 1.1 "Peel's Principles" of policing. [*Source:* W. L. Melville Lee, *A History of Police in England* (London: Methuen, 1901), Chapter 12.]

1840s, when industrialization began in earnest in America, U.S. officials were watching the police reform movement in England more closely.

To comprehend the blundering, inefficiency, and confusion that surrounded nineteenth-century police, we must remember that this was an age when the best forensic techniques could not clearly distinguish the blood of a pig from that of a human, and the art of criminal detection was little more than divination. Steamboats blew up, trains regularly mutilated and killed pedestrians, children got run over by wagons, injury very often meant death, and doctors resisted the germ theory of disease. In the midst of all this, the police would eventually be patrolling—men who at best had been trained by reading pathetic little rule books that provided little or no guidance in the face of human distress and disorder.[8]

New York Police Department officers initially refused to wear uniforms because they did not want to appear as "liveried lackeys." A blue frock coat with brass buttons was adopted in 1853. (*Courtesy* NYPD Photo Unit)

The movement to initiate policing in America began in New York City. (Philadelphia, with a private bequest of $33,000, actually began a paid, daytime police force in 1833; however, it was disbanded in three years.) In 1844, the New York state legislature passed a law establishing a full-time, preventive police force for New York City. This new body was very different from that adopted from Europe; it was deliberately placed under the control of the city government and city politicians. The mayor chose the recruits from a list of names submitted by the aldermen and tax assessors of each ward; the mayor then submitted his choices to the city council for approval. Politicians were seldom concerned about selecting the best people for the job; instead, the system allowed and even encouraged political patronage and rewards for friends.[9]

The police link to neighborhoods and politicians was so tight that the police of this era have been considered virtual adjuncts to political machines.[10] The relationship was often reciprocal: Political machines recruited and maintained police in the office and on the beat, whereas police helped political leaders maintain their political offices by encouraging citizens to vote for certain candidates. Soon other cities adopted the New York model. New Orleans and Cincinnati adopted plans for a new police force in 1852; Boston and Philadelphia followed in 1854,

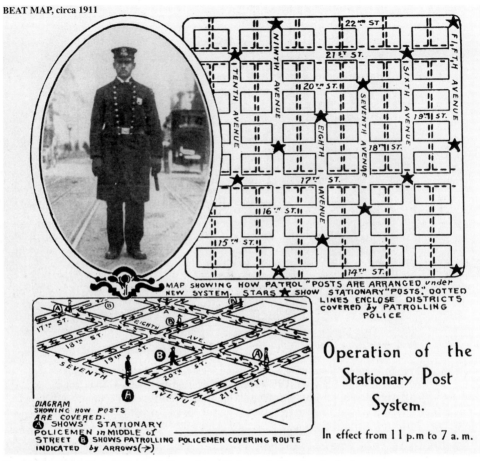

Foot patrol was the primary strategy for policing neighborhoods during the early 1900s. (*Courtesy* NYPD Photo Unit)

Chicago in 1855, and Baltimore and Newark in 1857.[11] By 1880, virtually every major American city had a police force based on Peel's model, pioneered in New York City.

From the East to the Wild, Wild West

These new police forces were born of conflict and violence. An unprecedented wave of civil disorders swept the nation from the 1840s until the 1870s. Few cities escaped serious rioting caused by ethnic and racial conflicts, economic disorder, and public outrage toward such things as brothels and medical school experiments. These occurrences often resulted in hostile interactions between citizens and the police, who were essentially a reactive force. Riots in many major cities actually led to the creation of the "new police." The use of the baton to quell riots, known as the "baton charge," was not uncommon.[12]

Whereas large cities in the East were struggling to overcome social problems and establish preventive police forces, the western half of the United States was anything but passive. When people left the wagon trains and their relatively law-abiding ways, they attempted to live together in communities. Many different ethnic groups—Anglo-Americans, Mexicans, Chinese, Indians, freed African Americans, Australians, Scandinavians, and others—competed for often scarce resources and fought one another violently, often with mob attacks. Economic conflicts were frequent between cattleherders and sheepherders, often leading to major range wars. There was constant labor strife in the mines. The bitterness of the slavery issue remained, and many men with firearms skills learned during the Civil War turned to outlawry, after leaving the service. (Jesse James was one such person.)[13]

Despite these difficulties, westerners established peace by relying on a combination of four groups who assumed responsibility for law enforcement: private citizens, U.S. marshals, businesspeople, and town police officers.[14] Private citizens usually helped to enforce the law by joining a posse or through individual efforts, such as vigilante committees.[15] Although it is true that they occasionally hanged outlaws, they also performed valuable work by ridding their communities of dangerous criminals.

Federal marshals were created by congressional legislation in 1789. As they began to appear on the frontier, the vigilantes tended to disappear. U.S. marshals enforced federal laws, so they only had jurisdiction over federal offenses, such as theft of mail, crimes against railroad property, and murder on federal lands. Their primary responsibility was in civil matters arising from federal court decisions. Finally, when a territory became a state, the primary law enforcement functions usually fell to local sheriffs and marshals. Sheriffs quickly became important officials, but they spent more time collecting taxes, inspecting cattle brands, maintaining jails, and serving civil papers than they did actually dealing with outlaws.[16]

Politics and Corruption

During the late nineteenth century, large cities gradually became more orderly. American cities absorbed millions of newcomers after 1900, without the social strains that attended the Irish immigration of the 1830s to 1850s.[17]

Partly because of their closeness to politicians, police during this era provided a wide array of services to citizens. Many police departments were involved in crime prevention and order maintenance as well as a variety of social services. In some cities they operated soup lines, helped find lost children, and found jobs and temporary lodging for newly arrived immigrants.[18] Police organizations were typically quite decentralized, with cities being divided into precincts and run like small-scale departments—hiring, firing, managing, and assigning personnel as necessary. Officers were often recruited from the same ethnic stock as the dominant groups in the neighborhoods, and they lived in the beats they patrolled, with considerable discretion in handling their individual beats. Decentralization encouraged foot patrol, even after call boxes and automobiles became available. Detectives operated from a caseload of "persons" rather than offenses, relying on their caseload to inform on other criminals.[19]

The strengths of the political era centered on the fact that police were integrated into neighborhoods. This strategy proved useful because it helped contain riots and the police assisted immigrants in establishing themselves in communities and finding jobs. There were weaknesses as well: The intimacy with the community, closeness to politicians, and a decentralized organizational structure (and its inability to provide supervision of officers) led to police corruption. The close identification of police with neighborhoods also resulted in discrimination against strangers—especially minority ethnic and racial groups. Police often ruled their beats with the "end of their nightsticks" and practiced "curbside justice."[20] The lack of organizational control over officers also caused some inefficiencies and disorganization; thus, the image of Keystone Cops—bungling police—was widespread.

The Emergence of Professionalism

The nineteenth-century police officer was essentially a political operative rather than a modern-style professional committed to public service. Because the police were essentially a political institution and perceived as such by the citizenry, they did not enjoy a widespread acceptance by the public. And, as political appointees, officers enjoyed little job security. Salaries were determined by local political factors. Primitive communications technology of the era meant that police chiefs were unable to supervise their captains at the precinct level; thus, policy was greatly influenced by the prevailing political and social mores of the neighborhoods. As a consequence, police behavior was very much influenced by the interaction between individual officers and individual citizens. The nature of that interaction, later termed the problem of police-community relations, was perhaps even more complex and ambiguous in the nineteenth century than in the late twentieth century.[21]

The idea of policing as a profession, however, began to emerge slowly in the latter part of the nineteenth century. Reform ideas first appeared as a reaction to the corrupt and politicized state of the police. Reformers agreed that partisan politics was the heart of the problem. Even reformers in the National Prison Association bemoaned the partisan politics that hindered the improvement of the police. Slowly, the idea of policing as a higher calling (higher than the concerns of local politics, that is), as a profession committed to public service, began to gain ground. Two other ideas about the proper role of the police in society also appeared. One emphasized improvement in the role of police with respect to scientific techniques of crime detection, and the other involved police playing more of a social work role; by intervening in the lives of individuals, police officers could reform society by preventing crime and keeping people out of the justice system. These reforms were closely tied to the emerging rehabilitative ideal in correctional circles.[22]

Movement toward Reform

New Developments and Calls for Reform

Several important developments in policing occurred during the late 1800s, including the beginning of a body of literature. Most authors were closely tied to the police and, thus, painted an inaccurate picture in some respects (e.g., ignoring the corruption that existed in many police departments), but their writings were also very illuminating. They provided glimpses into the informal processes that governed police departments and focused on the individual officer—a focus that would be lost in the later professionalization movement with its emphasis on impersonal, bureaucratic standards.

The late 1800s also witnessed improvements in the areas of testing and training. The physical and mental qualifications of police officers concerned new police commissioners, and formal schools of instruction were developed (the best being Cincinnati's, which required a total of 72 hours of instruction). Police conventions began to occur during the late 1800s, such as the National Police Chiefs Union [later named the International Association of Chiefs of Police (IACP)], and fraternal and benefit societies.[23] August Vollmer, pioneer of police professionalism from 1905 to 1932, rallied police executives around the idea of reform during the 1920s and 1930s, emerging as the leading national spokesperson for police professionalism. What is often overlooked among the abundance of Vollmer's contributions to policing is his articulate advocacy of the idea that the police should function as social workers. The belief that police officers should do more than merely arrest offenders, that they should actively seek to prevent crime by "saving" potential or actual offenders, was an important theme in police reform. It was an essential ingredient in the notion of professionalism. Indeed, in a series of addresses to the IACP Vollmer advanced his ideas in "The Policeman as a Social Worker" (1918) and "Predelinquency" (1921). He began by arguing that the "old methods of dealing with crime must be changed, and newer ones adopted."[24]

Vollmer's views were very prescient for today, especially given the contemporary movement toward community policing. Vollmer believed that traditional institutions and practices were no longer adequate for a modern and complex industrial society. He believed that the police should intervene and be involved with people before they entered lives of crime, and he suggested that police work closely with existing social welfare agencies and become advocates of additional reform proposals. Vollmer also suggested that police inform voters about overcrowded schools and support the expansion of recreational facilities, community social centers, and antidelinquency agencies. Basically, he was suggesting that the police play an active part in the political life of the community. Yet, the major

August Vollmer, a national spokesman for and early pioneer of police professionalism, established one of the first fingerprint bureaus and formal police schools while he was chief of police in Berkeley, California. (*Courtesy* Samuel G. Chapman)

thrust of police professionalization had been to insulate the police from politics. This contradiction illustrated one of the fundamental ambiguities of the whole notion of professionalism.[25]

Other reformers continued to reject political involvement by police, and civil service systems were created to eliminate patronage and ward off influences in hiring and firing police officers. In some cities, officers could not live in the same beat they patrolled. This tactic was intended to isolate the officers as completely as possible from political influences. Police departments, needing to be removed from political influence, became one of the most autonomous agencies in urban government.[26] However, policing also became a matter viewed as best left to the discretion of police executives to address. Police organizations became *law enforcement* agencies, with the sole goal of controlling crime. Any noncrime activities they were required to do were considered "social work." The "professional model" of policing was in full bloom.

The scientific theory of administration was adopted, as advocated by Frederick Taylor during the early twentieth century. Taylor had studied the work process, breaking down jobs to their basic steps and emphasizing time and motion studies, all with the goal of maximizing production. From this emphasis on production and unity of control flowed the notion that police officers were best managed by a hierarchical pyramid of control. Police leaders routinized and standardized police work; officers were to enforce laws and make arrests whenever possible. Discretion was limited to the extent possible. When special problems arose, special units (e.g., vice, juvenile, drugs, tactical) were created, rather than assigning those problem areas to patrol officers.

Crime Commissions and Early Police Studies

The early 1900s also became the age of the crime commission, including the Wickersham Commission reports in 1931. President Herbert Hoover, concerned with the lax enforcement of Prohibition and other forms of police corruption, created the National Commission on Law Observance and Enforcement—popularly known as the Wickersham Commission, after its chair, former U.S. Attorney General George W. Wickersham. This commission completed the first national study of crime and criminal justice, issuing 14 reports and recommending that the corrupting influence of politics be removed from policing, police chief executives be selected on merit, patrol officers be tested and meet minimal physical standards, police salaries and working conditions be decent, and that policewomen be used in juvenile and female cases. Many of these recommendations represented what progressive police reformers had wanted for the previous 40 years; unfortunately, President Hoover and his administration could do little more than report the Wickersham Commission's recommendations before leaving office.

The most important changes in policing during this decade were the advent of the automobile and its accompanying radio. Gradually the patrol car replaced foot patrol, expanding geographic beats and further removing people from neighborhoods. There was also Prohibition (which affected the police very little in the long term), a bloody wave of racial violence in American cities, and the rise and defeat of police unionism and strikes. Two-way radios also impacted policing; supervisors were able to maintain far closer supervision of patrol officers than previously; and the radio and telephone made it possible for citizens to make heavier demands for police service. The result was not merely a greater burden on the police but also an important qualitative redefinition of the police role.[27]

The 1930s marked an important turning point in the history of police reform. The first genuine empirical studies of police work began to appear, and O. W. Wilson emerged as the leading authority on police administration. The major development of this decade was a redefinition of the police role and the ascendancy of the crime-fighter image. Wilson, who took guidance from J. Edgar Hoover's transformation of the Federal Bureau of Investigation (FBI) into one of high prestige, became the principal architect of the police reform strategy.[28] Hoover, appointed FBI director in 1924, had raised eligibility and training standards of recruits, giving FBI agents stature as upstanding, moral crusaders and developing an incorruptible crime-fighting organization. He also developed impressive public relations programs that presented the Bureau in the most favorable light. Municipal police found Hoover's path a compelling one. Following

Wilson's writings on police administration, they began to shape an organizational strategy for urban police that was analogous to that pursued by the FBI.

Also by the 1930s the policewomen's movement, begun in the early 1900s, had begun losing ground. Professionalism came to mean a combination of managerial efficiency, technological sophistication, and an emphasis on crime fighting. The social work aspects of policing—the idea of rehabilitative work, which had been central to the policewomen's movement—fell into almost total eclipse. The result was a severe identity crisis for policewomen as they were caught between a social work orientation and a law enforcement ideology. Later, by the 1960s, women would occupy an extremely marginal place in American policing.[29]

Under the reform era's professional model of policing, officers were to remain in their "rolling fortresses," going from one call to the next with all due haste. As Mark Moore and George Kelling observed,

> In professionalizing crime fighting, the "volunteers," citizens on whom so much used to depend [were] removed from the fight. If anything has been learned from the history of American policing, it is that, whatever the benefits of professionalization (e.g., reduced corruption, due process, serious police training), the reforms . . . ignored, even attacked, some features that once made the police powerful institutions in maintaining a sense of community security.[30]

The Professional Crime Fighter

Emphasis on Efficiency and Control

The decade of the 1930s ended the first phase in the history of police professionalization. From the 1940s through the early 1960s, police reform continued along the lines that were already well established. Police professionalism was defined almost exclusively in terms of managerial efficiency, and administrators sought to further strengthen their hand in controlling rank-and-file officers. Many of the old problems persisted, however, such as racial unrest and an unclear definition of the police role. Nonetheless, by the late 1930s and early 1940s, there was a clear sense of mission for the police, a commitment to *public* service where one had not existed before.[31] Also, policing had begun to develop its own sense of professional autonomy. And, ironically perhaps, the most articulate groups and the most creative thinking were to be found in nonpolice groups: the National Prison Association, the social work profession, and the field of public administration. The efforts by reformers to remove political influence over police, though not entirely successful, were beginning to take hold as police boards and all-powerful police chiefs met their demise. Police unions reappeared, however, and the emergence of careerism among police officers significantly altered their attitudes toward the job and the public they served.

The professional model demanded an impartial law enforcer who related to citizens in professionally neutral and distant terms—personified by television's Sergeant Friday on *Dragnet:* "Just the facts, ma'am." The emphasis on

NYPD's Emergency Services was formed in 1926 to drive criminals, gangsters, and disorderly characters from the streets. *(Courtesy* NYPD Photo Unit)

professionalization also shaped the role of citizens in crime control. Like physicians caring for health problems, teachers for educational problems, and social workers for social adjustment problems, the police would be responsible for crime problems. Citizens became relatively passive in crime control, mere recipients of professional crime control services. Citizens' responsibility in crime control was limited to calling police and serving as witnesses when asked to do so. Police were the "thin blue line." The community "need" for rapid response to calls for service (CFS) was sold as efficacious in crime control. Foot patrol, when demanded by citizens, was rejected as an outmoded, expensive frill. Professionalism in law enforcement was often identified in terms of firearms expertise, and the popularity of firearms put the police firmly in the antigun control camp.[32]

Citizens were no longer encouraged to go to "their" neighborhood police officers or districts. Officers were to drive marked cars randomly through streets, to promote a sense of police omnipresence. The "person" approach ended and was replaced by the case approach. Officers were judged by the numbers of arrests they made or the number of miles they drove during a shift. The crime rate became the primary indicator of police effectiveness.

Reestablishing Communication: Police–Community Relations

Although much of the country was engaged in practicing and "selling" police reform embodied in the professional model of policing, a movement was beginning in Michigan to bring the police and community closer together. Louis Radelet served on the executive staff of the National Conference of Christians and Jews (NCCJ) from 1951 to 1963, when he became a professor in what was then the School of Police Administration and Public Safety at Michigan State University (MSU). In 1955, Radelet, having conducted many NCCJ workshops dedicated to reducing tensions among the various groups within the community, founded the National Institute on Police and Community Relations (NIPCR) at MSU; he served as the institute's director from 1955 to 1969 and was also coordinator of the university's National Center on Police and Community Relations, which was created to conduct a national survey on police–community relations, from 1965 to 1973.[33]

The institute held five-day conferences each May during its 15-year existence, bringing together teams of police officers and other community leaders to discuss common problems. In peak years, more than 600 participants came from as many as 165 communities, 30 states, and several foreign countries. As a result of the institute's work, such programs proliferated rapidly across the nation. We believe the stated purposes of the many programs initiated during this period are still applicable today and should be listed here:

1. To encourage the partnership of police and citizens in the cause of crime prevention.
2. To foster and improve communications and mutual understanding between the police and the total community.

During the 1960s, for the first time in history, Americans watched police on television respond to anti-war and civil rights demonstrations and were shocked at the treatment of students and minorities by the police. (A scene from the Walker Report of the 1968 Chicago Democratic National Convention)

3. To promote interprofessional approaches to the solution of community problems and to stress the principle that the administration of justice is a total community responsibility.

4. To enhance cooperation among the police, prosecution, courts, and corrections.

5. To assist police and other community leaders to achieve an understanding of the nature and causes of complex problems in people-to-people relations and especially to improve police–minority relationships.

6. To strengthen implementation of equal protection under the law for all persons.[34]

The NIPCR was discontinued at the end of 1969. Radelet wrote that its demise was

> a commentary on the evolution of issues and social forces pertinent to the field. The purposes, assumptions, and institute design of past years may have been relevant in their time. But it became imperative now to think about police–community relations programs in different terms, with more precise purposes that could be better measured.[35]

Problems Overwhelm the Professional Model

Problems with the professional model of policing arose during the late 1960s:

▪ *Crime began to rise and research suggested that conventional police methods were not effective.* The 1960s were a time of explosion and turbulence. Inner city residents rioted in several major cities, protestors denounced military involvement in Vietnam, assassins ended the lives of President John F. Kennedy, Robert F. Kennedy, and civil rights leader the Reverend Martin Luther King, Jr. The country was witnessing tremendous upheaval, and such incidents as the so-called "police riot" at the 1968 Democratic National Convention in Chicago raised many questions about the police and their function and role. Largely as a result of this turmoil, five national studies examined police practices during the 1960s and 1970s, each with a different focus: the President's Commission on Law Enforcement and the Administration of Justice (called the "President's Crime Commission," 1967); the National Advisory Commission on Civil Disorders (1968); the National Commission on the Causes and Prevention of Violence (1968); the President's Commission on Campus Unrest (1970); and the National Advisory Commission on Criminal Justice Standards and Goals (1973). Of particular note was the President's Crime Commission of 1967, charged by President Lyndon Johnson to find solutions to America's internal crime problems. The Commission's recommendations for the police included hiring more minorities as police officers to improve police–community relations, upgrading the quality of police officers by better educating them, and better applicant screening and intensive preservice training.[36] The President's Crime Commission brought policing full circle, restating several of the same principles that were laid out by Sir Robert Peel in 1829: that police should be close to the public, that poor quality of policing contributed to social disorder, and that the police should focus on community relations.

▪ *Police administrators became more willing to challenge traditional assumptions and beliefs and to open the door to researchers.* That willingness to allow researchers to examine traditional methods led to the growth and development of two important policing research organizations: the Police Foundation and the Police Executive Research Forum (PERF).

▪ *Fear rose.* Citizens abandoned parks, public transportation, neighborhood shopping centers, churches, and entire neighborhoods. What puzzled police and researchers was that levels of fear and crime did not always correspond: Crime levels were low in some areas but fear was high, and vice-versa. Researchers found that fear is more closely associated with disorder than with crime. Ironically, order maintenance was one of the functions that police had been downplaying over the years.

▪ *Many minority citizens did not perceive their treatment as equitable or adequate.* They protested not only police mistreatment but also lack of treatment, despite attempts by most police departments to provide impartial policing to all citizens.

▪ *The antiwar and civil rights movements challenged police.* The legitimacy of police was questioned: Students resisted police; minorities rioted against them for what they represented; and the public, for the first time at this level, questioned police tactics. Moreover, minorities and women insisted that they be represented in policing if police were to be legitimate.

▪ *Some of the myths on which the reform era was founded—that police officers use little or no discretion and their primary duty is law enforcement—could no longer be sustained.* Over and over, research underscored the use of discretion at all levels and the fact that law enforcement comprised but a small portion of police officers' activities.[37] Other research findings shook the foundations of old assumptions about policing; for example, two-person patrol cars are neither more effective nor more safe than one-person cars in reducing crime or catching criminals.[38] Other "sacred cows" of policing that were debunked by research are discussed later in the chapter.

▪ *Although managers had tried to professionalize policing, line officers continued to have low status.* Police work continued to be routinized; petty rules governed officer behavior. Meanwhile, line officers received little guidance in the use of discretion and had little opportunity for providing input concerning their work. As a result, many departments witnessed the rise of militant unionism.

▪ *The police lost a significant portion of their financial support.* Many police departments were reduced in size, reflecting an erosion of public confidence.

▪ *Police began to acquire competition: private security and the community crime control movement.* Businesses, industries, and private citizens began to seek alternative means of protecting themselves and their property—further suggesting a declining confidence in the capability of police to provide the level of services that citizens desired. Indeed, today more than 1.5 million private police personnel are employed in the United States—two to three times more personnel than there are in all federal, state, and municipal police agencies combined.[39] The social changes of the 1960s and 1970s obviously changed policing in America. The impact of the courts during this period should not be overlooked. A number of major landmark Supreme Court decisions curtailed the actions of police and, concurrently, expanded the rights of the accused.

THE CHANGING WISDOM OF POLICING

More Recent Studies of Police Work

As a result of the problems mentioned in the previous section and the civil unrest that occurred during the professional era of policing, research evolved a new "common wisdom" of policing. As will be shown, much of this research shook the foundation of policing and rationalizes the changes in methods we offer in later chapters. We discuss what might be called the two primary "clusters" of police research that illuminated where policing has been and what officers actually do.

The first cluster of research actually began in the 1950s and would ultimately involve seven empirical studies of the police: the early work of sociologist William Westley concerning the culture of policing;[40] the ambitious studies of the American Bar Foundation;[41] the field observations of Jerome Skolnick;[42] the work of Egon Bittner analyzing the police function on skid row;[43] Parnas's study of the police response to domestic disturbances;[44] James Q. Wilson's analysis of different policing styles;[45] and the studies of police–citizen contact by Albert Reiss.[46] These studies collectively provided a "new realism" about policing:

▪ Informal arrangements for handling incidents and behavioral problems were found to be more common than was compliance with formally established procedures.
▪ Workload, public pressures, interagency pressures, and the interests and personal predilections of functionaries in the criminal justice system were found in many instances to have more influence on how police and the rest of the criminal justice system operated than the Constitution, state statutes, or city ordinances.
▪ Arrest, commonly viewed as the first step in the criminal process, had come to be used by the police to achieve a whole range of objectives in addition to that of prosecuting wrongdoers, for example, to investigate, harass, punish, and provide safekeeping.

- A great variety of informal methods outside the criminal justice system had been adopted by the police to fulfill their formal responsibilities and to dispose of the endless array of situations that the public—rightly or wrongly—expected them to handle.

- Individual police officers were found to be routinely exercising a great deal of discretion in deciding how to handle the tremendous variety of circumstances with which they were confronted.[47]

These findings also underscored the fact that the police had, in the past, depended too much on the criminal law order to get their job done; that they were not autonomous, but rather accountable, through the political process, to the community; and that dealing with fear and enforcing public order are appropriate functions for the police.[48] Other early studies indicated that less than 50 percent of an officer's time was committed to CFS, and of those calls handled, more than 80 percent were noncriminal incidents.[49]

The five national studies of policing practices during the riots and Vietnam War of the 1960s and 1970s (discussed in the previous section) began a quest for new directions. Later, a second cluster of police research occurred that provided further knowledge about police methods. The Kansas City Preventive Patrol Experiment of 1973 questioned the usefulness of random patrol in police vehicles.[50] Other studies showed that officers and detectives are limited in their abilities to successfully investigate crimes[51] and that detectives need not follow up every reported unsolved crime.[52] In short, most serious crimes were unaffected by the standard police actions designed to control them.

The second group of studies began in the 1970s; they dispelled many assumptions commonly held by police about their efficiency and effectiveness. For example, preventive patrol has been shown to be costly, producing only minimal results toward a reduction of crime.[53] Rapid response to calls has been shown to be less effective at catching criminals than educating the public to call the police sooner after a crime is committed.[54] We now know that police response time is largely unrelated to the probability of making an arrest or locating a witness. The time it takes to report a crime is the major determining factor of whether an on-scene arrest takes place and whether witnesses are located.[55] And despite their best efforts, police have had little impact on preventing crime.[56] Figure 1.2 shows several studies and experiments in policing that were undertaken from 1972 to 2000.

Viewing "Sacred Cow" Police Methods with Caution

What did these studies mean for the police? Was the professional model of policing (discussed earlier) completely off base? No. In fact it still has a place in a police agency lacking organization, efficiency, control, and effectiveness. These studies, however, do show that the police erred in doggedly investing so much of their resources in a limited number of practices that were based on a rather naive and simplistic concept of the police role.[57] Furthermore, as noted earlier, the police got caught up in the "means over ends" syndrome, measuring their

Year	Subject	Focus
2000	COPS Program—National Evaluation	Federal Office of Community Oriented Policing Services (COPS) grants
2000	National Evaluation of the Problem Solving Partnerships Project for federal COPS office	Success of 447 police agencies receiving problem solving grants
1999	National Evaluation of Project Weed and Seed (discussed in Chapter 12)	Proactive drug enforcement and prevention
1998	National Evaluation of Youth Firearms Violence	Approaches to reduce firearms related violence
1998	Information Systems Technology Enhancement Project	Technology uses for COPPS
1997	Federal Study of Crime Prevention Programs	Broad range of programs
1995	Repeat Victimization	Prevention of revictimization
1995	Integrated Criminal Apprehension Program	Crime analysis based deployment
1993	"Tipping Point" Studies	Examination of crime epidemics
1992	Crime Prevention through Environmental Design	Designing out crime
1992	Situational Crime Prevention	Reducing crime opportunities
1991	Quality Policing in Madison, Wisconsin	Quality management study
1990	Minneapolis "Hot Spot" Patrolling	Intensive patrol of problem areas
1988	Police Decoy Operations	Criminal targeting tactic
1987	Problem Oriented Policing, Newport News, Virginia	Crime problem solving model
1987	Houston and Newark Fear of Crime Studies	Fear reduction study
1985	Repeat Offender Programs	Target career criminals
1984	Minneapolis Domestic Violence Experiment	Analysis of effective police action
1983	Differential Police Response Field Test	Call priority and alternative reporting
1982	Directed Patrol National Survey	Survey of patrol strategies
1981	Newark Foot Patrol Experiment	Cost benefits of foot patrol
1977	Split Force Patrol Experiment, Wilmington, Delaware	Patrol deployment study
1977	Patrol Staffing in San Diego	One- vs. two-officer cars
1976	Kansas City Response Time Study	Police response to crimes
1975	RAND Study of Investigations	Detective and patrol effectiveness
1975	Field Interview Study, San Diego	Linking field interviews to crime
1974	Kansas City Preventive Patrol Experiment	Effectiveness of random patrol
1973	Team Policing Experiment in Seven U.S. Cities	Team vs. traditional policing
1973	Police–Community Relations	Study of organizational orientation
1972	Policewomen on Patrol	Evaluation of women on patrol

FIGURE 1.2 Police studies and experiments, 1972–2000.

"success" by the number of arrests, quickness of responses, and so on, while often neglecting the outcome of their work—the ends.

As we have seen, the "We've always done it this way" mentality, still pervading policing to a large extent, may not only be an ineffective means of organizing and administering a police agency but may also be a costly squandering of valuable human and financial resources. For many police agencies today operating under the traditional, incident-driven style of policing, the *beat*, rather than the *neighborhood*, is, to borrow a term from research methodology, the "unit of analysis." Under this time-worn model, officers have been glued to their police radios, flitting like pinballs from one call for service to the next as rapidly as possible. Furthermore, police officers seldom leave their vehicles to address incidents except when answering CFS. They know very little about the underlying causes of problems in the neighborhoods on their beats.

The results of employing conventional police methods have been inglorious. Problems have persisted or gone unnoticed and grown while neighborhoods deteriorated. Officers become frustrated after they repeatedly handle similar calls, with no sign of progress. Petty offenses contributed to this decline and drove stable community members away once the message went out to offenders and vandals that "no one cares" about the neighborhood. Yet many in the police field are unaware of or refuse to accept the fact that the old ways are open to serious challenge.

Time for a New Approach

We believe it is clear from all we have discussed thus far that the time arrived long ago for police agencies to change their daily activities, their management practices, and even their view of their work in order to confront the changes that are occurring. We maintain that, given the current levels of violence and the public's fear of it, the disorder found in countless American neighborhoods, poor police–community relations in many cities, and the rapidly changing landscape of crime and demographics in America, the police need to seriously consider whether a "bureaucratic overhaul" is needed to meet the demands of the future.

Police research also demonstrated the need for agencies to evaluate the effectiveness of their responses. Both quantitative and qualitative data should be used as a basis for evaluation and change. Departments need to know more about what their officers are doing. Agencies are struggling to find enough resources for performing crime trend analyses; most also do not conduct proper workload analyses to discover how much uncommitted time their officers have.

Research has also provided the realization that policing consists of developing the most effective means for dealing with a multitude of troublesome situations. For example, problem solving is a whole new way of thinking about policing and carries the potential to reshape the way in which police services are delivered.[58]

One of several things the police must do to accomplish their mission is to reacquaint themselves with members of the community by involving citizens in the resolution of neighborhood problems. Simply stated, police must view the public as well as other government and social services organizations as "a part of," rather than "apart from," their efforts. This change in conventional thinking advocates efficiency with effectiveness and quality over quantity, and it encourages collaborative problem solving and creative resolutions to crime and disorder.

The Community Problem Solving Era

Team Policing, Foot Patrol, and Shattered Myths

In the early 1970s, it was suggested that the performance of patrol officers would improve more by using job redesign based on "motivators."[59] This suggestion later evolved into a concept known as "team policing," which sought to restructure police departments, improve police–community relations, enhance police officer morale, and facilitate change within the police organization. Its primary element was a decentralized, neighborhood focus to deliver police services. Officers were to be generalists, trained to investigate crimes and basically attend to all of the problems in their area. A team of officers would be assigned to a particular neighborhood and would be responsible for all police services in that area.

In the end, however, team policing failed for several reasons. Most of the experiments were poorly planned and hastily implemented, resulting in street officers not understanding what they were supposed to do. Many midmanagement personnel felt threatened by team policing and, as a result, some sabotaged the experiment. Furthermore, team policing did not represent a completely different view of policing. As Samuel Walker observed, "It was essentially a different *organizational approach* to traditional policing: responding to calls for service (CFS), deterring crime through patrol, and apprehending criminals" (emphasis in original).[60]

There were other developments for the police during the late 1970s and early 1980s. Foot patrol became more popular, and many jurisdictions (such as Newark, New Jersey; Boston; and Flint, Michigan) even demanded it. In Newark, an evaluation found that foot patrol was easily noticed by residents and that it produced a significant increase in the level of satisfaction with police service, led to a significant reduction of perceived crime problems, and resulted in a significant increase in the perceived level of safety of the neighborhood.[61] Flint researchers reported that the crime rate in the target areas declined slightly; CFS in these areas dropped by 43 percent. Furthermore, citizens indicated satisfaction with the program, suggesting that it had improved relations with the police.[62]

These findings and others discussed later shattered several long-held myths about measures of police effectiveness. In addition, research conducted during the 1970s suggested that *information* could help police improve their ability to deal with crime. These studies, along with those of foot patrol and fear reduction, created new opportunities for police to understand the increasing concerns of citizens' groups about disorder (e.g., gangs, prostitutes) and to work with citizens to do something about it. Police discovered that when they asked citizens about their priorities, citizens appreciated their asking and often provided useful information.

The Community Patrol Officer Program (CPOP), instituted by the New York City Police Department in 1984, was similar in many respects to the Flint foot patrol program. Officers involved in this program were responsible for getting to know the residents, merchants, and service providers in their beat area; identifying the principle crime and order maintenance problems confronting the people within their beat; and devising strategies for dealing with the problems identified.[63]

The public plays an important role in crime detection and prevention. (*Courtesy* Washoe County, Nevada, Sheriff's Office Photo Unit)

Principles of the New Model

Simultaneously, Herman Goldstein's problem oriented approach to policing was being tested in Madison, Wisconsin; Baltimore County, Maryland; and Newport News, Virginia. These studies found that police officers enjoy operating with a holistic approach to their work, have the capacity to do problem solving successfully, and can work with citizens and other agencies to solve problems. Also, citizens seemed to appreciate working with police. Moreover, this approach was a rethinking of earlier strategies of handling CFS: Officers were given more autonomy and trained to analyze the underlying causes of problems and find creative solutions. These findings were similar to those of the foot patrol experiments and fear reduction experiments.

The community oriented policing and problem solving model requires not only new police strategies but also a new organizational approach. There is a renewed emphasis on community collaboration for many police tasks. Crime control remains an important function, but equal emphasis is given to *prevention*. Police officers return to their wide use of discretion under this model and move away from routinization and standardization of addressing their tasks. This discretion pushes operational and tactical decision making to the lower levels of the organization.

Participative management is greatly increased, and fewer levels of authority are required to administer the organization; middle-management layers are reduced. Concurrently, many cities have developed what are, in effect, "demarketing" programs, actively attempting to rescind programs (such as in the area of rapid response to CFS, and 911 except for dire emergencies) that had been actively sold earlier.

Community problem solving has helped to explain what went wrong with team policing in the 1960s and 1970s. It was a strategy that innovators mistakenly approached as a tactic. Team policing also competed with traditional policing in the same departments, and they were incompatible with one another. A police department might have a small team policing unit or conduct a team policing experiment, but the reform, professional model of policing was still "business as usual."

The classical theory of police organization that continues to dominate many agencies is likewise alien to the community problem solving strategy. The new strategy will not accommodate the classical theory of traditional policing; the latter denies too much of the real nature of police work, continues old methods of supervision and administration, and creates too much cynicism in officers attempting to do creative problem solving.

Risks come with attempting the new strategy. The risks, however, "for the community and the profession of policing, are not as great as attempting to maintain a strategy that faltered on its own terms during the 1960s and 1970s."[64]

Why the Emergence of Community Oriented Policing and Problem Solving?

We discuss community oriented policing and problem solving in detail in Chapter 4; here we summarize this chapter and show the many factors that set the stage for its emergence:

- The narrowing of the police mission to crime fighting
- Increased cultural diversity in our society
- The detachment of patrol officers in patrol vehicles
- Increased violence in our society
- A scientific view of management, stressing efficiency more than effectiveness, quantitative policing more than qualitative
- A downturn in the economy and, subsequently, a "do more with less" philosophy toward the police
- Increased dependence on high-technology equipment, rather than contact with the public
- The emphasis on organizational change, including decentralization and greater officer discretion
- Isolation of police administration from community and officer input
- Concern with police violation of minority civil rights

- A yearning for personalization of government services
- Burgeoning attempts by the police to adequately reach the community through crime prevention, team policing, and police–community relations

Most of these elements contain a common theme: the isolation of the police from the public. The police got caught in the "means over ends" syndrome, wherein they measured their success by the numbers of arrests, quickness of responses, and so on. They often neglected the outcome of their work—the ends—which we believe now requires their utmost concentration in order to police the very complex needs of today's free and diverse society. This isolation resulted in the "we–they fallacy" or the "us versus them" mentality on the part of both the police and the citizenry. The notion of community policing, therefore, "rose like a phoenix from the ashes of burned cities, embattled campuses, and crime-riddled neighborhoods."[65] Known in the 1970s as foot patrol, then neighborhood policing, problem oriented policing, neighborhood oriented policing, community oriented policing, community-based policing, or community policing, this growing movement learned from the past and preserved the best aspects for each successive stage.

As will be seen in the following chapters, community oriented policing and problem solving (COPPS) has now reached what has been termed a *critical mass,* so that it is now recognized as being at the cutting edge of what is new in policing.[66] Indeed, the Violent Crime Control and Law Enforcement Act of 1994 authorized $8.8 billion over six years to create the Office of Community Oriented Policing Services (COPS) in the U.S. Department of Justice, add 100,000 more police officers to communities across the country, and create 28 regional community policing institutes (RCPIs) to develop and deliver community policing training to interested agencies and to provide technical assistance for implementation and technology throughout the nation. The COPS Office, the RCPIs, and other aspects of the act are discussed in more detail in Chapter 4.

As is discussed throughout this book, COPPS has been adopted as the culture of many police organizations, including their hiring processes, recruit academies, in-service training, promotional examinations, and strategic plans. COPPS is also having an impact on community oriented government and the criminal justice system. There is little doubt that COPPS is the future of policing. Table 1.1 summarizes the three eras of policing.

REWRITING POLICE AGENCY HISTORY

A casual look at the Internet Web pages of many city police departments and county sheriff's offices reveals many such agencies presenting a history of their organization, including their conversion to the COPPS initiative. In a sense, these agencies are explaining to the public—and their own employees—how they have evolved at the local level. This approach serves a twofold purpose. First, it serves to educate those persons *outside* the agency concerning the agency's history and identity, underscoring the fact that COPPS is not to be viewed as a temporary,

TABLE 1.1 The Three Eras of Policing

	Political Era 1840s to 1930s	Reform Era 1930s to 1980s	Community Era 1980s to present
Authorization	Politics and law	Law and professionalism	Community support (political), law and professionalism
Function	Broad social services	Crime control	Broad provision of services
Organizational design	Decentralized	Centralized, classical	Decentralized, task forces, matrices
Relationship to community	Intimate	Professional, remote	Intimate
Tactics and technology	Foot patrol	Preventive patrol and rapid response to calls	Foot patrol, problem solving, public relations
Outcome	Citizen, political satisfaction	Crime control	Quality of life and citizen satisfaction

Source: Adapted from George L. Kelling and Mark H. Moore, *The Evolving Strategies of Policing* (Washington, D.C.: U.S. Department of Justice, National Institute of Justice Perspectives on Policing, November 1988).

independent "program" but is a part of the agency's method of service delivery; second, it conveys to those persons who are employed *inside* the organization a sense of who they are and the agency's philosophy.

SUMMARY

This chapter has shown the evolution of policing in America. Problems with some of the old methods, as well as the willingness of police leaders to rethink their basic role and develop new strategies, led us to community oriented policing and problem solving. It is much more than a simple "return to the basics"; it is instead a retooling of the basics or coming full circle.[67]

We believe that the incorporation of past wisdom and the use of new tools, methods, and strategies via COPPS offers the most promise for crime detection and prevention, addressing crime and disorder, and improving relations with the public. These partnerships are essential for addressing the "broken windows" phenomenon[68]—an influential theory asserting that once the process of physical decay begins, its effects multiply until some corrective action is taken. The lesson, they argued, was that we should redirect our thinking toward improving police handling of "little" problems. In short, the police need to be thinking like street-level criminologists, examining the underlying causes of crime, rather than functioning like bureaucrats. This theme is echoed at various points throughout the book.

NOTES

1. David R. Johnson, *American Law Enforcement History* (St. Louis: Forum Press, 1981), p. 11.
2. *Ibid.*, p. 13.
3. *Ibid.*, p. 14–15.
4. Leon Radzinowicz, *A History of English Criminal Law and Its Administration from 1750*, Vol. IV: *Grappling for Control* (London: Stevens & Son, 1968), p. 163.
5. Johnson, *American Law Enforcement History*, pp. 19–20.
6. A. C. Germann, Frank D. Day, and Robert R. J. Gallati, *Introduction to Law Enforcement and Criminal Justice* (Springfield, Ill.: Charles C. Thomas, 1962), p. 63.
7. Clive Emsley, *Policing and Its Context, 1750–1870* (New York: Schocken Books, 1983), p. 37.
8. Eric H. Monkkonen, *Police in Urban America, 1860–1920* (Cambridge, Eng.: Cambridge University Press, 1981), pp. 1–2.
9. Johnson, *American Law Enforcement History*, pp. 26–27.
10. See K. E. Jordan, *Ideology and the Coming of Professionalism: American Urban Police in the 1920s and 1930s* (Dissertation, Rutgers University, 1972); Robert M. Fogelson, *Big-City Police* (Cambridge, Mass.: Harvard University Press, 1977).
11. Johnson, *American Law Enforcement History*, p. 27.
12. James F. Richardson, *Urban Policing in the United States* (New York: Oxford Press, 1970), p. 51.
13. Johnson, *American Law Enforcement*, p. 92.
14. *Ibid.*, p. 92.
15. *Ibid.*, p. 92.
16. *Ibid.*, pp. 96–98.
17. *Ibid.*
18. Monkkonen, *Police in Urban America, 1860–1920*, p. 158.
19. John E. Eck, *The Investigation of Burglary and Robbery* (Washington, D.C.: Police Executive Research Forum, 1984).
20. See George L. Kelling, "Juveniles and Police: The End of the Nightstick," in Francis X. Hartmann (ed.), *From Children to Citizens, Vol. II: The Role of the Juvenile Court* (New York: Springer-Verlag, 1987).
21. Samuel Walker, *A Critical History of Police Reform: The Emergence of Professionalism* (Lexington, Mass.: Lexington Books, 1977), pp. 8–9, 11.
22. *Ibid.*, p. 33.
23. *Ibid.*, pp. 33–34, 42, 47.
24. *Ibid.*, p. 81.
25. *Ibid.*, pp. 80–83.
26. Herman Goldstein, *Policing a Free Society* (Cambridge, Mass.: Ballinger, 1977).
27. Albert Reiss, *The Police and the Public* (New Haven, Ct.: Yale University Press, 1971).
28. See Orlando Wilson, *Police Administration* (New York: McGraw-Hill, 1950).
29. Walker, *A Critical History of Police Reform*, pp. 93–94.
30. Mark H. Moore and George L. Kelling, "'To Serve and Protect': Learning from Police History," *The Public Interest* 70 (Winter 1983):49–65.
31. Peter K. Manning, "The Police: Mandate, Strategies, and Appearances," in *Crime and Justice in American Society*, ed. Jack D. Douglas (Indianapolis, Ind.: Bobbs-Merrill, 1971), pp. 149–63.
32. Walker, *A Critical History of Police Reform*, p. 161.
33. Louis Radelet, *The Police and the Community*, 4th ed. (New York: Macmillan, 1986), p. ix.
34. *Ibid.*, p. 17.

35. *Ibid.*, p. 21.
36. William G. Doerner, *Introduction to Law Enforcement: An Insider's View* (Englewood Cliffs, N.J.: Prentice Hall, 1992), pp. 21–23.
37. Mary Ann Wycoff, *The Role of Municipal Police Research as a Prelude to Changing It* (Washington, D.C.: Police Foundation, 1982).
38. Jerome H. Skolnick and David H. Bayley, *The New Blue Line: Police Innovation in Six American Cities* (New York: The Free Press, 1986), p. 4.
39. William C. Cunningham, John J. Strauchs, and Clifford W. Van Meter, *The Hallcrest Report II: Private Security Trends, 1970–2000* (McLean, Va.: Hallcrest Systems, 1990).
40. William Westley, *Violence and the Police: A Sociological Study of Law, Custom, and Morality* (Cambridge, Mass.: MIT Press), 1970.
41. American Bar Foundation, *The Urban Police Function*. Approved draft. Chicago: American Bar Association, 1973.
42. Jerome Skolnick, *Justice without Trial: Law Enforcement in Democratic Society* (New York: John Wiley & Sons, 1966).
43. Egon Bittner, "The Police on Skid Row: A Study of Peace Keeping," *American Sociological Review* 32:699–715, 1967.
44. Raymond I. Parnas, "The Police Response to the Domestic Disturbance," *Wisconsin Law Review*, (1967): 914–955.
45. James Q. Wilson, *Varieties of Police Behavior: The Management of Law and Order in Eight Communities* (Cambridge, Mass.: Harvard University Press), 1968.
46. Albert J. Reiss Jr., *The Police and the Public* (New Haven, Conn.: Yale University Press), 1971.
47. Goldstein, *Policing a Free Society*, pp. 22–24.
48. *Ibid.*, p. 11.
49. Elaine Cumming, Ian Cumming, and Laura Edell, "Policeman as Philosopher, Guide, and Friend," *Social Problems* 12 (1965):285; T. Bercal, "Calls for Police Assistance," *American Behavioral Scientist* 13 (1970):682; Albert J. Reiss, *The Police and the Public* (New Haven, Conn.: Yale University Press, 1971).
50. George Kelling, Tony Pate, Duane Dieckman, and Charles E. Brown, *The Kansas City Preventive Patrol Experiment: A Summary Report*. Washington, D.C.: Police Foundation, 1974.
51. Peter W. Greenwood, Joan Petersilia, and Jan Chaiken, *The Criminal Investigation Process* (Lexington, Mass.: D. C. Heath, 1977); John E. Eck, *Managing Case Assignments: The Burglary Investigation Decision Model Replication* (Washington, D.C.: Police Executive Research Forum, 1979).
52. Bernard Greenbert, S. Yu Oliver, and Karen Lang, *Enhancement of the Investigative Function, Vol. 1, Analysis and Conclusions*, Final Report, Phase 1 (Springfield, Va.: National Technical Information Service, 1973).
53. Kelling, Pate, Dieckman, and Brown, *The Kansas City Preventive Patrol Experiment*.
54. *Ibid.*
55. Joan Petersilia, "The Influence of Research on Policing," in *Critical Issues in Policing: Contemporary Readings*, eds. Roger C. Dunham and Geoffrey P. Alpert (Prospect Heights, Ill.: Waveland Press, 1989), pp. 230–47.
56. James Q. Wilson, *Thinking about Crime* (New York: Vintage Books, 1975).
57. Herman Goldstein, *Problem-Oriented Policing* (New York: McGraw-Hill, 1990), p. 13.
58. *Ibid.*, p. 3.
59. Thomas J. Baker, "Designing the Job to Motivate," *FBI Law Enforcement Bulletin* 45 (1976):3–7.
60. Samuel Walker, *The Police in America: An Introduction*, 2nd ed. (New York: McGraw-Hill, 1992), p. 185.
61. Police Foundation, *The Newark Foot Patrol Experiment* (Washington, D.C.: Author, 1981).

62. Robert Trojanowicz, *An Evaluation of the Neighborhood Foot Patrol Program in Flint, Michigan* (East Lansing, Mich.: School of Criminal Justice, Michigan State University, 1982).

63. Michael J. Farrell, "The Development of the Community Patrol Officer Program: Community-Oriented Policing in the New York City Police Department," in *Community Policing: Rhetoric or Reality*, eds. Jack R. Greene and Stephen D. Mastrofski (New York: Praeger, 1988), pp. 73–88.

64. George L. Kelling and Mark H. Moore, "The Evolving Strategy of Policing" (Washington, D.C.: National Institute of Justice, November 1988), p. 14.

65. Robert Trojanowicz and Bonnie Bucqueroux, *Community Policing: A Contemporary Perspective* (Cincinnati, Ohio: Anderson, 1990), p. 67.

66. *Ibid.*, p. 71.

67. Stephanie Thompson, "Community Policing Comes Full Circle," *American City and County* (February 1991):33–41.

68. James Q. Wilson and George L. Kelling, "Broken Windows: The Police and Neighborhood Safety," *The Atlantic Monthly* (March 1982):29–38.

A NATION IN FLUX
Changing People, Crime, and Policing

> It was the best of times, it was the worst of times.
> —Charles Dickens,
> *A Tale of Two Cities*

INTRODUCTION

In what kind of country do we live? What is the nature of its demographics and crime, and where is it headed? Have conventional policing methods of the past been effective and are they sufficient for the future? Or, rather, do the police need to prepare for change and begin putting strategic plans into motion? This chapter examines some of the many changes occurring in America and explores what the police must do to confront them.

This chapter opens with an examination of the changes that are occurring in the United States, beginning with its people—including immigration trends, the elderly, the youth, and how technology is creating a bifurcated society. Next, we consider the changing nature of criminality in the United States, especially the recent decline in crime, the juvenile crime debate, crime accelerators (guns, drugs, and alcohol), computer crime, and the impact of prison and jail populations. Then we examine fear of crime and its effects on neighborhoods. The chapter concludes with a view of what all of this means for the police, whose charge is to keep our neighborhoods safe.

The Changing Face of America

Demographics and Jobs: A Bifurcated Society

Nearly 273 million people now live in the United States; a little more than half (51 percent) are female. The population of the United States grew nearly 10 percent during the 1990s. About 82 percent of all people in the United States are white, 13 percent are black, and 5 percent are Asian, Pacific Islander, Native American, Eskimo, and Aleut; about 12 percent are Hispanic. Nearly two in three of all U.S. citizens own their own homes; there are about 2.63 persons per household, and about one-fourth (27.6 percent) of all households are headed by one person.[1]

The mean age of U.S. citizens is 36.5 years; 25 percent of the population are under 18 years of age, whereas about 13 percent are over 65. About 56 percent of the population are married and live with their spouse; about 19.4 million adults (9.4 percent) are divorced.[2] Also, as a result of the divorce rate and the number of single-parent homes, there is an increasing number of fatherless children—children who are more prone to delinquency and other social pathologies. Between 1960 and 1990, the percentage of children living apart from their biological fathers increased from 17 to 36 percent. By 2000, that number had increased to about half. Today, of the 27 percent of all children less than 18 years old who live with one parent, about 88 percent of them live with their mother. Many problems in crime control are strongly related to father absence: 90 percent of all homeless and runaway youths are from fatherless homes, as are 71 percent of high school dropouts, 70 percent of youths in state institutions, 75 percent of adolescent patients in substance abuse centers, and 85 percent of rapists who were motivated by displaced anger.[3]

Nearly half (45.2 percent) of the women 65 years old and over are widowed; of those, 70.1 percent live alone.[4] The oldest old (persons 85 years old and over) are a small but rapidly growing group and are projected to be the fastest-growing part of the elderly population well into the twenty-first century.[5]

Many changes are expected in the demographics of the United States between now and the year 2035. For example, life expectancy is expected to increase from 76.0 years to 82.6 years, and the median age of the population will increase from 34.0 in 1994 to 39.1, the increase being driven by the aging baby boom population born after World War II (1946–1964).[6]

A police officer works with Asian business owners to improve a shopping center that was rundown and was experiencing increased crime. (*Courtesy Community Policing Consortium*)

Coming to America: Immigration Trends

Almost one-third of the current population growth is caused by immigration.[7] Each year, from 660,000 to nearly one million aliens are lawfully admitted into the United States for permanent residence; hundreds of thousands of others are legally residing in the United States with temporary immigrant visas, pending a decision on their residency applications.[8] Another estimated 5 million undocumented immigrants reside in the United States as well, and there is an estimated increase of about 275,000 illegal aliens entering and residing in the United States each year. Many, about 2.1 million (41 percent), entered legally on a temporary basis and failed to depart. Mexico is the leading country of origin of illegal aliens, with about 2.7 million (or 54 percent) of the illegal immigrant population. California is the leading state of residence for these immigrants, with about two million (or 40 percent) of the undocumented population.[9]

The influence of immigration to the United States and the growth of minority group populations in general cannot be overstated. As noted, the United States now accepts nearly one million newcomers each year (with a net immigration of about 880,000 persons, which could increase or decrease in future years), or about 10 million new residents each decade (excluding their offspring), even if immigration rates do not rise.[10]

Immigrants to this nation, however, are not more crime-prone than native-born U.S. citizens. Among 18–40-year-old men in the United States, immigrants are less likely than native-born U.S. citizens to go to prison. Furthermore, recent immigrants are much less likely than earlier immigrants to be institutionalized. These results are the opposite of what one would predict, based on immigrant earnings—earlier immigrants typically had better success in the labor market.[11]

The Graying of America: Implications and Concerns

As indicated earlier, we live in a "graying" country as well, in which the fastest-growing age group is between 55 and 65.[12] The golden years for baby boomers represents a graying of the population. The first boomers reached age 50, or midlife, in 1996; soon they will command the aging agenda as they prepare for retirement in 2010 through 2030.

The rapid growth of the elderly, particularly the oldest old, represents a triumph of efforts to extend human life, but these age groups also require a large share of special services and public support. There will be large increases in some very vulnerable groups, such as the oldest old living alone, older women, elderly racial minorities living alone, and elderly unmarried persons with no living children or siblings.[13]

Mexicans account for approximately 54 percent of the illegal immigrant population in the United States. (*Courtesy* Harold Beasley)

The good news is the elderly are less likely than younger people to become victims of violence, personal theft, and household crimes and less likely to be injured during a violent crime (but their injuries, because of their brittle bones, are more severe). Those who are victimized can be permanently disabled. Living on fixed incomes, they often cannot receive the best medical care. They also have a great fear of crime but are less likely than younger people to take protective measures against crime but are more likely to report a crime. They can also be victimized in nursing homes and hospitals. They are targeted more often than other people for fraud involving finances, which can lead to severe depression and other serious health problems. Their isolation leads to a high percentage of their victimization occurring in their homes.[14] On the positive side, the elderly offer a tremendous work force resource as volunteers, which is discussed in Chapter 3.

A Generational Divide

In addition to the "graying" of America, the United States also has a sizable youthful contingent that will affect the country's social fabric, work force, and crime in the future. These youthful cohorts are obviously significant in terms of their problems, size, and societal impact. The baby boomers, however—by virtue of their sheer numbers (a total of 76 million, constituting roughly a third of the total nation's population in the late nineties), age, and influence—can fairly be said to presently control U.S. politics and boardrooms. They are the nation's leaders—including its chief executive officers, sheriffs, and police chiefs; they are conservative, influential policy makers, and leaders in the nation's current get-tough-on-crime movement, carrying the banner for such movements as "three strikes" laws and zero tolerance for crime in general.

The Gen-X (also known as baby busters) cohort, born between 1965 and 1976, now consists of about 17 percent of the population. They are overall more knowledgeable about technology than earlier generational groups and are probably more mobile and less concerned at present about a long-term career and retirement.

There is also the baby boomlet generation, born between 1977 and 1995; these are offspring of the baby boomers, who created a generation that is approaching boom status in its size and scope. Boomlet births began to rise in the late 1970s and have surpassed four million a year since 1989.[15] These young people are high-technology oriented and very mobile as well, and they tend to be very concerned about real-world issues.

Finally, there are the echo boomers, known as Generation Y, constituting a massive demographic group born since 1990 and now believed to be behind a quiet revolution across the United States. It can be seen in their clothes, hair, and penchant for technology.[16]

How does this generational divide affect policing? First, the police need to understand the perspective of each group's members. Americans age 18 and younger will soon form a generation as big as the original baby boom. They will likely be quicker than earlier generations to challenge the status quo and higher authority and for that reason will make recruiting, hiring, and training of future police officers more difficult. They are also much more multicultural and opinionated; more accepting of shifting sex roles; and differ widely from their predecessors in race, living arrangements, and socioeconomic class.

Haves and Have-Nots

Today the world is also rapidly becoming more technological—to the extent that there now exists what can be termed a serious "digital divide" (see Exhibit 2.1). The ability to produce and analyze information has become as important to our country as economics in terms of a person's social standing or ability to get a job.

"Smokestack America" is largely gone; today, there are fewer blue-collar jobs and more white-collar positions. The fastest-growing careers are those requiring language, mathematics, and reasoning skills. Today's economy is based on knowledge and the ability to process information; whereas employers in the past mostly wanted muscle, today more and more jobs presuppose skills, training, and education.

For dropouts and unskilled workers, finding family wage jobs with benefits will become more difficult in the twenty-first century. The globalization of the economy and technology is producing greater productivity and competition, larger profits, and fewer family wage jobs. Technology will not only eliminate some jobs in industries, such as banking and manufacturing, it will also change the educational skills needed for the new jobs. Not everyone has, uses, or knows how to use technology.[17]

Many have-not Americans report bleak lifestyles. One Gallup study found that about a quarter of Americans consider themselves to be have-nots; they worry about household finances "most" or "all" of the time, have not had enough money to pay for basic necessities at some time during the past year, perceive their financial situation as being worse than that of their parents, and label their financial situation as "poor" or "lower income."[18] Furthermore, many Americans have seen little benefit from the much-hyped economic boom of the late 1990s and early twenty-first century. Although many stock and dot.com company owners did in fact become wealthy during that boom, there were many employee layoffs and relatively lower labor prices.

THE CHANGING NATURE OF CRIME

Crime in America: Reasons for Its Decline

We reside in a violent country. Although the rates of personal crimes of violence and household crimes have declined substantially in the past two decades, one only needs to look at the news, read the papers, or, in some cases, merely listen to or look at the environment to realize that life and the property of others are almost valueless to a large number of Americans (see Exhibit 2.2).

Exhibit 2.1   The "Digital Divide": Haves and Have-Nots in Information Technologies

Three-quarters of U.S. households with annual incomes greater than $75,000 have a computer, compared with only one-third of households with incomes between $25,000 and $35,000. Caucasian and Asian-American families have more than double the access to computers and on-line services than African American, Native American, and Hispanic families have. These numbers worry people who are serving on a 26-member President's Information Technology Advisory Committee, who have had extensive discussions on what is called the "digital divide."

The committee wants to ensure that economic or geographic barriers do not prohibit anyone from using advanced communication technologies, especially at this point in time when more women and minorities need to be trained for information technology careers.

One-third of the U.S. economic growth since 1992 is attributable to businesses in the computing and communication industries. A gulf in access to information will affect education, employment, and income for disadvantaged groups. More research is needed on how information resources are distributed, what the sources of inequities are, and how to remedy them. Overall, the federal government is underinvesting in research on information technology and is too focused on short-term problems, the committee found.

Americans spend about $113 billion per year for federal, state, and local criminal justice activities (including law enforcement, courts, and corrections agencies). Nearly half ($48.6 billion, or 43 percent) of this amount is for police protection, whereas $24.5 billion (21.7 percent) is for the courts, and $39.8 billion (35.3 percent) is for corrections.[19] On any given day there are about 1.8 million persons incarcerated in U.S. prisons and jails; state prisons hold about 1.1 million inmates, and federal prisons hold about 118,000. Local jails hold about 600,000 men and women.[20]

There are about 29 million violent and property crime victimizations in the United States per year.[21] (Figure 2.1 and Table 2.1 depict four measures of serious violent crime and the changes in crime rates from 1960 to 1998, respectively.) A number of factors contribute to these figures: immediate access to firearms, alcohol, substance abuse, drug trafficking, poverty, racial discrimination, and cultural acceptance of violent behavior (see Exhibit 2.3).[22]

Crime places an enormous tax on our civil society; it is responsible for neighborhood degradation and for keeping people in their homes, students out of school, and people out of parks. It forces increased taxes to pay for more police,

Exhibit 2.2   Signs of the Times: Crime Related Bulletins from across the Nation

Following are some "typical" crime news accounts that occurred in the nation during 1999 and 2000. They do not involve "household name" offenders or victims, but they reflect the kinds of crimes that are reported countless times each day. Although it might be easy to become accustomed and even hardened to such reports, we should not forget that each case represents a terrible tragedy. Behind each occurrence is a tremendous degree of trauma to be borne by the victims or their survivors. Reflected in some of the accounts is the viciousness on the part of some of our nation's youth.

- A grisly inventory of body parts inside nine gym bags that surfaced in the Mokelumne River, near Sacramento, California, in August 2000 showed the complete remains of three people; police believe two additional people were killed in a botched $100,000 extortion plot (Associated Press).
- A 52-year-old New Jersey police officer with 29 years of service was charged with committing nine sex crimes against five girls since early 1992 (*LEN*, September 15, 1999, p. 2).
- A 13-year-old Michigan boy was convicted of second-degree murder for shooting an 18-year-old stranger. He is believed to be the youngest American ever convicted of murder as an adult (*LEN*, November 30, 1999, p. 3).
- Cleveland's South High School was the target of a plot by four students to carry out a massacre similar to the Columbine High School shootings in Colorado. Four youths were charged with plotting a racially motivated massacre at the predominantly black school (*LEN*, November 30, 1999, p. 3).
- Washington, D.C., police arrested a 16-year-old boy for wounding seven youths in a shootout at the National Zoo. The boy is the son of a convicted enforcer for what is said to be the largest drug ring in the District's history (*LEN*, April 30, 2000, p. 2).
- The District of Columbia police chief said that more than half of the 1,200 murders committed in the capital during the past four years are unsolved, because drug and gang connections make witnesses reluctant to come forward (*LEN*, May 15/31, 2000, p. 2).
- A 58-year-old former Michigan county sheriff was sentenced to 3 to 15 years in prison for raping a 26-year-old woman during a law enforcement convention (*LEN*, May 15/31, 2000, p. 2).

■ Two Texas police officers, a lieutenant and his sergeant wife, face charges that they beat and sexually assaulted a 13-year-old boy in their foster care (*LEN*, April 15, 2000, p. 3).

■ A 13-year-old Florida boy will be tried as an adult for allegedly shooting his teacher to death after being sent home from school for throwing water balloons; he faces life without parole if convicted (*LEN*, June 15, 2000, p. 2).

Source: "LEN" refers to *Law Enforcement News,* a publication of John Jay College of Criminal Justice, New York, New York. Used with permission.

causes families and businesses to flee, and results in poverty. Crime reduces competition by weeding out merchants who are unable to harden their businesses against crime; high crime rates also cause families and businesses to flee urban communities; thus, cities become home to more transient individuals.[23]

Although the preceding discussion presents an overall dismal picture, a recent decline in crime has made America safer and reduced fear as well. Between 1994 and 1998, the murder rate declined 30 percent. For other violent crimes, the National Crime Victim Survey (NCVS) data showed a 7 percent decline from 1997 to 1998 and a decrease of 26.7 percent from 1993 to 1998, as well as a 12 percent decline in property crimes. Additionally, violent crimes are expected to continue to decline.[24] As shown in Exhibit 2.3, several large cities have recently experienced declines in crime.

Why this decline in crime? Possible reasons that have been offered include the fact that state legislators have imposed tougher sentences on violent criminals and local officials are implementing aggressive and intelligent methods of community policing. The effectiveness of good police work and extended incarceration of hardened criminals is beyond dispute.[25]

When crime drops substantially in a particular city in one year, as has occurred in several recent instances, it is not likely that changes in demographics are the explanation (indeed, there were no such changes during the 1990s). The war on drugs has not caused the dramatic decreases in crime. Changes in the economy, incarceration rates, and police initiatives do, however, appear to have had an effect. First, the nation has experienced slow but steady economic growth since 1970. Crime did not begin to drop until 1991, so the economy, although it explains some of the decrease, does not explain all of it. Second, fed up with persistently high crime rates, the public demanded that chronic offenders be locked up for long periods, which helps explain some of the decline.

Proactive approaches to policing that include enforcement, community oriented policing and problem solving (discussed in Chapter 4), and crime prevention (discussed thoroughly in Chapter 5) are working.[26]

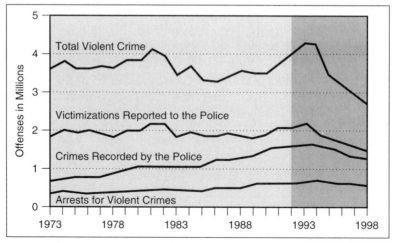

Note: The serious violent crimes included are rape, robbery, aggravated assault, and homicide. The light gray area indicates that, because of changes made to the victimization survey, data prior to 1992 are adjusted to make them comparable to data collected under the redesigned methodology. The adjustment methods are described in *Criminal Victimization 1973–95*. Estimates for 1993 and beyond are based on collection year while earlier estimates are based on data year.

FIGURE 2.1 Four measures of serious violent crime. (*Source:* The measures of serious violent crime come from two sources of data: The National Crime Victimization Survey (NCVS), a household survey ongoing since 1972, that interviews about 80,000 persons age 12 and older in 43,000 households twice each year about their victimizations from crime; and the *Uniform Crime Reports* (UCR) that collects information on crimes and arrests reported by law enforcement authorities to the FBI. U.S. Department of Justice, Bureau of Justice Statistics, "Serious Violent Crime Levels Continued to Decline in 1998." http://www.ojp.usdoj.gov/bjs/glance/cv2.htm

The Juvenile Crime Debate

In recent years there has been much fact, fiction, and debate about youth involvement in crime. Beginning in the mid-1990s, Americans were in a virtual panic over youth crime when some criminologists warned that a new wave of "superpredators" would soon hit the streets. Juvenile murder arrests were setting record after record (from 1984 to 1993, the number of homicides among juveniles that involved handguns increased fivefold),[27] as were arrests for aggravated assault and robbery. Several factors combined to cause this tide of youth violence, ranging from unsupervised children at home (57 percent of all children grow up without parental supervision after school because their parents are working), which led to many children learning values, ethics, and behaviors from peers and the popular culture, including the use of crack cocaine among the urban poor (with many youths involved in the drug market arming themselves as well).[28]

All of this, coupled with the impending increase in the numbers of young people entering crime-prone years (as discussed previously), led to predictions of

TABLE 2.1 **Change in Crime Rates, 1960–1998**

	Violent Crimes	Change in Number	Violent Crimes per 100,000	Change in Rate
1960	288,460	—	160	—
1970	738,820	156%	364	126%
1980	1,344,520	82	597	64
1990	1,820,130	35	732	23
1995	1,798,790	−1	684	−7
1998	1,531,044	−15	566	−17
	Total Crimes			
1960	3,384,200	—	1,887	—
1970	8,098,000	139%	3,985	111%
1980	13,408,300	66	5,950	49
1990	14,475,600	8	5,820	−2
1995	13,867,100	−5	5,277	−9
1998	12,475,634	−10	4,616	−13

Note: Change figure is the change from the previously listed year.

Sources: U.S. Department of Justice, Bureau of Justice Statistics. *Sourcebook of Criminal Justice Statistics, 1996;* Federal Bureau of Investigation, *Crime in the United States 1998: Uniform Crime Reports,* 1999.

an impending "crime storm" that set off a rash of tough-on-crime legislative initiatives, which sent more juveniles to adult court, put more metal detectors in schools, and resulted in many new curfews across the country.

Fortunately, however, the "superpredator" never materialized. In 1996 and 1997, there was a downturn in juvenile violent crimes, including the juvenile murder arrest rate and overall crime arrest rates. In 1998, the violent crime arrest rate for juveniles fell another 11 percent—30 percent less than 1994, with a murder rate that was half that of 1994.[29] Possible explanations include the tough crime measures taken by legislators, police, and courts; an improved economy; and the decline in the use of crack cocaine.[30]

Community policing, curfews, after-school activities, and conflict resolution classes have also been offered as reasons for the decline. Curfews probably had little overall effect, however, because studies show that most juvenile offenses are committed between 3:00 and 7:00 P.M.; furthermore, the value of conflict resolution programs in high school is probably negligible, because they miss the worst violators who are typically no longer in school. But, as one author noted, community policing mobilizes community resources to address the problems of our youth, "from clergy to women's clubs, mental health professionals and businesses, all tired of being victimized by a generation in crisis."[31]

Many people believe the jury is still out on juvenile crimes, however, especially given the future wave of new boomers that will arrive soon. Indeed, a 2000

Exhibit 2.3   Decreases in Crime: The Facts

- *FACT: New York City reduced crime by using tougher policies and better targeting of resources.* From 1993 through 1998, overall crime in New York City fell by 47 percent and murder fell by 60 percent because of tougher policies and better targeting of resources. The New York Police Department (NYPD) took a proactive approach to fighting crime. It sharply improved both the management of its 38,000 employees and its accountability practices. Regular meetings to analyze crime statistics help to tackle problems, whereas sophisticated computer models make it easy to identify hot spots. The NYPD sends some of its best police executives to neighborhood assignments.

- *FACT: Community policing, technology, and neighborhood crime watches have helped Boston reduce crime by 30 percent since 1996.* Boston's success in reducing crime may, in fact, be understated. Crime rates stand at their lowest levels since the city began using the current statistical methods in 1968. Boston officials took a new stance on public disorder and worked tirelessly to improve community contact with police. More than 1,000 citizen neighborhood crime watch programs now blanket the city, coordinated by citizens themselves. The neighborhoods sponsor regular community meetings, provide information to police, and participate in everything from street sign repair to neighborhood festivals. Police captains are held accountable for the crime rates in their own districts.

- *FACT: In Jacksonville, Florida, the crime rate has fallen despite an influx of nearly 60,000 new residents in the 1990s.* Only one other city (San Diego) has seen its crime rates fall as quickly as Jacksonville's during the 1990s. A recent survey revealed a 20 percent decrease in the number of people who felt unsafe walking in their communities at night between 1996 and 1998. Jacksonville police stress that increased community participation in police work helped them reduce crime. Seventeen advisory councils help the police get to know each community.

- *FACT: Crime is at a 25-year low in San Diego, which now has the reputation of being one of the safest large cities in America.* The San Diego Police Department (SDPD) has built impressive relationships with community organizations. There has been, according to one news account, "an unprecedented drop in crime, a veritable love-fest between neighborhoods and the Police Department, and a high level of pride among rank-and-file officers." The SDPD manages to combine toughness against criminals with a community-friendly public face. Officers got to know residents in their communities by name. Two-person teams developed effective ways of sharing information on specific problems. The police chief launched an immediate and thorough investigation whenever allegations of racial prejudice surfaced. Criminals live in justifiable fear. In 1998, civilian volunteers saved the SDPD $2.7 million by helping out with everything from litter control to crowd control.

Source: Robert E. Moffit and David B. Muhlhausen, *Issues 2000: The Candidate's Briefing Book* (Washington, D.C.: The Heritage Foundation, 2000). Used with permission.

report by the federal Office of Juvenile Justice and Delinquency Prevention cautioned that

> The decrease in juvenile crime will be fleeting, however, if we fail to temper the good news with caution. We need to continue focusing our efforts on combating juvenile crime with programs that have proven to be effective in reducing juvenile delinquency and violence.[32]

Whether we can expect a new and bigger juvenile violent crime crisis or, rather, more good news in the form of continued crime decreases depends largely on newly formed coalitions between police and communities, as is discussed more in later chapters.

Crime Accelerators: Guns, Drugs, and Alcohol

Notwithstanding the recent declining crime wave among juveniles with respect to violent crimes, as discussed previously, several ingredients for disaster will still afflict this nation unless dramatic changes are effected. Three possible "accelerators"—guns, drugs, and alcohol—might still increase the risk of victimization and a general fear of crime.

Nearly 200 million guns are in private hands in the United States, with 74 percent of gun owners possessing two or more. Interestingly, gun ownership is highest among middle-aged, college educated people of rural America who use them primarily for recreation. A little more than half of all privately owned firearms are stored unlocked.[33] Gun violence in the United States is both a criminal justice and a public health problem, with gun-related crime peaking in the late 1980s and early 1990s (in 1997, the national homicide rate declined to a 30-year low of 7 murders per 100,000 residents).

But homicide rates still remain unacceptably high, and firearms are still the weapons most frequently used for murder—they are the weapon of choice in nearly two-thirds of all murders. The impact of gun violence is even more

While the debate about juveniles continues, youth crime is at the forefront of the public's concerns. (*Courtesy* NYPD Photo Unit)

pronounced on juveniles and young adults. For persons ages 15 to 24, the U.S. homicide rate of 15.2 per 100,000 people is higher than the combined total homicide rate of 11 other industrialized nations. Strategies and programs to reduce gun violence include interrupting sources of illegal guns, deterring illegal possession and carrying of guns, and responding to illegal gun use.[34]

Alcohol and drugs are also major factors in crime and violence, with almost four in ten violent crimes involving alcohol. Nearly two million offenders (about 36 percent of the total) reported in 1996 that they were using alcohol at the time of their offense.[35] With respect to drugs, more than 277,000 offenders are in prison for a drug law violation—21 percent of state prisoners and more than 60 percent of federal prisoners. More than 80 percent of state prisoners and 70 percent of federal prisoners have engaged in some form of illicit drug use. One-third of state prison inmates and 22 percent of federal prisoners report they were under the influence of drugs when they committed the crime for which they are in prison.[36]

The New Challenge: Computer Crime

Certainly the advent of computer crime has changed the world of policing, posing new and extraordinary challenges. An estimated 144 million Americans are now plugged into cyberspace, and thousands more enter the on-line world each day.[37] The Internet has revolutionized the way people communicate, shop, entertain, learn, and conduct business.

But as the saying goes, "the fleas come with the dog"; this high-tech revolution in our homes and offices has opened a whole new world for the criminal element as well. Pornographers and pedophiles are now on the Web, as well as people who trade stolen credit card numbers, rig auctions, create viruses, and devise baby adoption scams, among many other crimes. In June 2000, the first Internet serial killer was charged with murdering five women in two states and stuffing their bodies into metal drums.[38]

CyberAngels, an organization founded by a 21-year-old man, assists victims of Internet crimes and receives 650 on-line stalking complaints every day. During 1999, the Federal Trade Commission received more than 18,000 Internet-related complaints—more than double the 1998 volume. The FBI opened 1,500 on-line child sex cases in 1999, an increase from 700 in 1998. And 70 percent of companies experienced cyberattacks during 1999, up from 42 percent in 1998. Nearly 300 companies reported losses of more than $265 million.[39] The Internet has at least 300 Web sites that offer counterfeit driver's licenses, law enforcement credentials, passports, social security cards, and military identification cards.[40]

Education would seem to be the best means to prevent computer crime. As one federal agency's motto reads, "A bit of prevention is worth a gigabyte of cure."[41] Many police-developed brochures are now available in the public sector, providing tips and ideas on how citizens can reduce their chances of being victimized by computer criminals. Specifically, pamphlets discuss copyright violations and pirated software, computer viruses, and tactics that are used to induce victims to disclose their passwords or other sensitive computer information. Tips are also provided on how to use caution when using cellular phones and automatic teller machine cards. In the private sector, hotlines now exist that allow employees to report such incidents as employees' taking home copies of software or stealing other computer equipment, downloading pornography onto their computers during work hours, and playing computer games at work.[42]

The Impact of Prison and Jail Populations

Another element to be reckoned with when policy analysts consider this country's contemporary crime problem involves those persons who are leaving its prisons and jails. From 1990 to 1997, the number of people in federal and state prisons or county jails rose by almost 680,000; despite decreasing crime rates and unprecedented economic expansion, the United States continues to lock up its citizens at a rate of six to ten times higher than any comparable industrialized democracy.[43]

Incarceration rates increase because states are tough on parole violators and because prisoners are now required to serve more of their sentences before their release. A small number of serious habitual offenders commit most of the violent crimes in America. They are typically young (15–24 years old), come from broken homes, are irreligious, have histories of drug and alcohol abuse and physical and sexual abuse, and possess low verbal skills and poor academic records.[44]

The high incarceration rates of the 1990s will result in a flood of unemployed ex-inmates from prisons and jails in the next two decades. When adult and juvenile parolees return to the community unemployed, they often attempt to make money through street crime, drug sales, and extortion from women on welfare (known as welfare pimps, some such men collect from five or six mothers on welfare per month). The current lack of sufficient reintegration programs, high recidivism rates, and the number of persons to be released from jails and prisons should signal an alarm to everyone.[45]

FEAR OF CRIME

Effects of Crime and Disorder

Crime and disorder can take many forms from neighborhood to neighborhood:

- The parking lots of fast-food restaurants in many downtown areas witness a nightly invasion of youths who gather to drink, fight, and vandalize; restaurant owners complain frequently of litter and damaged property.
- High-rise apartment complexes are plagued in many communities with crime, especially against the elderly and on weekends, with rapes and robberies continuing to rise in number.
- Young men sell drugs openly on street corners in front of residences. Drive-by shootings by gang members occur. Neighbors complain numerous times but to no avail; citizens, upset with the seemingly meaningless effect of an officer's occasional cruise by the area, threaten to take the law into their own hands.
- During a three-month period, detectives investigate a string of seemingly unrelated strong-armed robberies in one area of the city.
- Small bands of youths begin to commit a series of nighttime car burglaries, removing car stereos in less than two minutes.
- Middle-class married couples, apparently happy by day, commence drinking heavily each night; the police are summoned when the couple eventually begin shouting at and assaulting one another. Over time, officers are summoned to their domestic disturbances on numerous occasions.

Crime, fear, and disorder frighten Americans. Understandably, one of the greatest fears in the United States is the fear of crime (see Exhibit 2.4). The fear of crime is the number one factor keeping business out of high-poverty neighborhoods.[46] It costs America more than $1 trillion annually. Violent crime, including arson and drunk driving, costs an estimated $426 billion per year, including $105 billion in medical costs, lost earnings, and victim assistance.[47]

We know that neighborhood disorder affects a person's perception of safety as much as crime does. People express greater fear of strangers loitering near their homes than they do the threat of murder. They fear being bothered by people they view as sinister: panhandlers, drunks, addicts, rowdy teens, mental patients, and the homeless. They also fear physical disorder: litter, abandoned buildings, potholes, broken street lights and windows, wrecked cars, and other indicators of neighborhood decline.

Thomas Hobbes wrote in 1651 that the "fundamental purpose of civil government is to establish order, protecting citizens from a fear of criminal attack

Drunks, panhandlers, and the homeless add to people's perceptions of safety as much as do actual crimes.

Exhibit 2.4   "Body-Bag Journalism Fuels Cynicism and Fear"

Television journalism's preoccupation with bloody crimes and violent disaster footage is creating a nation of cynical, fearful viewers, according to two recent studies. "You get this body-bag journalism over and over again," said Joseph Angotti, director of a study by the University of Miami's School of Communication. The Miami study looked at local news during a four-month period in 1996 and 1997 in eight major cities; another study by Rocky Mountain Media Watch in Denver found that local news shows averaged 43 percent on its "mayhem index," meaning that nearly half the broadcast reported violent crimes or disasters.

"This kind of tabloid journalism is empty calories for the mind," said Paul Klite, head of the Denver organization. One station that was singled out, with an index of 74.5 percent, reported on two ambulance accidents, a robbery at an ATM, two sex offenders, a shooting, a truck being hit by a bullet, the trial of a negligent mother, and a father holding his daughter at knifepoint.

Barbara Cochran, president of the Radio and Television News Directors Association in Washington, said crime news appeals to TV news directors because it often involves good visuals and is easy to do; she added that it also provides a public service by warning people of dangerous situations.

Source: Adapted from " 'Body-Bag Journalism' Fuels Cynicism, Fear," *Law Enforcement News,* John Jay College of Criminal Justice, May 3, 1997, p. 6. Used with permission.

---

that can make life "nasty, brutish, and short."[48] It would appear, using this Hobbesian scale, that "the current level and distribution of fear indicate an important government failure."[49] For the past 30 years, the dominant police strategy has emphasized motorized patrol, rapid response time, and retrospective investigation of crimes. Those strategies were not designed to address root community problems but instead for criminal detection and apprehension—the "crime-fighter" cop.

People create organizations to carry out missions. In the United States, the police have adopted the notion that their principal mission is to control crime and maintain order. And they believe that they should carry out this mission through legal systems such as traffic courts, the criminal justice system, and the juvenile justice system.[50] Police administrators, in assessing their officers' effectiveness, ask questions such as how fast officers get to victims, how many arrests are made, and what percentage of cases are cleared.

Chapter 4 includes a discussion of what community oriented policing and problem solving (COPPS) can do to address the fear of crime.

SIGNIFICANCE FOR THE POLICE

What can the police do about all of these crime issues? Can they hold the line and diminish the spread of criminality? Next we explore these questions.

Keeping Neighborhoods Safe

Neighborhoods become vulnerable to the changing crime patterns surrounding them and vary in their capacity to resist crime. A neighborhood is less vulnerable if it is physically insulated from intrusion by outsiders (especially offenders) and if it is able to resist changes in commercial or other activities that attract offenders. Neighborhoods are also vulnerable to demographic changes, especially when a growing population must be accommodated in a housing market and in the trickle down of housing in that market. Especially important is the influx of single-parent households and of unrelated individuals.[51] As these transitional processes get under way, there is often little effort to repair the physical state of deterioration or to counter its symbolic significance. Albert Reiss stated that

> Inattention and its cumulative effects are rapid—a matter of a few years rather than of decades. Property crime . . . gives way to crimes against persons. The final stage in this transition to a high crime rate is a community that is physically deteriorated, has less residential and commercial property, and fewer residents. These rates eventually stabilize at a level that is high in relation to other neighborhoods in the city.[52]

From the standpoint of community life, the control of property crimes is important for quality of life and for preventing a transition to a high crime rate. This is true for several reasons. First, the destruction of property often leaves communi-

An abandoned residence vandalized with gang graffiti shows how quickly a neighborhood may decline. (*Courtesy* Sgt. Dominic Licavoli, LAPD)

ties with inadequate housing and the symbolic evidence of growing crime. Second, the effects are rapidly cumulative. Third, crimes against property are responsible for an exodus from the community. Finally, crimes against property from arson to malicious destruction of property and a disregard for its value (such as the abandonment of vehicles in the streets) are committed more often by juveniles than by adults.[53]

It has been shown that the police will certainly face powerful challenges in the years ahead. The methods of addressing those challenges must certainly change, also.

SUMMARY

This chapter examined a number of changes that are occurring in America, particularly with respect to its people and the nature of violence. Although violent crime has been declining of late, the years ahead certainly may not be tranquil. We cannot afford to "hurtle into the future with our eyes fixed firmly on the rearview mirror."[54] Social, political, and economic events of today are causing policing to change forever. A failure to strategically plan for what many police practitioners predict will be a turbulent and complex future could produce untenable consequences. Business as usual will probably not suffice.

In many ways these are, as Dickens said, "the worst of times" for American policing. The potential of problem solving, however, offers hope for those proactive police administrators who are strategically planning for the future of their agencies.

NOTES

1. U.S. Census Bureau, *Statistics in Brief: Population and Vital Statistics* (Washington, D.C.: Author, 2000).
2. *Ibid.*
3. *Ibid.*, p. 11.
4. U.S. Census Bureau, *Current Population Reports: Marital Status and Living Arrangements* (Washington, D.C.: Author, March 1998), p. 2.
5. Frank B. Hobbs, "The Elderly Population" (Washington, D.C.: U.S. Census Bureau, 1999), p. 2.
6. Jennifer Cheeseman Day, *National Population Projections* (Washington, D.C.: U.S. Census Bureau, 1999), pp. 1–2.
7. *Ibid.*, p. 2.
8. U.S. Department of Justice, Immigration and Naturalization Service, *Legal Immigration, Fiscal Year 1998* (Washington, D.C.: Author, May 1999), pp. 1–3.
9. U.S. Census Bureau, *Illegal Alien Resident Population* (Washington, D.C.: Author, 2000), p. 1.
10. Day, *National Population Projections*, p. 1.
11. Kristin F. Butcher and Anne Morrison Piehl, "Recent Immigrants: Unexpected Implications for Crime and Incarceration," National Bureau of Economic Research, *NBER Working Papers*, No. 6067, June 1997, p. 1.

12. Cicero Wilson, "Economic Shifts That Will Impact Crime Control and Community Mobilization," in U.S. Department of Justice, National Institute of Justice, *What Can the Federal Government Do to Decrease Crime and Revitalize Communities?* (Washington, D.C.: Author, 1998), p. 4.
13. Konrad M. Kressly, "Golden Years for Baby Boomers: America in the Next Century," *The Harbinger* (January 1998):1.
14. Andrew Karmen, *Crime Victims: An Introduction to Victimology*, 3rd ed. (Belmont, Calif.: Wadsworth, 1996), pp. 263–64.
15. Diane Crispell, "Where Generations Divide: A Guide," *American Demographics* (May 1993):2.
16. Christie Appelhanz, "Make Room—and Lots of It—for Generation Y," *The Topeka Capitol-Journal*, December 18, 1999, p. 1D.
17. Don Tapscott, *Growing Up Digital: The Rise of the Net Generation* (New York: McGraw-Hill, 1998), p. 255.
18. Gallup News Service, "Have and Have Nots" (Princeton, N.J.: The Gallup Organization, 2000), p. 1.
19. U.S. Department of Justice, Bureau of Justice Statistics, *Justice Expenditure and Employment in the United States, 1995* (Washington, D.C.: Author, November 1999), p. 1.
20. U.S. Department of Justice, Bureau of Justice Statistics Press Release, "Nation's Prison and Jail Population Reaches 1,860,520, Could Reach Two Million by Late 2001," April 19, 2000.
21. U.S. Department of Justice, Bureau of Justice Statistics Press Release, "National Violent Crime Rate Falls More Than 10 Percent—Violent Victimizations Down One-Third Since 1993," August 27, 2000.
22. Lee P. Brown, "Violent Crime and Community Involvement," *FBI Law Enforcement Bulletin* (May 1992):2–5.
23. Robert E. Moffit and David B. Mulhausen, "Crime: Making America Safer," *Issues 2000: The Candidate's Briefing Book* (Washington, D.C.: The Heritage Foundation), p. 5.
24. *Ibid.*, pp. 2–3.
25. *Ibid.*, p. 3.
26. Bill Blackwood Law Enforcement Management Institute of Texas, TELEMASP Bulletin, *Why the Drop in Crime? Part I: Measuring Crime* (Huntsville, Tex.: Sam Houston State University, January 1999), pp. 2–3.
27. Richard Abshire, "Facts and Fiction about Youth Violence," *Law Enforcement Technology* (July 1997):53.
28. *Ibid.*, pp. 53–54.
29. David Westphal, "Predicted Teen-Age Crime Wave Failed to Occur, Numbers Show," *Fresno Bee*, Washington Bureau, December 13, 1999, p. 1.
30. *Ibid.*, p. 2.
31. Abshire, "Fact and Fiction about Youth Violence," p. 56.
32. U.S. Department of Justice, Office of Juvenile Justice and Delinquency Prevention, Juvenile Justice Bulletin, 1999 National Report Series, *Challenging the Myths* (Washington, D.C.: Author), p. 1.
33. U.S. Department of Justice, National Institute of Justice, *Guns in America: National Survey on Private Ownership and Use of Firearms* (Washington, D.C.: Author, 1997), pp. 1–2.
34. David Sheppard, "Strategies to Reduce Gun Violence" (U.S. Department of Justice, Office of Juvenile Justice and Delinquency Prevention Fact Sheet 93, February 1999), p. 1.
35. U.S. Department of Justice, Bureau of Justice Statistics, *Alcohol and Crime* (Washington, D.C.: Author, 1998), p. 20.
36. U.S. Department of Justice, Bureau of Justice Statistics Press Release, "More Than Three-Quarters of Prisoners Had Abused Drugs in the Past," January 5, 1999.
37. Margaret Mannix, "The Web's Dark Side," *U.S. News and World Report*, August 28, 2000, p. 36.

38. *Ibid.*

39. *Ibid.*, pp. 37–38.

40. *Ibid.*, p. 45.

41. Matt Parsons, "Crime Prevention and the Electronic Frontier," *FBI Law Enforcement Bulletin* (October 1998):7.

42. *Ibid.*, p. 8.

43. Jenni Gainsborough, "What Happens after Prisons?" letter to the editor, *The Washington Post*, August 25, 1999, p. A16.

44. James Q. Wilson, "Crime and Public Policy," in *Crime*, eds. James Q. Wilson and Joan Petersilia (San Francisco: ICS Press, Institute for Contemporary Studies, 1995), p. 492.

45. Wilson, "Economic Shifts," p. 11.

46. See James K. Stewart, "The Urban Strangler: How Crime Causes Poverty in the Inner City," *Policy Review* (Summer 1986), p. 6.

47. Moffit and Mulhausen, "Crime," p. 5.

48. Thomas Hobbes, in *Leviathan*, ed. C. B. Macpherson (Baltimore, Md.: Pelican Books, 1968), p. 17.

49. Mark H. Moore and Robert C. Trojanowicz, "Policing and the Fear of Crime" (Washington, D.C.: National Institute of Justice, 1988), p. 2.

50. Robert Fogelson, *Big City Police* (Cambridge, Mass.: Harvard University Press, 1977).

51. Albert J. Reiss, "Crime Control and the Quality of Life," *American Behavioral Scientist* 27 (September/October 1983):52–53.

52. *Ibid.*, pp. 53–54.

53. *Ibid.*, p. 55.

54. Neil Postman, quoted in David Osborne and Ted Gaebler, *Reinventing Government: How the Entrepreneurial Spirit Is Transforming the Public Sector* (Reading, Mass.: Addison-Wesley, 1992), p. 19.

ATTENDING TO THE "CUSTOMER"
Community Oriented Government

INTRODUCTION

To better understand community oriented policing and problem solving (COPPS, discussed thoroughly in Chapter 4), this chapter examines one of the basic premises on which this strategy is founded: how government and the police should and do conduct business with respect to their "customers," and the need to "reinvent" government by empowering citizens to assist in reclaiming their neighborhoods from crime and disorder. Specifically, we discuss the independent nature of the American people and their occasionally forgotten ability to control their own problems. We include a discussion of how many government and police agencies have traditionally conducted business with the public.

We begin by discussing citizens as clients and customers, and as communitarians and volunteers. Next is a vital aspect of community oriented government: building partnerships. Following is a discussion of a concept that can assist in a COPPS initiative: total quality management (TQM). After reviewing how criminal justice organizations are often rewarded for their failures and should borrow ideas from business, we conclude the chapter with a discussion of how justice agencies can become partners in community justice and provide several illustrations of community oriented government.

CITIZENS AS CLIENTS AND CUSTOMERS

Individualism versus Clienthood

Do the majority of citizens today believe they are valued customers when they visit a police station or some other agency of criminal justice? Any agency of government? If we believe that question must be answered in the negative, it is because the public has been shut out of many of these agencies over time. Unfortunately, many public agencies would probably have considerable difficulty merely attempting to define exactly who their customers are. Furthermore, they may have forgotten long ago that quality is determined only by customers.[1] This situation must be corrected, supplanted with one in which the public and its government representatives and employees enjoy a closer relationship.

Indeed, it is important that the public be empowered by government to engage in the identification and resolution of neighborhood concerns. It is well established that people act more responsibly when they control their own environments than when they are controlled by others. Empowerment is an American tradition.[2] Yet, with the public's business, we seem to forget our independent spirit. We get locked into the "It's always been done this way" mind-set and bar the community from getting involved to any significant extent.

The community, for its part, allows government workers to dictate policy and procedure. This practice undermines public confidence in the community; it creates *dependency* and *clienthood*. From a COPPS perspective, clienthood is an undesirable trait of community life:

> Clients are people who are dependent upon and controlled by their helpers and leaders. Clients are people who wait for others to act on their behalf. Citizens, on the other hand, are people who understand their own problems in their own terms. Good clients make bad citizens. Good citizens make strong communities.[3]

Before 1900, local communities basically cared for themselves, because the majority of goods and services were produced and sold locally. Only with the emergence of an industrial economy did we begin to hire professionals and bureaucrats to do what families, neighborhoods, churches, and voluntary associations had formerly done. Then, after the depression, prosperity and mobility further diminished the bonds of the community and the "professionals" gained a foothold.

But the public reacted strongly. During the 1960s, neighborhoods fought against urban renewal, minorities battled for control over Great Society programs, the welfare rights movement had emerged to demand more control over the welfare system, and a tenants' rights movement demanded more control over public housing. Consumers wanted more control over products, a holistic health movement sought to give people more control over their health care, and a deinstitutionalization movement sought to give the mentally ill more control over their environments. There was a general effort to force authorities to share their power, through "sunshine" laws, freedom of information acts, rights-to-know laws, open-meeting laws, and so on.[4] People were convinced that control over their lives had been ceded to big business, big government, and big labor.

COMMUNITARIANISM AND VOLUNTEERISM

Citizens Fulfilling Responsibilities

A relatively new concept that has begun to attract the attention of academics and politicians alike—one that has application to problem solving and the general notion of community involvement in problem solving—is "communitarianism." This concept, promulgated by prominent sociologist Amitai Etzioni and other academics, argues that we have gone too far toward extending rights to our citizens and not far enough in asking them to fulfill responsibilities to the community as a whole. Focusing not so much on politics as on the process of government, "it is a mindset that says the whole community needs to take responsibility for itself. People need to actively participate, not just give their opinions . . . but instead give time, energy, and money."[5]

In this view, communitarianism is an attempt to nurture an underlying structure of "civil society"—sound families, caring neighbors, the whole web of churches, Rotary clubs, block associations, and nonprofit organizations that give individuals their moral compass and communities their strength. Communitarians have tapped into a rich vein of frustration with public behavior that has been eating away at the quality of community life, from drug dealing to aggressive panhandling. Communitarians believe our political culture is in very bad shape, not only because elected officials have done a bad job but also because citizens have not attended to the meaning of citizenship.[6]

As a result, communitarians support processes such as problem solving, in which neighborhoods have taken matters into their own hands, closing off streets and creating other physical barriers to disrupt the drug trade, working to overcome problems of homelessness and panhandling, and so on. This is where communitarians overlap with the objectives of community problem solving: the recognition that many of the answers to community problems lie not with government, but in the community at large.

Volunteerism in Action

A related concept is the need for greater support for volunteerism. It is estimated by Independent Sector, a group that studies and represents nonprofit organizations, that there are now 93 million volunteers in America, donating a stunning 20.3 billion hours of their time—a yearly average of 218 hours per person. Only about 8.4 percent of those 93 million volunteers, however, work in "human services," a broad category that includes aiding the homeless, family counseling, and helping the Red Cross; only about 1.2 percent volunteer as mentors or substance-abuse prevention counselors.[7]

Volunteers are believed by some to be people who do not have anything better to do with their time. Nothing could be further from the truth. Most are simply looking for a meaningful opportunity to contribute and give something back to their communities. Most prefer to have challenging assignments that combine the knowledge and skills they have developed in their professional careers with new applications in policing.[8]

Volunteering can build a sense of community, break down barriers between people, and raise our quality of life. Volunteers quickly lose interest if they are

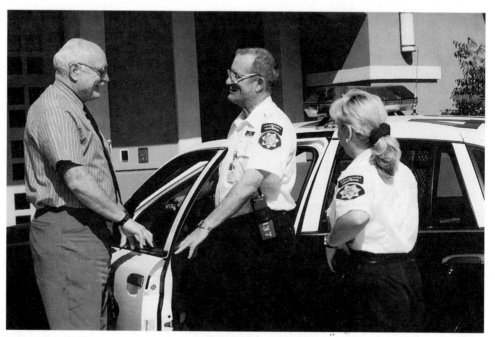

Volunteers provide a vital service to communities. (*Courtesy* Concord, California, Police Department)

not given meaningful work; therefore, police and other government agencies and nonprofit organizations need to ensure that their volunteers are active. Also, the attitude that "volunteers who work for free can't be valuable" must be cast aside. Such community efforts as COPPS need to be focused, powerful, and involve working with other people. This is the form of volunteering that is most likely to get at society's core problems.[9] Exhibit 3.1 provides examples of how some police agencies have used, and benefited from, the public's interest in volunteerism.

There are "Four R's" in volunteer programming: researching, recruiting, retaining, and recognizing.

1. *Researching* includes identifying needs and developing related job descriptions and handbooks (for both volunteers and supervisors).
2. *Recruiting*—at such places as job fairs, colleges, senior centers, and in newspaper and radio ads—entails putting volunteers through a complete background check, drug testing, fingerprinting, and polygraph testing.
3. *Retaining* involves showing the volunteers that they are valued and needed, so that they will continue to give of their time.
4. *Recognizing* occurs in the form of service awards, social events, birthday cards, and so on; volunteers must be rewarded on a regular basis, because recognition is the volunteer's paycheck.[10]

BUILDING PARTNERSHIPS

Why should the police be interested in forging partnerships? Isn't their job to enforce the law and solve crime problems rather than nurture relationships? It is true: Partnerships are difficult. Indeed, one official with the U.S. Conference of Mayors stated

> I think that among the biggest obstacles is the resistance of police departments and police officers to change what they see as their jobs, and mistrust on the part of the community.[11]

A small town, an industrial city, a capital city, a university town, a metropolis—all differ radically in terms of crime rate, types of crime, the degree of cultural homogeneity or heterogeneity, financial and organizational resources, political conditions, and the fear of crime. Under these circumstances, it will take time for police and nonpolice people to build relationships, to learn to trust each other, to find mutual interests and concerns, and to learn a common language. But police officers all across the country are learning that long-term solutions to problems require partnerships.[12]

A partnership, according to *Webster's*, is "a relationship involving close cooperation between parties having specified and joint rights and responsibilities."[13] The community is not the only potential partner; partnerships may also be forged with social agencies, religious and business groups, educational institutions, and

EXHIBIT 3.1   Volunteers in Action

Volunteering in Concord, California

The Concord, California, Police Department (PD) believes that the police have been "losing out" for many years because of their failure to recognize the many skills and abilities that volunteers have acquired in their professional careers. For example, Concord PD has a volunteer who was the former director of information systems for a large national company for more than 20 years. With the department's increased use of information systems and interest in various software programs (such as Excel or Lotus), this is an area just waiting to be tapped. Former school teachers give tours of the police headquarters, and persons experienced as nurses and ham radio operators are being used to develop a citywide disaster plan in the event of an emergency. Volunteers are also involved with neighborhood watch programs, compiling crime statistics for individual neighborhoods and coordinating meetings. Others assist in the domestic violence unit by designing computer programs for data, compiling information and working with victims (some are specially trained to work directly with victims and provide support during court appearances).

Using Volunteers to Track Deadbeat Parents

Special posses, under the direction of the county sheriff in Maricopa County, Arizona, set out to find and arrest deadbeat parents who ignore their financial obligations to their families. Posse and reserve members work closely with the warrants unit, conducting background checks once the court issues an action against a parent for back child support. The group researches the individual's previous residences, locates information on former employers, and attempts to find friends and associates. These volunteers contact the motor vehicle department, run criminal history checks, and scan jail and prison rosters for possible leads. Frequently, as many as 150 volunteers participate. To date, their efforts have resulted in more than 60 arrests.

Running the Gamut: Other Volunteers Making a Difference

Volunteer programs in Phoenix, Arizona, and Los Angeles both began in 1982. In Phoenix, 120 volunteers do everything from helping stranded motorists and serving as liaisons between the department and the families of homicide victims to following up on missing person cases. Los Angeles's sheriff's office has the largest volunteer program in the country, with 4,300 members who donate about 350,000 hours a year in a variety of programs.

Sources: Karen Siemsen, "For a Full Menu of Policing Services, Partner with Volunteers," *Community Policing Exchange* (September/October 1998), p. 8; Joe Arpaio, "Arizona Posse Tracks Deadbeat Parents," in *Partnerships* (Washington, D.C.: Community Policing Consortium, 1995–1998 Edition), p. 49; Ronnie L. Paynter, "Helping Hands," *Law Enforcement Technology* (March 1999), p. 30; and Marilyn Jensen, "Volunteers Can Make a Difference, *Law and Order* (September 1998), p. 102.

individuals. Community policing partnerships make sense when they are formed to solve problems.[14]

Imagine the following scenario: You are a police officer and have been invited to attend a neighborhood meeting. At the meeting, residents complain about prostitution and drug dealing and wish to form a partnership with the police. Using a problem solving approach, the following six steps represent the systematic process that you might follow to form a partnership and reduce or solve these problems.[15]

Step 1: Build a relationship. The first step before seeking partnerships is to find out where the problem areas are and then ask, "Who is directly involved? Who has a stake in getting this problem cleaned up?" Answering these questions might lead a police agency to the most productive partnerships for addressing a specific problem. Once a specific issue and potential allies have been identified, police can then try to engage people as partners. These kinds of "strategic partnerships" help ensure that the right people will be brought together to solve the problem. And the partners are fluid; the people the police need to partner with will always change. One begins with the problem and then decides who is best suited to help. Those problems that can be solved quickly or most easily should be addressed first. Nonprofit agencies can be valuable partners; let them handle the paperwork, assist with grantwriting, and develop timelines.[16]

You might open the meeting by explaining that you are there to listen and will try to understand the problems from the community's perspective. Record each problem on a large sheet of paper that is visible to everyone in the room. Once the problems have been listed, ask if people are willing to work with you to solve the problems. Also, state clearly that the police will do everything possible to help but that the problems cannot be solved without help from the community.

Step 2: Define the problem. Next, go through the list of problems one by one with the community, identifying whether or not the problems may be influenced or controlled. Ask the community to focus on and prioritize the problems identified. The number one priority is the starting point for the group's problem solving efforts.

SAN DIEGO POLICE DEPARTMENT

Neighborhood Policing

*A Guide for Building a
Police/Community Partnership*

PD-1175 (Rev. 2-93)

This guide to partnerships explains the San Diego Police Department's Neighborhood Policing Program and emphasizes the importance of collaborative partnerships with the public. (*Courtesy* San Diego Police Department)

Step 3: Ask questions about the problem. Analyzing the problem begins by asking, "Who is affected by the problem?" Brainstorm to create a list of everyone who is affected; this list may include children, families, police, prostitutes, drug dealers, social service agencies, probation and parole officers, prosecutors, and so on. From this list, have the group decide who should be included in the problem solving effort. Invite the appropriate people to future meetings. The next question is, "What do we want to know about the problem?" List everything that the group can think of that they want to know. Then go back over this list and ask,

"Where do we go to get the information?" Once you identify the source of the information, people can volunteer to get the answers to the questions. Delegate the responsibility for finding information to a number of people. When most questions have been answered, redefine the problem based on the information gathered. Is the group clear about the specific problem (such as drug dealing or prostitution at specific locations)? If the problem is defined too broadly (such as prostitution in the city), ask the group to narrow it.

Step 4: Set short-term and long-term goals. Aim for small wins initially. What short-term goal can the group reach that will create hope and enthusiasm? Then look at the big picture. What underlying conditions or root causes of the problem need to be addressed? Is it possible to eliminate the problem (such as prostitution, for example)? Only the group can decide. The community knows what the problem is now.

Step 5: Take action. If the right questions have been asked and the group understands what it can influence, responses to problems become clear. If one short-term goal is to get used condoms and syringes out of the neighborhood, whose responsibility is it to do so? Who should trim the overgrown shrubs and bushes that hide illegal activity on the street? Get the action rolling.

Step 6: Assess effectiveness. Was the problem solved? If more work needs to be done, do you need to start with Step 1 or can you reenter the problem solving process at another step? The most important question at this point is, "Where does the group want to go from here?" If the problem is solved, the group may want to stay in place to monitor the situation and begin work on another problem.

Exhibit 3.2 provides other examples of how the police have forged successful partnerships with other individuals and groups.

IMPROVING CUSTOMER SERVICE: TOTAL QUALITY MANAGEMENT

Definition and Rationalization

It was suggested earlier that as we begin the twenty-first century, the American public appears to be increasingly cynical toward—and even suspicious of—all levels of government. Citizens want to know what services government provides, how much these services actually cost, how effectively they are delivered and how performance is measured, and whether these services can be provided more efficiently.

What can be done to improve the problems experienced by government agencies described previously? Total quality management (TQM) is a philosophical concept for organizations that provides a practical means of meeting these challenges.

Following are key characteristics of the TQM process: customer focus, alignment, total involvement, continuous improvement, and leadership commitment.

Exhibit 3.2   Examples of Partnerships

Street Drinking Gets Curbed in Portland

The Portland Police Bureau's Central Precinct witnessed increasing numbers of transients and, consequently, an increase in alcohol-related crimes in the Old Town area. Contributing to these incidents was the availability of large-size containers of beer and malt liquor—each with the alcohol equivalent of a six-pack of regular beer or five glasses of wine. For more than a decade, Portland officials tried various strategies to deal with alcohol availability; not a lot of progress was made, largely because of the difficulty of pinpointing street drinking to a particular business. Two Old Town convenience stores came up for liquor review before the city council. The police and license bureaus asked the stores to stop selling large containers of beer. These stores declined, but the idea caught on, and six major retailers agreed to a voluntary ban on large containers of alcoholic substances. Their agreement stated that the community and the police would seek to expand this partnership to all retailers within the same geographic area. City council members reviewed the agreement and initiated a plan to encourage the participation of additional businesses. Once agreements had been reached with 40 businesses, a committee was formed to bring together all of the city bureaus and community representatives who had a vested interest in liquor issues. Since the agreement was enacted, retailers have experienced fewer problems with loitering, panhandling, public urination, harassment, and littering; citizen complaints have also diminished.

Sheriff's Office Uses Tax-Exempt Status to Empower Community

The Broward Sheriff's Office, Fort Lauderdale, Florida, is convinced that "the key ingredient in a successful community policing program is the partnership formed between police agencies and the community." The sheriff's office recently formed a community council in each of its jurisdiction's 10 districts. Each council consisted of informed and active citizens who represented the businesses and neighborhoods in their respective areas. The community councils meet frequently with their district's commander to discuss mutual problems and jointly plan possible remedies. Each council was incorporated as a 501(c)(3), tax-exempt, nonprofit organization. This status freed the councils to raise funds for crime prevention and other community needs. The sheriff, using confiscated funds, gave each council a $10,000 grant to get started. In a twist of fate, the monies that had been illegally taken by offenders from these neighborhoods were returned through grants.

Aurora, Colorado, Says "Bye, Bye, Bad Guys"

A community police officer and a property manager stroll the grounds of a crime-riddled, multifamily housing complex in Aurora, Colorado. The officer frequently makes broad pointing gestures to various areas of the grounds and buildings while the manager takes notes. It's a quiet, uneventful afternoon. The next day, the Aurora Police Department receives a typical phone call. "Thanks," the manager says, "four of my worst tenants moved out during the night." Since that day, 911 calls from that property have declined 61 percent. Criminal activity in the complex is almost gone. The manager and police consider themselves a team rather than adversaries. Undesirable tenants are screened out before they get a chance to move in. There is no more loitering in stairwells. Most important, the police have created a ripple effect throughout the neighborhood to bring other multifamily properties up to higher standards. What happened was just one of the successful steps in the new Social Weapons and Tactics (SWAT) program. SWAT works with city officials to make existing ordinances more powerful; it provides day-long seminars for police representatives, 16 hours of training for landlords and property managers, and on-site evaluations and suggestions.

Community Policing Catches Fire in Tampa

Tampa, Florida, has practiced community policing for years. In the early 1980s, the police created specific squads to focus on areas that generated a disproportionate number of the city's calls for service. A shortcoming remained, however, because the squads focused on specific areas; other areas of Tampa were excluded from the benefits of these efforts. Tampa's mayor brought the police and fire departments' executive staffs together, resulting in the birth of the firehouse–cop concept. The fire department is divided into 20 sections across the city, each having a station that is able to provide immediate response. The police department assigned two officers to each of the 20 firehouses and made them responsible for servicing those particular areas. The firehouse officers remain in their area, unless an emergency arises, assisting regular officers with incidents occurring within their area and providing additional preventive patrolling throughout the night. They also coordinate and conduct community meetings that address crime prevention, problem solving, dispute resolution, and an increased familiarization with governmental services and available resources. The major strength of the program is the relationships that have developed between the firehouse areas and surrounding neighborhoods, which previously had not existed. The department's ultimate goal is for each officer to have substantial time for problem solving.

Sources: Kelly Lewis and Greg Hendricks, "Street Drinking Gets Curbed in Portland," in *Partnerships* (Washington, D.C.: Community Policing Consortium, 1995–1998 Edition), p. 7; Norman Botsford, "Sheriff's Office Uses Tax-Exempt Status to Empower Community," in *Partnerships* (Washington, D.C.: Community Policing Consortium, 1995–1998 Edition), p. 14; Allison St. Claire, "Aurora, Colorado, Says 'Bye, Bye, Bad Guys,'" in *Partnerships* (Washington, D.C.: Community Policing Consortium, 1995–1998 Edition), p. 18; and Bennie R. Holder and Scott A. Cunningham, "Community Policing Catches Fire in Tampa," in *Partnerships* (Washington, D.C.: Community Policing Consortium, 1995–1998 Edition), p. 26.

Customer focus means realizing that the customer or client is the most important ingredient in the feedback loop of all organizational processes.

Alignment is both internal (having each employee and department understand the organization's vision) and external (the organization is capable of meeting the customer's requirements).

Total involvement rests on the assumptions that people want to do good work and can identify the problems that keep work from being accomplished, and that leadership must remove the barriers to getting work done effectively and efficiently.

Continuous improvement means that people in every part of the organization must believe that it is part of their job to continuously improve all they do.

Leadership commitment is also important, as TQM requires people who can see the big picture and work for their people.[17]

TQM was developed by W. Edwards Deming in 1950. Deming, born in Wyoming in 1900, took a doctorate in physics at Yale University in 1924 and then distinguished himself as a government statistician. After World War II, Deming was summoned to Japan by General Douglas MacArthur to help the Japanese rebuild their completely destroyed industrial base. Using Deming's teachings, the Japanese completely expanded the statistical side of quality control into a broad management philosophy that involved all members of the organization.[18]

Entrepreneurial governments that have adopted the TQM concept promote competition among service providers, measure the performance of their agencies by outcomes rather than inputs, and are driven by their goals instead of their rules and regulations. They redefine their clients as customers and espouse participatory management. They use quantitative "community condition indicators," which provide information about current conditions in the city. Objectives set the specific targets for each unit of government. For example, in policing, a Sunnyvale, California, objective is to keep the city "within the lowest 25 percent of Part I crimes for cities of comparable size, at a cost of $74.37 per capita."[19]

It is clear that TQM *can* be adapted to the public sector and is growing rapidly. The basics of TQM have been applied in many disparate kinds of government agencies; and cities, counties, and states now have official offices of quality, directors of quality services, or offices of excellence. They have started

Police storefronts and substations provide convenience and improved customer service to neighborhoods. (*Courtesy* Huntington Beach, California, Police Department)

"quality institutes" to train personnel and established "quality networks" to share resources and information. They are giving out quality awards.[20]

TQM involves the complete rethinking and redesigning of the way a job is performed or a service is rendered, with the goal of improving the process. Proponents say to begin with two things: a list of desired outcomes and a clean sheet of paper. Then design the process as if it did not already exist. Be merciless. Ask not how better to handle situations with a particular method, but whether a particular method is needed at all. Avoid projects that amount to little more than glorifying or automating the old bureaucratic routine. In short, do not engage in "paving cowpaths."[21]

As demands for better services increase and budgets decrease or stabilize, managers look for ways to "do more with less" and achieve improved products and services with fewer resources. Many private businesses, as well as all levels of government, have embraced this approach, which seeks to make their services synonymous with excellence, allegiance to customers, and the highest standards of public service.

TQM relies on well-established principles of quality assurance, using the creativity of all employees. Managers and employees continuously strive to "do the right thing the first time" and to achieve ever higher standards of quality, timeliness, and efficiency. And, according to the Federal Quality Institute and the FBI, this means *searching out and listening to the customer*.[22] Table 3.1 shows what TQM is and is not.

Next we discuss TQM's principal elements and its application to COPPS, use by leadership, and some success stories. As will be seen, there are several common elements between the processes and philosophies of TQM and COPPS.[23]

TABLE 3.1 What Total Quality Management Is and Is Not

It Is	It Is Not
A structured approach to solving problems	"Fighting fires"
A systematic way to improve products and services	A new program
Long term	Short term
Conveyed by management's actions	Conveyed by slogans
Supported by statistical quality control	Driven by statistical quality control
Practiced by everyone	Delegated to subordinates

Source: U.S. Department of Justice, Federal Bureau of Investigation, Administrative Services Division, *Total Quality Management* (October 1990), no page number.

Principal Elements

The principal elements of TQM—the customer, a long-term commitment, teamwork, internal communication, measurement, training, and rewards and recognition—embrace a commonsense approach to management. TQM has two primary concepts at its foundation: participative management and total involvement. Merely paying "lip service" to quality improvement by using quality slogans to exhort workers is nonproductive. As Deming stated, "Quality cannot be shouted."[24] And who decides what "quality" is? The answer is the customers, inside and outside each organization.

Every functional unit has a *customer*, and the police are no different. In its customer orientation, TQM

> stands the traditional organization on its head; it says that the customers are the most important people for an organization; those who serve customers directly are next; and management is there to serve those who serve customers.

Every question becomes, "How does this add value to the customer?[25] TQM forces organizations to listen and has, therefore, become very effective in changing their cultures.

An aspect of TQM that is also central to community problem solving is decentralization. In TQM, managers listen to all voices in the organization, including dissenters, and are always open to ideas for improvement from all sources. Managers also push power and decision making in the organization downward by delegating authority and encouraging problem solving at the lowest appropriate levels. In TQM (as with the COPPS strategy), managers demonstrate respect for people by treating everyone in the organization with honor and dignity and by recognizing each one's potential for growth and development. The manager also allows subordinates the freedom to make mistakes and, sometimes, even to fail.

A *long-term commitment* is also essential; substantial gains can be attained in customer satisfaction and organizational efficiency only after management becomes committed—usually after five years or more—to improving quality. Top management, therefore, must be the driving force behind TQM. Full employee involvement is also key. Each employee must be a partner in achieving quality goals. *Teamwork* involves managers, supervisors, and employees in improving service delivery, solving systemic problems, and correcting errors in all parts of work processes. Together, managers emphasize planning rather than "fighting fires."

Internal communication, both vertical and horizontal, is also central for employee involvement. Regular and meaningful communication must occur at all levels, allowing the agency to adjust its ways of operating and reinforcing its commitment to TQM at the same time. In the old style of management (including policing), information was something to be guarded. Information begat knowledge, which begat power, which was not to be shared. There is no shame in making mistakes, only in trying to hide them.

Measurement is the backbone of involvement, allowing the organization to initiate corrective action, set priorities, and evaluate progress. As with community problem solving, an evaluation of success cannot use conventional measures. Nothing will kill a TQM program faster than using it as a budget tool or productivity program. It does allow quality managers, however, to lead their organizations by using statistical data rather than a "gut feeling." Standards and measures should reflect customer requirements and changes that need to be introduced in the internal business of providing those requirements.

Training is also vital to the success of TQM. This usually includes "awareness" training concerning the concept for teams of top-level managers, courses for teams of midlevel managers, and courses for nonmanagers. This is followed by an identification of areas of concentration. TQM is a process and not a program. There is no magic formula. One can learn TQM only by education and training, followed by practice.

Rewards and recognition are also part of the package. Most private sector companies and federal agencies practicing TQM have given wide latitude to managers in issuing rewards and recognition. Here, a common theme is that individual financial rewards are not as appropriate as awards to groups or team members, because most successes are group achievements.

TQM asks police managers to accept ownership of the environment and "culture" of their organizations. They must realize that a shift to TQM will, in many cases, require a substantive shift in management approaches and a cultural change. TQM means working collectively to resolve problems in an environment of mutual responsibility. This notion is consistent with problem solving. Much like TQM, the problem solving process seeks to identify the role of all parties that may have responsibility for solving a problem. At its simplest level, TQM involves identifying problems, assessing needed corrective action, and taking those actions. It also requires that someone take responsibility for solving a problem and then resolve it.

Experience has shown that midlevel management is the slowest group to accept TQM. It requires special help in adjusting to its new role as facilitators of problem recognition and problem solving.

Implementing principles of TQM into an organization does not occur overnight. It presents a difficult and challenging task for police leadership. As Deming stated, "A big ship, travelling at full speed, requires distance and time to turn."[26]

Exhibit 3.3 provides several principles of quality leadership that assisted the Madison, Wisconsin, Police Department with implementing TQM into the organization.

USE OF SURVEYS

A number of communities have found that a beneficial method of facilitating community participation is the survey process. In fact, a key part of both COPPS and TQM is for organizations to constantly ask their customers what they want, then to shape their entire service and production processes to produce it.

As an example, since 1987 the Reno, Nevada, Police Department has engaged in a semiannual, scientific, telephone survey of the community, seeking to reach 1 percent of the total city population of 150,000, or about 1,500 completed surveys per year. And in 1987, the Madison, Wisconsin, Police Department began mailing a survey to every 35th person it encountered, whether a victim of a crime, a witness, a complainant, or even a criminal. Further discussion of community surveys is provided in Chapter 11.

CRIMINAL JUSTICE: ORGANIZATIONS IN NEED OF ATTENTION

As previously indicated, there is a need for community involvement at government's invitation and with government's persuasion. And in no segment of government is this involvement needed more than in policing and criminal justice generally.

Citizen surveys provide police departments with vital information about their performance and citizens' concerns. (*Courtesy* Reno, Nevada, Police Department)

EXHIBIT 3.3   Principles of Quality Leadership

The following principles of quality leadership were developed by the Madison, Wisconsin, Police Department:

1. Believe in, foster, and support TEAMWORK.
2. Be committed to the PROBLEM SOLVING process; use it and let DATA, not emotions, drive decisions.
3. Seek employees' INPUT before you make key decisions.
4. Believe that the best way to improve the quality of work or service is to ASK and LISTEN to employees who are doing the work.
5. Strive to develop mutual RESPECT and TRUST among employees.
6. Have a CUSTOMER orientation and focus toward employees and citizens.
7. Manage on the BEHAVIOR of 95 percent of employees and not on the 5 percent who cause problems. Deal with the 5 percent PROMPTLY and FAIRLY.
8. Examine PROCESSES before placing individual responsibility when problems arise.
9. Avoid top down, POWER-ORIENTED decision making whenever possible.
10. Encourage CREATIVITY through RISK-TAKING and be TOLERANT of honest MISTAKES.
11. Be a FACILITATOR and COACH. Develop an OPEN atmosphere that encourages providing and accepting FEEDBACK.
12. Using TEAMWORK, develop with employees agreed-on GOALS and a PLAN to achieve them (emphases in original).

Source: David C. Couper, "Management for Excellence," International Association of Chiefs of Police, *The Police Yearbook 1988*:76–84.

Wanted: A Different "MO"

Notwithstanding the good news concerning the recently declining crime rates in the United States, there is still much room for concern. We still have some of the highest murder, rape, and robbery rates in the world. Our courts and prisons are so full that criminals know real punishment is unlikely. Yet the system is bankrupting state and county governments. Much of the problems stem in part from an outmoded way of approaching the situation. Radical change is afoot in some places, but for the most part our policing system is made up of large, rule-bound bureaucracies. Osborne and Gaebler described it this way:

For the most part, our governments do not play a catalytic role, trying to work with other sectors of society to strengthen families and communities and thus reduce crime. They simply hire more public employees to staff the assembly line. . . . Our governments rarely give communities and citizens any control over public safety; they leave that to the . . . police. They rarely offer their customers any choices. They rarely let the police . . . define a mission and go after it; they tie them up in rules and red tape.[27]

The key, then, is the ability of the police to act as a catalyst to coalesce community resources and to provide resources, education, and training to the community. The police must realize that if they empower citizens, they help themselves. This invitation by the police to the community is basically a commonsense approach. It involves community empowerment, which actually began in 1829 when Robert Peel recognized that the police alone could not control crime.

Rewarding Failure

Under the traditional method of government, agencies can spend blindly. Police departments frequently make this mistake. For example, studies show that doubling the number of patrol officers or vehicles on the streets has no effect on the level of serious crime or the public's fear of crime; yet, when crime rates rise, more patrol officers and vehicles are purchased. One writer described this situation, which is certainly not unique to the police sector, "Inasmuch as we have lost sight of our objectives, we are going to redouble our efforts."[28]

Budgeted funds that are not spent by the end of the budget year typically "revert back" (in other words, they are lost); thus, with no incentive to save money and a "spend it or lose it" mentality, instead of "save it and invest it," an irrational flurry of spending often occurs toward the end of the budget year. Entrepreneurial governments reward thrifty organizations by allowing them to carry over saved funds and provide rewards for being fiscally responsible. Conventional methods of doing business provide little incentive for agency heads to be creative with their funds or ideas; successful ideas and creative expenditures of funds often go unrewarded.

There is little incentive for police agencies to experiment with new crime-fighting methods. If crime rises, the agencies are given more money; if crimes continue to rise, they are given more money. This "rewarding failure" approach discourages police departments from attacking neighborhood crimes at their sources. Why would a police department want to seriously consider a problem solving strategy if it is continually "rewarded" with more funds because of increases in crime?

Furthermore, administrators are generally constrained by narrow, compartmentalized line-item budgets that allow only for a certain amount of funds to be expended out of each compartment. Administrators are, therefore, constrained in trying to find money to "fix" problems as they arise and have little opportunity to use their funds in innovative, money-saving ways. At a minimum, a new budget system, incentives to save money, and quantitative, performance-based budgets would not only allow administrators to redefine "success" but would also encourage them to strive to achieve it.

Borrowing Ideas from Business

A maxim in the private sector says, "The customer is always right." Certainly not all "customers" with whom the police deal on a day-to-day basis are always right; there is, however, an important lesson here for the police. Private industry thrives on consumer information. It believes that the more information an organization has about customer needs, the better equipped that organization is to provide quality service. We believe COPPS holds customer service in similar esteem, conveys the importance of good customer relations, and improves the quality of police service. Conventional police methods, however, can be likened to the bus line that bankrupted itself by speeding past queues of customers standing at bus stops: "It is impossible for the drivers to keep their timetables if they have to stop for passengers."[29]

Traditional policing has often functioned not unlike this bus line. Goldstein wrote that such a condition has been found in traditional policing, because "the police have been particularly susceptible to the 'means over ends' syndrome, placing more emphasis on their organization and operating methods than on the substantive outcome of their work."[30] The conventional model has also considered patrol as "at best, what officers do until promoted or, at worst, the dumping ground for officers who are incompetent, suffering from alcoholism, or simply burned out."[31]

PARTNERS IN COMMUNITY JUSTICE

In the late 1980s and early 1990s, when the police began to rethink their mission and approach, and community policing and problem solving began to develop and be diffused around the country, the courts and corrections components also began to change strategies and combine the lessons learned from the past with the "modern" approaches of better educated people and better equipped methods. In short, they became more attuned to the concept of "community justice."

Community justice is a new way of thinking about the criminal justice system; it is a systemic approach to public safety, emphasizing problem solving and focusing on community concerns. It seeks to bring the police, courts, and other governmental agencies back into direct contact with the community, and to seek input from and partner with community resources, agencies, and the community itself.

Increasingly, all segments of society, as well as the nation's criminal justice system, are realizing that the only viable approach to mediating their problems is communitywide participation and cooperation. The primary, underlying tenet for this movement is that people matter. In reaction to a bureaucratic society in which we have often become mere numbers or statistics, community collaboration is gaining popularity, because it emphasizes the needs, desires, and dreams of individual citizens.[32]

Criminal justice executives must plan a systematic approach to be in a strategic position to focus on community cooperation. The following steps are essential: *identifying the issues* (knowing what specific problems are facing the community and what is being done to address them), *identifying key partners* (persons who are key to the solution of problems), *formulating a message* (communicating what needs to be done to accomplish goals), *establishing relationships* (using friendships, common interests, social service agencies, the corporate sector, other justice agencies, and so on), and *establishing evaluation procedures* (monitoring and measuring community efforts according to previously established criteria).[33]

Community justice services aim to identify and solve the problems that foster crime and injustice. The transformation from machine to service is most advanced in police departments. Next, though, we present some of the means by which courts and corrections agencies have also worked successfully to revitalize their communities.

Prosecution

Community prosecution, a concept begun in Multnomah County (Portland), Oregon, in 1990,[34] has now spread to many other states. An experienced special prosecutor, known as a Neighborhood District Attorney (NDA), is assigned to work on a neighborhood-based prosecution project in an inner-city district and performs duties that go well beyond prosecution, conducting behind-the-scenes negotiations and often acting as a facilitator, legal counselor, negotiator, problem solver, and community advocate.

Community policing and community prosecution share many similarities. Both strive to prevent crime before it occurs, rather than to react to crime after it happens. Both empower communities to take control of their own destinies. The presence of community police officers and community prosecutors in the neighborhoods, in attendance at community meetings, and accessible to community members shows their human side and makes them seem less intimidating to the average citizen.

An example of community prosecution in operation is a situation involving skateboarders in Portland, Oregon. In the mid-1990s, business owners in an industrial area began complaining to the police department that skateboarders were grabbing onto their trucks, which presented a real liability issue for the business owners and their truck drivers as well. The business owners wanted the police to close down the skateboarding; the skateboarders were also littering and acting unruly in the area. Both parties approached the NDA and asked that the area be closed to skateboarders. The NDA, however, proposed to include the skateboarders in discussions in an effort to reach an accord that would satisfy all parties. The outcome was an initiative that kept the skateboard area where it was but required the youths to abide by established guidelines, such as not grabbing onto trucks, littering, or leaving a delineated area. The business owners paid for the signage that was placed around the skateboarding area and provided the youths with a portable toilet. This partnership is a testament to the effectiveness of community prosecution and community policing—both of which use clever, innovative strategies in response to neighborhood problems.[35]

Defense

A Neighborhood Defender Service (NDS) experiment in Harlem, New York,[36] aimed to develop and test new ways of organizing and deploying public defenders that could solve problems of justice in the community. The NDS was based in the community rather than a courthouse and represented indigent defendants, encouraging citizens to call the office at any time—thus giving lawyers more time to visit with their clients and creating a new attorney-client relationship. Each client is represented by a team, consisting of attorneys, community workers (who helped former clients avoid problems and thereby not produce new cases while on probation and parole), an administrative assistant, and a senior attorney/team leader.

Defenders know about their clients and the communities from which they come; the staff began to see Harlem as a series of interconnected family networks, and NDS became a family service. Relatives often called the office out of concern for a person's safety as he or she entered the justice system. The program provides a deep understanding of clients through continuity of representation and better investigation, better presentation of sentencing options through greater connection to community resources, and greater ability to represent residents' support for a less severe sentence. Program savings through shorter sentences alone were about 150,000 bed days or about $10 million.

Courts

From police to corrections, education to job training, probation to parole, the courts are in a unique position among service agencies. And increasingly, the community is believed to have a major stake in how well the courts adjudicate cases involving quality of life crimes, and the courts are heavily dependent on the active involvement of community groups.

We discussed in Chapter 2 the deep influence that drug abuse has on criminality in our country. For what may be termed community courts—specifically, drug courts and domestic violence courts—community justice involves developing a systemwide approach to the supervision and rehabilitation of offenders, with judges accepting an active leadership role and responsibility for communitywide antidrug and domestic violence programs. These special court judges hold an important position in their communities; they have political influence, contacts with other local government agencies, moral authority, expertise, and fairness and impartiality to bring leadership to antidrug, domestic violence, and other crime efforts.[37]

Following are some examples of how the community policing philosophy can "feed into" community drug court initiatives:

- In Macon, Illinois, police officers are trained to identify individuals who would make good drug court participants.
- In Las Vegas, a phone system allows officers from multiple jurisdictions to call in the activities of drug court participants, reporting their good or bad behavior. The district attorney's office and treatment facilities have access to this system.
- In Thurston County, Washington, each drug court participant is assigned a police officer, who must know the participant's address, vehicles, and associates; make monthly contact with the participant; and report any relevant information to the drug court coordinator.
- In Las Cruces, New Mexico, police officers act as mentors to youths who participate in the juvenile drug court program; officers use ride-alongs, visits to the police station, and trips to the movies to try to change the youths' perceptions of police.[38]

Other partnerships that can involve the courts and citizens include child care during trials for victims and witnesses, law-related education, and job training and referral for offenders and victims. A community-focused court practices *restorative justice*, emphasizing the ways in which disputes and crimes adversely affect relationships among community residents, treating parties to a dispute as real individuals rather than abstract legal entities, and using community resources in the adjudication of disputes.[39]

Corrections

With the advent of Megan's Law and other related types of legislation, the public is demanding more information about who the offenders are, where they are living, and what the criminal justice system is doing about them. As a result, the corrections end of the criminal justice spectrum—probation and parole—is steadily taking on a more visible role within the community policing strategy. Collaborative efforts are being made to make communities safer. Interagency groups are monitoring offenders who are at risk of committing new offenses and finding ways to direct them away from criminal activity—and engaging the community in the process. Community corrections officers and police officers are working as teams, with the community as a partner, to provide a range of prevention, intervention, and support services to the offenders.

A good example of such an initiative is in an area of Maricopa County, Arizona, where probation officers saw community blight (graffiti, crack houses, and vandalism) as an opportunity to make a visible, positive impact on the area. The officers mobilized work crews of neighborhood probationers and set about

Sentencing low-risk offenders to community work projects is one
community-based corrections strategy. (*Courtesy* Washoe County, Nevada,
Sheriff's Office)

replacing a damaged community center roof. They also landscaped the grounds
and made repairs inside the center. "Reformed" gang members performed community service by assisting police and neighborhood youth organizations in
speaking to "at-risk" teens on the dangers of gang involvement. Select residents
and probation and police officers work side by side in the ongoing effort to close
down and clean up crack houses. Vacant lots are kept clean, and graffiti is
painted over with murals.[40]

Maricopa County's ability to make offenders repay their social debt by completing unpaid community service in their own neighborhoods served to break
down barriers and prejudice. As community members and police came to know
the probationers in a social context and on a somewhat more personal level, they
were no longer viewed as merely criminals but as neighbors who, under proper
supervision, can safely remain in a community setting and make a meaningful
contribution to the community as well.[41]

In other jurisdictions, such as Richmond, Virginia, where 820 probation and
parole officers supervise more than 36,000 offenders, officers have frequent interaction with the police and often work side by side with community policing officers.
One very successful program in Bristol, Virginia, involves a probation and parole
services office in a housing project, where officers work closely with local police
and simply walk or bicycle through the community, talking with local residents.[42]

SOME ILLUSTRATIONS OF COMMUNITY ORIENTED GOVERNMENT

Next we discuss the kinds of activities and successes communities are realizing
when their local governments become determined to empower their citizens in
decision making and work with citizens to improve their quality of life.

Mason, Ohio: Reinventing Government and Customer Service

Recent growth placed a strain on the ability of the Mason, Ohio, governing board to provide superior services. Understanding that citizen perceptions are vital to government performance and credibility, the city manager and his staff decided to embark on a program designed to emphasize excellent customer service as the hallmark of a well-run organization.

The city first undertook to raise the morale of the city employees. The manager believed that incorporating such values as trust, teamwork, innovation, a respect for the worth of the individual, and a desire to provide high-quality service in the day-to-day life of the organization would improve employees' performance. The first step was to show the "Excellence in the Public Sector" videotape to all 75 employees. Then employees were surveyed as to their suggestions and needs for city government. The results were that most of the employees wanted to feel more appreciated and involved, and wanted management to demonstrate a stronger interest in their welfare. The manager's staff initiated new strategies, including more frequent departmental meetings between directors and employees; a Public Service Recognition Week and an annual employee excellence award; an employee wellness program; and employee development of their own departmental values, mission statement, and goals for the coming year.[43]

The next step was to improve external customer service. A slogan, "Commitment to Excellence in Public Service," was chosen and put on the doors to the municipal building as well as all department stationary, memos, and business cards. Additionally, the following steps were among many that were taken:

- Distributed a customer service survey concerning courtesy, helpfulness, and problem resolution to every fifth person (except arrestees) having contact with the police, engineering, building, utility billing, and tax departments—all of which have high volumes of pedestrian traffic.
- Prepared materials to inform citizens about city activities.
- Initiated a breakfast program for citizens with three council members, the city manager, and other government officials who get feedback on the community and its services.
- Introduced annual open houses in the police, engineering, and building departments and city garages.
- Used a publication entitled "How to Get It Done" for the police department to distribute to citizens. Topics include reporting suspicious or criminal activity, forming a neighborhood watch group, and other information.
- Initiated a program to help students understand their local form of government.
- Distributed a directory of city officials, which includes all local, school, township, county, state, and federal officials.[44]

The results have been very positive. The city learned that before changing the organization and making total quality customer service a top priority, officials must first check the pulse of employees. They must first identify and attempt to remedy any pressures and demands their employees are experiencing.

Exhibit 3.4 presents an example of a community oriented government in the Midwest.

Lawrence, Massachusetts: TQM and Focusing on Customer Needs

Serving a diverse community of 70,000 people, the Lawrence, Massachusetts, Police Department had begun to feel out of touch with its citizens, and its managers believed that its authoritarian management style had led department members to feel disenfranchised. A commitment was made to customers. The first step was to meet and exceed customers' needs. The second step was to obtain valuable input using a variety of means, including customer surveys (done annually), citizen advisory committees, customer comment cards, and small focus groups. Other tools used to identify true customer needs included a flow chart, cause-and-effect diagram, affinity diagram, check sheet, and run chart. These in-depth means of identifying needs have been fruitful. For example, using an affinity diagram the department found that although its customers were calling for more foot patrol and more police officers, what they really wanted was to feel safe in neighborhoods free of disorder.

Techniques employed in small groups for obtaining citizen input included the nominal group technique (individuals silently develop ideas and prioritize by voting and ranking), idea writing, brainstorming, and the Delphi technique (ideas of a panel of experts result in a consensus being reached). The department believes that using TQM methods has allowed it to become more focused on customers; it has also found that citizens are happier with the services provided, that employees are more satisfied because of their input, and that the "job is done not only better but often more cheaply."[45]

Other Examples

Following are other brief examples of problem solving and a new government approach working with citizens and saving money. Each example is but a portion of the overall efforts and accomplishments achieved in each venue.

- The Visalia, California, Police Department pioneered a lease-purchase program for squad cars that cut its energy consumption by 30 percent. In a few years, the department had saved $20 million in cash—almost its entire operating budget.[46]
- The St. Louis County Police Department developed a system that allows officers to call in their reports; the department licensed the software to a

---

Exhibit 3.4   Community Oriented Government in Fort Wayne, Indiana

During the 1980s, the Fort Wayne, Indiana, Police Department experienced a 95 percent increase in calls for service, and crime was on the rise. The city's mayor began looking for ways to stem the increase in violence. Part of the answer was in the initiation of community policing. Then, in the early 1990s, a task force was established and charged with implementing the philosophies of community policing throughout the city government. Out of the task force grew Community Oriented Government, an approach that takes community policing one step further and gives primary responsibility for problem solving to neighborhood leadership. Community Oriented Government encourages individual citizens to take issues to one of 197 organized neighborhood associations. Associations prioritize concerns and work with city staff to find solutions. Issues that concern more than one neighborhood are addressed in one of four Area Partnerships, a coalition of neighborhood leaders that meets monthly to discuss and solve problems. This system makes citizens the true "boss." They dictate up the chain of command and tell their "employees"—city staff—which issues require the most attention.

Source: Paul Helmke, "Community-Oriented Government," http://www.fwi.com/cofw/community-oriented_government/cog.html, July 9, 2000.

---

private company, and earns $25,000 each time the package is sold to another department.[47]

- Paulding County, Georgia, built a 244-bed jail when it needed only 60 extra beds, so that it could charge other jurisdictions $35 a night to handle their overflow. In the first year of business, the jail brought in $1.4 million, $200,000 more than its operating costs.[48]
- Some enterprising police departments in California earned money renting out motel rooms as weekend jails. They reserved blocks of rooms at cheap motels, paid someone to sit outside to ensure inmates stay in their rooms, and rented the rooms to convicted drunk drivers for $75 a night.[49]

These examples demonstrate what can happen when administrators begin thinking "out of the box," like entrepreneurs rather than strict bureaucrats. More and more government agencies are giving thought to entrepreneurship, looking for better methods and ways to enhance revenues.

Lease-purchase programs can save agencies thousands of dollars in their budgets. (*Courtesy* Reno, Nevada, Police Department)

CLOSURE

What is needed is nothing short of a shift in the basic model of governance that is used in America—a shift that is already under way. Justice administrators must look beyond tomorrow and anticipate the future. As Peter F. Drucker observed,

> Every government agency, every policy, every program, every activity should be confronted with these questions: "What is your mission? Is it still the right mission? Is it still worth doing? If we were not already doing this, would we now go into it?"[50]

A shift to consideration of the client/customer perspective creates opportunities for police administrators to rethink what their organizations really do and how they do it—to steer rather than row, with a clear map in hand.

TQM and COPPS give police officers enough free rein to experiment and see what works. And the police must continually communicate to people—both those within and without the department—that community problem solving is in everybody's best interest.

We must also emphasize the important role of persons working with other government agencies (including social services). The police do not function in a vacuum; representatives from other agencies must be mobilized in the problem solving endeavor. These agencies include but are not limited to housing, zoning, health, street, fire, and other justice system agencies.

These are important partnerships for problem solving. Representatives from these agencies are key problem solving agents who must know how they can best assist the police in eliminating crime and disorder, and they must be trained in the philosophy and methods that underlie problem solving. We address the issue of training in Chapter 8.

SUMMARY

We propose in this chapter that it is time for government—specifically criminal justice and especially the police—to "get under the hood of its car" to see where problems might be repaired. The theme of this chapter is that government must expand its commitment to customer service—much of which can be achieved through partnerships and borrowed wholly or in part from the total quality management philosophy. It is time for a new, cooperative partnership between the public and its government. This partnership is essential for mending the "broken windows" that plague many of our neighborhoods. This new relationship offers hope for the future and is based on shared accountability for outcomes. It empowers citizens to take charge of their own destiny and reclaim their neighborhoods. In turn, citizens may indeed be safer and realize an improvement in their quality of life.

NOTES

1. David Couper and Sabine Lobitz, *Quality Policing: The Madison Experience* (Washington, D.C.: Police Executive Research Forum, 1991), p. 65.
2. David Osborne and Ted Gaebler, *Reinventing Government: How the Entrepreneurial Spirit Is Transforming the Public Sector* (Reading, Mass.: Addison-Wesley, 1992), p. 51.
3. Tom Dewar, quoted in *The Saint Paul Experiment: Initiatives of the Latimer Administration,* eds. David A. Lanegran, Cynthia Seelhammer, and Amy L. Walgrave (St. Paul, Minn.: City of St. Paul, 1989), p. xxii.
4. Osborne and Gaebler, *Reinventing Government,* p. 53.
5. Rob Gurwitt, "Communitarianism: You Can Try It at Home," *Governing* 6 (August 1993):33–39.
6. *Ibid.,* p. 39.
7. Michael J. Gerson, "Do Do-Gooders Do Much Good?" *U.S. News and World Report,* April 28, 1997, p. 27.
8. Karen Siemsen, "For a Full Menu of Policing Services, Partner with Volunteers," *Community Policing Exchange* (September/ October 1998), p. 8.
9. *Ibid.,* pp. 33–34.
10. Ronnie L. Paynter, "Helping Hands," *Law Enforcement Technology* (March 1999):30–34.
11. Quoted in William B. "Duke" Whiteside, "Initiating Action," in *Partnerships* (Washington, D.C.: Community Policing Consortium, 1995–1998 Edition), p. 45.
12. Nancy McPherson, "Solution-Driven Partnerships: Just Six Steps Away." In *Partnerships* (Washington, D.C.: Community Policing Consortium, 1995–1998 Edition), p. 10.
13. Quoted in *ibid.,* p. 10.
14. *Ibid.*
15. Adapted from Nancy McPherson, "Solution-Driven Partnerships," pp. 10–11.
16. "Getting the Job Done through Partnerships," in *Partnerships,* p. 4.

17. Stephen J. Harrison, "Quality Policing and the Challenges for Leadership," *The Police Chief* (January 1996):26, 31–32.
18. *Ibid.*, p. 26.
19. City of Sunnyvale, California, *Resource Allocation Plan: 1989–90 to 1998–99 Fiscal Years, 10 Year Operating Budget* (Sunnyvale, Calif.: Author, no date).
20. Jonathan Walters, "TQM: Surviving the Cynics," *Governing* (September 1994):40.
21. John Martin, "Reengineering Government," *Governing* (March 1993):27–30.
22. U.S. Department of Justice, Federal Bureau of Investigation, Administrative Services Division, *Total Quality Management* (October 1990), no page number.
23. The reader is also encouraged to see Howard S. Gitlow and Shelly J. Gitlow, *The Deming Guide to Quality and Competition* (Englewood Cliffs, N.J.: Prentice Hall, 1987).
24. *Ibid.*, p. iv.
25. *Ibid.*, p. 172.
26. W. Edwards Deming, quoted in U.S. Department of Justice, Federal Bureau of Investigation, *Total Quality Management*, p. 1.
27. Osborne and Gaebler, *Reinventing Government*, p. 319.
28. Stan Jordan, quoted in Osborne and Gaebler, *Reinventing Government*, p. 148.
29. Philip Ryan, "Get Rid of the People, and the System Runs Fine," *Smithsonian* (September 1977):140.
30. Herman Goldstein, "Problem-Oriented Policing" (University of Wisconsin Law School: Conference on Policing, 1987).
31. George L. Kelling, "Police and Communities: The Quiet Revolution" (Washington, D.C.: National Institute of Justice, 1988), p. 4.
32. Laurie J. Wilson, "Placing Community-Oriented Policing in the Broader Realms of Community Cooperation," *The Police Chief* (April 1995):127.
33. *Ibid.*, p. 128.
34. Adapted from David M. Kennedy, "Neighborhood Revitalization: Lessons from Savannah and Baltimore" (U.S. Department of Justice, National Institute of Justice, *Communities: Mobilizing against Crime, Making Partnerships Work*, August 1996), pp. 35–40.
35. Cynthia E. Tompkins, "Prosecutors Are Part of the Community, Too!" *Community Policing Exchange* (May/June 1999):8.
36. *Ibid.*, pp. 41–45.
37. The National Association of Drug Court Professionals, *Community Policing and Drug Courts/Community Courts Project: A Two-Year Progress Report* (Washington, D.C.: Author, no date), p. 1.
38. *Ibid.*, pp. 2–5.
39. *Ibid.*, pp. 46–51.
40. Leslie D. Ebratt, "Giving Probation a Stake in the Neighborhood," *Community Policing Exchange* (May/June 1999):5.
41. *Ibid.*
42. Ray Arp Sr., "COPPS: Crossing over Boundary Lines," *Community Policing Exchange* (May/June 1999):5.
43. Patrick Ibarra, "Empowering Employees to Improve Customer Service," in International City Management Association, *MIS Report*, "Responsive Service Delivery: A Community Orientation for Problem Solving" (Volume 25, May 1993), pp. 12–13.
44. *Ibid.*, pp. 13–14.
45. Allen W. Cole, "Better Customer Focus: TQM and Law Enforcement," *The Police Chief* (December 1993):23–26.
46. Osborne and Gaebler, *Reinventing Government*, p. 4.
47. *Ibid.*, p. 197.
48. *Ibid.*
49. *Ibid.*
50. Peter F. Drucker, "Really Reinventing Government," *The Atlantic Monthly* (February 1995):49–61.

COMMUNITY ORIENTED POLICING AND PROBLEM SOLVING "COPPS"

> No problem can be solved by the same consciousness that created it. We must learn to see the world anew.
>
> —Albert Einstein
>
> Before we can communicate, let us define our terms.
>
> —Voltaire

INTRODUCTION

According to one source, community oriented policing "has become a mantra for police chiefs and mayors in cities big and small across the country."[1] What is this concept that is sweeping the nation? How did it develop, and how does it operate? What are its component parts?

This chapter, the "heart and soul" of the book, addresses those questions. First we discuss the concept of community policing, examining basic principles of the concept and how community oriented and traditional policing differ, and how community policing is distinguished from earlier attempts to engage the community. Next we analyze problem oriented policing, including its origin, how it broadened the role of the street officer, and the four-stage problem solving process.

Although the two concepts, community policing and problem oriented policing, are commonly treated as separate and distinct, we maintain here and throughout the remainder of the book that they are complementary core components. Therefore, we devote considerable attention in this chapter to an examination of community oriented policing and problem solving—COPPS—which we believe to be the most effective and efficient approach to policing for the future. We conclude the chapter with a review of the types of tools that can be used by police problem solvers: crime mapping, police reports, call for service (CFS) analysis, surveys, and software.

It should be noted that Chapter 5 examines a concept that is integral to COPPS—crime prevention—and offers a cost-effective means of making communities safe. As with COPPS, today's police are shifting their emphasis to one of crime prevention as an agencywide philosophy, not as an add-on program or a mere appendage. Two very important components of crime prevention and COPPS are analyzed in Chapter 5: crime prevention through environmental design and situational crime prevention.

COMMUNITY POLICING

As we discussed in Chapter 3 (and will necessarily revisit from time to time in later chapters), there is a growing awareness that the community can and *must* play a vital role in problem solving and crime fighting. A fundamental aspect of community policing has always been that the public must be engaged in the fight against crime and disorder. As we noted in Chapter 1, Robert Peel emphasized the police and community working together in the 1820s when setting forth his principles of policing: "The police are the only members of the public who are paid to give full-time attention to duties which are incumbent on every citizen in the interest of the community welfare."[2]

Unfortunately, as Herman Goldstein posited, the police have erred in recent decades by pretending that they could take on and successfully discharge all of the responsibilities that are now theirs:

> It is simply not possible for a relatively small group of individuals, however powerful and efficient, to meet those expectations. A community must police itself. The police, at best, can only assist in that task. We are long overdue in recognizing this fact.[3]

Basic Principles

In the early 1980s, the notion of community policing emerged as the dominant direction for thinking about policing. It was designed to reunite the police with the community: "It is a philosophy and not a specific tactic; a proactive, decentralized approach, designed to reduce crime, disorder, and fear of crime, by involving the same officer in the same community for a long-term basis."[4]

Working partnerships with residents to create safer and more secure neighborhoods are vital in community policing. (*Courtesy* Keith Richards, City of Charlotte, North Carolina)

No single program describes community policing. It has been applied in various forms by police agencies in the United States and abroad and differs according to the community needs, politics, and resources available. A few examples are the Neighborhood Oriented Policing and the Directed Area Responsibility Team programs (Houston); Community Patrol Officer Program (Brooklyn); Citizen-Oriented Police Enforcement (Baltimore County); and the Community Mobilization Project, the Basic Car Plan, and the Senior Lead-Officer programs (Los Angeles).

Community policing goes much further than being a mere police–community relations program (discussed later) and attempts to address crime control through a working partnership with the community. Here, community institutions such as families, schools, and neighborhood and merchants associations are believed to be key partners with the police in creating safe, secure communities. The community's views have greater status under community policing.[5]

Differences in Community Policing and Traditional Policing

The major points at which community policing departs from traditional policing may be seen in Table 4.1. Note that the definition, role, priorities, and assessment of the police differ considerably between the two models.

TABLE 4.1 Traditional versus Community Policing: Questions and Answers

Question	Traditional Policing	Community Policing
Who are the police?	A government agency principally responsible for law enforcement.	Police are the public and the public are the police: The police officers are those who are paid to give full-time attention to the duties of every citizen.
What is the relationship of the police force to other public service departments?	Priorities often conflict.	The police are one department among many responsible for improving the quality of life.
What is the role of the police?	Focusing on solving crimes.	A broad problem solving approach.
How is police efficiency measured?	By detection and arrest rates.	By the absence of crime and disorder.
What are the highest priorities?	Crimes that are high value (e.g., bank robberies) and those involving violence.	Whatever problems disturb the community most.
With what, specifically, do police deal?	Incidents.	Citizens' problems and concerns.
What determines the effectiveness of police?	Response times.	Public cooperation.
What view do police take of service calls?	Deal with them only if there is no real police work to do.	Vital function and great opportunity.
What is police professionalism?	Swift effective response to serious crime.	Keeping close to the community.
What kind of intelligence is most important?	Crime intelligence (study of particular crimes or series of crimes).	Criminal intelligence (information about the activities of individuals or groups).
What is the essential nature of police accountability?	Highly centralized; governed by rules, regulations, and policy directives; accountable to the law.	Emphasis on local accountability to community needs.
What is the role of headquarters?	To provide the necessary rules and policy directives.	To preach organizational values.
What is the role of the press liaison department?	To keep the "heat" off operational officers so they can get on with the job.	To coordinate an essential channel of communication with the community.
How do the police regard prosecutions?	As an important goal.	As one tool among many.

Source: Malcolm K. Sparrow, "Implementing Community Policing" (Washington, D.C.: U.S. Department of Justice, National Institute of Justice: U.S. Government Printing Office, November 1988), pp. 8–9.

Many past and present practitioners have become staunch proponents of the concept. For example, former New York City Police Commissioner Lee P. Brown, who had implemented community policing in Houston, wrote

I believe that community policing—the building of problem solving partnerships between the police and those they serve—is the future of American law enforcement. In essence, we are bringing back a modern version of the "cop on the beat." We need to *solve* community problems rather than just *react* to them. It is time to adopt new strategies to address the dramatic increases in crime and the fear of crime. I view community policing as a better, smarter and more cost-effective way of using police resources.[6]

It should be emphasized, however, that community oriented policing is a long-term process that involves fundamental institutional change. One scholar warned police managers that "if you approach community oriented policing as a program, you will likely fail. Beware of the trap that seeks guaranteed, perfect, and immediate results."[7]

Community policing goes beyond simply implementing foot and bicycle patrols or neighborhood stations. It redefines the role of the officer on the street from crime fighter to problem solver and neighborhood representative. It forces a cultural transformation of the entire department, including a decentralized organizational structure and changes in recruiting, training, awards systems, evaluation, promotions, and so forth. Furthermore, this philosophy asks officers to break away from the binds of incident-driven policing and to seek proactive and creative resolution to crime and disorder.

To demonstrate how community policing and problem solving are different from traditional policing, see Table 4.1 and Figures 4.1 and 4.2.

PROBLEM ORIENTED POLICING

Early Beginnings

Problem solving is not new; police officers have always tried to solve problems (we define "problem" later). The difference is that in the past, officers received little guidance, support, or technology from police administrators for dealing with problems. The routine application of problem solving techniques is new. It is premised on two facts: Problem solving can be applied by officers throughout the agency as part of their daily work, and routine problem solving efforts can be effective in reducing or resolving problems.

Problem oriented policing (POP) was grounded on different principles than community oriented policing (COP), but they are complementary. POP is a strategy that puts the COP philosophy into practice. It advocates that police examine the underlying causes of recurring incidents of crime and disorder. The problem solving process, discussed in later chapters, helps officers to identify problems, analyze them completely, develop response strategies, and assess the results.

Herman Goldstein is considered by many to be the principal architect of problem oriented policing. His book *Policing a Free Society* (1977)[8] is among the most frequently cited works in police literature. A later work, *Problem-Oriented Policing* (1990),[9] provides a rich and complete exploration into problem oriented

TRADITIONAL POLICING
Emphasis on enforcing laws and making arrests provides short-term solutions to problems

VS.

COMMUNITY ORIENTED POLICING AND PROBLEM SOLVING
COPPS is a philosophy, management style, and organizational strategy that promotes proactive problem solving and police–community partnerships to address the causes of crime and fear as well as other community issues

COMMUNITY POLICING	PROBLEM SOLVING
A philosophy that emphasizes effective working partnerships *Code Enforcement, Health Department, Other City Agencies, Local Business, Dangerous Buildings, Community Groups, Code Enforcement, Narcotics Task Force, Social Service Agencies, Fire Department, and so on . . .*	A process to identify, analyze, and respond on a routine basis to the underlying causes of crime and disorder

FIGURE 4.1 Traditional Policing versus Community Oriented Policing, Problem Oriented Policing, and Neighborhood Police Officers

policing. Goldstein first coined the term *problem oriented policing* in 1979 because of frustration with the dominant model for improving police operations: "More attention [was] being focused on how quickly officers responded to a call than on what they did when they got to their destination."[10] He also bemoaned the association between the police and the telephone: "The telephone, more than any public or internal policy, dictates what a police agency does. And that problem has been greatly aggravated with the installation of 911."[11]

As a result, Goldstein argued for a radical change in the direction of efforts to improve policing—a new framework that would help move the police from their past preoccupation with form and process to a much more direct, thoughtful concern with substantive problems. To focus attention on the nature of police business and to improve the quality of police response in the course of their business, Goldstein argued that several steps must be taken:

1. Police must be equipped to define clearly and to understand fully the problems they are expected to handle. They must recognize the relationships between and among incidents—for example, incidents involving the same behavior, the same address, or the same people.

In addition to traditional law enforcement activities, such as patrol and responding to calls for service, the day might include

- Operating neighborhood substations
- Meeting with community groups
- Analyzing and solving neighborhood problems
- Conducting door-to-door surveys of residents
- Talking with students in schools
- Meeting with local merchants
- Making security checks of businesses
- Dealing with disorderly people

FIGURE 4.2 A Community Police Officer's Day *(Source:* Stephen D. Mastrofski, "What Does Community Policing Mean for Daily Police Work?" *National Institute of Justice Journal* [August 1992]:23–27.)

2. Police must develop a commitment to analyzing problems. This requires gathering information from police files, from the minds of experienced officers, from other agencies of government, and from private sources as well. It requires conducting house-to-house surveys and talking with victims, complainants, and offenders.

3. Police must be encouraged to conduct an uninhibited search for the most effective response to each problem, looking beyond the criminal justice system to a wide range of alternatives; they must try to design a customized response that holds the greatest potential for dealing effectively with a specific problem in a specific place under specific conditions.[12]

Basic Principles

Earlier chapters mentioned the limitations of traditional methods of policing in trying to deal with incidents. The first step in problem oriented policing, therefore, is to move beyond simply handling incidents, recognizing that incidents are often merely overt symptoms of problems. It requires that officers take a more in-depth interest in incidents by acquainting themselves with some of the conditions and factors that cause them. Everyone in the department contributes to this mission, not only a few innovative officers or a special unit or function.[13]

Figure 4.3 shows incident-driven policing as it attempts to deal with each incident. Like a Band-Aid application, this symptomatic relief is valuable but limited. Because police leave unresolved the underlying condition that created the incidents, the incidents are likely to recur.

A problem oriented police agency would respond as described in Figure 4.4. Officers use the information in their responses to incidents, along with information obtained from other sources, to get a clear picture of the problem. Then they

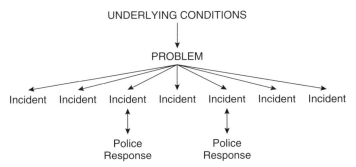

FIGURE 4.3 Incident-Driven Policing (*Source:* John E. Eck and William Spelman, *Problem-Solving: Problem-Oriented Policing in Newport News* [Washington, D.C.: U.S. Department of Justice, National Institute of Justice, 1987], p. 4.)

address the underlying conditions. As James Fyfe asked, "Can anyone imagine the surgeon general urging doctors to attack AIDS without giving any thought to its causes?"[14] If successful, fewer incidents may occur; those that do occur may be less serious. The incidents may even cease.[15]

Chris Braiden, former superintendent of police in Edmonton, Alberta, Canada, described problem oriented policing with an analogy from the medical community:

> The doctor (police officer) talks to the patient (community) to identify a problem. Sometimes the solution lies solely with the patient (community); for example, a change of diet (the owner agrees to remove an eyesore or an abandoned automobile). Sometimes it calls for the doctor (police officer) and patient (community) to work together, i.e., a change of diet plus medicine (organizing the neighborhood to help shut down a "blight" establishment). Sometimes only the doctor (police) alone can solve the problem, i.e., surgery (heavy law enforcement). Sometimes we have to accept the fact that the problem simply cannot be solved, e.g., terminal illness (poverty).[16]

The problem oriented approach also addresses a major dilemma for the police: the lack of meaningful measures of their effectiveness in the area of crime and disorder. Crime rate statistics are virtually useless, because they collapse all the different kinds of crime into one global category and they are an imperfect measure of the actual incidence of criminal behavior.[17]

Goldstein also maintained that the police should "disaggregate" the different problems they face and then attempt to develop strategies to address each one.[18] Domestic disturbances, for instance, should be separated from public intoxication; murder should be separated from sexual assault. In this respect, problem oriented policing is primarily a *planning process*. As the name suggests, it asks the police to think in terms of specific problems.

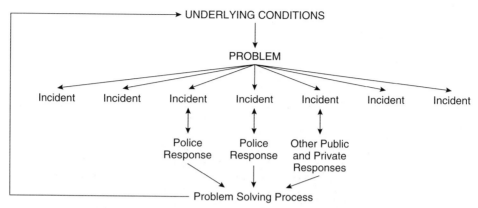

FIGURE 4.4 Problem Oriented Policing (*Source:* John E. Eck and William Spelman, *Problem-Solving: Problem-Oriented Policing in Newport News* [Washington, D.C.: U.S. Department of Justice, National Institute of Justice, 1987], p. 4.)

A Broader Role for the Street Officer

A major departure of problem oriented policing from the conventional style lies with POP's view of the line officer, who is given much more discretion and decision-making responsibility and, in general, is trusted with a much broader array of responsibilities.

Problem oriented policing values "thinking" officers, urging that they take the initiative in trying to deal effectively with problems in the areas they serve. This concept uses the potential of college-educated officers, "who have been smothered in the atmosphere of traditional policing." [19] It also gives officers a new sense of identity and self-respect; they are more challenged and have opportunities to follow through on individual cases—analyzing and solving problems—which gives them greater job satisfaction. Using patrol officers in this manner also allows the agency to provide sufficient challenge for the better-educated officer as well as for those who remain patrol officers throughout their entire careers. We ought to be recruiting as police officers people who can "serve as mediators, as dispensers of information, and as community organizers."[20]

Under problem oriented policing, officers continue to handle calls, but they also do much more. They use the information gathered in their responses to incidents, together with information obtained from other sources, to get a clear picture of the problem. They then address the underlying conditions. If they are successful in ameliorating these conditions, fewer incidents may occur; those that do occur may be less serious. The incidents may even cease. At the very least, information about the problem can help police to design more effective ways of responding to each incident.

Seeking information from a variety of resources (e.g., business owners) will assist officers in understanding the underlying conditions and factors related to problems. (*Courtesy* Community Policing Consortium)

Testing Problem Oriented Policing

The National Institute of Justice (NIJ) selected Newport News, Virginia, as a funded project to design and implement the problem solving process. In January 1982, Newport News had a moderately sized agency of 280 employees serving a population of 155,000. It was small enough that changes could be made in a reasonably short period of time, but it served an urban population with many of the crime problems of big cities. Because Newport News was close to Washington, D.C., Police Executive Research Forum staff could spend a great deal of time in the field. And its chief of police, Darrel Stephens, was well versed in the background research, believed the project would be worthwhile, and was committed to its success.[21]

To design the system, the police department assembled a task force of 12 department members, representing all ranks and units. Because this group had no experience at solving problems, it was decided to test the system design with several problems, including robberies downtown, burglaries from an apartment complex, and thefts from vehicles. It was understood, however, that all subsequent problems would be handled by officers in their normal assignments.

The results of the experiment were encouraging: Downtown robberies were reduced by 39 percent, burglaries in an apartment complex were reduced 35 percent, and thefts from parked vehicles outside a manufacturing plant dropped 53 percent.[22] Another important finding was that street officers are capable of applying the problem solving process on a routine, daily basis. By June 1986, some two dozen problems had been identified and were in various stages of analysis, response, and assessment. The Newport News experiment was the first significant research using problem oriented policing and the problem solving process. The work at Newport News provided important information to the field in addition to a problem solving process that is being used by many other agencies.

"S.A.R.A.": The Problem Solving Process

The Newport News task force designed a four-stage problem solving process (depicted in Figure 4.5); known as S.A.R.A., the process involves *scanning, analysis, response,* and *assessment.*[23]

Scanning: Problem Identification

Scanning means problem identification. As a first step, officers should identify problems on their beats and look for a pattern or persistent, repeat incidents. At this juncture the question might well be asked, "What is a 'problem'?" A problem has been defined as:

> *A group of two or more incidents that are similar in one or more respects, causing harm, and, therefore, being of concern to the police and the public.*

Incidents may be *similar* by various means, including

- *Behaviors* (this is the most frequent type of indicator, including such activities as drug sales, robberies, thefts, graffiti, and so on)
- *Location* (problems occur in area hot spots, such as downtown, housing complexes plagued by burglaries, parks where gangs commit crimes, and so forth)
- *Persons* (including repeat offenders or victims; both account for a high proportion of crime)

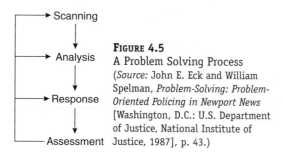

FIGURE 4.5
A Problem Solving Process
(*Source:* John E. Eck and William Spelman, *Problem-Solving: Problem-Oriented Policing in Newport News* [Washington, D.C.: U.S. Department of Justice, National Institute of Justice, 1987], p. 43.)

- *Time* (seasonal, day of week, hour of day; examples include rush hours, bar closings, tourist activity during holidays)
- *Events* (crimes may peak during events such as university spring break, rallies, gatherings, and so on)

There does not appear to be any inherent limit to the types of problems on which patrol officers can work; several types of problems are appropriate for problem solving. The following list presents the diversity of problems identified and addressed in several jurisdictions:

- A series of burglaries from trailers at a construction site
- Drug activity, drinking, and disorderly conduct at a community park
- Suspected drug activity at a private residence
- Thefts from autos at a shopping mall
- Juvenile loitering at a shopping center and near a bar
- Vagrants panhandling downtown
- Problems with false and faulty alarms at commercial addresses
- Parking and traffic problems

Motels converted to daily and weekly rentals often result in an increase in calls for service and crimes in the area.

- Street prostitution and related robberies in a downtown neighborhood
- A high rate of burglaries at a rundown apartment complex
- Repeat domestic assault calls to certain addresses[24]

If the incidents police are responding to do not fall within the definition of a problem, then the problem solving model is not applicable, and police should handle the incident according to normal procedure.

Numerous resources are available to the police to identify problems, including CFS data, especially repeat calls from the same location or a repeated series of similar incidents. Other ways include citizen complaints, census data, data from other government agencies, newspaper and media coverage of community issues, officer observations, and community surveys.

The primary purpose of scanning is to conduct a preliminary inquiry to determine if a problem really exists and if further analysis is needed. During this stage, priorities should be established if multiple problems exist, and a specific officer or team of officers should be assigned to handle each problem. Scanning initiates the problem solving process.

Analysis: The Heart of Problem Solving

Determining Problem Nature and Extent. The second stage, *analysis*, is the heart of the problem solving process. For this reason, we dwell on it at greater length. Comprehensively analyzing a problem is critical to the success of a problem solving effort. Effective, tailor-made responses cannot be developed unless people know what is causing the problem. Thus, the purpose of analysis is to learn as much as possible about problems in order to identify their causes; officers must gather information from sources inside and outside their agency about the scope, nature, and causes of problems. A complete analysis includes identifying the seriousness of the problem, all the persons or groups involved and affected, all of the causes of the problem, and assessing current responses and their effectiveness.

Many people essentially skip the analysis phase of S.A.R.A., believing that the nature of the problem is obvious and succumbing to pressure to solve the problem quickly, or believing that the pressure of CFS precludes their having time for detailed inquiries into the nature of the problem. Problem solvers must resist these temptations, or they risk addressing a problem that does not exist and implementing solutions that are ineffective in the long run.

For example, computer-assisted dispatch (CAD) data in one southeastern police department indicated that there was a large auto theft problem at a local shopping mall. After reviewing incident reports and other records, however, it became clear that many of the reported "thefts" actually involved shoppers misplacing their cars and then mistakenly reporting them as stolen.[25]

Identifying the Harms. A discussion of harms is important to analyzing problems and responding to them. The problem of gangs serves as an example. We begin by asking why gangs are a problem. We can find the answer to this question by focusing on harmful behaviors. Not all gang members are criminals or engage in harmful behaviors. It is, therefore, important that each community examine the behaviors of its gangs, determine which behaviors are harmful, and design responses appropriate to deal with those behaviors.

Common gang behaviors may include wearing "colors," spreading graffiti, using and selling drugs, and creating a threatening presence. For example, the wearing of colors to school creates fear among students and teachers and may result in fights among rival gang members.

These behaviors present harm to the community and should be the focus of police problem solving efforts. By identifying harmful behaviors, *gangs*—a huge, nondescriptive term and problem—is broken down into smaller, more manageable problems. This helps to identify the underlying causes or related conditions that contribute to illegal gang activity and is the basis for officers' responses.

Seeking "Small Wins." Karl Weick explained that people often look at social problems on a massive scale. The public, media, elected officials, and government agencies often become fixated on problems and define them by using the simplest term (gangs, homelessness, poverty, mental illness, violent crime, and so on). Viewing problems in this manner leads to defining problems on a scale so massive that they are unable to be addressed, thus overwhelming attempts to solve them. For this reason, Weick introduced the concept of "small wins." One must understand that some problems are too deeply ingrained, or too rooted in other complex social problems, to be eliminated. Conversely, adopting the "small wins" philosophy helps to understand the nature of our analysis and response to problems.

As indicated previously, a more appropriate response to these problems is to break them down into smaller more controllable problems. Although an individual, small win may not seem important, a series of small wins may have a substantial impact on the overall problem. Eliminating the harms (graffiti, drug sales, and so on) is a sensible and realistic strategy for reducing the impact of gang behaviors. Therefore, it makes sense to address a large problem at a level at which there can be a reasonable expectation of success.

The idea of small wins is also helpful when prioritizing problems and working together in a group. We have discussed the benefits of collaborating with the community and other outside agencies to address problems. Small wins can help the group understand the problem better, select realistic objectives, and formulate effective strategies. It also helps to build confidence and trust among group members.[26] Next we discuss a tool developed to further analyze problems.

The Problem Analysis Triangle. Generally, three elements are needed for a problem to occur: an *offender*, a *victim*, and a *location*. The "problem analysis triangle" helps officers visualize the problem and understand the relationships among the three elements. Additionally, it helps officers analyze problems, suggests where more information is needed, and helps with crime control and prevention.

The relationships among these three elements can be explained as follows: If there is a victim, and the victim is in a place where a crime occurs, but there are no offenders, no crime occurs; if there is an offender, and the offender is in a place where crimes occur, but there is nothing or no one to be victimized, then no crime will occur; and if an offender and victim are not in the same place, there will be no crime. Part of the analysis phase involves finding out as much as possible about the victims, offenders, and locations where problems exist in order to understand what is prompting the problem and what to do about it.

The three elements must be present before a crime or harmful behavior—the problem—can occur (see Figure 4.6): an *offender* (someone, in this case, a gang member, who is motivated to commit harmful behavior), a *victim* (a desirable and vulnerable target), and a *location* (the victim and offender must both be in the same place at the same time; we discuss location later in the chapter). If these three elements recur over and over again in patterns, removing one of the elements can stop the pattern and prevent future harms.[27]

As an example, let us apply the analysis triangle to the problem of graffiti. The "location" is marked buildings and areas immediately around them. The "victims" are the owners and users of the buildings; the "offenders" are the people who write the graffiti (see Figure 4.7). Removing one or more of these elements will remove the problem. Strategies for removing one of these elements are limited only by an officer's creativity, the availability of resources, and the ability to formulate collaborative responses.

Some jurisdictions are setting aside an area for graffiti "artists," even having graffiti contests, or using nonadhesive paint on buildings and property (protecting locations) to discourage taggers ("offenders") or give them an outlet for their illegal tagging activities; other jurisdictions have contemplated outlawing the sale of spray paint or limiting the sale of broad-tip markers to juveniles; whereas still others have enacted graffiti ordinances to help business owners ("victims") keep their "locations" graffiti free.

Spelman described the significance of attending to all three areas of the triangle when analyzing a problem and developing crime detection and prevention strategies:

> The primary implication of repeat offenders, vulnerable victims, and dangerous places has always been that long-term activities make sense. In the absence of special attention, these high-risk people and places would remain at high risks. Thus they had a claim on a disproportionate share of police

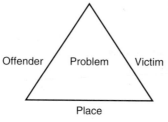

FIGURE 4.6
Problem Analysis Triangle
(*Source:* U.S. Department of Justice, Bureau of Justice Assistance, *Comprehensive Gang Initiative: Operations Manual for Implementing Local Gang Prevention and Control Programs* [Draft, October 1993], p. 3.)

FIGURE 4.7
Graffiti Problem Triangle
(*Source:* U.S. Department of Justice,
Bureau of Justice Assistance,
*Comprehensive Gang Initiative:
Operations Manual for Implementing
Local Gang Prevention and Control
Programs* [Draft, October 1993],
pp. 3–11.)

resources. Programs to target certain offenders, provide assistance to certain victims, and solve recurring problems at certain locations seem appropriate.[28]

The Role of Third Parties. Police engaged in problem solving also need to be aware of the three types of "third parties" that can either help or hinder the problem solving effort, by attempting to act on behalf of one or more of the three elements discussed in the problem analysis triangle in Figure 4.6. We will again use examples to explain the role of third parties:

1. *Controllers:* people who, acting in the best interests of the potential offenders, try to prevent offenders from committing crimes. Controllers of gang members might be parents, adult neighbors, peers, teachers, and employers. Offending youths, however, may live in poor, one-parent homes or may not be attending school or working. Controllers can often restrict the tools used by gang members, such as retailers putting spray cans in locked bins, school administrators restricting the wearing of "colors," and governing bodies passing laws obstructing the sale of semiautomatic and automatic weapons.[29]

2. *Guardians:* people or things that exercise control over each side of the triangle, making crime less likely. For instance, if the crime problem is drug dealing in a house, and the offender side of the triangle includes dealers and buyers, then a list of guardians would include police, parents of the dealers and buyers, probation and parole officers, the landlord, city codes, health and tax departments, and neighbors. Tools used by guardians include crime prevention techniques (discussed further later).[30]

3. *Managers:* people who oversee locations. For example, apartment managers can help prevent or solve problems by installing security equipment in their buildings, screening tenants carefully, and evicting troublemakers or criminals. Conversely, when managers are absent or lax, risks will be higher.[31]

Police should constantly look for ways to improve the effectiveness of third parties, because these groups of individuals have the authority to deal with the problem. There will always be the temptation on the part of society to use the police as controllers, guardians, or managers. Although this may be effective for a short time, there are rarely enough officers to control a recurring problem in the long run.

The problem analysis triangle allows officers to dissect a problem and find out what allows it to persist. Crafting a solution (the "response") comes next. An important adjunct to our discussion of analysis is a look at situational crime prevention (including crime prevention through environmental design—CPTED) and crime analysis under community policing, both of which are addressed in Chapter 5.

Response: Formulating Tailor-Made Strategies

After a problem has been clearly defined and analyzed, the officer confronts the ultimate challenge in problem oriented policing: the search for the most effective way of dealing with it. This stage of the S.A.R.A. process focuses on developing and implementing *responses* to the problem. Before entering this stage, an agency must overcome the temptation to implement a response prematurely and be certain that it has thoroughly analyzed the problem; attempts to fix problems quickly are rarely effective in the long term.

To develop tailored responses, problem solvers should review their findings about the three sides of the crime triangle—victims, offenders, and location—and develop creative solutions that address at least two sides of the triangle.[32] It is also important to remember that the key to developing tailored responses is making sure the responses are very focused and *directly linked* to the findings from the analysis phase of the project.

Responses may be wide ranging and often require arrests (however, apprehension may not be the most effective solution), referral to social service agencies, or changes in ordinances. Potential solutions to problems can be organized into five groups:

1. *Totally eliminating the problem.* Effectiveness is measured by the absence of the types of incidents that a problem creates. It is unlikely that most problems can be totally eliminated, but a few can.
2. *Reducing the number of incidents the problem creates.* A reduction of incidents stemming from a problem is a major measure of effectiveness.
3. *Reducing the seriousness of the harms.* Effectiveness for this type of solution is demonstrated by showing that the incidents are less harmful.
4. *Dealing with a problem more effectively.* Participants can be treated more humanely, costs can be reduced, or the effectiveness of handling incidents can be improved. Improved victim satisfaction, reduced costs, and other measures can show that this type of solution is effective.
5. *Removing the problem from police consideration.* The effectiveness of this type of solution can be measured by examining why the police were handling the problem originally and the rationale for shifting the problem to others.[33]

Figure 4.8 provides an elaboration on the possible alternative responses to problems. Problem solving officers will often seek the assistance of the community, other city departments, businesses, private and social service organizations, and anyone else who can help. Figure 4.9 is a guide to collaboration to help officers develop networks with people and work with other agencies.

Assessment: Evaluating Overall Effectiveness

Finally, in the *assessment* stage, officers evaluate the effectiveness of their responses. A number of measures have traditionally been used by police agencies and community members to assess effectiveness. These include numbers of arrests, levels of reported crime, response times, clearance rates, citizen complaints, and various workload indicators, such as CFS and the number of field interviews conducted.[34]

Several of these measures may be helpful in assessing the impact of a problem solving effort; however, a number of nontraditional measures, such as the following, will shed light on whether a problem has been reduced or eliminated:

- Reduced instances of repeat victimization
- Decreases in related crimes or incidents
- Neighborhood indicators, which can include increased profits for businesses in the target area, increased usage of the area, increased property values, less loitering and truancy, and fewer abandoned cars
- Increased citizen satisfaction regarding the handling of the problem, as determined through surveys, interviews, focus groups, electronic bulletin boards, and so on
- Reduced citizen fear related to the problem[35]

Assessment is obviously key in the S.A.R.A. process; knowing that we must assess the effectiveness of our efforts emphasizes the importance of documentation and baseline measurements. Supervisors can help officers with this assessment.

If the responses implemented are not effective, the information gathered during analysis should be reviewed. New information may need to be collected before new solutions can be developed and tested.[36] We discuss assessment (evaluation) in depth in Chapter 11.

A Collaborative Approach: "COPPS"

Basic Principles

As mentioned in the introduction, our view is that the two concepts of community policing and problem oriented policing are separate but complementary notions that can work together. We believe the police are severely hampered

1. *Concentrate attention on the individuals accounting for a disproportionate share of the problem.* A relatively small number of individuals usually account for a disproportionate share of practically any problem, by causing it (offenders), facilitating it (controllers, managers, guardians), or suffering from it (victims).

2. *Connect with other government and private services.* A thorough analysis of a problem often leads to an appreciation of the need for (a) more effective referrals to existing governmental and private services, (b) improved coordination with agencies that exert control over some of the problems or individuals involved in the incidents, and (c) initiative for pressing for correction of inadequacies in municipal services and for development of new services.

3. *Use mediation and negotiation skills.* Often the use of mediation and negotiation teams can be effective responses to conflicts.

4. *Convey information.* Relating sound and accurate information is one of the least used responses. It has the potential, however, to be one of the most effective for responding to a wide range of problems. Conveying information can help (a) reduce anxiety and fear, (b) enable citizens to solve their own problems, (c) elicit conformity with laws and regulations that are not known or understood, (d) warn potential victims about their vulnerability and advise them of ways to protect themselves, (e) demonstrate to people how they unwittingly contribute to problems, (f) develop support for addressing a problem, and (g) acquaint the community with the limitations on government agencies and define realistically what can be expected of those agencies.

5. *Mobilize the community.* Mobilizing a specific segment of the community helps implement a specific response to a specific problem for as long as it takes to deal with the problem.

6. *Make use of existing forms of social control.* Solve problems by mobilizing specific forms of social control inherent in existing relationships—for example, the influence of a parent, teacher, employer, or church.

7. *Alter the physical environment to reduce opportunities for problems to recur.* Adapt the principles of crime prevention through environmental design and situational crime prevention to the complete range of problems.

8. *Increase regulation, through statutes or ordinances, of conditions that contribute to problems.* An analysis of a specific problem may draw attention to factors contributing to the problem that can be controlled by regulation through statutes or ordinances.

9. *Develop new forms of limited authority to intervene and detain.* Examination of specific problems can lead to the conclusion that a satisfactory solution requires some limited authority (e.g., to order a person to leave) but does not require labeling the conduct criminal so that it can be dealt with through a citation or a physical arrest followed by a criminal prosecution.

10. *Make more discriminate use of the criminal justice system.* Use of the criminal justice system should be much more discreet than in the past, reserved for those problems for which the system seems especially appropriate, and used with much greater precision. This could include (a) straightforward investigation, arrest, and prosecution; (b) selective enforcement with articulated criteria; (c) enforcing criminal laws that, by tradition, are enforced by another agency; (d) defining with greater specificity that behavior which should be subject to criminal justice prosecution or control through local ordinances; (e) intervention without making

(figure continues)

Figure 4.8 Range of Possible Response Options

FIGURE 4.8 Range of Possible Response Options *(continued)*

---

an arrest; (f) use of arrest without the intention to prosecute; and (g) attaching new conditions to probation or parole.

11. *Use civil law to control public nuisances, offensive behavior, and conditions contributing to crime.* Because most of what the police do in the use of the law involves arrest and prosecution, people tend to forget that the police and local government can initiate a number of other legal proceedings, including those related to (a) licensing, (b) zoning, (c) property confiscation, (d) nuisance abatement, and (e) injunctive relief.

Source: Adapted from Herman Goldstein, *Problem-Oriented Policing* (New York: McGraw-Hill, 1990, pp. 104–141). Used with permission of McGraw-Hill.

when attempting to solve neighborhood and community problems without the full cooperation—a partnership and collaboration—of the community and other resources.

Both community and problem oriented policing share some important characteristics: (1) decentralization (to encourage officer initiative and the effective use of local knowledge), (2) geographically defined rather than functionally defined subordinate units (to encourage the development of local knowledge), and (3) close interactions with local communities (to facilitate responsiveness to, and cooperation with, the community).[37]

Goldstein did not believe problem oriented policing was an alternative to community policing or in competition with it. He asserted, however, that much of what is occurring in community policing projects begs for application of all that has been described under the concept of problem oriented policing.

A Definition and Illustration

What exactly is COPPS? How does it function? How would we know it if we saw it? Following is a definition we believe accurately captures the essence of this concept:

 Community oriented policing and problem solving (COPPS) is a proactive philosophy that promotes solving problems that are criminal, affect our quality of life, or increase our fear of crime, as well as other community issues. COPPS involves identifying, analyzing, and addressing community problems at their source.

To assist in our understanding of this definition, following is an example of how a neighborhood problem is treated under the traditional, reactive style of policing versus the community problem solving approach:

Police have experienced a series of disturbances in a relatively quiet and previously stable residential neighborhood. Although the neighborhood's zoning had for years provided for late-night, cabaret-style businesses, none

General Background

1. Develop personal networks with members of other agencies who can give you information and help you with problems on which you may be working.
2. Become familiar with the workings of your local government, private businesses, citizen organizations, and other groups and institutions that you may need to call on for help in the future.
3. Develop skills as a negotiator.

Getting Other Agencies to Help

1. Identify agencies that have a role (or could have a role) in addressing the problem early in the problem solving process.
2. Determine whether these other agencies perceive that there is a problem.
   a. Which agency members perceive the problem and which do not?
   b. Why is it (or isn't it) a problem for them?
   c. How are police perceptions of the problem similar to and different than the perceptions of members of other agencies?
3. Determine whether there is a legal or political mandate for collaboration.
   a. To which agencies does this legal mandate apply?
   b. What are the requirements needed to demonstrate collaboration?
   c. Who is checking to determine whether collaboration is taking place?
4. Look for difficulties that these other agencies face that can be addressed through collaboration on this problem.
   a. Are there internal difficulties that provide an incentive to collaborate?
   b. Are there external crises affecting agencies that collaboration may help address?
5. Determine how much these other agencies use police services.
6. Assess the resource capabilities of these agencies to help.
   a. Do they have the money?
   b. Do they have the staff expertise?
   c. Do they have the enthusiasm?
7. Assess the legal authority of these other agencies.
   a. Do they have special enforcement powers?
   b. Do they control critical resources?
8. Determine the administrative capacity of these agencies to collaborate.
   a. Do they have the legal authority to intervene in the problem?
   b. What are the internal procedures and policies of the stakeholders that help or hinder collaboration?

Working with Other Agencies

1. Include representatives from all affected agencies, if possible, in the problem solving process.
2. Look for responses to the problem that maximize the gains to all agencies and distribute costs equitably.
3. Reinforce awareness of the interdependence of all agencies.

(figure continues)

FIGURE 4.9 Problem Solving: Guide to Collaboration

FIGURE 4.9 Problem Solving: Guide to Collaboration *(continued)*

---

4. Be prepared to mediate among agencies that have a history of conflict.
5. Develop problem information sharing mechanisms, and promote discussion about the meaning and interpretation of this information.
6. Share problem solving decisions among stakeholders, and do not surprise others with already-made decisions.
7. Develop a clear explanation as to why collaboration is needed.
8. Foster external support for collaborative efforts, but do not rely on mandates to further collaboration.
9. Be prepared to negotiate with all involved agencies as to their roles, responsibilities, and resource commitments.
10. When collaborating with agencies located far away, plan to spend time developing a working relationship.
11. Try to create support in the larger community for collaborative problem solving.

When Collaboration Does Not Work

1. Always be prepared for collaboration to fail.
2. Have alternative plans.
3. Assess the costs and benefits of unilateral action.
4. Be very patient.

Source: Adapted from John E. Eck, "Implementing a Problem-Oriented Approach: A Management Guide," mimeo, draft copy (Washington, D.C.: Police Executive Research Forum, 1990), pp. 69–70.

had existed until "Nite Life," a live-music dance club, opened. Within a few weeks the police dispatcher received an increased number of complaints about loud music and voices, fighting, and screeching tires late into the night. Within a month's time, at least 50 CFS had been dispatched to the club to restore order. Evening shift officers responded to calls and restored order prior to midnight but graveyard shift officers would have to again restore order when they were called back to the scene by complaining neighbors after midnight.

Under the COPPS approach, this same matter might be handled as follows:

The evening shift area patrol sergeant identified the disturbances as a problem. The initial scanning phase provided the following information: data showed huge CFS increases in the area on both the evening and graveyard shifts, several realtors had contacted council members to complain about declining market interest in the area and to say that they were considering suing both the owner of the new business and the city for the degradation of the neighborhood, and a local newspaper was about to run a story on the increase in vehicle burglaries and damage done to parked vehicles in and around the cabaret's parking lot. The team also determined that the consolidated narcotics unit was investigating both employees and some of the late-night clientele of the business as a result of several tips that narcotics were being used and sold in the parking lot and inside the business.

The officers and their sergeant gathered information from crime reports, a news reporter about to publish the story, neighboring business owners, and the department's crime analysis unit. Information was also gathered concerning possible zoning and health department violations. Officers then met with the business owner to work out an agreement for reestablishing the quality of life in the neighborhood to its previous level and to decrease the department's CFS. First, the business licensing division and the owner were brought together to both reestablish the ground rules and provide for a proper licensing of all the players. This resulted in the instant removal of an unsavory partner and, in turn, his "following" of drug users and other characters at the business. The landlord agreed to hasten landscaping and lighting of the parking lots and provide a "sound wall" around the business to buffer the area residents. Agreements were reached to limit the hours of operation of the live music of the business. The cabaret's owner and all of his employees were trained by the area patrol teams in pertinent aspects of the city code (such as disturbing the peace, minors in liquor establishments, and trespassing laws). The police experienced a reduction in CFS in the area. Area residents, although not entirely happy with the continuing existence of the business, acknowledged satisfaction from their complaints; no further newspaper stories appeared regarding the noise and disorder in the neighborhood.

In this example, the police not only responded to the concerns of the neighborhood residents, but they also developed a better understanding of both the area's businesses and residents and established a working relationship with all involved. By co-opting the services of the other municipal entities, police also discovered new and valuable resources with whom they could share some of the burden of future demands for government service.

One of the strongest advocates of this kind of approach to policing is the California Department of Justice, which has published several monographs on the subject and has taken the position that

Community Oriented Policing and Problem Solving is a concept whose time has come. This movement holds tremendous promise for creating effective police–community partnerships to reclaim our communities and keep our streets safe. COPPS is not "soft" on crime; in fact, it is tougher on crime because it is smarter and more creative. Community input focuses police activities; and, with better information, officers are able to respond more effectively with arrests or other appropriate actions. COPPS can unite our communities and promote pride in our police forces.[38]

In order for COPPS to succeed, however, the following measures are required:

- Conducting accurate community needs assessments
- Mobilizing all appropriate players to collect data and brainstorm strategies
- Determining appropriate resource allocations and creating new resources where necessary
- Developing and implementing innovative, collaborative, comprehensive programs to address underlying causes and causal factors
- Evaluating programs and modifying approaches as needed[39]

Figure 4.10 sets forth the basic principles of COPPS as developed by the California Department of Justice.

CRIME ANALYSIS TOOLS

It is important for officers who are engaged in problem solving to understand *how, when, where,* and *why* criminal events occur, rather than merely responding to them. We are not suggesting that patrol officers should develop expertise in understanding the mental processes and theories that are involved in a person's choosing to commit crimes (although criminology or psychology courses at a college or university would certainly benefit the problem solving officer); rather, we are referring to what might be termed *street-level criminology*. It is relatively new to policing, and it requires that we learn more about crime occurrences through analysis and experimentation with the problem solving process.

Analyzing Crime: Definition, Functions, and Types

Crime analysis has been defined as "a set of systematic, analytical processes providing timely and pertinent information to assist operational and administrative personnel."[40] There are basically three types of crime analysis:

1. *Tactical:* An analytical process that provides information used to assist operations personnel (patrol and investigative officers) in identifying specific and immediate crime trends, patterns, sprees, and hot spots, providing investigative leads. Criminal activity is associated by the method, time, date, location, suspect, vehicle, and other types of information.
2. *Strategic:* Analysis that is concerned with long-range problems and projections of long-term increases or decreases in crime (crime trends), including the preparation of crime statistical summaries, resource acquisitions, and allocation studies.
3. *Administrative:* Analysis that focuses on the provision of economic, geographic, or social information.

1. *Reassesses who is responsible for public safety and redefines the roles and relationships between the police and the community.* Community policing recognizes that the community at large shares responsibility with the police for social order. Both must work cooperatively to identify problems and develop proactive communitywide solutions.

2. *Requires shared ownership, decision making, and accountability, as well as sustained commitment from both the police and the community.* Police management styles must be adjusted to include diverse public feedback into the decision-making process. In turn, the community—neighborhoods, families, schools, churches, organizations, elected officials, and businesses—must become empowered to accept the challenge and responsibility to assume ownership of their community's safety and well-being.

3. *Establishes new public expectations of and measurement standards for police effectiveness.* With the current incident-driven system of policing—especially with the 911 emergency system—a majority of officers' time is spent responding to calls for service. The community policing approach reprioritizes police efforts to focus on customer satisfaction and service. These deal with qualitative rather than simply quantitative factors and effectiveness as well as efficiency.

4. *Increases understanding and trust between police and community members.* With rapidly changing demographics in our communities, the police must become culturally competent and literate for the neighborhoods in which they work; they must be aware of and sensitive to the multicultural populations they serve. Assigning officers to one beat for extended time periods ("beat integrity") promotes daily, direct, and positive contact and fosters friendship and understanding.

5. *Supports community initiative by supplying community members with necessary information and skills, reinforcing their courage and strength, and ensuring them the influence to impact policies and share accountability for outcomes.* A mobilized community can send messages about how people are to behave that will be more powerful in constraining inconsiderate, ill-considered, abusive, and criminal behavior than anything police can do on their own.

6. *Requires constant flexibility to respond to all emerging issues.* Developing new and alternative authority (i.e., new policies, regulations, and ordinances) to respond to specific situations is often more effective or more suitable than using the criminal law. COPPS greatly expands the prevention and intervention alternatives available to police and requires a full-scale, ongoing search for effective solutions to community problems.

7. *Requires an ongoing commitment to develop long-term and proactive strategies and programs to address the underlying conditions that cause community problems.* To maintain the long-term struggle of addressing the complex and chronic underlying issues that plague our society and communities, police need accurate community needs assessments; review of existing community resource allocations; collaborative, comprehensive programs that address the underlying issues and causal factors in question; and evaluation and modification of programs and strategies as necessary.

8. *Requires knowledge of available community resources and how to access and mobilize them and the ability to develop new resources within the community.* Police must recognize and mobilize the untapped resources within a community. Increased communication and cooperation among local government agencies enhances

(figure continues)

Figure 4.10 The Basic Principles of COPPS

FIGURE 4.10 The Basic Principles of COPPS *(continued)*

problem solving by providing diverse perspectives. Being "resource knowledge-able" is a unique skill that will enhance any COPPS effort.

9. *Requires buy-in of the top management of the police and other local government agencies, as well as a sustained personal commitment from all levels of management and other key personnel.* COPPS encourages creativity and risk taking. It is a value-driven rather than rule-driven management approach. Its "quality leadership" focuses on actively modifying and improving the systems that serve us. In turn, police executives must have the support and cooperation of local government. This entails training elected officials, directors, and department heads.

10. *Decentralizes police services/operations/management, relaxes the traditional "chain of command," and encourages innovation and creative problem solving.* The officers on the beat become the most important persons in the department and the managers of their areas. The role of the first-line supervisors on up to the chief is to provide the beat officers with the resources they need to solve the problems in their areas. The internal reward and performance evaluation systems must be revised so that officers are evaluated for community development and problem solving in addition to enforcement activities.

11. *Shifts the focus of police work from responding to individual incidents to addressing problems identified by the community as well as by the police.* The *problem* becomes the main unit of police work. A careful analysis of the problem precedes the development of specific responses. Follow-up and feedback between the police and the community follows. However, community policing is still law enforcement. It is not soft on crime. Consulting the community focuses police activities more effectively; with community input, police receive more information and are able to respond more effectively with arrests or other appropriate actions.

12. *Requires commitment to developing new skills through training.* There are a number of skills officers must be taught to make the transition viable, including problem analysis and problem solving, facilitation, community organization, communication, mediation and conflict resolution, resource awareness and development, networking and linkages, and cultural competency and literacy. Training in COPPS must be comprehensive and ongoing to bring about a transition in skills, attitudes, and values that reflect community policing and problem solving approaches.

Source: Adapted from the California Attorney General's Office, Crime Prevention Center, *Community Oriented Policing and Problem Solving,* "Community Oriented Policing and Problem Solving (COPPS) Definition and Principles" (Sacramento, Calif., 1992), pp. 4–12.

In more closely dissecting crime, crime analysis is also indispensable in identifying the underlying characteristics of criminal behavior. Unfortunately, much of our attempts to control crime attempt to treat the symptoms and ignore the disease:

[R]emember "The Iceberg, or 80/20 Rule" . . . no matter how large the tip of an iceberg seems, 80% of it lies below the surface of the water. If you want to eliminate the problem, you have to attack the 80% that is not so visible, yet is the underlying cause and condition that allows the 20%, or tip of the iceberg, to exist. When analyzing crime problems, consideration must be given to the characteristics of all the people involved, the environment in

Crime analysis information led these repeat offender program officers to the arrest of suspects in a car theft ring. (*Courtesy* Reno, Nevada, Police Department)

which they live and interact with one another, and the community reaction to those factors.[41]

Another reason for engaging in crime analysis is that career criminals are more mobile than the average criminal, often crossing city and even state lines to commit their crimes.[42] As William Spelman indicated, "The offenders we would most like to catch are also the ones we are least likely to catch, at least using present police methods."[43] If we stop concentrating on individual crimes and instead think about series of crimes, all committed by the same offender, we may be able to forecast when and where the offender will commit the next crime, and we may be able to link together clues from several crimes to help identify the responsible offender.

Crime analysis has the potential to become increasingly useful to police engaged in problem solving. There are four kinds of analysis functions that may be performed:

- *Crime series/pattern detection*: Crime series detection is identification of offenses that are believed to be committed by the same person or group; crime pattern detection, in contrast, is the number of offenses that have some common characteristics but are not necessarily unique to a given person or group. The objective of crime series detection is apprehension, and the objective of crime pattern detection is suppression.
- *Suspect–crime correlations*: These identify perpetrators of known crimes by systematically matching a suspect's physical, vehicle, or MO information from crime reports with similar information from offender-based files.

- *Target and suspect profiles*: Target profiles attempt to forecast the nature of the objects that might be attacked or descriptions of the types of structures and victims for a given crime problem. Suspect profiles can be established in the same manner.
- *Crime potential forecasts*: Attempts to determine future crime events based on the historical analysis of cyclical, periodic, or special events and information from crime series/pattern detection.[44]

The value of crime analysis to problem solving also depends on the time crime analysts are allotted to respond to individual officer requests and their ability to become *problem* analysts.

Next we discuss the crime analysis tools that are available to crime problem solvers, including crime mapping, police reports, CFS analysis, and surveys.

Crime Mapping

Conclusive evidence from clay tablets found in Iraq proves that maps have been around for several thousand years—perhaps tens of millennia.[45] Crime mapping has long been an integral part of the crime analysis process. The New York City Police Department, for example, has traced the use of maps back to at least 1900.

The traditional crime map was a jumbo representation of a jurisdiction with pins stuck in it. The old pin maps were useful for showing where crimes occurred, but they had several limitations. As they were updated, the prior crime patterns were lost; the maps were static, unable to be manipulated or queried. Also, pin maps could be quite difficult to read when several types of crime were mixed together. They also occupied considerable wall space (as an example, to make a single wall map of the 610 square miles of Baltimore County, 12 maps had to be joined, covering 70 square feet).[46] Consequently, during the 1990s pin maps largely gave way to desktop computer mapping, which has now become commonplace and fast, aided by the availability of inexpensive color printers.[47]

Computerized crime mapping has been called *policing's latest hot topic*.[48] For officers on the street, mapping puts street crime into an entirely new perspective; for administrators, it provides a way to involve the community in addressing its own problems by observing trends in neighborhood criminal activity (see Exhibit 4.1). Crime mapping also offers crime analysts graphic representations of crime-related issues. Furthermore, detectives can use maps to better understand the hunting patterns of serial offenders and to hypothesize where these offenders might live.[49]

Computerized crime mapping combines geographic information from global positioning satellites with crime statistics gathered by the department's computer-aided dispatching (CAD) system and demographic data provided by private companies or the U.S. Census Bureau. (Some agencies acquire information from the Census Bureau's Internet home page.) The result is a picture that combines disparate sets of data for a whole new perspective on crime. For example, a map showing crime locations can be overlaid with maps or layers of causative data,

---

Exhibit 4.1   The Crime Mapping Research Center

In 1997, the National Institute of Justice established the Crime Mapping Research Center (CMRC) to promote research, evaluation, development, and dissemination of geographic information systems technology for criminal justice research and practice. The CMRC holds annual conferences on crime mapping to provide researchers and practitioners an opportunity to gain both practical and state-of-the-art information on the use and utility of computerized crime mapping. The CMRC provides fellowships; NIJ-funded grant awards; evaluation of best practices and current criminal justice applications and needs; training programs; a national geocoded data archive; and information through conferences, workshops, a Web site, and a listserv. The CMRC Web site address is http://www.ojp.usdoj.gov/cmrc.

Source: U.S. Department of Justice, National Institute of Justice, *Crime Mapping Research Center* (Washington, D.C.: Author, 2000).

---

such as unemployment rates in the high-crime areas, abandoned housing sites, population density, drug activity reports, or geographic features (such as alleys, canals, or open fields), which might be contributing factors.[50] Hardware and software are available to nearly all police agencies for a few thousand dollars.

In 1995 the Chicago Police Department implemented a system called Information Collection for Automated Mapping, or ICAM—a flexible, user-friendly system that enables all police officers to quickly generate maps of their beats, sectors, or districts, and to search for and analyze crime patterns. ICAM (now officially ICAM2, with 20 enhancements) is now in use in all of the city's 25 policing districts and can query up to two years and map from a selection of 300 crimes within specific time ranges; it can also reveal important neighborhood establishments, such as schools, abandoned buildings, and liquor stores. It provides mugshot images within a minute. ICAM is also an informative tool for the community; many COPPS officers are providing maps detailing crime on a beat during community meetings.[51]

Another example of mapping success is the New York Police Department's highly touted CompStat program, which provides up-to-the-minute statistics and maps patterns and establishes causal relationships among crime categories. CompStat also puts supervisors in constant communication with the department's administration, provides updates to headquarters every week, and makes supervisors responsible for responding to crime in their assigned areas.[52]

Crime mapping is an important tool in smaller jurisdictions as well. Following are case studies involving successful outcomes using crime mapping:

- When an armored car was robbed in Toronto, dispatchers helped officers chase the suspects through a sprawling golf course using the mapping feature of the CAD system.

- The Illinois State Police map fatality accidents throughout the state and show which districts have specific problems. It can correlate such data with citations written, seatbelt usage, and other types of enforcement data.

- The Salinas, California, Police Department maps gang territories and correlates socioeconomic factors with crime-related incidents. Murders are down 61 percent; drive-by shootings, 31 percent; and gang-related assaults, 23 percent.[53]

A wealth of information and other successful case studies about crime mapping are available from the NIJ[54] and the Police Executive Research Forum.[55] Furthermore, the NIJ's CMRC, established in 1997, provides information concerning research, evaluation, and training programs through its Web site at http://www.ojp.usdoj.gov/cmrc.

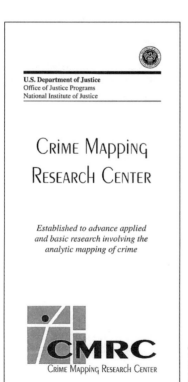

U.S. Department of Justice
Office of Justice Programs
National Institute of Justice

CRIME MAPPING
RESEARCH CENTER

*Established to advance applied
and basic research involving the
analytic mapping of crime*

CMRC
CRIME MAPPING RESEARCH CENTER

The Crime Mapping Research Center is a national clearinghouse for information about crime analysis and mapping. The CMRC Web site address is http://www.ojp.usdoj.gov/cmrc

Exhibit 4.2 shows the Tempe, Arizona, Police Department Crime Analysis Unit's Web site home page, which allows citizens to learn about crime analysis, view a wide variety of crime statistics and demographics, and learn about on-going crime studies and available reports and bulletins concerning crime in their community. Figure 4.11 (p. 116) provides an example of crime mapping of street gang motivated homicide in Chicago.

Police Reports

Police offense reports can be analyzed for suspect characteristics, MOs, victim characteristics, and many other factors. Offense reports are also a potential source of information about high-crime areas and addresses, because they capture exact descriptions of locations. In a typical department, however, patrol officers may write official reports on only about 25 to 30 percent of all calls to which they respond. Another limitation is that there may be considerable lag time between when the officer files a report and when the analysis is complete.[56]

Call for Service Analysis

With the advent of CAD systems, a more reliable source of data on CFS has become available. CAD systems, containing information on all types of calls for service, add to information provided by offense reports, yielding a more extensive account of what the public reports to the police.[57] The data captured by CAD systems can be sorted to reveal hot spots of crime and disturbances—specific locations from which an unusual number of calls to the police are made.

One study on hot spots analyzed nearly 324,000 CFS for a one-year period covering all 115,000 addresses and intersections in Minneapolis. The results showed relatively few hot spots accounting for the majority of calls to the police:

- Fifty percent of all calls came from 3 percent of places.
- All robbery calls came from 2.2 percent of places.
- All rape calls came from 1.2 percent of places.
- All auto thefts came from 2.7 percent of places.[58]

Many police agencies have the capability to use CAD data for repeat call analysis. The repeat call locations identified in this way can become targets of directed patrol efforts, including problem solving. For example, a precinct may receive printouts of the top 25 CFS areas to review for problem solving assignments. In Houston, the police and Hispanic citizens were concerned about violence at cantinas (bars). Through repeat call analysis, police learned that only 3 percent of the cantinas in the city were responsible for 40 percent of the violence. The data narrowed the scope of the problem and enabled a special liquor control squad to better target its efforts.[59]

EXHIBIT 4.2   Tempe, Arizona, Police Department Crime Analysis Unit's Web Site Home Page

Crime Analysis Unit

              Home   Site Map   Search

Tempe Police Department's Crime Analysis Unit

Table of Contents

-
-
-
-
-
-

Featured Pages:

(Please contact the   with questions on this page).

About Crime Analysis

Historically, the causes and origins of crime have been the subject of investigation by varied disciplines. Some factors known to affect the volume and type of crime occurring from place to place are:

- Population density and degree of urbanization with size locality and its surrounding area.
- Variations in composition of the population, particularly youth concentration.
- Stability of population with respect to residents' mobility, commuting patterns, and transient factors.
- Modes of transportation and highway system.
- Economic conditions, including median income, poverty level, and job availability.
- Cultural factors and educational, recreational, and religious characteristics.
- Family conditions with respect to divorce and family cohesiveness.

- Climate.
- Effective strength of law enforcement agencies.
- Administrative and investigative emphases of law enforcement.
- Policies of other components of the criminal justice system (e.g. prosecutorial, judicial, correctional, and probational).
- Citizens' attitudes toward crime.
- Crime reporting practices of the citizenry.

Crime Analysis is defined as...

A set of systematic, analytical processes directed at providing timely and pertinent information relative to crime patterns and trend correlations to assist the operational and administrative personnel in planning the deployment of resources for the prevention and suppression of criminal activities, aiding the investigative process, and increasing apprehensions and the clearance of cases. Within this context, Crime Analysis supports a number of department functions including patrol deployment, special operations, and tactical units, investigations, planning and research, crime prevention, and administrative services (budgeting and program planning). --Steven Gottlieb et al., 1994, "Crime Analysis: From First Report To Final Arrest."

Types of Crime Analysis

- **Tactical crime analysis:** An analytical process that provides information used to assist operations personnel (patrol and investigative officers) in identifying specific and immediate crime trends, patterns, series, sprees, and hotspots, providing investigative leads, and clearing cases. Analysis includes associating criminal activity by method of the crime, time, date, location, suspect, vehicle, and other types of information.
- **Strategic:** Concerned with long-range problems and projections of long-term increases or decreases in crime (crime trends). Strategic analysis also includes the preparation of crime statistical summaries, resource acquisition, and allocation studies.
- **Administrative:** Focuses on provision of economic, geographic, or social information to administration.

Crime Analysis Personnel

The Tempe Police Department's Crime Analysis Unit is comprised of three full-time crime analysts and a full-time crime analysis clerk.   and   are the current Crime Analysts. The Tempe Police Department's Crime Analysis Unit performs all three types of Crime Analysis: Tactical, Strategic, and Administrative.

Interesting Statistics

The following reflect 2000 figures unless otherwise noted:

- The population of Tempe is 163,000.
- There were a total of 122,830 citizen generated calls for service 2000, up 3% from 1999.
- The citizen generated calls for service rate per person is 754 per 1,000 persons. It was 734 per 1,000 persons in 1999.
- The most common type of citizen generated call for service is the "burglary alarm" call. These calls are 11.6% of the total calls for service. Approximately 84.5% of alarm calls are false, 1.7% result in a report, and the remaining 15.6% of alarm calls are unknown in outcome (no evidence of a false alarm or of a crime committed). Officers spend an average of 18 minutes on an alarm call.
- The average amount of time it took an officer to respond to an emergency call for service is 6 minutes and 28 seconds.
- Approximately one report is generated for every five calls for service (not necessarily a criminal report).

- Tempe's crime rate is 9,353 Part I crimes per 100,000 persons.

Reports and Bulletins

Thematic map which shades neighborhoods according to number of Part I crimes reported that month. Part I crimes include Murder, Rape, Robbery, Aggravated Assault Burglary, Motor Vehicle Theft, Larceny, and Arson. Available monthly after the 20th for the previous month. Recently, the crime data have been somewhat behind due to processing which is beyond the control of the Crime Analysis Unit.

This page begins with a map of all the beats in the city. From there, you can click on the beat you are interested in and a "Beat Information" page about that beat will come up. These individual beat pages include a detailed map of reporting districts (RDs), links to annual information, and the Monthly Part I Crime report for the most recent month (available).

Thematic map which shades neighborhoods according to number of calls for service that month. A call for service is any request for police service. Available monthly after the 10th for the previous month.

Monthly ranking of apartment communities including location and number of units rated according to the ratio of calls for service per unit. Available monthly after the 10th for the previous month.

Note that the rankings included in this reports do not imply that any one apartment community is "worse" than the others. These rankings are only a relative measure of calls for service reported to the police and are not a measure of the safety or quality of the apartment community.

2000 Reports!!! 1) Ranking of apartment communities according to calls for service per unit, also includes location and number of units. 2) Ranking of apartment communities according to Part I Property Crime per unit 3) Ranking of apartment communities according to Part I Violent Crime per unit.

Note that the rankings included in this reports do not imply that any one apartment community is "worse" than the others. These rankings are only a relative measure of crime and other activity reported to the police and are not a measure of the safety or quality of the apartment community.

This report is a list of the top five types of calls for service and the frequencies for each of the 173 apartment communities (included in the monthly and annual ranking reports). This is a more detailed report than the Apartment Community Rankings that do not distinguish between types of calls for service at a community.

This report is a list of ALL of the Part I crime and the frequencies for each of the 173 apartment communities (included in the monthly and annual ranking reports). This is a more detailed report than the Apartment Community Rankings that do not distinguish between types of Part I crime at a community.

List of mobile home communities including location and number of units rated according to the ratio of calls for service per unit.

Note that the rankings included in this reports do not imply that any one apartment community is "worse" than the others. These rankings are only a relative measure of calls for service reported to the police and are not a measure of the safety or quality of the apartment community.

List of the number of calls for service at each elementary, middle, and high school in Tempe.

List of the number of calls for service at each Park in Tempe.

1999 Report on Policing

The 1999 Report on Policing in Tempe is here!!! This report includes information about 1999 crime and calls for service in Tempe. It also contains the results of the **1999 Citizen Survey**! It contains historical information as well as includes analyses of specific types of crimes, e.g. theft from vehicle, motor vehicle theft, domestic violence, and calls for service, e.g. burglary alarms, traffic accidents. Additionally, it contains information on specific types of locations like parks, schools, apartment communities, mobile home communities, the Arizona Mills Mall and others. Finally, individual beat analyses are included in the report that contain the number of crimes, number of calls for service, top five types of each and a month chart for each beat. The file is in PDF Format and requires Acrobat Reader.

The 1998 Report on Policing in Tempe is here!!! This report includes information about 1998 crime and calls for service in Tempe. It contains historical information as well as includes analyses of specific types of crimes, e.g. robbery, theft from vehicle, motor vehicle theft, domestic violence, and calls for service, e.g. burglary alarms, traffic accidents. Additionally, it contains information on specific types of locations like parks, schools, apartment communities, mobile home communities, the Arizona Mills Mall and others. Finally, individual beat analyses are included in the report that contain the number of crimes, number of calls for service, top five types of each and a month chart for each beat.

Crime Analysis Unit
Copyright © [Tempe Police Department]. All rights reserved.
Revised: April 25, 2001.
Please send feedback to:

We hope you found this page helpful. Drop us a line and let us know what you liked, didn't like, or would like to see on this page. Thanks.

/ / /

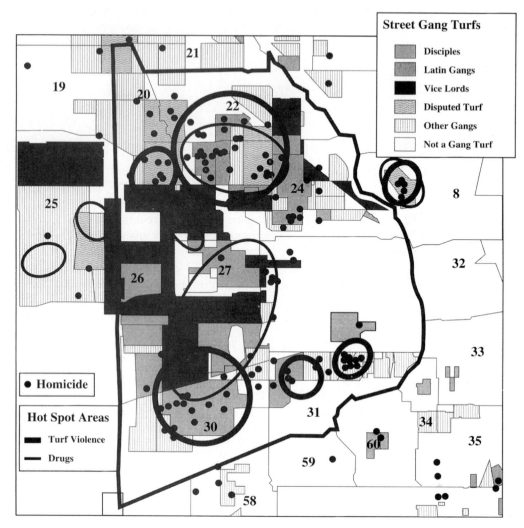

FIGURE 4.11 A Crime Map of Street Gang Motivated Homicide, Chicago

Repeat alarm calls are another example of how CAD data can be used to support patrol officer problem solving. In fact, when the Baltimore County experiment began, some commanders preferred that officers start with alarm projects. Data documenting repeat alarm calls by address were readily available, and commanders anticipated that solving alarm problems would be relatively simple, with considerable benefits compared to the investment of time.[60]

Surveys

Not to be overlooked in crime analysis is the use of community surveys to identify or clarify problems. For example, an officer may canvass all the business proprietors in shopping centers on his or her beat. One variation on this theme occurred in Baltimore when an officer telephoned business owners to update the police department's after-hours business contact files. Although the officer did not conduct a formal survey, he used this task to also inquire about problems the owners might want to bring to police attention.

On a larger scale, a team of officers may survey residents of a housing complex or neighborhood known to have particular crime problems. The survey could assist in determining residents' priority concerns, acquiring information about hot spots, and learning more about residents' expectations of police.[61] Residents are also more likely to keep the police abreast of future problems when officers leave their cards and encourage residents to contact them directly.

Another approach to the survey process involves developing a beat profile. In Tempe, Arizona, COPPS officers began by conducting a detailed profile of a target beat. This involved both door-to-door surveys of residents and businesses and detailed observations of the environment. A survey instrument was developed and pilot tested and all survey team members were trained and given a uniform protocol to follow. The instrument contained questions about sociodemographic characteristics of residents, observed crime and drug problems, fear of crime, perception of city and police services, willingness to participate in and support community policing objectives, and other information. Survey team members also recorded information about the surroundings—conditions of buildings, homes, streets, and yards; presence of abandoned vehicles; possible zoning and other code violations; and the existence of graffiti, trash, loiterers, gang members, and other signs of disorder.[62]

Obviously a wide range of survey techniques and instruments are available for use, from the very elementary, as discussed, to the very scientific. Several of the latter are available from the FBI and other police agencies.

Software for COPPS

Computer software has analytic power that can work with the S.A.R.A. problem solving process. Systems, such as the Dynamic Community Policing System (DCPS) offered by Analysis Central Systems in Tiburon, California, have been specially developed for COPPS and are adaptable to laptop computers. These systems are used by many large and medium-size police departments in the United States and Canada, including Dallas, Miami, Austin, Long Beach, Sacramento, Virginia Beach, and Vancouver, British Columbia. As advertised, this system is a "proactive computer companion to the officer in finding problems and implementing solutions."[63]

This system can automate beat profiling and demographics, find patterns of problems, help plan daily officer activities, balance beat and officer workloads, and identify current levels of performance. Downloaded information from agency computers is transferred to powerful microcomputers and notebook computers. The system continuously analyzes data using its proprietary decision tools, mathematical analyses, statistical tools, and expert systems. It can scan hundreds of millions of pieces of data for patterns, trends, or clusters in beats and neighborhoods while ranking and reranking problems. The computer constantly asks itself thousands of questions and develops answers.

In the field, the officer simply highlights the neighborhood, beat, or grid to consider, then selects the problem(s) to be worked on from a menu the computer has composed. The emphasis for COPPS shifts from "What are the problems in this area?" to "Which of the ranked problems do I want to work on and what options do I want to use to solve them?"

See Exhibit 4.3 for another example of COPPS software.

Contemporary Community Policing Activities of Local Agencies

The U.S. Department of Justice, Bureau of Justice Statistics, recently published survey findings in its *Law Enforcement Management and Administrative Statistics* report[64]—commonly referred to as the LEMAS survey—with funding provided by the federal Office of Community Oriented Policing Services. Included in the survey were more than 700 state and local law enforcement agencies that employed 100 or more full-time sworn officers; these agencies employed about 402,000 full-time sworn officers.

The survey found that as of mid-1999, 66 percent of county and 62 percent of municipal police agencies with 100 or more officers had a formal written community policing plan, as did nearly half (46 percent) of sheriff's departments. Nearly all larger county (97 percent) and municipal (95 percent) agencies had full-time community policing officers, as did 88 percent of sheriff's departments.

Furthermore, 60 percent of these agencies had formed problem solving partnerships through written agreements, while 64 percent actively encouraged officers to become involved in problem solving projects that utilized community policing concepts. Nearly all larger local police agencies had met with community groups during the previous year, and local police agencies were most likely to meet with neighborhood associations (96 percent), school groups (88 percent), and business groups (84 percent). About a third of these agencies provided citizens with routine access to crime statistics or crime maps over the Internet.

Additional findings from the LEMAS survey concerning officer and citizen training in community policing are provided in Chapter 8.

Summary

This chapter, dubbed at the outset as the "heart and soul" of this book, has set out the basic principles and strategies of the community policing and problem oriented policing concepts. It also offered a combined approach that we believe is the best philosophy for the future of policing: community oriented policing and problem solving, or COPPS. We believe that blending these two concepts results in a better, more comprehensive approach to providing quality police service—

EXHIBIT 4.3 POP TRACK: A Problem Solving Tracking and Resource System

POP TRACK was developed by police practitioners, in conjunction with the Law Enforcement Assistance Network (LEAN), to maintain agencies' COPPS files. It features pull-down menus and increases access to agency-wide information; assists in tracking all stages of problem solving; offers a variety of easy to read reports and forms; allows users to export text files for mapping, spreadsheets, and databases; and is customized to fit each agency's needs. It provides field names, report formats, and graphics. A free demonstration disk is available from LEAN at P.O. Box 2171, Crestline, California, 93235.

---

combining the emphasis on forming a police–community partnership to fight crime with the use of the S.A.R.A. process to solve problems. Other very important elements of this strategy are the expanded role of the street officer and the focus on crime analysis.

NOTES

1. Gordon Witkin and Dan McGraw, "Beyond 'Just the facts, ma'am'," *U.S. News and World Report* (August 2, 1993):28.
2. W. L. Melville Lee, *A History of Police in England* (London: Methuen, 1901), Chapter 12, p. 178.
3. Herman Goldstein, "Toward Community-Oriented Policing: Potential, Basic Requirements, and Threshold Questions," *Crime and Delinquency* 33 (1987):17.
4. Robert Trojanowicz and Bonnie Bucqueroux, *Community Policing: A Contemporary Perspective* (Cincinnati: Anderson, 1990), p. 154.
5. Mark H. Moore and Robert C. Trojanowicz, *Corporate Strategies for Policing*. U.S. Department of Justice, National Institute of Justice (Washington, D.C.: U.S. Government Printing Office, 1988), pp. 8–9.
6. Lee P. Brown, "Community Policing: Its Time Has Come," *The Police Chief* 62 (September 1991):10.
7. Jerald R. Vaughn, *Community-Oriented Policing: You Can Make It Happen* (Clearwater, Fla.: National Law Enforcement Leadership Institute, no date), p. 8.
8. Herman Goldstein, *Policing a Free Society* (Cambridge, Mass.: Ballinger, 1977).
9. Herman Goldstein, *Problem-Oriented Policing* (New York: McGraw-Hill, 1990).
10. Herman Goldstein, "Problem-Oriented Policing," paper presented at the Conference on Policing: State of the Art III, National Institute of Justice, Phoenix, Ariz., June 12, 1987, p. 4.
11. *Ibid.*
12. *Ibid.*, pp. 5–6.

13. John Eck and William Spelman, "A Problem-Oriented Approach to Police Service Delivery," in *Police and Policing: Contemporary Issues*, ed. Dennis Jay Kenney (New York: Praeger, 1989), pp. 95–111.

14. Quoted in Roland Chilton, "Urban Crime Trends and Criminological Theory," in *Criminal Justice: Concepts and Issues*, ed. Chris W. Eskridge (Los Angeles: Roxbury, 1993), p. 49.

15. *Ibid.*, p. xvii.

16. Chris Braiden, "Community Policing: Nothing New under the Sun," in *Community Oriented Policing and Problem Solving* (Sacramento, Calif.: California Department of Justice, November 1992), p. 21.

17. Samuel Walker, *The Police in America: An Introduction*, 2nd ed. (New York: McGraw-Hill, 1992), p. 177.

18. Goldstein, *Problem-Oriented Policing*, pp. 38–40.

19. Goldstein, "Toward Community-Oriented Policing," p. 10.

20. *Ibid.*, p. 21.

21. William Spelman and John E. Eck, "Problem-Solving," *Research in Brief* (Washington, D.C.: National Institute of Justice, January 1987) p. 4.

22. William Spelman and John E. Eck, "Problem-Oriented Policing" (Washington, D.C.: U.S. Department of Justice, National Institute of Justice, January 1987), pp. 2–3.

23. *Ibid.*, pp. 43–52.

24. Goldstein, *Problem-Oriented Policing*, p. 18.

25. U.S. Department of Justice, Office of Community Oriented Policing Services, *Problem Solving Tips: A Guide to Reducing Crime and Disorder through Problem-Solving Partnerships*, p. 10.

26. Karl E. Weick, "Small Wins: Redefining the Scale of Social Problems," *American Psychologist*, Vol. 39, no. 1 (January 1984):40–49.

27. John Eck, "A Dissertation Prospectus for the Study of Characteristics of Drug Dealing Places," November 1992.

28. William Spelman, "Once Bitten, Then What?: Cross-Sectional and Time Course Explanations for Repeat Victimization," *British Journal of Criminology* 35, no. 3 (March 1995):380.

29. Marcus Felson, "Linking Criminal Career Choices, Routine Activities, Informal Control, and Criminal Outcomes," in *The Reasoning Criminal: Rational Choice Perspectives on Offending*, eds. Derek Cornish and Ronald Clarke (New York: Springer-Verlag, 1986).

30. Lawrence E. Cohen and Marcus Felson, "Social Change and Crime Rate Trends: A Routine Activity Approach," *American Sociological Review* 44 (August 1979):588–608.

31. John Eck, "A Dissertation Prospectus for the Study of Characteristics of Drug Dealing Places" (College Park: University of Maryland, November 1992).

32. Rana Sampson, "Problem Solving," in *Neighborhood-Oriented Policing in Rural Communities: A Program Planning Guide* (Washington, D.C.: U.S. Department of Justice, Office of Justice Programs, Bureau of Justice Assistance, 1994), p. 4.

33. William Spelman and John E. Eck, "Problem-Solving," *Research in Brief* (Washington, D.C.: National Institute of Justice, January 1987):6.

34. Darrel Stephens, "Community Problem-Oriented Policing: Measuring Impacts," in *Quantifying Quality in Policing*, ed. Larry T. Hoover (Washington, D.C.: Police Executive Research Forum, 1995).

35. U.S. Department of Justice, Office of Community Oriented Policing Services, *Problem Solving Tips: A Guide to Reducing Crime and Disorder through Problem-Solving Partnerships*, p. 20.

36. Sampson, "Problem Solving," p. 5.

37. Moore and Trojanowicz, *Corporate Strategies for Policing*, p. 11.

38. California Department of Justice, Attorney General's Office, *Community Oriented Policing and Problem Solving: Definitions and Principles* (Sacramento, Calif.: Author, 1993), p. iii.

39. *Ibid.*
40. Noah Fritz, "Crime Analysis" (Tempe, Arizona: Tempe Police Department, no date), p. 9.
41. Jerald R. Vaughn, *Community-Oriented Policing: You Can Make It Happen* (Clearwater, Fla.: National Law Enforcement Leadership Institute, no date), p. 5.
42. Mark A. Peterson and Harriet B. Braiker, "Doing Crime: A Survey of California Prison Inmates" (Santa Monica, Calif.: RAND Corporation, 1980), pp. 131–135.
43. William Spelman, "Crime Analysis: A Review and Assessment" (Washington, D.C.: Police Executive Research Forum, May 1985), p. 3.
44. Bill Blackwood Law Enforcement Management Institute of Texas, TELEMASP Bulletin, "Crime Analysis: Administrative Aspects" (Huntsville, Tex., January 1995), p. 1.
45. J. Campbell, *Map Use and Analysis*, 2nd ed. (Dubuque, Ia.: William C. Brown, 1993).
46. U.S. Department of Justice, National Institute of Justice, Crime Mapping Research Center, *Mapping Crime: Principle and Practice* (Washington, D.C.: Author, 1999), p. 1.
47. *Ibid.*, p. 2.
48. Lois Pilant, "Computerized Crime Mapping," *The Police Chief* (December 1997):58.
49. Dan Sadler, "Exploring Crime Mapping" (Washington, D.C.: U.S. Department of Justice, National Institute of Justice, Crime Mapping Research Center, 1999), p. 1.
50. Pilant, "Computerized Crime Mapping," p. 58.
51. Chicago Police Department, *CAPS News* (October 1995), pp. 1, 6.
52. Pilant, "Computerized Crime Mapping," pp. 64–65.
53. *Ibid.*, pp. 66–67.
54. See U.S. Department of Justice, National Institute of Justice, Crime Mapping Research Center, *Mapping Crime*, 1999.
55. See Nancy LaVigne and Julie Wartell (eds.), *Crime Mapping Case Studies: Successes in the Field* (Washington, D.C.: Police Executive Research Forum, 1998).
56. Barbara Webster and Edward F. Connors, "Community Policing: Identifying Problems" (Alexandria, Va.: Institute for Law and Justice, March 1991), p. 9.
57. See Lawrence W. Sherman, Patrick R. Gartin, and Michael E. Buerger, "Hot Spots of Predatory Crime: Routine Activities and the Criminology of Place," *Criminology* 27 (1989):27.
58. *Ibid.*, p. 36.
59. William Spelman, *Beyond Bean Counting: New Approaches for Managing Crime Data* (Washington, D.C.: Police Executive Research Forum, January 1988).
60. Webster and Connors, "Community Policing," p. 11.
61. For an example of this type of survey process, see William H. Lindsey and Bruce Quint, *The Oasis Technique* (Fort Lauderdale, Fla.: Florida Atlantic University/Florida International University Joint Center for Environmental and Urban Problems, 1986).
62. Webster and Connors, "Community Policing," pp. 14–15.
63. Analysis Central Systems, "Dynamic Community Policing System: Proactive Neighborhood Oriented Systems" (Tiburon, Calif.: Author, no date), p. 3. Also see J. J. Campbell, "Computer Support for Community-Oriented Policing," *FBI Law Enforcement Bulletin* 62 (February 1994):16–18.
64. Brian A. Reaves and Timothy C. Hart, *Law Enforcement Management and Administrative Statistics, 1999: Data for Individual State and Local Agencies with 100 or More Officers* (Washington, D.C.: U.S. Department of Justice, Bureau of Justice Statistics, November 2000), p. v.

CRIME PREVENTION
For Safe Communities

> The test of police efficiency is the absence of crime and disorder, not the visible evidence of police action dealing with them.
>
> —Sir Robert Peel's ninth principle of policing, 1829

INTRODUCTION

Crime prevention has been defined by the Crime Prevention Coalition of America as

> A pattern of attitudes and behaviors directed both at reducing the threat of crime and enhancing the sense of safety and security to positively influence the quality of life in our society and to help develop environments where crime cannot flourish.[1]

Crime prevention once consisted primarily of exhorting people to "lock it or lose it" and advice from the police on door locks and window bars for their homes and businesses. It typically was (and often still is) an add-on program or appendage to the police agency, which normally included a few officers who were trained to go to citizens' homes and perform security surveys or engage in public speaking on prevention topics.

But times have changed dramatically in this respect. We know that attempting to investigate and solve crimes and prosecute and punish offenders is much more expensive than preventing the offense from occurring in the first place. We are also aware that as the costs of public safety have skyrocketed, governments are extremely hard pressed to continue to afford to build, staff, and operate more jails and prisons. In an era of decreasing resources, crime prevention offers a cost-effective means of making communities safer. Therefore, crime prevention now involves the police and government seeking to influence the civil behavior of individuals, corporations, businesses, and others that are responsible for the creation of criminal opportunities or motivation.[2]

This chapter examines the multifaceted domain of what contemporary crime prevention has become. We begin with a brief history of how crime prevention evolved and then discuss how today's police are shifting their emphasis to that of crime prevention as an agencywide philosophy. Then the essential role of the community in preventing crime is explored, followed by an overview of how crime prevention relates to community oriented policing and problem solving (COPPS, examined in Chapter 4).

Two very important components of crime prevention and COPPS are then analyzed: crime prevention through environmental design and situational crime prevention. Following that, we review several issues and problems that can accompany crime prevention efforts: the implementation of crime interventions, the displacement of crime when interventions are undertaken, and the evaluation of results. Finally, we view which crime prevention strategies work, do not work, and hold promise and present examples from six cities.

Throughout the chapter the emphasis and common thread—from strategy to strategy, community to community—is the acknowledgment by the police that they alone cannot prevent or address crime and disorder; the community *must* be engaged in a collaborative effort if the physical and social problems that plague communities are to be reduced or eliminated.

A BRIEF HISTORY

Crime prevention is not a new idea. Humans have long known that crime is not simply a matter of motivation; it is also a matter of opportunity. Indeed, for as long as people have been victimized, there have been attempts to protect one's self and family. The term *crime prevention*, however, has only recently come to signify a set of ideas for combatting crime.[3]

Our earliest ancestors maximized lighting from the sun and moon and employed defensive placement of homes on the side of cliffs, with only one entrance and exit.[4] Cave dwellers established ownership of a space by surrounding it with large boulders. The Romans developed and enforced complex land laws. Walled cities and castles exist throughout the world. It is a natural human impulse to claim and secure an area to prevent problems.[5]

Under COPPS, crime prevention is evolving to more comprehensive situational and environmental intervention strategies. This photo depicts a Neighborhood Watch sign vandalized by local gangs.

A more contemporary form of early preventive action was the Chicago Area Project (CAP), based on the research of Shaw and McKay in the 1930s and 1940s, which concerned the altering of the social fabric. Crime and delinquency were concentrated in the central areas of Chicago. Identifying a high level of transiency and an apparent lack of social ties in these areas as the root cause of the problems, Shaw and McKay labeled the problem as "social disorganization," meaning that the constant turnover of residents resulted in the inability of the people to exert any informal social control over the individuals in the area. Consequently, offenders could act with some degree of impunity in these neighborhoods.[6]

Shaw's proposed solution to the problem was to work with the residents to build a sense of pride and community, thereby prompting people to stay and exert control over the actions of the people in the area. CAP was founded in 1931 and generated community support by using volunteers and existing neighborhood institutions.[7]

The 1970s saw the rise of community-based crime prevention programs, such as the Neighborhood or Block Watch. These programs used the same premise as physical design approaches—potential offenders will not commit a crime if they perceive citizen activity, awareness, and concern in an area. The focus is on citizen surveillance and action (such as cutting back bushes, installing lighting, removing obstacles to enhance sight lines, organizing security surveys, and distributing crime and crime prevention news). Signs of resident activity and cohesion should work to protect the neighborhood. The police also recognized that they could not stop crime or solve problems on their own; they needed the help of the citizenry.[8]

Crime prevention experienced perhaps its biggest boost, however, with the emergence of physical design as a topic of debate. Led by the work of Oscar Newman in 1972, flaws in the physical environment were identified as causes of, or at least facilitators for, criminal behavior.

In 1969 Newman first coined the term *defensible space,* which, in his mind, did not mean ugly, fortresslike buildings where occupants were prisoners. (Table 5.1 depicts Newman's suggestions for defensible space.) Rather, buildings that are properly designed promote a sense of safety and power to their occupants, making them less afraid and vulnerable.[9]

Newman, an architect, argued that the physical characteristics of an area have the potential to suggest to residents and potential offenders that the area is either well cared for and protected or it is open for criminal activity. Design features conducive to criminal behavior—allowing offenders to commit a crime and escape with minimal risk of detection—would include common entrances for a large number of people, poorly placed windows inhibiting casual surveillance of grounds and common areas, hidden entrances, easy access for illegitimate users, and isolated buildings.[10]

Then, in the 1970s and 1980s, theories of crime were developed that gave added importance to the role of opportunity in crime. Cohen and Felson's "routine activity theory" seeks to explain how physical and social environments create crime opportunities by bringing together in one place at a particular time a "likely" offender, a "suitable" target, and the absence of a "capable guardian" against crime (e.g., a police officer or security guard).[11] Routine activity theory was used to explain how large increases in burglary rates occurred in the United States in the 1960s and 1970s, because (1) home electronic goods became lighter, and (2) women increasingly entered the labor force, resulting in more empty homes during the day, which could be entered by burglars.

Another opportunity theory is the "rational choice" perspective, which holds that all crime is purposive behavior designed to benefit the offender.[12] In committing an offense, the offender makes the choice to balance the effort, risks, and rewards with the costs and benefits of alternative legal means of achieving an end.

TABLE 5.1 Oscar Newman's Defensible Space Suggestions

1. Reduce the size of a housing estate or block.
2. Reduce the number of dwellings sharing an entrance way.
3. Reduce the number of stories in a building block.
4. Arrange dwellings in groups to encourage social contact.
5. Minimize the degree of shared public space inside and near blocks.
6. Make the boundaries between public and private space very clear.
7. Make public areas clearly visible to nearby housing.
8. Use external rather than internal corridors in blocks of housing so that they are visible.
9. Make entrances flush with the street rather than set back.
10. Do not have entrances facing away from the street because they are not open to surveillance.
11. Avoid landscaping and vegetation that impedes surveillance.
12. Reduce escape routes (elevators, staircases, and multiple exits) for criminals.

Source: U.S. Department of Housing and Urban Development, *Crime Prevention Brief*, "Crime Prevention Through Environmental Design" (no date), p. 2.

Wilson and Kelling's 1982 "broken windows" theory extended Oscar Newman's focus on housing projects to entire neighborhoods. "Broken windows" refers to physical signs that an area is unattended: There may be abandoned vehicles and buildings in the area, trash and litter may be present, and there may be broken windows and lights and graffiti.[13] In addition to these physical indicators are social manifestations of the same problems, such as loitering youths, public drunkenness, prostitution, and vagrancy. Both the physical and social indicators are typically referred to as signs of "incivility" that attract offenders to the area.[14]

The most recent movements in crime prevention focus efforts and interventions on attacking specific problems, places, and times. Ronald V. Clarke proposed "situational prevention" as "measures directed at highly specific forms of crime that involve [environmental changes that] reduce the opportunities for crime and increase its risk."[15] Examples of situational prevention include the installation of surveillance equipment in a parking lot experiencing vandalism, erecting security screens in banks to stop robberies, altering traffic patterns in a drug market neighborhood, using electronic tags for library materials, and using caller ID for obscene phone calls.[16] The physical environment as it relates to crime prevention is discussed shortly. Next we discuss the contemporary crime prevention–based philosophy.

TODAY'S SHIFTING EMPHASIS

A simple but profound shift in thinking in contemporary times may help American police organizations to realize new gains in reducing crime, victimization, and fear. Many police agencies now conceive of prevention as the overarching

The glass stairwell in this parking garage demonstrates how natural surveillance can be designed into a facility. People using the stairwell are easily seen by passers-by, thus reducing the likelihood of victimization.

goal of policing rather than as a set of activities. We discuss the following benefits of crime prevention:

- Deterrence of specific kinds of crimes
- Mobilization of residents
- Development of physical and social environments inhospitable to crime[17]

The concept of prevention shifts a police organization's purpose. Police agencies that are operating in a prevention framework must be organized to prevent the next problem from occurring. This reflects Herman Goldstein's call for replacing efficiency with effectiveness as the goal of policing. Once the question becomes "How can we prevent the next crisis?" all kinds of approaches become possible. Police departments and their partners will find themselves embracing approaches that would have been unimaginable under the reactive, traditional policing model.[18]

The Boston Police Department, for example, partners with probation officers to conduct joint curfew checks on gang members and other high-risk probationers. As the police commissioner noted, "First we tried conventional, police heavy enforcement tactics. Then we realized we needed a better strategy. We realized the kids needed jobs and opportunities. At that point we gained a new appreciation of our mission."[19]

The focus on effective prevention has spurred new and innovative practices within criminal justice agencies. The Montreal-based International Centre for Crime Prevention (ICCP) has found that a preponderance of research indicates "recreating social bonds, bringing agencies to work in concert and transforming attitudes and practices hold considerable potential to strengthen citizenship, reduce crime, and improve the quality of life."[20]

Understanding prevention as the strategic goal of the policing process, rather than as a set of activities for police officers, puts into practice Sir Robert Peel's ninth principle of policing, quoted at the beginning of this chapter.[21] Today, prevention means more than simply warning citizens about crime. It means strategically maximizing police resources with those of the community for tangible outcomes.

The core mission of the police is simply to preserve the peace. But they cannot do so alone. Crime prevention is much broader than the confines of the police station house. Still, there is much important work for the police to do in the area of crime prevention. As the International Association of Chiefs of Police Crime Prevention Committee has stated, "Community safety is everyone's responsibility, and crime prevention is everyone's business."[22]

The mission is clear: "Establish the prevention of crime as fundamental to a free and safe society; anchor crime prevention in each department's organizational policy.[23]

Needed: Community Involvement

A number of critical elements must be in place before the community as a whole can be mobilized effectively into positive energy. First, the causes of the problems that contribute to diminished community safety must be identified in order to define appropriate, community-based solutions (see Exhibit 5.1). Second, a community-based, shared vision must be developed with appropriate strategies, including resource allocation, the implementation of specific programs and services, and the identification of measurable results. Third, communitywide mobilization—including the private and corporate sectors, schools, churches, governments, and institutions—must be achieved to solve problems. Finally, dynamic, visionary leaders are needed to provide a voice and example.[24]

Exhibit 5.1 Using the World Wide Web to Educate the Community in Rochester

In an effort that has expanded awareness of community safety beyond traditional crime issues, the city of Rochester, New York, has posted vital information on its Web site that has helped parents, children, and the elderly avoid becoming victims of accidents and crimes. The site links browsers to practical information on issues such as

10 Tips for Fire Safety	How to Praise/Complain about Policing
911 Tips	How to Protect Your Neighborhood
Baby Sitter Guide	Latchkey Children
Beware the Stranger at the Door	Neighborhood Watch
Child Safety Forum	Preventing Child Sexual Abuse
Community Services	Internet Sexual Assault Information
Exploring Law Enforcement	Shoplifting
Guidelines for Gun Owners	Teenage Driver Safety

Source: National Institute of Justice, Office of Community Policing Services, *Technology for Community Policing: Conference Report* (Rockville, Md.: Author, 1997), p. 19.

These are complex issues. The strategic question, however, is not "Can we do it?" but "Can we afford not to do it?" It is no longer realistic to expect the police to be solely responsible for controlling crime.[25]

Community oriented policing and problem solving (COPPS) argues that the police and the community must stop treating the symptoms of the problem. COPPS requires a "new age" of prevention—as well as improvement of prevention efforts.

Altering physical designs of buildings, for example, is not in itself generally sufficient for altering the level of crime; physical design changes cannot stop a truly motivated offender. Furthermore, altering the physical environment does not guarantee that residents will become involved and take action. Direct efforts to enhance active citizen involvement are necessary.[26]

Chapter 3 introduced the concept of communitarianism, a mind-set for the whole community to take responsibility for itself, actively participating and giving of time, energy, and money.[27] We noted that communitarians support processes, such as crime prevention and community policing, taking matters into their own hands and closing off streets and creating other physical barriers to disrupt the drug trade, working to overcome problems of homelessness and panhandling, and so on. Communitarians recognize that many of the answers to community problems lie not with government but in the community at large. Volunteerism can also provide a much needed boost for the police, building a sense of community, breaking down barriers between people, and raising quality of life.

CRIME PREVENTION AND COPPS

Crime prevention and COPPS are close companions, attempting to define a problem, identify contributing causes, seek out the proper people or agencies to assist in identifying potential solutions, and work as a group to implement the solution. The problem drives the solution.[28]

At its heart, COPPS is about preventing crime. COPPS and crime prevention are linked in several areas.

Crime prevention efforts provide information and skills that are essential to community policing. Furthermore, crime prevention and community policing have six major points in common:

- *Each deals with the health of the community.* They acknowledge the many interrelated issues that contribute to crime.

- *Each seeks to address underlying causes and problems.* Although short-term and reactive measures (such as personal security and response to CFS) are necessary, they are insufficient if crime is to be significantly reduced. Looking beyond symptoms to treat the causes of community problems is a strategy that both, at their best, share in full measure.

- *Each deals with the combination of physical and social issues that are at the heart of many community problems.* An abandoned building may attract drug addicts; bored teens may become area burglars. Both approaches examine the broadest possible range of causes and solutions.

- *Each requires active involvement by community residents.* Both have the chief task of enabling people to make themselves and their communities safer by helping them gain appropriate knowledge, develop helpful attitudes, and take useful actions.

- *Each requires partnerships beyond law enforcement to be effective.* Both efforts can and have involved schools, community centers, civic organizations, religious groups, social service agencies, public works agencies, and other elements of the community.

- *Each is an approach or a philosophy, rather than a program.* Neither is a fixed system for delivery of a specific service. Rather, each is a way of doing business and involves the development of an institutional mind-set.[29]

The following list of initiatives represents some of the types of crime prevention activities that can help to support community policing. These programs in and of themselves are neither research-based approaches nor community policing; rather, they further the implementation of community policing at the local level. Cooperation is needed among community organizations, government, and police agencies to create and maintain such activities.

- *Adopt-a-School/Adopt-an-Officer:* The police increase their communication with local schools by having each officer select a school to sponsor. The school has the officer as a primary contact to assist with various service needs.

- *Community Crime Patrol:* Organized citizen patrols in specific neighborhoods provide additional exposure for police services and assistance for police in desired areas.

- *Crime Prevention Month Celebration:* National celebration of crime prevention month in October heightens the awareness and need for crime prevention. Each year a new theme is developed to promote local programming.

- *Cops and Cons:* A coordinated program by the police in which convicts discuss with citizens and businesses why and how they committed their particular

Comprehensive crime prevention resource guides for municipal and rural agencies are available through the National Crime Prevention Council at http://www.ncpc.org (*Courtesy* National Crime Prevention Council)

crimes; this approach provides awareness of crime prevention and indicates some intervention strategies.

- *Domestic Violence/Sexual Assault Prevention:* Efforts raise the awareness that domestic violence is a crime and should not be tolerated. It also educates victims and others about prevention strategies.

- *Foot Beat/Walk and Talk:* Foot patrol is the oldest method of police patrol; it is an excellent way to get acquainted with citizens and learn about potential neighborhood problems.

- *Hate Crime Prevention:* An initiative designed to address the understanding of bias-motivated crimes and the prevention of criminal acts aimed at particular groups within a neighborhood.

- *Homeless Outreach:* The police and community work together to provide transportation to homeless individuals from city streets to shelter areas.

- *Home Safety and Security Surveys:* Police officers conduct home safety and security surveys to educate community residents on how to better protect their homes.

- *National Night Out:* A community event celebrated nationally by citizens displaying outdoor lights on a designated night in August to represent a unified effort against criminal activity.

- *Safe Haven:* An identified area in a public housing community that provides residents a safe place to live and activities for youths as a positive alternative to gang involvement. It engages residents in meaningful partnerships with many of the youth they may otherwise fear or distrust and provides students with a safe place to go after school.

- *Together for a Safer Campus:* An initiative to raise the awareness and importance of crime prevention measures on a college campus to encourage students to take appropriate precautions for their personal safety.

- *Turn Off the Violence:* An initiative to raise the awareness levels among children, teens, and adults so that violence in all of its forms is recognized and dealt with before it escalates beyond control.

- *Weed and Seed:* An initiative of the U.S. Department of Justice, it focuses on the elimination of criminal activity in a particular neighborhood through enforcement and adjudication, while providing a prevention and intervention component to eliminate the illicit activity from recurring in the community.[30]

Crime prevention provides knowledge about ways to involve the entire community in reducing crime, both individually and collectively; community policing practices can spread that knowledge. Community policing officers need to understand and apply techniques to educate and motivate citizens; crime prevention offers these techniques. Because crime prevention addresses both physical and social aspects of neighborhoods, it offers numerous ways for community policing officers to gain entry into community circles. Crime prevention offers resources to help change community attitudes and behaviors.

The Chicago Police Department made crime prevention one of its guiding principles for change to community policing:

> Crime control and prevention must be recognized as dual parts of the fundamental mission of policing. Solving crimes is, and will continue to be, an essential element of police work. But preventing crimes is the most effective way to create safer environments in our neighborhoods.[31]

Exhibit 5.2 provides an example of crime prevention and community policing working hand-in-hand to address a serious set of problems in Bridgeport, Connecticut.

CRIME PREVENTION THROUGH ENVIRONMENTAL DESIGN

Crime prevention through environmental design (CPTED) is defined as the "proper design and effective use of the environment that can lead to a reduction in the fear and incidence of crime, and an improvement in the quality of life."[32] At its core are three principles that support problem solving approaches to crime:

- *Natural access control.* Natural access control uses elements such as doors, shrubs, fences, and gates to deny admission to a crime target and to create a perception among offenders that there is a risk in selecting the target.
- *Natural surveillance.* Natural surveillance includes the proper placement of windows, lighting, and landscaping to increase the ability of those who care to observe intruders as well as regular users, allowing them to challenge inappropriate behavior or report it to the police or the property owner.
- *Territorial reinforcement.* Using such elements as sidewalks, landscaping, and porches helps distinguish between public and private areas and helps users exhibit signs of "ownership" that send "hands off" messages to would-be offenders.[33]

Ironically, in the past the police were not involved in design planning, whereas fire departments have promulgated and enforced national fire codes for about a half-century. Today, in cities such as Tempe, Arizona, if the police are not involved in the preliminary stages of planning a building, they often become very involved afterward, when crimes are committed in or around the structure. Police departments in 8 of the nation's 10 largest cities have followed Tempe's lead to some degree, including those in New York, Los Angeles, Detroit, Houston, San Antonio, Dallas, Phoenix, and San Diego.[34]

Exhibit 5.2   Crime Prevention and Community Policing in Bridgeport, Connecticut

Once a major industrial center on the shore of Long Island Sound, Bridgeport, Connecticut, lost a great deal of its tax base during the 1970s and 1980s. By 1991 the city had filed for bankruptcy. The population of 143,000 included a highly diverse population of 54 separate ethnic groups. The city also faced a major crime crisis, with the highest homicide rate in New England—50 to 60 per year. Many of the victims were juveniles. Drug markets were blatant. There was a long history of police–resident animosity. The police department decided to focus efforts on the toughest area of the city—Eastside, a 1.75-square-mile, high-density area of burned buildings, plagued nightly by automatic weapon gunfire. Gang members walked around openly. Almost half of Eastside's residents were under age 18; most families were too poor to relocate. The police department initiated an outreach to the community, based on community policing and emphasizing that the police wanted to hear residents' concerns. Meanwhile, police stepped up enforcement and surveillance in the area, curbing narcotics traffic by disrupting both sellers and buyers and rescheduling officers to provide for more intensive patrolling in the critical period, 7:00 P.M. to 3:00 A.M. Eventually, community meetings were drawing as many as 200 people. Residents began to more readily report suspicious activities and call 911 or page community officers to report crimes. Community policing was implemented on a neighborhood-by-neighborhood basis, and the emphasis was placed on eradicating blight. Seventy abandoned houses in Eastside were boarded up and vacant lots and graffiti were cleaned up. Crime prevention through environmental design (CPTED, discussed later in the chapter) tactics were employed, including the installation of concrete diverters and low curbs (to prevent easy access to drug markets by suburban junkies). A sense of community developed, and new programs sprang up from the community policing efforts (such as the group of seniors who conduct a life-skills course for girls ages 13 to 14). Between 1993 and 1997, crime declined 40 percent overall and 75 percent in Eastside; murder rates were down by one-third, as were robberies, burglaries, stolen cars, and fired shots—figures that are even more remarkable because reporting rates in Eastside have increased.

Source: U.S. Department of Justice, Bureau of Justice Assistance, *Crime Prevention and Community Policing: A Vital Partnership* (Washington, D.C.: U.S. Government Printing Office, 1997), pp. 8–9.

Some cities, such as Tempe, have become leaders in expanding policing's new role in "designing out crime." In 1997 Tempe enacted an ordinance requiring that no commercial, park, or residential building permit be issued until the police department had approved it, ensuring that the building fully protected its

This gated storage facility uses an electronic keyed gate for access control.

occupants. The department now makes several recommendations, such as keeping landscaping and plants that will be more than two feet high away from parking islands, inside perimeter, or screening walks or within 50 feet of access doors.

Tempe's CPTED officers advocate that walls around the perimeter of a building be at least eight feet high to make them more difficult to scale. Decorative wrought iron should not provide a foothold to assist someone jumping a fence. River rocks are banned from parking lots, as they can be used as weapons. Natural surveillance, which can be obtained from proper lighting and window placement, helps to oversee nearby activities. Transparent fences are better than walls to monitor activities. Light switches in rest rooms should be keyed or remotely controlled to prevent tampering, thus perhaps facilitating a possible hiding place for an attacker; rest rooms should not be located at the ends of hallways where they are isolated. Defensive architecture includes "target hardening" through quality deadbolts and other mechanical means. It also includes proper landscaping—thorny bushes, for example, help to keep burglars away.[35] Five types of information are needed for CPTED planning:

1. *Crime analysis information.* This can include crime mapping, police crime data, incident reports, and victim and offender statistics.
2. *Demographics.* This should include resident statistics such as age, race, gender, income, and income sources.

Advertising obstructions create poor natural surveillance and may contribute to a location's being an attractive target to offenders.

3. *Land use information.* This includes zoning information (such as residential, commercial, industrial, school, and park zones) as well as occupancy data for each zone.
4. *Observations.* These should include details of parking procedures, maintenance, and residents' reactions to crime.
5. *Resident information.* This includes resident crime surveys and interviews with police and security officers.[36]

See Exhibit 5.3 for other successful CPTED case studies.

Criticisms of CPTED fall into two categories. First, some people believe that CPTED is a stopgap measure and not a long-term solution. They argue that the elimination of opportunities for criminals does not change their desire to commit crimes. Second, there is the concern about displacement (discussed later). As noted previously, a crime decrease in one area does not necessarily mean that crime will increase in another area. According to Marcus Felson's rational choice theory (discussed in more detail later in the chapter), a criminal will not commit a crime if the effort involved outweighs the rewards from the crime.[37]

SITUATIONAL CRIME PREVENTION

Situational crime prevention (SCP) departs radically from most criminology in its orientation. It is focused on the settings for crime, rather than on persons committing criminal acts. It seeks to forestall the occurrence of crime, rather than

Exhibit 5.3 Successful CPTED Case Studies

Following are brief descriptions of three successful applications of CPTED strategies for solving problems.

Knoxville, Tennessee's "Deal Street," as the name implies, was the locus of drive-through drug dealing for as many as 1,200 cars per day. Based on the neighborhood analysis, the following programs and activities were adopted:

- Cleaning up the area and replacing broken street lights and fixtures
- Closing streets, creating cul-de-sacs, and adding speed bumps in the neighborhoods
- Redesigning parks and rescheduling recreational activities to encourage the use of park facilities
- Training police officers to work with other city staff in CPTED objectives, and volunteers in how to conduct security surveys

The result was that only 50 cars per day came into the neighborhood, and children now cross the streets safely to get to and from school.

Gainesville, Florida, was faced with a tremendous increase in the number of convenience store robberies. The police department carried out an evaluation of the problems and possible solutions. Nearly every store in the community (96 percent) had been robbed—most (81 percent) more than once, and some as many as 14 times in a six-year period. The city commission enacted an ordinance that required store operators to remove signs from windows to offer clear views to and from cash registers, locate the sales area and cash registers in a place visible from the street, post signs declaring limited cash availability, provide lighted parking areas, install security cameras, and train all employees in robbery prevention. Afterward, the city enjoyed a 64 percent decrease in convenience store robberies.

Richmond, Virginia, had one branch of a bank in a declining area that contained numerous vacant properties and abandoned businesses. The bank installed bullet-resistant enclosures for tellers inside the bank; another problem arose, however; ATM patrons were being robbed an average of once a month. Robbers would come to the bank after hours and hide around the corner from the ATM, under cover of the darkened drive-up teller area. When a patron conducted the ATM business on foot, the offender would jump from cover and rob the patron. After the bank's officers rejected a number of expensive options for addressing the problem, one of the bank's employees suggested a very simple and cost-effective solution: construction of a fence at the corner of the building to remove any opportunity to jump out and surprise ATM patrons. The bank installed an 8-feet tall, 16-feet long ornamental aluminum picket fence at a cost of $800, totally eliminating robberies at the location.

Source: National Crime Prevention Council, *Designing Safer Communities: A Crime Prevention through Environmental Design Handbook* (Washington, D.C.: Author, 1997), pp. 7–8.

to detect and sanction offenders. It seeks not to eliminate criminal or delinquent tendencies through improvement of society or its institutions but merely to make criminal action less attractive to offenders.[38]

SCP is a targeted means of reducing crime. It provides an analytical framework for strategies to prevent crime in varying settings. It is an "environmental criminology" approach that seeks to reduce crime opportunity by making settings less conducive to unwanted or illegal activities, focusing on the environment rather than the offender.[39] The commission of a crime requires not merely the offender, but, as every detective story reader knows, it also requires the opportunity for crime.[40]

Although the concept of SCP was British in origin, its development was influenced by two independent, but nonetheless related, strands of policy research in the United States: defensible space and crime prevention through environmental design—both of which preceded SCP and were discussed earlier in the chapter. Because of the trans-Atlantic delay in the dissemination of ideas, however, there was no stimulus for the development of SCP.[41]

SCP is a problem oriented approach that examines the roots of a problem and identifies a unique solution to the problem. Experience has shown that successful SCP measures must be directed against specific crimes and must be designed with a clear understanding of the motives of offenders and the methods they employ. SCP relies on the rational choice theory of crime, which asserts that criminals choose to commit crimes based on the costs and benefits involved with the crime. For example, a potential offender will commit a high-risk crime only if the rewards of the crime outweigh the risks.[42]

In his 1992 book, *Situational Crime Prevention*,[43] Ronald V. Clarke divided crime prevention goals into four primary objectives, each of which is designed to dissuade the criminal from committing the offense by making the crime too hard to commit, too risky, or too small in terms of rewards to be worth the criminal's time. Next we discuss each of these four objectives.

1. *Increasing the effort needed to commit the crime.* Crimes are typically committed because they are easy to commit. A person might see an easy opportunity to commit a crime and do so. Casual criminals are eliminated by increasing the effort needed to commit a crime. Following are different methods for increasing the effort needed to commit a crime:

Target hardening: installing physical barriers (such as locks, bolts, protective screens, and mechanical containment and antifraud devices to impede an offender's ability to penetrate a potential target).

Access control: installing barriers and designing walkways, paths, and roads so that unwanted users are prevented from entering vulnerable areas.

Deflecting offenders: discouraging crime by giving people alternate, legal venues for their activities (such as decreasing littering by providing litter bins or separating fans of rival teams after athletic events).

Controlling facilitators: facilitators are accessories who aid in the commission of crimes. Controlling them is achieved by universal measures (such as firearm permit regulations) and specific measures (metal detectors in community centers).

2. *Increasing the risks associated with the crime.* Increasing the risks associated with a crime reduces the incidence of that crime, because criminals believe they will not be caught; offenders who believe that they will be caught are less likely to offend. For example, if a video camera monitors all entrances and exits to a convenience store or bank, potential robbers who know of such surveillance will be less likely to rob such establishments.

Entry and exit screening: screening methods include guest sign-ins or a required display of identification; they ensure that residents and visitors meet entrance requirements.

Formal surveillance: using security personnel and hardware (such as CCTV and burglar alarms) is a deterrent to unwanted activities.

Informal surveillance: the presence of building attendants, concierges, maintenance workers, and attendants increases site surveillance and crime reporting.

Natural surveillance: the surveillance provided by people as they go about their daily activities, making potential offenders feel exposed and vulnerable.

3. *Reducing the rewards.* Reducing the rewards from crime makes offending not worthwhile to offenders. Methods of reducing rewards include making targets of crime less valuable by the following means:

Target removal: eliminating crime purposes from public areas. Examples include a no-cash policy and keeping valuable property in a secure area overnight.

Identifying property: using indelible marks, establishing ownership, and preventing individuals from reselling the property.

Removing inducements: related to target removal; involves removing temptations that offenders have not targeted in advance but that are likely to become the targets of a spontaneous crime (such as vacant houses or other living units or broken windows and light fixtures).

4. *Removing the excuses.* Many offenders say, "I didn't know any better" or "I had no choice." This strategy involves informing individuals of the law and rules and offers them alternatives to illegal activity by eliminating their excuses for committing crime. For example, a "no trespassing" sign is enforceable if posted. It also involves "rule-setting," such as clearly stating the rules, say, of a housing development, which establishes the procedures of punishment for violators. Such methods prevent offenders from excusing their crimes by claiming ignorance or misunderstanding.

Table 5.2 presents a situational crime prevention matrix for CPTED, specifically the four CPTED objectives discussed. Included are organized (procedural measures), mechanical (providing or removing certain physical objects), and natural (using native aspects of the environment) means of facilitating each. Exhibit 5.4 also provides situational prevention successes.

Signage at the entrance to this apartment complex and high school parking lot serves to remove offenders' excuses for loitering and trespassing.

TABLE 5.2 Situational Crime Prevention Matrix for CPTED

	Increasing the Effort (Access Control and Territorial Reinforcement)			
	Target Hardening	*Access Control*	*Removing/Deflecting Offenders*	*Closing Windows to Crime Facilitators*
Organized		Kiosks, reception desks	Bus stop placement and stop times, alternate cruising areas	Controlled spray can sales, gun control, alcohol ban, nonbreakable containers, occupying vacant apartments
Mechanical	Locks, bandit screens, tough glass, tamperproof seals, safes, slug rejectors	Locked gates, fences, entry phones, card keys, ID badges, PINs, vehicle decals, parking lot barriers	Graffiti boards, moving bars and pubs, litter bins, spittoons, public urinals, moving recreational space locations	Credit card photos, Breathalyzer, caller ID, rotary dials on pay phones, removing shopping carts from the premises
Natural	Remove trees that can enable access to upper level units	Shrubbery "fences"	Plants or steep slopes near windows to prevent entry	Greenery or planters in front of graffiti-prone areas
	Increasing the Risk (Surveillance)			
	Entry and Exit Screening	*Formal Surveillance*	*Surveillance by Employees*	*Improving Natural Surveillance*
Organized	Guest sign-ins, registration	Police patrol, security guards, informant hotline	Bus conductors, place administrative offices in view of development, front desk clerks, maintenance crews	Neighborhood watch, passive surveillance by "eyes on the street"
Mechanical	ID badges, PIN entry, metal sensors	Burglar alarms, hidden cameras, CCTV, radar speed traps	CCTV systems, pay phones in locations visible to employees	Interior and exterior lighting, windows on high-crime areas
Natural	Gates	Remove greenery that obstructs view of crime-ridden areas	Place frequently used service drives in crime-ridden areas	Remove greenery that obstructs view of crime-ridden areas

(table continues)

Table 5.2 *(continued)*

	Removing Crime Targets	Identifying and Tagging Property	Removing Inducements for Crime	Boundary and Rule Setting
	Reducing the Rewards of Crime			
Organized	Exact change requirements, limited or no-cash policy, pay by check, safe in administrative offices	Vehicle and bike registration	Rapid graffiti removal, gender-neutral phone lists, off-street parking	Drug-free school zone, public park use sign-up, enforced evictions, applicant screening
Mechanical	Removable car radios in maintenance vehicles, tokens for laundry and vending machines, phone card public phones, remove vending machines, antigraffiti treatments	Property marking, operation ID, Lojack, property serial number databases	Replace metal signs with plastic or wood signs to reduce "drive-by shootings," remove damaged signs, remove abandoned cars	Signs and posted notices of policies and local laws
Natural	Cover graffiti-prone areas with ivy or thorny bushes	Use greenery to define private areas surrounding individual units (gardens, flowers, etc.)	Remove greenery such as trees near windows that can hide or enable criminal activities	Use greenery to define public and private areas

	Removing Excuses and Increasing Shame
Organized	Public posting of trespasser pictures and names, sending postcards to suspected drug purchasers, impounding vehicles of drug purchasers, sign upkeep.

Source: U.S. Department of Housing and Urban Development, *Crime Prevention Brief,* "Situational Prevention" (no date), pp. 2–3.

In some cases, cultural attitudes prevent the adoption of particular SCP measures, even though they might have been accepted elsewhere. For example, the use of photo radar with traffic offenders is enthusiastically supported in some cities in the United States and abroad, but in the mid-1990s it was made illegal in New Jersey and discontinued in many other U.S. cities. Even for the same population, what is found objectionable or obtrusive today can change over time, such as changed attitudes toward wearing seat belts and motorcycle helmets.[44]

Exhibit 5.4 Situational Prevention Successes

Following are several of more than 50 studies of successful crime interventions that have been evaluated documenting declines in crime following the implementation of situational interventions:

- The elimination of graffiti on the New York City subway system through a program of immediate cleaning of fresh attacks[45]
- The substantial reduction of aircraft hijackings achieved by baggage screening and associated measures at airports around the world[46]
- The virtual elimination of robberies of bus drivers in 20 U.S. cities following the introduction of exact fare systems[47]
- Reductions in convenience store robberies in Florida as a result of having two sales persons on duty at all times[48]
- Reductions in fraudulent use of phones (and in fights between inmates over access to the phones) in a New York City jail through the introduction of "smart" phones[49]
- Reductions in thefts of car radios following the introduction of security-coded radios that are operable only with knowledge of the PIN[50]

ISSUES AND PROBLEMS

Next we look at three areas that can be problematic for crime prevention: implementation of programs, crime displacement, and evaluation of results.

Implementation

A key issue for any type of intervention is the degree to which it is adequately implemented. Unless implemented properly, interventions have a good chance of failure. For example, a Neighborhood Watch initiative in a crime-ridden, ethnically divided area that gains participation from only 20 percent of the residents, and that number from only one of three ethnic groups, could not be expected to have much of an impact on the entire neighborhood or community.

Another potential problem is the possibility that key agencies, actors, or community members will only halfheartedly participate. The police and public might develop a "we-versus-them" attitude, there may be a sense that the police have the necessary training and the public does not, or there might be a fear of a return to vigilante justice. Breaking through such attitudes and fears is not easy, but cooperation between the police and public is essential for successful crime prevention programs.[51]

Canada's National Crime Prevention Council asked, "How do we get started?" and developed the following practical answer:

> Crime prevention efforts must begin with an understanding of the under-lying causes of crime . . . knowledge that the roots of crime lie, in large part, within the broad social and economic environment of the child. Develop-ment of a comprehensive and workable crime prevention strategy will require involvement and improved coordination of all levels of govern-ment, criminal justice organizations, social and health services, and com-munity agencies and groups.[52]

Julian Fantino, chief of the London Police Force, Ontario, Canada, argued that one of the critical components concerns children and youth:

> We must move quickly, before the promise of childhood is poisoned by exploitation and neglect. Many chronic young offenders have been victims as children. Clearly, a link exists between child abuse or neglect and later delinquency and antisocial behavior. Society as a whole must embrace the challenge to become more proactive in protecting its most vulnerable citizens—especially children who are preyed upon by adults.[53]

We discuss planning and implementation for COPPS in Chapter 6; many of those same methods, considerations, and approaches can be applied to crime pre-vention as well.

Displacement of Crime

An issue that emerges in any serious discussion of crime prevention is crime dis-placement, which refers to the idea that rather than eliminate crime, interventions simply result in the movement of crime to another area, shift offenders to new tar-gets in the same area, alter the methods used to accomplish a crime, or prompt offenders to change the type of crime they commit.[54] Displacement has, therefore, been the Achilles' heel of crime prevention in general. Efforts to control drug deal-ing and crime in neighborhoods and places are often criticized for having dis-placed the offending behavior instead of reducing it. If crime or drug dealing has only been moved around without any net reduction in harmful behavior, then that would be a valid criticism.

Research indicates, however, that displacement is not inevitable but is con-tingent on the offender's judgments about alternative crimes. If these alternatives are not viable, the offender may well settle for smaller criminal rewards or for a lower rate of crime. Few offenders are so driven by need or desire that they have to maintain a certain level of offending, whatever the cost. For many, the elimina-tion of easy opportunities for crime may actually encourage them to explore non-criminal alternatives.[55] There are six commonly recognized types of displacement:

- *Temporal:* Offenders change the time when they commit crimes (e.g., switching from dealing drugs during the day to dealing at night).
- *Spatial:* Offenders switch from targets in one location to targets in other locations (e.g., a dealer stops selling drugs in one community and begins selling them in another community).
- *Target:* Offenders switch from one type of target to another type (e.g., a burglar switches from apartment units to single-family, detached homes).
- *Method:* Offenders change the way they attack targets (e.g., a street robber stops using a knife and uses a gun).
- *Crime type:* Offenders switch from one form of crime to another (e.g., from burglary to check fraud).
- *Perpetrator:* New offenders replace old offenders who have been removed by police enforcement (e.g., a dealer is arrested and a new dealer begins business with the same customers).[56]

A review of the evidence for displacement shows that when attempts to detect displacement have been made, it is often not found, and, if found, it is far less than 100 percent.[57] Though numerous studies of enforcement and crime prevention tactics have been made, relatively few present data on displacement effects. John Eck reviewed the literature and found that of 33 studies that looked for displacement effects, only 3 found evidence of much displacement;[58] Eck concluded that, "There is more reason to expect no displacement than a great deal. A reasonable conclusion is that displacement can be a threat, but that it is unlikely to completely negate gains due to an enforcement crackdown or a crime prevention effort."[59]

Research has shown that offenders generally begin offending at places they are familiar with and explore outward into increasingly unfamiliar areas.[60] If opportunities are blocked (by increased enforcement, target hardening, or some other means) close to a familiar location, then displacement to other targets close to familiar areas is most likely. Displacement is most likely to occur in the direction of familiar places, times, targets, and behaviors. Offenders may desist for varying periods of time, or they may even stop offending, depending on how important crime is to their lives.[61]

Though studies have indicated that displacement may not pose a major threat to crime prevention efforts, it is still a phenomenon that police officials must take into account. Unfortunately, researchers have observed that the police seem either to be extremely pessimistic or to ignore the problem,[62] being intent on cleaning up a problem site and moving on to other problems. Ignoring this problem can lead to inequitable solutions to problems; this is particularly true of problem solving tactics designed to displace offenders from specific locations. Efforts must be made to track those individuals to ensure that they do not create a problem somewhere else.[63]

Another concept that relates to displacement is *diffusion of benefits,* which means that some crime prevention measures have the additional unexpected benefit of reducing crimes over a wider range than those immediately targeted by the preventive action.[64] Two examples are the installation of closed circuit television (CCTV) cameras in Britain to reduce thefts from parking lots and the installation of CCTVs to reduce vandalism and graffiti on double-deck buses. The "benefits" in the former situation diffused to other parking lots that were not equipped with CCTVS, and in the latter case to other buses that had no CCTVs. These results probably occurred because potential offenders thought they would be seen in the adjacent areas as well.[65]

Evaluation of Results

Crime prevention also suffers from the same malady from which many other interventions suffer: poor or nonexistent evaluation. The evaluation component of many programs is poorly conceived, marginally funded, and short lived. A useful form of evaluation is an "outcome" or "impact" evaluation to determine whether the intervention accomplished the expected outcome. Assessments of this type require more planning and effort, and consideration must be given to the selection of comparison groups, time frames, outcome variables, potential confounding factors, and analytic techniques.[66] (Evaluations are discussed more thoroughly in Chapter 12.)

Giving community leaders and residents an indication of the success or failure of crime prevention efforts is critical to maintaining strong ties, ensuring their continued participation, and documenting that headway is being made in efforts to improve the safety and quality of neighborhoods.[67] (See the following discussion of what works and does not work in crime prevention.)

WHAT WORKS AND DOES NOT WORK IN CRIME PREVENTION

Many crime prevention programs work. Others do not. Most programs have not yet been evaluated with enough scientific evidence to draw conclusions. Enough evidence is available, however, to create tentative lists of what works, what does not work, and what is promising.

Following are the major conclusions of a 1997 report to Congress, based on a systematic review of more than 500 scientific evaluations of crime prevention practices by the University of Maryland's Department of Criminology and Criminal Justice.[68] This is the first major evaluation of crime prevention programs, resulting in much attention and debate in the field. There are some surprising findings, particularly in the list of programs that do not hold promise—several of which have become pet projects of police agencies and political leaders.

What Prevents or Reduces Crime

The following are programs that researchers believed with reasonable certainty would prevent crime or reduce risk factors for crime; these programs are thus likely to be effective in preventing some form of crime:

Although both adult and juvenile military style boot camps are increasing in number, they have poor results in reducing repeat offending. (*Courtesy* Washoe County, Nevada, Sheriff's Office)

- Providing extra police patrols in high-crime hot spots
- Monitoring repeat offenders to reduce the time on the streets of known high-risk repeat offenders and returning them to prison quickly
- Arresting domestic abusers to reduce repeated abuse by employed suspects
- Offering rehabilitation programs for adult and juvenile offenders that are appropriate to their risk factors to reduce their repeat offending rates
- Offering drug treatment programs in prison to reduce repeat offending after release

What Does Not Appear to Be Successful

Sufficient evidence indicated to the University of Maryland researchers that the following programs failed to reduce crime or reduce risk factors:

- Gun buyback programs failed to reduce gun violence in cities (as evaluated in St. Louis and Seattle).
- Community mobilization of residents' efforts against crime in high-crime, inner-city areas of concentrated poverty were not effective.
- Neighborhood Watch programs organized with police failed to reduce burglary or other target crimes, especially in higher-crime areas where voluntary participation often fails.
- Arrests of unemployed suspects for domestic assault caused higher rates of repeat offending over the long term than nonarrest alternatives.
- Increased arrests or raids on drug markets failed to reduce violent crime or disorder for more than a few days, if at all.
- Storefront police offices failed to prevent crime in the surrounding areas.

- Police newsletters with local crime information failed to reduce victimization rates (as evaluated in Newark, New Jersey, and Houston, Texas).
- Correctional boot camps using traditional military training failed to reduce repeat offending after release compared to similar offenders serving time on probation and parole, both for adults and juveniles.
- "Scared Straight" programs that bring minor juvenile offenders to visit maximum security prisons to see the severity of prison conditions failed to reduce the participants' reoffending rates and may increase crime.
- Shock probation, shock parole, and split sentences, in which offenders are incarcerated for a short period of time at the beginning of the sentence and then supervised in the community, did not reduce repeat offending compared to the placement of similar offenders only under community supervision, and increased crime rates for some groups.
- Home detention with electronic monitoring for low-risk offenders failed to reduce offending compared to the placement of similar offenders under standard community supervision without electronic monitoring.
- Intensive supervision on parole or probation did not reduce repeat offending compared to normal levels of community supervision.

What Holds Promise

Researchers determined that the level of certainty for the following programs is too low for there to be positive, generalizable conclusions, but some empirical basis exists for predicting that further research could show positive results.

- Problem solving analysis is effective when addressed to the specific crime situation.
- Proactive arrests for carrying concealed weapons in gun crime hot spots, using traffic enforcement and field interrogations, can be helpful.
- Community policing with meetings to set priorities reduced community perceptions of the severity of crime problems in Chicago.
- Field interrogations of suspicious persons reduced crime in a San Diego experiment.
- Gang offender monitoring by community workers and probation and police officers can reduce gang violence.
- Community-based mentoring by Big Brothers/Big Sisters of America substantially reduced drug abuse in one experiment, although evaluations of other similar programs showed that it did not.
- Battered women's shelters were found to reduce at least the short-term (six-week) rate of repeat victimization for women who take other steps to seek help.

Many more impact evaluations using stronger scientific methods are needed before even minimally valid conclusions can be reached about the impact on crime of programs. Again, as previously noted, there is much debate in the field about the research findings. The Maryland report to Congress, however, has raised the consciousness of the crime prevention discipline and will, it is hoped, bring about much more needed research and inquiry.

SIX SAFER CITIES AND THEIR PATHBREAKING WORK

The National Crime Prevention Council (NCPC) of Washington, D.C., has worked with about three dozen cities to help them examine their resources and needs and craft coalitions with community leaders to address priorities and plan for the future. Several of these cities have distinguished themselves in the fight to reduce crime during the past decade. These cities have surpassed national decreases and dramatically reduced crime through collaborative partnerships, and they have addressed priority crime and quality of life concerns; they have demonstrated a capacity to fuse grassroots support, political and bureaucratic will, and crime prevention practices as a way of doing business.[69]

The NCPC selected six cities to participate in the Municipal Crime Reduction Working Group (MCRWG). Following is a listing of the cities along with their *total* percentage of crime reduction from 1986 to 1996 and the percentage of reductions for both *property* and *violent* crimes during the same time period:

Boston, Massachusetts (29 percent, 31 percent, and 16 percent)
Denver, Colorado (8, 6, and 18)
Fort Worth, Texas (56, 57, and 48)
Hartford, Connecticut (30, 31, and 24)
New York City (41, 43, and 32)
San Diego, California (46, 40, and 1)[70]

How did these municipalities achieve such substantial crime reductions at a time when there was a gradual decline in national crime trends? It is difficult to identify with certainty any causes for the reductions, and crime rates can fluctuate as a result of many social and economic factors. Furthermore, no single, "cookie-cutter" set of solutions will cause crime to decline in all jurisdictions. Some initiatives and approaches employed in the venues, however, indicate a clear connection between practice and crime reduction (see Table 5.3).[71]

All of the cities shared a similar experience: the use of certain processes and practices (shown in the table) that target the key situational and social causes of local crime. Each also recognized the need to develop partnerships with neighborhood leaders and ordinary citizens, and to improve collaboration among institutions. There was also a drive to hold offenders, the community, municipal government, and the police accountable by not allowing crime and the conditions that foster it to continue.[72]

TABLE 5.3 Crime Prevention Matrix

Best Practice Crime Prevention Programs	Boston	Denver	Fort Worth	Hartford	New York City	San Diego
Communities and Crime Prevention						
• Gang violence prevention focused on reducing gang cohesion, but not increasing it	■	■	■	■	■	■
• Volunteer mentoring (Big Brothers/Big Sisters) reduces substance abuse, but not delinquency	■	■	■	■	■	■
• Restorative justice, such as police referral of vandalism cases to repair damage and to community rehabilitation programs	■	■		■		■
• "Coaching" to reduce crime at sporting venues ("Hooliganism")					■	■
Family-Based Crime Prevention						
• Long-term, frequent home visitation combined with preschool prevents later delinquency	■	■				
• Infant weekly home visitation reduces child abuse and injuries	■	■				
• Family therapy by clinical staff for delinquent/predelinquent youth	■	■	■			■
• Reeducation program for men convicted of wife battering	■		■			■
• Battered women's shelters for women who take other steps to change their lives	■	■	■	■		■
• Orders of protection for battered women	■		■	■	■	■
School-Based Crime Prevention						
Crime and Delinquency						
• Programs aimed at building school capacity to initiate and sustain innovation	■	■	■	■		■
• Programs aimed at clarifying and communicating norms about behaviors—by establishing school rules, improving the consistency of their enforcement (particularly when they emphasize positive reinforcement of appropriate behavior), or communicating norms through schoolwide campaigns (e.g., antibullying campaigns) or ceremonies	■	■		■		■

(table continues)

TABLE 5.3 *(continued)*

• Comprehensive instructional programs that focus on a range of social competency skills (e.g., developing self-control, stress-management, responsible decision making, social problem solving, and communication) and that are delivered over a long period of time	■	■	■	■	■	■
• Coordinated action between schools and social services		■		■		■
• Antibullying programs using coordinated work between schools, families, and social services				■		■
• Programs that group youth into smaller "schools-within-schools" to create smaller units, more supportive interactions, or greater flexibility in instruction	■			■		
• Behavior modification and programs that teach "thinking skills" to high-risk youth	■	■		■	■	■
Substance Abuse						
• Programs aimed at clarifying and communicating norms about behaviors	■	■	■	■	■	■
• Comprehensive instructional programs using a range of social competency skills (see above) delivered over a long period of time to continually reinforce skills	■	■	■	■	■	■
• Programs aimed at building school capacity to initiate and sustain innovation	■	■			■	■
• Programs that group youth into smaller "schools-within-schools" to create smaller units, more supportive interactions, or greater flexibility in instruction	■			■		
• Programs that improve classroom management and that use effective instructional techniques	■	■			■	■

Labor Markets and Crime Risk Factors

• Vocational programs aimed at older male ex-offenders no longer in the justice system	■		■	■		
• Job Corps	■	■		■		■
• Prison-based vocational education programs aimed at adults	■			■	■	■
• Dispersed housing for poverty-level households		■		■		■

(table continues)

TABLE 5.3 *(continued)*

Preventing Poverty at Places

Nuisance abatement	■		■	■	■	■
Microneighborhood watch				■		■
Housing design standards						■
Supervision by caretakers	■					
Reduction of access to firearms	■			■	■	
Burglary reduction programs using the Safer Cities model					■	
Multiple clerks in commercial stores	■					■
Store design	■					■
Server training in bars and taverns	■					
Metal detectors and guards in airports	■		■	■	■	■
Street closures in open public spaces	■		■	■	■	■
Target hardening in public facilities	■		■	■	■	■
Closed circuit television in public places	■			■	■	
City guards in public streets				■	■	

Policing for Prevention

Increased directed patrols in street-corner hot spots of crime	■	■	■	■	■	■
Proactive arrests of serious repeat offenders	■		■	■	■	■
Proactive drunk driving arrests	■		■	■	■	■
Arrests of employed suspects for domestic assault	■		■	■		■
Police traffic enforcement patrols against illegally carried handguns	■		■	■		
Community policing with community participation in priority setting	■	■	■	■	■	■
Community policing focused on improving police legitimacy	■		■	■		■
Zero tolerance of disorder, if legitimacy issues can be addressed	■		■	■	■	
Problem oriented policing generally	■	■	■	■	■	■
Adding extra police to cities, regardless of assignments	■		■	■		■
Warrants for arrest of suspect absent when police respond to domestic violence	■			■	■	■

Criminal Justice and Crime Prevention

Rehabilitation programs with particular characteristics	■	■		■		■
Prison-based therapeutic community treatment of drug-involved offenders	■				■	■

(table continues)

TABLE 5.3 *(continued)*

• Incapacitating offenders who continue to commit crimes at high rates	■				■
• Effective rehabilitation programs that	■	■			■
• Are structured and focused, use multiple treatment components, focus on developing skills (social, academic, and employment), and use behavioral and cognitive methods (with reinforcements for clearly identified, overt behaviors as opposed to nondirective counseling focusing on insight, self esteem, or disclosure)	■			■	■
• Provide for substantial, meaningful contact with the treatment personnel	■			■	■
• Providing intensive community-based treatment for drug addicts	■	■	■	■	■
• Drug courts combining both rehabilitation and criminal justice control	■		■	■	■
• Day fines	■			■	
• Juvenile aftercare	■	■	■	■	■
• Drug treatment combined with urine testing	■	■	■	■	■

SUMMARY

It is clear that the field of crime prevention has "matured" from its earlier forms, originally involving strategic placement of rocks by early cave dwellers, or more recently having to do primarily with target hardening one's home with better locks. This chapter has shown its various elements as well as the results of research efforts concerning what good can occur when measures are taken to prevent crimes.

The police are realizing that they alone cannot prevent or address crime and disorder, and that a partnership with the community is essential if the physical and social problems that plague communities are to be reduced or eliminated.

NOTES

1. Crime Prevention Coalition of America, *Crime Prevention in America: Foundations for Action* (Washington, D.C.: National Crime Prevention Council, 1990), p. 64.
2. Ronald V. Clarke, *Situational Crime Prevention: Successful Case Studies*, 2nd ed. (Monsey, N.Y.: Criminal Justice Press, 1997), p. 2.
3. Steven P. Lab, "Crime Prevention: Where Have We Been and Which Way Should We Go?" In Steven P. Lab (ed.), *Community Policing at a Crossroads* (Cincinnati: Anderson, 1997), pp. 1–13.

4. Cynthia Scanlon, "Crime Prevention through Environmental Design," *Law and Order* (May 1996):50.
5. U.S. Department of Housing and Urban Development, "Crime Prevention through Environmental Design," Crime Prevention Brief (Washington, D.C.: Author, no date), p. 2.
6. Lab, "Crime Prevention," p. 5.
7. *Ibid.*
8. *Ibid.*, p. 7.
9. Scanlon, "Crime Prevention through Environmental Design," p. 50.
10. Lab, "Crime Prevention," p. 6.
11. L. E. Cohen and M. Felson, "Social Change and Crime Rate Trends: A Routine Activity Approach," *American Sociological Review* 44 (1997):588–608.
12. D. B. Cornish and R. V. Clarke, *The Reasoning Criminal: Rational Choice Perspectives on Offending* (New York: Springer-Verlag, 1986).
13. James Q. Wilson and George Kelling, "Broken Windows." *The Atlantic Monthly* 211 (1982):29–38.
14. Lab, "Crime Prevention," p. 6.
15. Ronald V. Clarke, "Situational Crime Prevention: Its Theoretical Basis and Practical Scope," In *Crime and Justice: An Annual Review of Research* Vol. 4, eds. Michael Tonry and Norval Morris (Chicago: University of Chicago Press, 1983), p. 225.
16. Lab, "Crime Prevention," pp. 8–9.
17. U.S. Department of Justice, Bureau of Justice Assistance, *Crime Prevention and Community Policing: A Vital Partnership* (Washington, D.C.: U.S. Government Printing Office, 1997), p. 4.
18. Jim Jordan, "Shifting the Mission: Seeing Prevention as the Strategic Goal, Not a Set of Programs," *Subject to Debate* (Washington, D.C.: Police Executive Research Forum, December 1999), pp. 1–2.
19. *Ibid.*, p. 3.
20. *Ibid.*
21. *Ibid.*
22. Quoted in Julian Fantino, "Taking Crime Prevention Back to the Future!" *The Police Chief* (May 1999):18.
23. *Ibid.*
24. *Ibid.*, p. 20.
25. *Ibid.*
26. Lab, "Crime Prevention," p. 6.
27. Rob Gurwitt, "Communitarianism: You Can Try It at Home," *Governing* 6 (August 1993):33–39.
28. *Ibid.*, p. 8.
29. U.S. Department of Justice, Bureau of Justice Assistance, *Crime Prevention and Community Policing: A Vital Partnership* (Washington, D.C.: U.S. Government Printing Office, 1997), p. 3.
30. Adapted from The Ohio Crime Prevention Association, *A Citizen Guide to Community Policing* (Dublin, Oh.: Author, 1998), pp. 21–24.
31. Chicago Police Department, *Together We Can* (Chicago: Author, 1992), p. 6.
32. C. R. Jeffrey, *Crime Prevention through Environmental Design* (Beverly Hills, Calif.: Sage, 1971), p. 117.
33. National Crime Prevention Council, *Designing Safer Communities: A Crime Prevention through Environmental Design Handbook* (Washington, D.C.: Author, 1997), pp. 7–8.
34. "Building a More Crime-Free Environment: Tempe Cops Have the Last Word on Construction Projects," *Law Enforcement News*, November 15, 1998, p. 7.
35. Scanlon, "Crime Prevention through Environmental Design," pp. 51–52.
36. *Ibid.*, p. 3.

37. Marcus Felson, "Routine Activities and Crime Prevention: Armchair Concepts and Practical Action," *Studies on Crime and Crime Prevention* 1, No. 1 (1992):30–34.
38. Clarke, *Situational Crime Prevention*, p. 3.
39. U.S. Department of Housing and Urban Development, "Situational Prevention," Crime Prevention Brief (Washington, D.C.: Author, no date), p. 1.
40. Clarke, *Situational Crime Prevention*, p. 3.
41. *Ibid.*
42. *Ibid.*
43. Ronald V. Clarke, *Situational Crime Prevention: Successful Case Studies* (Albany, N.Y.: Harrow and Heston, 1992), p. 27.
44. Clarke, *Situational Crime Prevention*, 2nd ed., p. 17.
45. M. Sloan-Howitt and G. Kelling, "Subway Graffiti in New York City: 'Gettin' Up' vs. `Meanin' It and Cleanin' It," *Security Journal* 1 (1990):131–36.
46. P. Wilkinson, *Terrorism and the Liberal State*, 2nd ed. (New York: New York University Press, 1986).
47. Stanford Research Institute, *Reduction of Robbery and Assault of Bus Drivers, Vol. III: Technological and Operational Methods* (Stanford, Calif.: Author, 1970).
48. R. D. Hunter and C. R. Jeffrey, "Preventing Convenience Store Robbery through Environmental Design," in *Situational Crime Prevention: Successful Case Studies*, ed. R. V. Clarke (Albany, N.Y.: Harrow and Heston, 1992), pp. 219–22.
49. N. G. LaVigne, "Rational Choice and Inmate Disputes over Phone Use on Rikers Island," in *Crime Prevention Studies*, Vol. 3, ed. R. V. Clarke (Monsey, N.Y.: Criminal Justice Press, 1994), pp. 147–49.
50. A. Braga and R. V. Clarke, "Improved Radios and More Stripped Cars in Germany: A Routine Activities Analysis," *Security Journal* 5 (1994):154–59.
51. *Ibid.*, pp. 9–10.
52. *Ibid.*, p. 21.
53. *Ibid.*
54. Lab, "Crime Prevention," p. 12.
55. Clarke, *Situational Crime Prevention*, 2nd ed., p. 2.
56. Robert Barr and Ken Pease, "Crime Placement, Displacement, and Deflection," in *Crime and Justice: A Review of Research*, Vol. 12, eds. Michael Tonry and Norval Morris (Chicago: University of Chicago Press, 1990), pp. 146–75.
57. John E. Eck, "The Threat of Crime Displacement." *Criminal Justice Abstracts* 25, No. 3 (September 1993):529.
58. Pat Mayhew, Ronald V. Clarke, A. Sturman, and J. M. Hough, *Crime as Opportunity*. Home Office Research Study No. 34 (London: Her Majesty's Stationery Office, 1976); J. Lowman, "Prostitution in Vancouver: Some Notes on the Genesis of a Social Problem," *Canadian Journal of Criminology* 28, no. 1 (1997):1–16; Barry Poyner and Barry Webb, "Reducing Theft from Shopping Bags in City Center Markets," in Ronald V. Clarke (ed.), *Situational Crime Prevention: Successful Case Studies* (Albany, N.Y.: Harrow and Heston, 1992).
59. Eck, "The Threat of Crime Displacement," pp. 534–36.
60. *Ibid.*, p. 537.
61. *Ibid.*, p. 537.
62. Barr and Pease, "Crime Placement, Displacement, and Deflection," p. 147.
63. Eck, "The Threat of Crime Displacement," pp. 541–42.
64. R. V. Clarke and D. Weisburd, "Diffusion of Crime Control Benefits: Observations on the Reverse of Displacement," in *Crime Prevention Studies*, Vol. 2, ed. R. V. Clarke (Monsey, N.Y.: Criminal Justice Press, 1994), pp. 89–129.
65. See B. Poyner, "Situational Crime Prevention in Two Parking Facilities," *Security Journal* 2 (1991):96–101; and B. Poyner, "Video Cameras and Bus Vandalism," *Journal of Security Administration* 11 (1988):44–51.

66. *Ibid.*, pp. 11–12.
67. John E. Eck and William Spelman, *Problem Solving: Problem-Oriented Policing in Newport News*, Appendix B., p. 83.
68. Lawrence W. Sherman, Denise C. Gottfredson, Doris L. MacKenzie, John Eck, Peter Reuter, and Shawn D. Bushway, *Preventing Crime: What Works, What Doesn't, What's Promising.* National Institute of Justice, *Research in Brief* (Washington, D.C.: Author, 1998), pp. 1–27.
69. National Crime Prevention Council, *Six Safer Cities: On the Crest of the Crime Prevention Wave* (Washington, D.C.: Author, 1999), p. 3.
70. *Ibid.*, pp. 8–18.
71. *Ibid.*, p. 20.
72. *Ibid.*, pp. 20–21.

Read For 3-26

PLANNING AND IMPLEMENTATION
Translating Ideas into Action

> Alice: Cheshire Puss, would you tell me, please, which way I ought to go from here?
> Cheshire Cat: That depends a good deal on where you want to get to.
> Alice: I don't much care where . . .
> Cheshire Cat: Then it doesn't matter which way you go.
> —Lewis Carroll, in *Alice's Adventures in Wonderland*, 1865, Chapter 6

INTRODUCTION

Having identified the core components and elements of community oriented policing and problem solving (COPPS) in Chapter 4, we now look at how to strategically plan for and implement this concept.

To help conceptualize strategic planning, one might view it as maintaining the tension on the line while fishing—if you reel it in too fast, the line might snap; but if you go too slowly, the fish will not be landed. The strategic plan that the police agency "holds in its hands" outlines bold milestones spread over the next several years.[1]

This chapter begins with a look at the general need for strategic thinking, and for police organizations to manage their resources and engage in the strategic planning process. This section also discusses the planning cycle, and how to assess local needs and develop a planning document.

Then we shift to the implementation of COPPS per se, considering some principal components: leadership and administration, human resources, field operations, and external relations. All of this is then brought fully into focus by an example, with a view of an actual agency strategic plan that includes vision, mission, and values statements; goals and objectives; and related strategies (other, more brief examples are provided as well, in tables and figures throughout the chapter). We conclude the chapter by considering several general obstacles to implementation, and by delineating 10 ways that COPPS can be undermined.

STRATEGIC THINKING

In order for a chief executive to engage in strategic planning, he or she must first become engaged in strategic *thinking* and then assist the organization in thinking strategically. This means seeing both the big picture and its operational implications. As one author observed,

> The purpose of strategic thinking is to discover novel, imaginative strategies which can rewrite the rules of the competitive game and to envision potential futures, significantly different from the present.[2]

Strategic thinking refers to a creative, divergent thought process. It is a mode of strategy making that is associated with reinventing the future.[3]

Strategic thinking is, therefore, compatible with strategic planning. Both are required in any thoughtful strategy-making process and strategy formulation. The creative, groundbreaking strategies emerging from strategic thinking still have to be operationalized through convergent and analytical thought (strategic planning). Thus, both strategic thinking and strategic planning are necessary, and neither is adequate without the other for effective strategic management (see Figure 6.1).[4] As Herocleous observed,

> It all comes down to the ability to go up and down the ladder of abstraction, and being able to see both the big picture and the operational implications, which are signs of outstanding leaders and strategists.[5]

STRATEGIC PLANNING

Basic Elements

Strategic planning is a leadership tool and a process (as shown in Figure 6.2); furthermore, as with most tools, it is primarily used for one purpose: to help an organization do a better job—to focus its energy, ensure that members of the organization are working toward the same goals, and assess and adjust an organization's

Montgomery County, Maryland's multiyear strategic plan
was designed for adaptability and continual evaluation.
(*Courtesy* Montgomery County, Maryland, Police Department)

direction in response to a changing environment. In short, strategic planning is a disciplined effort to produce fundamental decisions and actions that shape and guide what an organization is, what it does, and why it does it, with a focus on the future.[6]

The history of strategic planning begins in the military, in which strategy is "the science of planning and directing large-scale military operations." Although our understanding of strategy as applied to management has been transformed, one element remains: aiming to achieve competitive advantage. Strategic planning also includes the following elements:

- It is oriented toward the future and looks at how the world could be different five to ten years in the future. It is aimed at creating the organization's future.
- It is based on thorough analysis of foreseen or predicted trends and scenarios of possible alternative futures.
- It thoroughly analyzes the organization, its internal and external environment, and its potential.
- It is a qualitative, idea-driven process.
- It is an ongoing, continuous learning process.
- When it is successful, it influences all areas of operations, becoming a part of the organization's philosophy and culture.[7]

Excellent examples of strategic planning abound. For example, see the strategic plan of the U.S. Department of Justice.[8]

For police leaders, strategic planning holds many benefits. It can help an agency anticipate key trends and issues facing the organization, both currently and

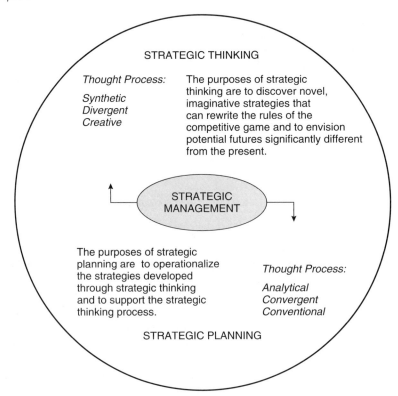

Figure 6.1 Strategic Thinking and Strategic Planning (*Source:* Loizos Heracleous, "Strategic Thinking or Strategic Planning?" *Long Range Planning* 31 [June 1998]:485. Used with permission.)

in the future. The planning process explores options, sets directions, and helps stakeholders make appropriate decisions. It facilitates communication among key stakeholders who are involved in the process and keeps organizations focused on outcomes while battling daily crises. Planning can be used to develop performance standards to measure an agency's efforts. Most important, it helps leaders facilitate and manage change (which is the subject of the following chapter).

The Planning Cycle

A fundamental cycle is used for strategic planning—the initial steps to be taken in the process—with appropriate involvement by all stakeholders. The process is not fixed, however; it must be flexible enough to allow rapid revision of specific strategies as new information develops:

1. Identify the planning team: include the involvement of several key stakeholders, both internal and external to the organization.

a. *Department and city leadership*
b. *Department personnel*: supervisors, officers, nonsworn staff members, and all members of the department should be included.
c. *The community*: The plan must be developed in partnership with the community it is designed to serve.
d. *Interagency partners*: These include both staff and other government agencies and representatives of key social welfare agencies.

2. *Environmental scanning*: Conduct a needs assessment (discussed later).
3. Development of a planning document (discussed later).

Figure 6.2 depicts the various steps that are involved in the planning cycle.

Environmental Scanning: A Needs Assessment

Environmental scanning is a part of the planning cycle that deserves special attention, because it refers to the collection and analysis of information required to determine the nature and extent of crime in a community, community residents' perceptions of crime and how they are affected by it, and information about the environment or conditions of a community. The purpose of the needs assessment is to determine and exchange information about specific types of community crime and disorder problems, their causes and effects, and the resources available to combat them. The needs assessment provides the foundation for a community's entire COPPS effort.

Therefore, in order to develop a comprehensive implementation plan for community policing, a needs assessment should be completed at the earliest possible time. There are several reasons for conducting a community needs assessment:

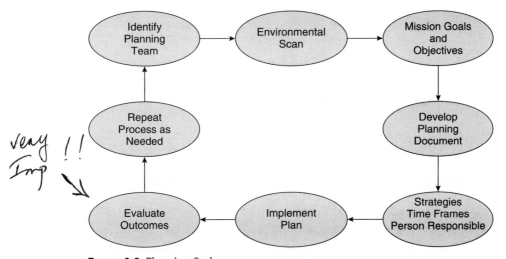

very !!
Imp

FIGURE 6.2 Planning Cycle

- To list in order of priority and clarify the existing crime and drug problems
- To provide a view of resident perceptions about the crime and drug problems, and to provide an excellent means of involving the community in problem identification
- To provide information to the public about problems
- To provide initial direction for developing a workplan, and to assist in setting program goals, strategies, and objectives
- To provide baseline data for evaluation

Needs assessment is ultimately a process conducted by collaborating staff agencies that outlines the current issues of the community and the resources needed to resolve those issues. This document will

- Result in a clearer picture of community needs and resources
- Allow the planning team to develop a strong rationale for decision making
- Ground agencies' deliberations in fact
- Dispel myths about crime issues

Information sources for needs assessment include the following:

- City planning reports
- Newspaper articles
- Police reports [including local crime analysis and dispatch calls for service (CFS) data, as well as police officers' knowledge of the community, the Federal Bureau of Investigation's *Uniform Crime Reports,* and other related sources]
- Interviews with community leaders
- Community surveys (see "A Strategic Plan Survey in Portland, Oregon" in Appendix C)
- Employment, housing, education, and health information

THE PLANNING DOCUMENT: A GUIDE FOR IMPLEMENTATION

Elements and Issues

A written document or plan is the product of a planning team's efforts, is helpful for organizing key objectives, and serves as a guide for those persons involved in the implementation process. The detail and structure of a plan may vary greatly. It may be highly detailed and cover goals, objectives, tasks, and timelines, or it may be less formal, identifying general areas targeted for change.

The structure and formality of a plan will depend largely on the needs and capacity of the organization (based on the environmental scanning and needs

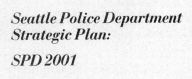

"*Our Mission, together with the communities of Seattle, is to make our city a place where all people live safely and without fear.*"

The Seattle, Washington, Police Department's Strategic Planning document displays its mission statement and illustrates police commitment to working in partnership with the community. (*Courtesy* Seattle, Washington, Police Department)

assessment). Large organizations with funding and staff support may desire a more comprehensive plan to keep track of the many details and numbers of people involved in implementation. Conversely, smaller police organizations may be capable of implementing change with less detailed plans (see Exhibit 6.1).

Following are some format and content issues for the planning process and the development of a planning document.

1. *Develop statements of vision, mission, and values*:
   - The *vision* is a scenario or description of how the agency and community will change if the plan is successful.
   - The *mission* defines the "business" of COPPS. The statement can be expected to include both traditional aspects of policing (such as public safety, enforcement, "protect and serve") and aspects of COPPS philosophy (community engagement, shared responsibility for public safety).
   - *Values* guide decisions and actions. Prioritize and develop a short list of key principles that people who are involved in COPPS implementation should consider.

Exhibit 6.1   Shifting to COPPS in Mount Pleasant, South Carolina

Mount Pleasant, South Carolina, is a small oceanside community of about 36,000 citizens. For several years the city's police department—with 71 sworn officers and 28 civilians—had been moving from the traditional policing model to COPPS. The command staff in the police department began a comprehensive training process that included visits to departments in three other states. Staff members met with the agency leaders and observed various COPPS initiatives in action. Each command staff member was given a set of materials to review and critique pertaining specifically to Mount Pleasant. Then the staff developed an implementation process that included

- Redefining the department's mission
- Researching COPPS
- Setting goals, objectives, and tasks for implementation

After the goals, objectives, and tasks were identified, the department was in a position to establish time frames for completing the tasks associated with program implementation. Time frames allowed agency personnel and community members to schedule program activities around their normal responsibilities. The implementation plan also specified the process by which everyone was to be informed about the work to be done and the changes necessary to get it done.

Based on this process, the plan included 133 tasks that the staff was to undertake over a three-year period to ensure a complete transition to COPPS. These tasks included everything from training personnel to seeking alternative sources of revenue to fund agency operations. The plan was presented to the city council and a number of community organizations. COPPS training was completed by January 1993. To obtain citizen input, the department worked closely with a planning committee throughout the process. CFS management, performance evaluations, training, and a rewards system consumed a considerable amount of time during implementation. Today, however, every patrol team in the department practices COPPS, performing research, analyzing data, and developing potential solutions for problems.

Source: Thomas J. Sexton, "Mount Pleasant Plans Strategy for Shift to Community Policing," *Community Policing Exchange* (November/December 1995), p. 5.

2. *Identify primary objectives* that define critical outcomes anticipated from the change to COPPS.

3. *Select strategies* from among various options outlined during the process that clearly outline the primary avenues and approaches that will be used to attain objectives.

4. *Set goals* that are general statements of intent. They are the first step in translating a mission statement into what can realistically be attained. Goals should be obtainable and measurable, often beginning with such phrases as "to increase," "to reduce," or "to expand."

5. *Set objectives*—specific statements of what must be done to achieve a goal or desired outcomes. Usually, several objectives are developed for each goal. A meaningful and well-stated objective should be

   Specific: stating precisely what is to be achieved

   Measurable: answering how much, how many, how well

   Time-bound: indicating when results will be achieved

6. *Set activities*, or detailed steps necessary to carry out each strategy; they should be time framed and measurable.

7. *Identify a responsible person* for every task.

8. *Set timelines* for the completion of tasks.

IMPLEMENTING **COPPS**

Departmentwide versus Experimental District

Since COPPS came into being, most police executives have implemented the strategy throughout the entire agency; some executives, however, have attempted to implement the concept by introducing it in a small unit or an experimental district[9] and often in a specific geographic area of the jurisdiction.

It is strongly argued that COPPS be implemented on a departmentwide basis. When COPPS has been established as a distinct unit within a patrol rather than departmentwide, the introduction of this "special unit" seems to exacerbate the conflict between community policing's reform agenda and the more traditional outlook and hierarchical structure of the agency (see Exhibit 6.2). A perception of elitism is created—a perception that is ironic, because COPPS is meant to close the gap between patrol and special units and to empower and value the rank-and-file patrol officer as the most important functionary of police work.

As can be seen in Exhibit 6.2, explaining implementation challenges in a study of eight cities, this perception of elitism is indeed a problem. As the Ministry of the Solicitor General in Canada put it,

A department-wide approach attempts to change all members of the department into problem-solvers, irrespective of rank or function. Creating

Exhibit 6.2   Implementation Challenges

A recent study sponsored by the National Institute of Justice evaluated what were termed "INOP" ("Innovative Neighborhood Oriented Policing") initiatives in eight cities (Hayward, California; Houston; Louisville; New York City; Norfolk, Virginia; Portland; Prince George's County, Maryland; and Tempe, Arizona) that focused on drug problems. The initiatives attempted to lower the demand for illegal drugs. Implementation issues received special emphasis in the study. The findings were as follows:

- The major implementation challenges were resistance by police officers to INOP, the difficulty of involving other public agencies, and the need to organize the community.
- The involvement of other public agencies was limited.
- Police officers generally did not understand INOP; they believed problem solving assignments conferred elite status and perceived the strategy as more time consuming, less productive, and more resource-intensive than traditional policing. They also believed that their power to enforce the law was restrained.
- Average citizens had less knowledge than community leaders about INOP and were reluctant to participate because of fear of drug dealers' retaliation and cynicism about the short duration of the initiative.
- The perceived effects of INOP on drug trafficking were mixed; they resulted in displacement of markets.
- Most site residents believed their relationship with the police had improved, even when the effect on drugs, crime, and fear was believed to be minimal.

Source: Susan Sadd and Randolph M. Grinc, *Implementation Challenges in Community Policing: Innovative Neighborhood-Oriented Policing in Eight Cities* (Washington, D.C.: U.S. Department of Justice, National Institute of Justice Research in Brief, February 1996), pp. 1–2.

special problem solving units . . . may marginalize COPPS as a specialized function and have a limited impact on the effectiveness of the department as a whole.[10]

The key lesson from research on implementation, however, is that there is no "golden" or "bright-line" rule or any universal method to ensure the successful adoption of COPPS. Two general propositions are important, however, for consideration in implementing the concept: the role of the rank-and-file officer and the role of the environment (or "social ecology") in which COPPS is to be implemented.[11] The social ecology of COPPS includes both the internal/organizational and external/societal environments. Both of these factors are discussed later in the chapter.

We also believe that TQM (discussed in Chapter 3) supports our notion of putting the responsibility for implementation of COPPS at the door of everyone in the organization. If rank-and-file officers are able to show positive results with COPPS projects, their success can become difficult to criticize among those with whom the philosophy is unpopular. Indeed, turning implementation over to practitioners has been found to have the effect of depoliticizing potential implementation hurdles.[12]

Principal Components of Successful Implementation

Moving an agency from the reactive, incident-driven mode to COPPS is a complex endeavor. Four principal components of implementation profoundly affect the way agencies do business: leadership and administration, human resources, field operations, and external relations.[13] Information provided in these four components may serve as a basis for conducting an organizational assessment and identifying key issues and areas to be included in a planning document.

Leadership and Administration

Management Approaches. COPPS requires changing the *philosophy of leadership* and management throughout the entire organization. This begins with the development of a *new vision/values/mission statement*. Leadership should be promoted at all levels, and a shift in management style from *controller to facilitator* is necessary. The organization should invest in *information systems* that will assist officers in identifying patterns of crime and support the problem solving process. Progressive leaders will need to prepare for the future by *engaging in long-term, strategic management and developing continuous evaluation processes*, but at the same time these leaders should be flexible and comfortable with change. *Finances and resources* will no longer be firmly established within boxes in the organizational chart. Rather, they will be commonly shared across the organization, with other city departments and the public engaged in neighborhood problem solving.

Role of the Chief Executive. It is essential that chief executives communicate the idea that COPPS is departmentwide in scope. To get the whole agency involved, the chief executive must adopt four practices as part of the implementation plan:

1. Communicate to all department members the vital role of COPPS in serving the public. Executives must describe why handling problems is more effective than simply handling incidents.

Arlington County, Virginia, Police Chief Ed Fynn "walks the talk" of COPPS by appearing at neighborhood clean-up efforts to show his support to residents and officers. (*Courtesy* Arlington County, Virginia, Police Department)

2. Provide incentives to all department members to engage in COPPS. This includes a new and different personnel evaluation and reward system, as well as positive encouragement.
3. Reduce the barriers to COPPS that can occur. Procedures, time allocation, and policies all need to be closely examined.
4. Show officers how to address problems. Training is a key element of COPPS implementation. The executive must also set guidelines for innovation. Officers must know they have the latitude to innovate.[14]

The top management of a police agency must consciously address these four concerns. Failure to do so will result in the COPPS approach being conducted by a relatively small number of officers; as a result, relatively few problems will be addressed.

The general task of the chief executive is to challenge the fundamental assumptions of the organization, its aspirations and objectives, the effectiveness of the department's current technologies, and even the chief's own self-perception. This is an awkward stage in the life of the organization. It seems to be a deliberate attempt by the chief to upset the agency. The remedy lies in the personal commitment of the chief and his or her senior managers and supervisors.

Ensuing surveys may well find that morale improves once it becomes clear that the change in direction and style was more than a "fleeting fancy," that the chief's policies have some longevity.[15]

Middle Managers. In the early twentieth century, a powerful midlevel management group emerged that extended the reach of chiefs throughout the department and became the locus of the practice and skill base of the occupation. As such, middle managers—captains and lieutenants—became the leading edge in the establishment of decentralized control over police departments' internal environment and organizational operations.[16] Furthermore, in the past one of the basic functions and practices of middle managers was to forestall creativity and innovation.

Times have changed in this regard, however; today these middle managers play a crucial role in planning and implementing COPPS, as well as encouraging their officers to be innovative, to take risks, and to be creative.[17] As George Kelling and William Bratton observed, "Ample evidence exists that when a clear vision of the business of the organization is put forward, when mid-managers are included in planning, when their legitimate self-interests are acknowledged, and when they are properly trained, mid-managers can be the leading edge of innovation and creativity."[18]

First-Line Supervisors. Research has provided additional information for leaders to consider when implementing a COPPS philosophy. To begin, first-line supervisors and senior patrol officers seem to generate the greatest resistance to community policing, largely because of long-standing working styles cultivated from years of traditional police work and because these officers can feel disenfranchised by a management system that takes the best and brightest out of patrol and (they often believe) leaves them behind. The press of 911 calls also makes it difficult to meet the need for community outreach, problem solving, and networking with other agencies. Officers may also become concerned about the size of the area for which they are responsible; community policing beats are typically smaller than those of radio patrols.

We discuss the role of middle managers and first-line supervisors in greater detail in Chapter 7, on changing the culture of the organization.

Examining the Organization. An important aspect of COPPS is that its implementation occurs not over a period of days or weeks but more likely over many months or even years. Like small boats that can shift their direction more quickly than large ships, the bigger the organization the longer it will take to change. Also, throughout the period of change the office of the chief executive is going to be surrounded by turbulence. An executive may be fortunate enough to inherit an organization that is already susceptible to change; however, the executive who inherits a smoothly running bureaucracy, complacent in the status quo, has a tougher job.

With regard to the organization, one of the first steps the executive and managers must take is an *analysis of existing policies and procedures*. Although a need remains for some standing orders and some prepared contingency plans and procedures, in the past such manuals have been used more to allocate blame retrospectively after some error has been discovered. It is not surprising that street officers have adopted a mind-set of doing things "by the book." Many executives have deemphasized their policy and procedure manuals in implementing community policing. As an extreme example, the manual of an English police force had grown to four volumes, each more than three inches thick, totaling more than 2,000 pages of instructions. Under COPPS, the manual was discarded in favor of a one-page "Policy Statement" that gave 11 brief "commandments." (Many chief executives may consider this to be unreasonably brief because of the complexities of the job.) These commandments related more to initiative and "reasonableness of action" than to rules and regulations. Each officer was issued a pocket-size laminate copy of the policy statement.[19]

The organization should conduct an *in-depth analysis of the existing departmental rank structure*, which itself can be a principal obstacle to the effective communication of new values and philosophy throughout the organization. A large metropolitan police force may have 10 or more layers of rank. Contrast this with the Roman Catholic Church (with more than 860 million members), which manages its work with only five layers. The chief executive must talk with the officers. Therefore, it is necessary to ensure that the message not be filtered, doctored, or suppressed.[20]

Human Resources

Human resources constitutes the basis of organizational culture. Developing COPPS as a part of daily police behaviors and practices presents a major challenge. To accomplish this requires that the mechanisms that motivate, challenge, reward, and correct employees' behaviors comport with the principles of COPPS. They include *recruiting, selection, training, performance evaluations, promotions, honors and awards*, and *discipline*, all of which should be reviewed to ensure that they promote and support the tenets of COPPS.

Modeling Behaviors. Recruiting literature should reflect the principles of COPPS. Agencies should actively recruit students, minorities, and women into their organization. Community groups may be helpful in this respect. Advertisements in newspapers or on television and radio shows that target certain populations are also wise. A job task analysis identifying the new knowledge, skills, and abilities needed for the work should be conducted and become a part of the testing process for entry-level employees.

COPPS should be integrated into academy training, field training programs, and in-service training. As was discussed in previous chapters, it is also important to provide training and education to the other city agencies and community, business, and social service organizations so that they understand COPPS. Performance evaluations and reward systems should reflect new job descriptions and officers' application of their COPPS training.

Promotion systems should be expanded from their usual focus on tactical decision making to include knowledge of the research on community policing, and they should test an officer's ability to apply problem solving to various crime and neighborhood problems.

Labor Relations. Another challenge for leadership and administration in the implementation of COPPS centers on labor unions. Since the 1960s police unions and associations have evolved quickly, making great strides in improving wages, benefits, and working conditions. Yet there is a concern about police administrators' ability to run their agencies and the impact of unions on police–community partnerships. Unions are often viewed by administrators and the public as a negative force, focusing only on financial gain and control over administrative policy making without regard for the department or community.

The question relevant to this situation is, "How is the implementation of COPPS affected by this situation?" Or, perhaps more important, "Can COPPS benefit both labor and management?" These questions are important for police administrators who are strategically planning the future of their agencies and considering the initiation of COPPS. The power and influence of unions cannot be overlooked by police administrators.

Does COPPS conflict with the philosophy of police unions? It is understandable that this approach could be construed as antithetical to union interests. For example, COPPS asks officers to assume a proprietary interest in the neighborhoods where they work and to be flexible and creative in their work hours and solutions to problems. This approach often conflicts with collective bargaining contracts in which unions have negotiated for stability of work hours and compensation when working conditions are altered. The idea of civilianization, reductions of rank, and decentralized investigations can also be viewed as a threat to officers' lateral mobility, promotional opportunities, and career development. Labor organizations are also concerned with any proposed changes in shifts, beats, criteria for selection, promotion, discipline, and so on.

It is wise to include labor representatives in the planning and implementation process from the beginning. When the unions are excluded from the planning process, officers perceive the implementation of COPPS as a public relations gimmick in management's interests. It is also important that union leaders understand management's concerns and collaborate in planning an agency's future.

Remember, COPPS is important from both the labor and management perspectives. Both sides are interested in creating a quality work environment for employees. This translates to a healthy and productive work force. COPPS provides officers the opportunity to use their talents. It removes layers of management and quota-driven evaluations that are often opposed by officers.

Field Operations

Specialists or Generalists? The primary concern with field operations is to structure the delivery of patrol services so as to assist officers in dealing with the root causes of persistent community problems. The first issue raised is whether a *specialist or a generalist* approach will be used. As we noted previously, it is not uncommon, especially in larger police agencies, to implement COPPS in an experimental district comprised of a team of specially trained officers. Departmentwide implementation should occur as quickly as possible, however, to eliminate the common criticism that COPPS officers do not do "real police work" and that they receive special privileges.

Decentralized Services. The need for available time to engage in problem solving presents a supervisory challenge that begins with managing CFS. This requires comprehensive workload analysis, call prioritization, alternative call handling, and differential response methods (discussed in Chapter 4). This information helps an agency when its managers are considering a decentralized approach to field operations that involves assigning officers to a beat and shift for a minimum of one year to learn more about a neighborhood's problems. It is also helpful in reconstructing beat boundaries to correspond more closely with neighborhoods.

Decentralized service is an important part of the general scheme of COPPS. Under the traditional, incident-driven style of policing, officers have little permanent territorial responsibility. They know that they may be dispatched to another area at any time and that they are not responsible for anything that occurs on their beat when they are off duty. This responsibility for their area only during a specific period of time reinforces the officer's focus on incidents rather than on long-term area problems. When the chief executive says to the officer, "This area is yours, and nobody else's," however, the territory becomes personalized. The officer's concern for the beat does not end with a tour of duty. Concerned officers will want to know what occurred on their beat while they were off duty and will often make unsolicited follow-up visits, struggling to find causes of incidents that would otherwise be regarded as inconsequential.[21]

Detectives. A matter that relates to field operations and COPPS involves detectives. The detective division may easily view the introduction of COPPS as a matter strictly for the patrol officers; the detectives might believe that "Our job is still to solve crime."[22] Detectives might maintain that attitude until they are removed from the group that reinforces that perception. They have to be incorporated into the COPPS system (see Exhibit 6.3). Valuable intelligence information gained by detectives through investigations can be fed to the patrol division. Also, detectives must believe that crime prevention is their principal obligation and not the exclusive responsibility of the patrol force.

Detectives have opportunities to establish and enhance positive working relationships with victim-advocacy groups, civic organizations, police district advisory councils, and other stakeholders in the system. Detectives, like patrol officers, attend regular community meetings and impart valuable knowledge relating to criminal activities, trends, and patterns. In addition, quicker, easier investigative responses can be realized.

The Top Priority: Patrol Personnel. There is one very important positive aspect of considering whether to implement a COPPS philosophy, one that all chief executives should remember: It encourages many of the activities that patrol officers would like to do, that is, to engage in more inquiry of crime and disorder and get more closure from their work. When asked why they originally wanted to enter policing, officers consistently say that they joined in order to help people.[23] By emphasizing work that addresses people's concerns and giving officers the discretion to develop a solution, COPPS helps make police work more rewarding.

Among the most frequent complaints voiced by patrol officers, however, are that patrol is given little support, they are accorded low esteem by their

---

EXHIBIT 6.3   Investigations in the COPPS Context

One problematic issue for police departments that are implementing COPPS is the appropriate organization of investigative functions. How can agencies structure investigations to best support these approaches? Who in the organization should conduct which types of investigations? Should agencies decentralize investigative functions? Should there be a separate command structure for detectives?

A group of chiefs leading organizations through the change process first identified this whole issue. The National Institute of Justice will fund a research project surveying 900 law enforcement agencies, all those serving populations of at least 50,000 and having at least 100 sworn personnel. The Police Executive Research Forum will ask these agencies about their status with respect to COPPS, as well as detailed questions about the structure of their investigative functions. Researchers will then develop several models of the investigative function in the COPPS context.

Source: Workshop presentation, Mary Ann Wycoff, Police Executive Research Forum, "The 8th Annual International Problem Oriented Policing Conference: Problem Oriented Policing 1997," November 16, 1997, San Diego, California.

---

organization, and they are simply a pool of employees from which to draw for other special assignments. For COPPS to be successful, the agency must ensure that patrol staffing is maintained and that its officers believe that their work is most important to the organization's success.

External Relations

In Chapter 4 we discussed the various stakeholders and partners that police will find in the community for assistance in the COPPS initiative. As was shown in Exhibit 6.2, enlisting the assistance of the community is often a more complex undertaking than one might assume.

Collaborative responses to neighborhood crime and disorder are essential to the success of COPPS. This requires new relationships and the sharing of information and resources among the police and community, local government agencies, service providers, and businesses. Also, police agencies must educate and inform their external partners about police resources and neighborhood problems using surveys, newsletters, community meetings, and public service announcements. The media also provide an excellent opportunity for police to educate the community. Press releases about collaborative problem solving efforts should be sent to the media, and news conferences should be held to discuss major crime reduction efforts.

Another essential consideration of implementing COPPS is the solicitation and establishment of political support for the concept. The political environment

Allowing officers to identify and resolve neighborhood problems can improve morale by making the job more rewarding. (*Courtesy* Community Policing Consortium)

varies considerably, say, with the strong mayor and council-manager forms of government. These and other rapidly changing political environments make the implementation of COPPS more difficult—especially when we add to the cauldron the at-will employment of most police executives.

Exhibit 6.4 shows how Sacramento, California, approached external relations by providing neighborhood services.

Elected officials must provide direction and support through policy development and resource allocation. This may be accomplished in several ways. For instance, in Tempe, Arizona, the city council passed a resolution that established guidelines for the creation of a Neighborhood Assistance Office. The program's goal was "fostering a partnership among the city council, city staff and residents, and the creation of an environment in which citizens are afforded an opportunity to participate in city affairs in an advisory or advocacy role."[24] In essence, the Neighborhood Assistance Office was to be a conduit for communication between the city government and citizens:

> Implementation of the Neighborhood Associations included several important steps on the part of the City: maintaining a register and mailing list of existing organizations and their officers and bylaws; mailing newsletters for Neighborhood Associations; providing insurance coverage for use of

---

Exhibit 6.4 External Relations: Neighborhood Services in Sacramento

Recently Sacramento, California, decided to reorganize its city services into four geographically based system areas. This configuration mirrored the Sacramento Police Department's (SPD) patrol deployment boundaries. A new city department called Neighborhood Services was developed that included such elements as recreation, housing and building inspections, nuisance abatement, community centers, planning, parks, human services, and code enforcement. The four area managers of this new department and the four SPD patrol captains cooperated to implement new levels of problem solving. The increased contact between the departments and community members occurred simultaneously at several levels. Problem solving is a collaboration among the SPD, Neighborhood Services, and the community, facilitating the dissemination of information and enabling them to identify issues quickly. Community mobilization has spread from community associations to business associations, recreation programs, political action committees, and redevelopment project boards. With this increase of community input, a variety of responses enhances and continues the problem solving cycle.

Source: Workshop presentation, Mike Busch, Sacramento Police Department, "The 8th Annual International Problem Oriented Policing Conference: Problem Oriented Policing 1997," November 16, 1997, San Diego, California.

---

school facilities for neighborhood meetings; coordinating annual citywide informational meetings; arranging for city staff and officials to speak at association meetings; and responding to concerns and questions raised by individual associations.[25]

TYING IT ALL TOGETHER

Figure 6.3 ties together these four key areas—leadership and administration, human resources, field operations, and external relations—illustrating the principle components of implementation.

An Example: Montgomery County, Maryland

Exhibits 6.5 through 6.11 show the Montgomery County, Maryland, Department of Police Strategic Implementation Plan for moving to COPPS. Provided are the plan's vision statement (Exhibit 6.5), mission statement (Exhibit 6.6), statement of

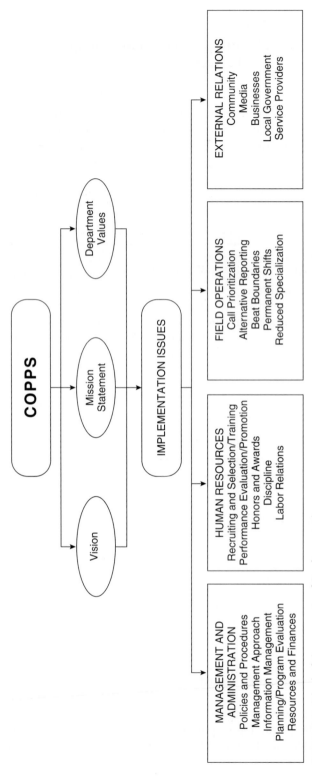

Figure 6.3 Principal Components of Implementation

EXHIBIT 6.5   Vision Statement

The Montgomery County Police will provide the highest quality of police services by working in partnership with the community to improve the quality of life within Montgomery County, while at the same time maintaining respect for individual rights and human dignity. The Department recognizes the value and importance of its employees and will ensure that all employees are treated equitably and fairly. The Department is committed to providing its members with the quality of leadership, training, and equipment necessary to perform its mission.

EXHIBIT 6.6   Mission Statement

We, the Montgomery County Department of Police, are committed to providing the highest quality of police services by empowering our members and the community to work in partnership with the goal of improving the quality of life within Montgomery County, while at the same time maintaining respect for individual rights and human dignity.

---

organizational values (Exhibit 6.7), goals and objectives for empowering the community and police employees (Exhibit 6.8), and goals and objectives for the problem solving strategy (Exhibit 6.9); additional goals and objectives are provided in the agency's planning document for accountability, partnership, and organizational development.

Exhibits 6.10 and 6.11 are examples of some of the *strategies* to be employed by the department to achieve its goals. Exhibit 6.10 shows the strategies for *empowerment* and presents the desired time frame (in years), fiscal impact, and assignment of responsibility for the strategies to occur. There are actually more than 70 strategies listed in the agency's goal for empowerment. Shown in the exhibit are such diverse matters as developing media interest; creating a Speakers Bureau; developing Neighborhood Watch Groups and a newsletter; and creating a cable television program and citizens' police academy open forums. Other strategies that are not shown include such tasks as decentralizing the organization, establishing satellite police facilities, creating a police cadet program, revising agency policies, developing logos and slogans, and amending the police recruiting and hiring process.

Exhibit 6.11 provides Montgomery County's strategies for implementing problem solving. The strategies are quite diverse and number about 30. In addition to the strategies shown in the exhibit, including training personnel, creating relevant manuals, expanding Neighborhood Watch Programs, and developing a Community

---

Exhibit 6.7 Organizational Values

Partnership

We are committed to working in partnership with the community and each other to identify and resolve issues which impact public safety.

Respect

We are committed to respecting individual rights, human dignity, and the value of all members of the community and the department.

Integrity

We are committed to nurturing the public trust by holding ourselves accountable to the highest standards of professionalism and ethics.

Dedication

We are committed to providing the highest quality of professional law enforcement service to the community with the goal of enhancing the quality of life within Montgomery County.

Empowerment

We are committed to empowering our members and the community to resolve problems by creating an environment that encourages solutions that address the needs of the community.

. . . pride in our community, pride in our department, pride in ourselves

---

Services Section within each policing district, others include such tasks as using foot and bicycle patrols, initiating a new Arrest Processing and Transport Unit, adjusting patrol boundaries and beats following workload studies, beefing up the planning unit, and coordinating with other governmental agencies.

To further demonstrate the implementation process, Table 6.1 shows the specific sequential steps taken by the Baltimore, Maryland, Police Department toward implementation of its COPPS philosophy, following the development of appropriate vision, mission, and values statements for the department.

Exhibit 6.8   Goal 1.0: Empowerment

Empowerment includes the delegation of the authority and responsibility necessary to identify and resolve those public safety related issues confronting our communities. Empowerment requires that all of the participants in this effort share the responsibility for its success or failure. Empowerment involves not only police employees, but also members of the community and local government.

Community policing recognizes that the community should have input into matters which affect its quality of life. An empowered community shares the responsibility to better itself and can assist the police in defining and prioritizing problem areas and designing and implementing strategies to reduce or eliminate these problems. Through this process a sense of partnership with the police is created and strengthened.

Police employees are empowered to analyze problems and design effective solutions. Most community problems can best be resolved by allowing individual beat officers the flexibility to solve the problem rather than just "clear the call." The resources of the agency must be focused on assisting their officers in problem resolution. In order to be successful, the active support and participation of the local government is essential.

1.0 Empowerment

The process of delegating to the police and the community the responsibility for prioritizing concerns, decision making and distribution of resources.

Goal Objectives

1.1 Decentralize department decision making to ensure that this process occurs at the lowest level possible.

1.2 Decentralize, where and when possible, the department in function and structure.

1.3 Increase community involvement in identifying and resolving issues which impact public safety.

1.4 Develop equitable recruiting practices within the department consistent with community characteristics and needs.

1.5 Develop equitable promotional practices and career opportunities within the department consistent with community characteristics and needs.

Exhibit 6.9 Goal 2.0: Problem Solving

Community policing emphasizes the need for a problem solving approach to reduce the incidence and the fear of crime. In many instances, it will be more effective and efficient to spend several hours (or even days) to thoroughly address and eliminate a problem than it will be to repeatedly dispatch cars to the same call day after day, week after week, month after month, and in some cases, year after year.

Problem solving requires that officers be allowed to not only try the safe and proven traditional solutions, but also new, imaginative, and even unorthodox solutions. Not all solutions will be successful, as with any solution there is the risk of failure.

Risk taking is a necessity in community policing. Problem solving requires that the department not only accept risk taking but encourage it. Employees should be commended for their successes and not chastised for their failures. A common axiom in community policing is "zero risk equals zero success."

2.0 Problem Solving

The analysis of a recurring problem to determine its cause and to devise solutions to permanently eliminate it. Problem solving also includes implementing the chosen solution. Problem solving involves risk taking.

Goal Objectives

2.1 Reduce fear of crime and conditions that contribute to crime and disorder through community policing strategies.

2.2 Reallocate individual and unit workloads to facilitate innovation and problem solving opportunities.

2.3 Establish a permanent planning unit to support and facilitate current and future departmental planning strategies.

2.4 Identify changes needed to existing laws and ordinances and propose new legislation to facilitate community policing strategies.

Exhibit 6.10   Goal 1.0: Empowerment

Strategies	Time Frame (Years)	Fiscal Impact	Assignment of Responsibility
1.3.5 Develop media interest by providing examples of community policing successes and human interest stories involving the community. CALEA 54.1.1, 54.2.1, 54.2.8	Immediate	No	Media Services
1.3.6 Create a Speakers Bureau by utilizing trained officers and citizens to initiate a communications link to the community. CALEA 54.2.5	Immediate	No	Office of Comm. Policing
1.3.7 Provide established neighborhood watch groups and citizen associations with an overview of community policing and use of problem solving in the community. CALEA 54.2.1	.5	No	Office of Comm. Policing Speakers Bureau
1.3.8 Provide a newsletter for citizen groups at the district level, published on a regular basis. CALEA 54.2.3	Ongoing	Yes	Field Svcs. Bureau District Commanders
1.3.9 Utilize a local newspaper to reach a large section of our county by securing a regular column. CALEA 54.1.4	.5	Yes	Media Services
1.3.10 Create a monthly cable television program to promote community policing. CALEA 54.1.4	1	Yes	Media Services Office of Comm. Policing
1.3.11 Provide one telephone number that utilizes a tree flow to provide information and referral service for county citizens.	.5	Yes	Media Services Volunteer Services Office of Comm. Policing

1.3.12 Develop an improved resource guide for the community. (Also identified under *Partnership 4.1.32*.) CALEA 4.1.5	.5	Yes	Volunteer Serices Office of Comm. Policing
1.3.13 Provide a Citizens Academy at the PSTA to involve citizens in various topics. CALEA 54.2.3	1	Yes	Training Office of Comm. Policing
1.3.14 Provide reality tapes to the library system on various police topics. CALEA 54.2.3	.5	Yes	Media Services Office of Comm. Policing
1.3.15 Provide open forums to allow citizens to address problems and provide suggestions. CALEA 54.2.3	.5	No	Field Svcs. Bureau District Commanders

GENERAL OBSTACLES

Several possible obstacles that can militate against the implementation of COPPS have been identified:

1. *Police leadership.* Many police executives pride themselves on being hard-line disciplinarians, unbending in the governance of their organizations. They may rule through coercion, fear, and intimidation. Their officers may be legalistic in style and reactive in nature. There may be a distinct separation between labor and management, as well as an "us-versus-them" schism between the police and the public.

2. *Police organization.* Traditional crime-fighting organizational values provide a strong barrier to COPPS because, in order for implementation of COPPS to occur, the very core of the organization's culture must change (discussed in Chapter 7). There also exists in some organizations what has been termed a "small cadre of nonproductive, abusive, malcontents." Not until police officers at all levels begin to clean house will the community accept them as trusting, civil, sensitive, and responsive representatives, which is a vital step toward implementing COPPS.

3. *Political leadership.* Politics are involved in every aspect of policing in America. Every jurisdiction is beholden to some extent to elected politicians, who in turn serve at the pleasure of their constituents. Politicians set the tone for the policing of a community.

4. *Community diversity.* Until officers can fully embrace our diverse communities, it is not likely that the concept can be implemented in those neighborhoods.[26]

Exhibit 6.11   Goal 2.0: Problem Solving

Strategies	Time Frame (Years)	Fiscal Impact	Assignment of Responsibility
2.1.1 Institute a training program to train all members of the department in the concepts and philosophies of community policing. CALEA 33.6.2	Ongoing	Yes	Office of Comm. Policing Training
2.1.2 Develop a training manual for problem solving techniques. CALEA 33.6.2	Completed	No	Field Svcs. Bureau Office of Comm. Policing Training
2.1.3 Assign beat officers the responsibility of identifying problems within their beat and developing plans to remedy the problem. CALEA 41.2.1, 41.2.5, 54.2.4, 54.2.5	Immediate	No	Field Svcs. Bureau District Commanders
2.1.4 Increase district crime analysts' interaction with beat officers by jointly identifying crime patterns or problem areas through analysis. CALEA 15.1.6	Ongoing	No	Field Svcs. Bureau Central Crime Analyst District Crime Analysts District Commanders
2.1.5 Expand and publicize the Neighborhood Watch Programs. CALEA 45.2.2	1–2	Yes	Field Svcs. Bureau District Commanders Community Svcs. Section District Comm. Svcs. Officer
2.1.6 Reinstitute and publicize "Operation ID." CALEA 45.2.2	1–2	Yes	Field Svcs. Bureau District Commanders Crime Prevention Section District Comm. Svcs. Officer
2.1.7 Train patrol officers in specific skill areas of investigations and innovative investigative techniques. CALEA 33.6.2	1–2	Yes	Training Investigative Svcs. Bureau

2.1.8	Develop and maintain a Community Services Section within each district. This section will coordinate community meetings and serve as a liaison. CALEA 45.2.1	Completed	No	Field Svcs. Bureau District Commanders
2.1.9	Implement a training program to educate resident managers and rental property owners. CALEA 33.7.1	2–3	No	District Comm. Svcs. Officer

Notwithstanding these conceivable obstacles, the potential for their coming into play and creating problems for COPPS implementation will be minimized if the guidelines provided earlier in this chapter are followed.

TEN WAYS TO UNDERMINE COPPS

In closing this chapter on implementation, Exhibit 6.12 offers for the tradition-bound chief John Eck's[27] "ten things you can do to undermine" COPPS—a prescription for preventing COPPS from gaining a foothold for many years to come. Many of these tactics are being practiced today, sometimes out of ignorance and sometimes intentionally. With apologies to the U.S. Surgeon General, we issue a prefatory warning: "Practicing these techniques in a police department may be hazardous to the health of community policing and problem solving."

SUMMARY

This chapter has shown how to plan and implement the COPPS concept after assessing community needs and developing a planning document. Four keys to successful implementation—leadership and administration, human resources, field operations, and external relations—were examined, and we considered several obstacles that can undermine COPPS.

It should be evident that there is no substitute for having a well-thought-out, laid-out plan of implementation for the COPPS philosophy. As with any new venture, there must be a "road map" to show the executive and the agency how to travel the highway, in order to reach the ultimate destination.

Table 6.1 Implementation in Baltimore, Maryland

Several implementation issues had to be addressed. The values statement was widely disseminated across the community and the department. The public was challenged to come forth when they believed a value standard had been violated. The policing strategy became neighborhood based and officers were shown that they were respected for the enormous contributions they could and did make to the community. Restructuring of the department, especially the Operations Bureau, was necessary. Each commander was given total responsibility for policing the neighborhoods in that district. There were a number of other important steps in the implementation sequence:

- *Fiscal support:* A commitment by the city was necessary to provide the department with the capital needed for maximum effectiveness, as well as a commitment by the department that resources would be carefully and effectively utilized.
- *Organizational structure and management systems:* The organizational hierarchy was flattened so that there was a minimum of supervisory and management levels between the police commissioner and the officers assigned to field service delivery in the city's neighborhoods. Investigative functions were decentralized as well, and civilianization was increased.
- *Community policing district deployment model:* Decisions had to be made concerning such matters as duties and job descriptions of COPPS officers, functions to be performed, staffing levels, and neighborhood boundaries.
- *Internal and external marketing:* The philosophy had to be marketed in order to succeed. All members of the department had to be oriented to the philosophy and massive changes had to be undertaken with regard to the department's handling of 911 CFS. The city council, other government agencies, and citizens were made fully aware of the changes proposed and positive results to be expected.
- *Deployment:* A new set of district and post boundaries were created that matched the major neighborhood areas of the city, ensuring that key "activity" centers (those areas generating the greatest number of CFS) were in the middle of districts and posts, thus providing for strong accountability for policing those areas. Patrol staffing was given the highest priority in the department.
- *Training:* COPPS training was developed for patrol officers and detectives, based on nationally recognized, state-of-the-art police problem solving methodology. To support the curricula, new materials were developed reflecting the department's new orientation. Lieutenants, sergeants, and patrol officers were trained in facilitation and COPPS skills.
- *Interagency support:* A problem solving methodology was developed to link all levels of the department with other agencies of government.
- *Quality control:* A new system was developed for evaluating police success at all levels—as a department, within a district, and on individual posts. A new set of performance standards was developed.
- *Recruitment and personnel management:* A new recruitment strategy was initiated that attracted young men and women to join the department, desiring to serve the community and become neighborhood COPPS officers. This ensured that the department remained on a "fast track" toward guaranteeing that the diversity of the community was reflected in all ranks.
- *Profiling neighborhoods:* Officers in each neighborhood of the city profiled their post, developing a "picture" of the neighborhood's priorities, resources, institutions, and problems of crime, fear, and violence. They also developed an action plan to address the neighborhood's concerns, in collaboration with local residents and business people.

Source: Baltimore Police Department, *Implementation Task Force Report: Assessment of the Department* (Baltimore, Md.: Author, no date), pp. 10–12.

Exhibit 6.12 Ten Ways to Undermine COPPS

1. *Oversell it:* COPPS should be sold as the panacea for every ill that plagues the city, the nation, and civilization. Some of the evils you may want to claim COPPS will eliminate are crime, fear of crime, racism, police misuse of force, homelessness, drug abuse, gangs, and other social problems. COPPS can address some of these concerns in specific situations, but by building up the hopes and expectations of the public, the press, and politicians, you can set the stage for later attacks on COPPS when it does not deliver.

2. *Don't be specific:* This suggestion is a corollary of the first principle. Never define what you mean by the following terms: community, service, effectiveness, empowerment, neighborhood, communication, problem solving. Use these and other terms indiscriminately, interchangeably, and whenever possible. At first, people will think the department is going to do something meaningful and won't ask for details. Once people catch on, you can blame the amorphous nature of COPPS and go back to what you were doing before.

3. *Create a special unit or group:* Less than 10 percent of the department should be engaged in this effort, lest COPPS really catch on. Since the "grand design" is possibly the return to conventional policing anyway (once everyone has attacked COPPS), there is no sense in involving more than a few officers. Also, special units are popular with the press and politicians.

4. *Create a soft image:* The best image for COPPS will be a uniformed female officer hugging a small child. This caring and maternal image will warm the hearts of community members suspicious of police, play to traditional stereotypes of sexism within policing, and turn off most cops.

5. *Leave the impression that COPPS is only for minority neighborhoods:* This is a corollary of items 3 and 4. Since a small group of officers will be involved, only a few neighborhoods can receive their services. Place the token COPPS officers in areas like public housing. With any luck, racial antagonism will undercut the approach. It will appear that minority, poor neighborhoods are not getting the "tough on crime" approach they need.

6. *Divorce COPPS officers from "regular" police work:* This is an expansion of the soft image concept. If the COPPS officers do not handle calls or make arrests, but instead throw block parties, speak to community groups, walk around talking to kids, visit schools, and so on, they will not be perceived as "real" police officers to their colleagues. This will

further undermine their credibility and ability to accomplish anything of significance.

7. *Obfuscate means and ends:* Whenever describing COPPS, never make the methods for accomplishing the objective subordinate to the objective. Instead, make the means more important than the ends, or at least put them on equal footing. For example, to reduce drug dealing in a neighborhood, make certain that the tactics necessary (arrests, community meetings, etc.) are as important as, or more important than, the objective. These tactics can occupy everyone's time but still leave the drug problem unresolved. Always remember: The means are ends, in and of themselves.

8. *Present community members with problems and plans:* Whenever meeting with community members, officers should listen carefully and politely and then elaborate on how the department will enforce the law. If the community members like the plan, go ahead. If they do not, continue to be polite and ask them to go on a ride-along or witness a drug raid. This avoids having to change the department's operations while demonstrating how difficult police work is, and why nothing can be accomplished. In the end, they will not get their problems solved, but will see how nice the police are.

9. *Never try to understand why problems occur:* Do not let officers gain knowledge about the underlying causes of the problems; COPPS should not include any analysis of the problem and as little information as possible should be sought from the community. Keep officers away from computer terminals; mandate that officers get permission to talk to members of any other agency; do not allow COPPS officers to go off their assigned areas to collect information; prevent access to research conducted on similar problems; suppress listening skills.

10. *Never publicize a success:* Some rogue officers will not get the message and will go out anyway and gather enough information to solve problems. Try to ignore these examples of effective policing and make sure that no one else hears about them. When you cannot ignore them, describe them in the least meaningful way (item 2). Talk about the wonders of empowerment and community meetings. Describe the hours of foot patrol, the new mountain bikes, or shoulder patches. In every problem solved, there is usually some tactic or piece of equipment that can be highlighted at the expense of the accomplishment itself. When all else fails, reprimand the COPPS officer for not wearing a hat.

Source: John E. Eck, "Helpful Hints for the Tradition-Bound Chief," *Fresh Perspectives* (Washington, D.C.: Police Executive Research Forum, June 1992), pp. 1–7.

NOTES

1. Robert Trojanowicz, quoted in Harry Sloan, Grand Rapids, Michigan, Police Department Web page, http://www.grpolice.grant-rapids.mi.us/default.htm, October 20, 2000, p. 1.
2. Eton Lawrence, "Strategic Thinking: A Discussion Paper," Research Directorate, Policy, Research, and Communications Branch, Public Service Commission of Canada, Ottawa, Ontario, Canada, April 27, 1999, p. 6.
3. *Ibid.*, pp. 6–7.
4. *Ibid.*
5. L. Herocleous, "Strategic Thinking or Strategic Planning?" *Long Range Planning* 31:481–87.
6. Internet Nonprofit Center, "What Is Strategic Planning?" (San Francisco, Calif.: Author, Support Center, 2000), p. 1.
7. "Brief History of Strategic Planning," http://www.des.calstate.edu/glossary.html, September 24, 2000, p. 2.
8. http://www.usdoj.gov/jmd/mps/strategic2000_2005/index.htm.
9. Herman Goldstein, *Problem-Oriented Policing* (New York: McGraw-Hill, 1990), p. 172.
10. Solicitor General of Canada, Ministry of the Solicitor General of Ontario, *Problem Oriented Policing: A Manual for the Development and Implementation of Problem Oriented Policing* (Ontario, Canada: Author, 1991), p. 36.
11. Gregory Saville and D. Kim Rossmo, "Striking a Balance: Lessons from Community-Oriented Policing in British Columbia, Canada" (unpublished manuscript, June 1993), pp. 29–30.
12. Charles S. Bullock and Charles M. Lamb (eds.), *Implementation of Civil Rights Policy* (Monterey, Calif.: Brooks/Cole, 1984).
13. Ronald W. Glensor and Kenneth J. Peak, "Implementing Change: Community-Oriented Policing and Problem Solving," *FBI Law Enforcement Bulletin* 7 (July 1996):14–20.
14. John E. Eck and William Spelman, *Problem-Solving: Problem-Oriented Policing in Newport News* (Washington, D.C.: Police Executive Research Forum, 1987), pp. 100–101.
15. Malcolm K. Sparrow, *Implementing Community Policing* (Washington, D.C.: National Institute of Justice, "Perspectives on Policing," no. 9, November 1988), pp. 2–3.
16. George L. Kelling and William J. Bratton, *Implementing Community Policing: The Administrative Problem* (Washington, D.C.: U.S. Department of Justice, National Institute of Justice, "Perspectives on Policing," no. 17, July 1993), p. 4.
17. *Ibid.*, p. 9.
18. *Ibid.*, p. 11.
19. Sparrow, *Implementing Community Policing*, pp. 4–5.
20. *Ibid.*, p. 5.
21. *Ibid.*, p. 6.
22. *Ibid.*, p. 7.
23. Jesse Rubin, "Police Identity and the Police Role," in *Issues in Police Patrol: A Book of Readings*, eds. Thomas J. Sweeney and William Ellingsworth (Kansas City, Mo.: Kansas City Police Department, 1973); John Van Maanen, "Police Socialization: A Longitudinal Examination of Job Attitudes in an Urban Police Department," *Administrative Science Quarterly* 20 (1975):207–28.
24. Don Cassano and Carol Smith, *Establishing and Sustaining Political Support for Problem Oriented/Community Policing* (Tempe, Ariz.: Tempe City Council Representatives, 1992), p. 74.
25. *Ibid.*, pp. 74–75.
26. Adapted from George E. Rush, "Community Policing: Overcoming the Obstacles," *The Police Chief* (October 1992):50, 52, 54–55.
27. John E. Eck, "Helpful Hints for the Tradition-Bound Chief," *Fresh Perspectives* (Washington, D.C.: Police Executive Research Forum, June 1992), pp. 1–7.

From Recruit to Chief
Changing the Agency Culture

> **Where there is no vision, a people perish.**
> —Ralph Waldo Emerson

Introduction

Police agencies have a life and culture of their own. Powerful forces have a much stronger influence over how a department conducts its business than do managers of the department, the courts, legislatures, politicians, and members of the community. As Herman Goldstein observed, "Against this background, many of the exhortations for change do, indeed, look naive, and the elaborate schemes for 'improving the police' unlikely to succeed."[1] Nonetheless, willingness to change is a fundamental requirement of community oriented policing and problem solving (COPPS); police agencies must modify their culture from top to bottom. This chapter addresses that agency imperative. Change is never easy, however, because there is so much uncertainty accompanying it.

We begin this chapter with a discussion of change within organizations generally, including some obstacles to innovation and the requirements of effecting smooth, planned change. Then we turn specifically to change in police organizations, beginning with a look at the traditional culture and management style that prevail in many agencies, focusing on how change must occur to accommodate COPPS. The roles of three key leaders in this process—chief executives (and their precarious political position as innovators), middle managers, and rank-and-file officers—are then covered, including how sufficient time may be allocated for the latter to engage in problem solving activities. In this vein we also examine some methods and challenges involved with recruiting problem solvers under the COPPS philosophy. We conclude the chapter with some case studies of agencies that have modified their culture for adopting the COPPS approach.

CHANGE IN ORGANIZATIONS: A FORMULA

Organizational change occurs when an organization adopts new ideas or behaviors.[2] Any change in the organization involves an attempt to persuade employees to change their behavior and their relationships with one another. Therefore, it is not surprising that most people find change uncomfortable. Studies on change in organizations have shown that only about 10 percent of the people in most organizations will actively embrace change. Approximately 80 percent will wait to be convinced or wait until the change is unavoidable. The remaining 10 percent will actively resist change. For these people, change is very upsetting; they may even seek to subvert or sabotage the process.[3]

This resistance to change is reflected in the "change equation":[4] Discomfort (the case for change) + Vision + Steps must be greater than Resistance to change).

$$D + V + S >> R$$

Managers and supervisors must communicate with officers to ensure that the values they express reflect those of the department.
(*Courtesy* NYPD Photo Unit)

D includes those compelling reasons for and against change in an agency or community, such as existing supports for and barriers against change. The *V* requires the leadership to consider changes that will have to occur with respect to related public institutions, management practices, individual behaviors, organizational culture, and the community at large. The *S* includes those steps that must be developed in order to leverage supports and overcome barriers to change.[5]

Usually when change is proposed, an innovative idea is introduced and behavioral changes are supposed to follow. Consequently, the ultimate success of any organizational change depends on how well the organization can alter the behavioral patterns of its employees. Employee behavior is influenced by factors such as leadership styles, motivational techniques, informal relationships, and organization and job design. To bring about timely change, managers need to consider why people resist change and how resistance can be overcome.[6]

As indicated earlier, probably the most common characteristic of change is people's resistance to it. Generally, people do not like to change their behavior, and adaptation to a new environment or methods often results in feelings of stress or other forms of psychological discomfort. Resistance to change is likely when employees do not clearly understand the purpose, mechanics, or consequences of a planned change because of inadequate or misperceived communication. If employees are not told how they will be affected by change, rumors and speculation will follow, and resistance and even sabotage can ensue.[7]

Those who resist change are sometimes coerced into accepting it. Although coercion may be immediately effective and lead to compliance, the long-range results will certainly be harmful. Change in police agencies, particularly major changes, are frequently characterized by the use of centralized decision making and coercive tactics. Management and employees often have an adversarial relationship. Management might assume that because many employees do not understand the need for the change and will resist it anyway, there is no need to involve them in the process, and they must be forced to go along. Some managers might even hope that those persons resisting the change will retire or resign. These are inappropriate assumptions; coercion should be used as a last resort.[8]

By using task forces, ad hoc committees, group seminars, and other participatory techniques, employees can become directly involved in planning for change. By thoroughly discussing and debating the issues, an accurate understanding and unbiased analysis of the situation is likely to result.[9]

REQUIREMENTS FOR PLANNED CHANGE

Radical versus Gradual Change

Psychologist Kurt Lewin is often considered the father of modern organizational change theory. He coined the term *group dynamics* and was one of the first people to observe that leader behavior could shape culture during organizational change. Working with anthropologist Margaret Mead during World War II, Lewin established the concept of participative management: People are more likely to modify their own behavior and carry out decisions when they participate in problem analysis and solution.

Lewin believed change was a three-phase process: unfreezing, changing, and refreezing (see Table 7.1). He believed that people are naturally resistant to change, but meanwhile the environment is changing. To create change, "unfreezing" the organization is necessary; this includes overcoming the negative forces that cause people to resist change through new or disconcerting information. "Changing" is the change in attitudes, values, feelings, and behaviors of the people, and it occurs when people discuss and plan new actions. "Refreezing" occurs when the organization reaches a new status quo, with the support mechanisms in place to maintain the desired behaviors.

Any police executive contemplating change should do so in a manner that offers the greatest possibility of success. As Charles Swanson, Leonard Territo, and Robert Taylor noted:

> Conventional wisdom about change states that the way to change an organization is to bring in a new top executive, give the individual his or her head (and maybe a hatchet), and let the individual make the changes that he or she deems necessary. What the conventional wisdom overlooks are the long-term consequences of unilateral, top-down change.[10]

The problem, then, with radical and unilateral change is the possibility of a severe backlash in the organization; a complementary problem for changes that are made very gradually is that after many months or a few years of meetings, discussion, and planning sessions, nothing much has actually happened in the organization. Finding an appropriate pace for change to occur—neither too quickly and radically nor too slowly and gradually—is one of the most critical problems of planned organizational change. The readiness of the organization for change is a problem for which no easy resolutions are available.[11]

Sometimes a great deal can be learned by studying the success and failure patterns of organizations that have undertaken planned change. A survey of 18 studies of organizational change found the following "successful" change patterns:

- Being spread throughout the organization
- Producing positive changes in line and staff attitudes
- Prompting people to behave more effectively in solving problems
- Resulting in improved organizational performance[12]

TABLE 7.1 **Lewin's Process Model of Change**

Unfreezing	Changing	Refreezing
The process by which people become aware of the need for change	The movement from the old way of doing things to a new way	Making new behaviors relatively permanent and resistant to change

Avoiding the "Bombshell" Technique

Police organizations develop considerable inertia and can develop a resistance to change. Having a strong personal commitment to the values with which they have "grown up" in the organization, patrol officers may find any hint of proposed change in the department extremely threatening. Therefore, the chief executive who simply announces that COPPS is now the order of the day—dropping the "bombshell"—without a carefully designed plan for implementing that change is in danger of "losing traction" and of throwing the entire force into confusion. Additionally, the chief executive confronts a host of difficult issues: What structural changes are needed, if any? How do we get the people on the beat to behave differently? What should we tell the public and when? How fast can we bring about this change? Do we have enough external support?[13]

Changing Organizational Values

A related subject is that of values in police organizations, discussed briefly in Chapter 6. All organizations have values—the beliefs that guide an organization and the behavior of its employees.[14] Police departments are powerfully influenced by their values, and policing styles reflect a department's values.

The Honolulu Police Department displays its values—"Integrity/Respect/
Fairness"—on its vehicles.

COPPS reflects a set of values, rather than a technical orientation toward the police function. There is a service orientation, which means that citizens are to be treated with respect at all times. And when riding in patrol vehicles, supervisors and managers must listen for the "talk of the department" to determine whether values expressed by officers reflect those of the department.

Also, values are no longer hidden but serve as the basis for citizen understanding of the police function, judgments of police success, and employee understanding of what the police agency seeks to achieve.[15] Values are a guidepost by which the agency will provide service to the community and a means by which the community can evaluate the agency.

THE PREVAILING POLICE CULTURE

Although we discussed the professional model of policing in Chapter 1, we briefly revisit it to see how it can and often does operate to choke the life out of innovative efforts.

Debilitating Beliefs

We need to remember that the cornerstone of contemporary policing remains that the police exist, in their own view, as impartial and professional crime fighters. This image is what is discussed at budget time and at civic dinners; it is the face that is presented to the public. Moreover, behind this belief are several other more powerful beliefs that often run counter to what is printed in operating manuals or stated as values (when they exist). These other beliefs, the building blocks of contemporary police culture, are said to be "the truths that officers feel in their bones, the touchstones that—unless changed—will continue to govern their behavior and attitudes."[16] According to Malcolm Sparrow, Mark Moore, and David Kennedy, they are as follows (we have inserted some parenthetical comments as well):

1. *We are the only real crime fighters. Crime fighting is what the public wants from us. Other agencies, public or private, only play at it.* In practice, this belief prevents the police from wanting to share their crime fighting burden with the public; it also isolates the police from the citizens and groups who share their concern about crime and would be quite willing to engage in crime-control efforts.

2. *No one else understands the real nature of police work. That is no one outside the police service—academics, politicians, and lawyers in particular—can comprehend what we have to do. The public is generally naive about police work.* This belief is true—the public is actually quite uninformed about the nature of police work and crime fighting. But the maintenance of this belief by the police also works to prevent any kind of meaningful, open discussion with the community about the police role. (This belief also denies the police a valuable resource and information in their efforts.)

3. *Loyalty to colleagues counts above everything else. We have to stick together. Everyone else—including the public, politicians, and especially senior officers— seems to be out to make our job difficult.* (This elitist and parochial attitude breeds corrupt values and ignores the real purpose of policing: to serve the public, not the self.)

4. *It is impossible to win the war against crime without bending the rules. We are hopelessly shackled by unrealistic constraints foisted on us by civil liberties groups, thanks to the fecklessness of politicians.* Beliefs 3 and 4 serve to shield and encourage corruption in police agencies. Even the truly incorruptible officers are prevented from reporting their less honorable colleagues. These beliefs also, on occasion, create the kind of police behavior the public fears the most: use of forged evidence, falsified warrants, and "street justice."

5. *Members of the public are basically unsupportive and unreasonably demanding. They all seem to think they know our job better than we do. They only want us when they need something done.* This belief works to create a bunker mentality. It combines a pessimistic outlook on the community in general with a cynical view of human nature. It can work to make officers callous and even brutal. (This belief also ignores the many successful problem solving efforts surfacing around the country that show the public's legitimate interest in helping the police.)

6. *Patrol work is the pits. The detective branch and other specialties are relatively glorious, because they tackle serious crime. Patrol work is only for those who aren't smart enough to get out of it.* The work of detectives is viewed as superior to crime prevention, thereby reducing the importance of contact with the general public. This belief also condemns all of the noncrime functions patrol officers perform—traffic control, emergency medical treatment, welfare tasks, and so on. Officers engaged in COPPS work are the "grin-and-wave" or "rubber gun" squads.[17]

At worst, these six beliefs can encourage and legitimize insensitive, unproductive, and even illegal behavior. At best, they promote organizational insularity, introspection, and detachment. Unfortunately, these beliefs fashion the behavior of the police and reflect the values that are taught recruits informally. Replacing them with more open, realistic, productive, and honorable beliefs must be a priority of any new policing model or philosophy.

The traditional police culture (discussed next) must change if agencies are to become open to new ideas and be successful in the eyes of their "customers." By way of analogy, one only need look at General Motors and Harley Davidson during the 1970s and 1980s. The quality of their products was poor, customer satisfaction was low, profits were dropping, and their sales were being outstripped by Japanese imports. The problem was that the corporate vision was not what consumers wanted. Eventually, by listening to what customers wanted, implementing TQM (discussed in Chapter 3), and empowering assembly line workers to use more discretion to ensure quality manufacturing, the corporate culture in both

The notion of adventure and winning the "war on crime" permeates police culture and is supported by the print media and in the movies. (*Courtesy* Reno, Nevada, Police Department)

organizations changed to a quality management style. This analogy to policing should be clear: Organizations need to evolve with society and their clientele.[18]

YE OLDE MANAGEMENT STYLE

The Bureaucracy of Policing

Many police departments maintain voluminous policy and procedures manuals, covering a wide range of circumstances and crimes that can occur. They set forth who is to make which decisions and whose approval must be obtained before certain actions may be taken. They are believed to be both useful reference books and, for many officers, instruments of control, to be used when something goes wrong and "you need to be able to turn to it to find out whose head goes on the block."[19] Thus, tight control, with clear-cut rules enforced by rigorous disciplinary systems, remains the predominant management style. The persistence of this style has been ensured by the propensity of many police agencies to hire ex-military personnel, for whom familiarity with weapons, military bearing, chain-of-command, and physical fitness are stressed. Precision marching is still taught at some police academies, although it obviously has little application on the job.

The professional era of policing (discussed in Chapter 1) inculcated this militaristic style of management and established rigid hierarchical lines of control. As a result, chief executives often place great emphasis on their officers to "go by the book" (the operations manual) and try to avoid any chance of something going awry that would make their department (and themselves) look bad. Change can bring about criticism, thus tight control with strict discipline becomes their watchword. Their shift commanders feel the same pressures, often being praised by the chief if they "run a tight ship." They are naturally loathe for their subordinates to initiate changes. Their sergeants are expected to maintain strict control over patrol officers. It is hardly surprising, then, that management style often surpasses riots, fatal accidents, violent confrontations, and shootings as the major cause of stress for police officers.[20]

This dominant form of police management represents a steep hurdle for any new form of policing. As a consequence,

> No one can expect a department to risk innovation, however promising, when the entire organizational culture is poised to attack the first sign of failure or error. Creativity, innovation, and experimentation . . . are all stifled. If policing is to change and progress, police management, like police culture, must also change. Making such changes in . . . culture . . . can only, in contemporary policing, be the job of chiefs of police. Chiefs . . . can no longer afford simply to keep things running smoothly. They must pioneer.[21]

This new, required leadership style also means (1) a shift from telling and controlling employees to helping them develop their skills and abilities; (2) listening to the customers in new and more open ways; (3) solving problems, not just reacting to incidents; (4) trying new things and experimenting, realizing that risk taking and honest mistakes must be tolerated to encourage creativity and achieve innovation; and (5) avoiding, whenever possible, the use of coercive power to effect change.[22] Next we discuss in greater depth the roles of key agency leaders.

Changing to COPPS

Potential for Resistance and Conflict

If COPPS is to flourish and succeed, the powerful orthodoxy of policing described earlier, rooted in the traditions of military command and scientific management theory, must be changed. In short, the traditional orthodoxy must become "taboo."[23] This includes management style, performance measures (as one author put it, "Bean-counting performance measures have little meaning in such a system"[24]), and disciplinary measures.[25] Obviously, today's police managers should be aware of, and attempt to deal with, these types of resistance when substantive changes in organizational structures and styles of operation are planned.

Similarly, a Washington state graduate student determined that the three most significant reactions by Spokane officers to the shift to community policing were

Meaning: Some officers saw community policing as a way of validating who they were, allowing them to do the kind of policing they believed they should have been doing all along.

Resistance: Community policing, being a philosophy rather than a program, made it more difficult for management to describe, so some officers who were said to be resistant were merely trying to determine what community policing meant in relation to how they were currently doing their jobs.

Sabotage: Some employees went beyond resistance, engaging in sabotage and being obstructionist; some supervisors wait until a ranking officer is out of earshot and then proceed to tell their staff "how it's really going to be."[26]

"We're Too Busy to Change"

It is not uncommon for consultants to go into police agencies to assist in implementing or training COPPS and be told, "We're too busy for community policing and problem solving." As William Geller and Guy Swanger noted, it may be true in some organizations that people are too busy to change; this, they said, may be the case

> if the senior leadership insists that middle managers continue doing all the old things they shouldn't be doing plus all the new things they should. The classic problem here is being too busy bailing out the boat to fix the hole in the hull.[27]

Indeed, preoccupation with the task at hand prevents people from pausing to reflect critically on whether what they are doing has any value. As Price Pritchett and Ron Pound observed, "Ditch those duties that don't count much, even if you can do them magnificently well."[28] Beliefs that police are too busy to change can be compounded by fears that COPPS will only intensify the workload. But when the community is an organized, active partner in problem solving, the problem solving process is not so labor intensive for the police as some have asserted.[29] (Exhibit 7.1 shows how one police department got the community involved in its change to COPPS.)

Sometimes the "too busy to change" objection may actually be a form of opposition to change. Middle management's resistance to change is usually covert, including such statements as, "We tried that idea and it didn't work," or "That idea will never fly." As a St. Louis police officer put it, "The sum total of all the excuses could be summed up as I just don't want to change, because I know how I fit into the way we do it now."[30] As a Native American proverb states, "It is better to limp in the right direction than to run in the wrong direction."

Former Canadian police chief D. D. McNally cautioned his own middle managers, as they strove to find better ways to serve the public, not to let the "process . . . overwhelm the task."[31] And Herman Goldstein called on the

---

Exhibit 7.1   Time for a Change in Santa Clara

Following is part of the "Community Policing Tutorial" home page of the Santa Clara, California, Police Department. It presents the reasons the department believes it is time to change to COPPS:

- Public safety is a citywide concern. Crime and disorder in our neighborhoods, parks, and business districts cause citizen frustration, uneasiness, and fear.
- Traditionally, police respond to calls, investigate crimes, and make arrests. This process alone does not reduce crime.
- Crime and public safety issues are community problems. They require the commitment of the community and the police to solve them together.
- The police department is committed to developing a strong relationship with the citizens of Santa Clara through community policing.

---

police to "go beyond taking satisfaction in the smooth operation of their organization" and to "extend their concern to dealing effectively with the problems that justify creating a police agency in the first instance."[32]

ROLES OF KEY LEADERS

In Chapter 6 we discussed briefly the roles of chief executives, middle managers, and first-line supervisors in the implementation process of COPPS. Here we briefly examine their respective roles in the change process.

The Chief Executive as Change Agent

Risk Takers and Boat Rockers

Of course, the police chief executive is ultimately responsible for all of the facets of COPPS, from implementation to training to evaluation. Therefore, what is needed are chief executives who are willing to do things that have not been done before, or, as one writer put it, "risk takers and boat rockers within a culture where daily exposure to life-or-death situations makes officers natural conservators of the status quo."[33] These are chief executives who become committed to getting the police and neighborhoods to work together to attack the roots of crime. For them, "Standing still is not only insufficient . . . it is going backwards."[34]

Therefore, police executives must be *viable change agents.* In any hierarchy the person at the top is responsible for setting both the policy and tone of the organization. Within a police agency the chief or sheriff has the ultimate power to make change, particularly one as substantive as COPPS. The chief executive must be both visible and credible and must create a climate conducive to change. Under COPPS, chief executives must focus on the values, mission, and long-term goals of policing in order to create an organizational environment that enables officers, government officials, and community members to work together. By building consensus, they can establish programs, develop timelines, and set priorities. They should honor the good work done in the past but exhibit a sense of urgency about implementing change while involving people from the community and the department in all stages of the transition. The chief executive's roles and responsibilities during the change to COPPS include the following:

- Articulating a clear vision to the organization
- Understanding and accepting the depth of change and time required to implement COPPS
- Assembling a management team that is committed to translating the new vision into action
- Being committed to removing bureaucratic obstacles whenever possible

Many police organizations boast talented and creative chief executives who, when participating in the change process, will assist in effecting change that is beneficial and lasting. As James Q. Wilson put it,

The police profession today is the intellectual leadership of the criminal justice profession in the United States. The police are in the lead. They're showing the world how things might better be done.[35]

Middle Managers

Middle managers—lieutenants and captains—also play a crucial role in the operation of a COPPS philosophy. COPPS's emphasis on problem solving necessitates that middle managers draw on their familiarity with the bureaucracy to secure, maintain, and use authority to empower subordinates, helping officers to actively and creatively confront and resolve issues, sometimes using unconventional approaches on a trial-and-error basis.

There are many really significant contributions middle managers can make to the changing culture of the agency to embrace and sustain COPPS. First, they must *build on the strengths* of their subordinates, capitalizing on their training and competence.[36] They do so by treating people as individuals and creating talented teams.[37] They must "cheerlead," encouraging supervisors and patrol officers to actually solve the problems they are confronting.[38] It is also imperative that middle managers *not* believe they are serving the chief executive's best interests by preserving the status quo. The lieutenants are the gatekeepers and must develop the system, resources, and support mechanisms to ensure that the officers, detectives, and supervisors can perform to achieve the best results. The officers and supervisors cannot perform without the necessary equipment, resources, and reinforcement.[39]

Middle managers, like their subordinates, must be allowed the freedom to make mistakes. And good middle managers protect their subordinates from organizational and political recrimination and scapegoating when things go wrong. Put another way, middle managers cannot stand idly by while their people are led to the guillotine, and they must protect their officers from the political effects of legitimate failure.[40] They must not allow their problem solving officers to revert to traditional methods. They must be diplomats and facilitators, using a lot more persuading and negotiating (toward win-win solutions) than they did under the traditional, "my way or the highway" management style.

The roles and responsibilities of middle managers during the change to COPPS include the following:

- Assuming responsibility for strategic planning
- Eliminating red tape and bottlenecks that impede the work of officers and supervisors
- Conducting regular meetings with subordinates to discuss plans, activities, and results
- Assessing COPPS efforts in a continuous manner

The general role and outlook for middle managers in a COPPS environment were well described by Kelling and Bratton, who stated that

The idea that mid-managers are spoilers, that they thwart project or strategic innovation, has some basis in fact. Mid-managers improperly directed can significantly impede innovation. Yet, ample evidence exists that when a clear vision of the business of the organization is put forward, when mid-managers are included in planning, when their legitimate self-interests are acknowledged, and when they are properly trained, mid-managers can be the leading edge of innovation and creativity.[41]

First-Line Supervisors

The Ultimate Challenge

It is widely held that the most challenging aspect of changing the culture of a police agency lies in changing the attitudes and beliefs of first-line supervisors. The influence of first-line supervisors is so strong that their role warrants special attention.

The primary contact of street officers with their organization is through their sergeant. Indeed, the quality of an officer's daily life is often dependent on his or her immediate supervisor. Most officers do not believe their sergeants are sources of guidance and direction but rather are authority figures to be satisfied (by numbers of arrests and citations, manner in which reports are completed, officer's ability to avoid citizen complaints, and so on). There is just cause for the reluctance of first-line supervisors to avoid change. Herman Goldstein stated that

> Changing the operating philosophy of rank-and-file officers is easier than altering a first-line supervisor's perspective of his or her job, because the work of a sergeant is greatly simplified by the traditional form of policing. The more routinized the work, the easier it is for the sergeant to check. The more emphasis placed on rank and the symbols of position, the easier it is for the sergeant to rely on authority—rather than intellect and personal skills—to carry out [his or her] duties. . . . [S]ergeants are usually appalled by descriptions of the freedom and independence suggested in problem oriented policing for rank-and-file officers. The concept can be very threatening to them. This . . . can create an enormous block to implementation.[42]

Supervisors must be convinced that COPPS makes good sense in today's environment. And they should possess the "Characteristics of a Good Problem Oriented Supervisor," as shown in Exhibit 7.2.

The roles and responsibilities of first-line supervisors during a change to COPPS include the following:

- Understanding and practicing problem solving
- Managing time, staff, and resources
- Encouraging teamwork
- Helping officers to mobilize stakeholders
- Tracking and managing officers' problem solving
- Providing officers with ongoing feedback and support

Coaching subordinates in their daily work is an important characteristic of good supervision for COPPS. (*Courtesy* Washoe County, Nevada, Sheriff's Office)

EXHIBIT 7.2 Characteristics of a Good Problem Oriented Supervisor

1. Allowing subordinates freedom to experiment with new approaches.
2. Insisting on good, accurate analyses of problems.
3. Granting flexibility in work schedules when requests are appropriate.
4. Allowing subordinates to make most contacts directly and paving the way when they are having trouble getting cooperation.
5. Protecting subordinates from pressures within the department to revert to traditional methods.
6. Running interference for subordinates to secure resources, protect from criticism, and so on.
7. Knowing what problems subordinates are working on and whether the problems are real.
8. Knowing subordinates' beats and important citizens in it, and expecting subordinates to know it even better.
9. Coaching subordinates through the process, giving advice, helping them manage their time.
10. Monitoring subordinates' progress and, as necessary, prodding them along or slowing them down.
11. Supporting subordinates even if their strategies fail, as long as something useful is learned in the process and the process was well thought through.
12. Managing problem solving efforts over a long period of time; not allowing efforts to die simply because they get sidetracked by competing demands for time and attention.
13. Giving credit to subordinates and letting others know about their good work.
14. Allowing subordinates to talk with visitors or at conferences about their work.
15. Identifying new resources and contacts for subordinates and making them check them out.
16. Stressing cooperation, coordination, and communication within the unit and outside it.
17. Coordinating efforts across shifts, beats, and outside units and agencies.
18. Realizing that this style of policing cannot simply be ordered; officers and detectives must come to believe in it.

Source: Police Executive Research Forum, "Supervising Problem-Solving" (Washington, D.C.: Author, training outline, 1990).

Another matter implicating police supervisory personnel concerns the amount of time required for patrol officers to engage in problem solving activities. Next we examine that issue.

"Recapturing Officers' Time" for Problem Solving

One of the ongoing controversies with respect to COPPS—as noted in the "We're Too Busy to Change" section earlier—concerns whether police officers can garner the time required to engage in problem solving activities. On the one hand, officers complain that they are going from call to call and have little time for anything else. On the other hand, administrators say there is plenty of time for problem solving because calls account for only 50 to 60 percent of an officer's time.

Who is right? According to Tom McEwen,[43] both sides are correct. Table 7.2 describes a hypothetical workload during a unit's shift. In the example shown in the table, the unit starts the shift at 4:00 P.M. and receives an accident call at 4:14 P.M., which takes until 4:44 P.M. (30 minutes). The next call (robbery) comes in at 5:02 P.M., which means 18 minutes elapsed between calls. The pattern continues throughout the shift, alternating between handling calls for service and having time for other activities. In total, the unit devotes 4 hours 46 minutes (286 minutes) to calls, with the remaining 3 hours 14 minutes (194 minutes) available for other activities.

The time between calls is the key element of the argument as to whether officers have time for problem solving. In this example, more than three hours are available for other activities. An administrator would be correct in pointing out that there is plenty of time available. However, the available time is spread throughout the shift, varying from 10 minutes between calls to 47 minutes. If we assume a problem solving project takes 45 minutes, then the officer in this unit has only one block of uninterrupted time for an assignment. (Note: Clearly not all problem solving projects take 45 minutes each day. Some days, all that is needed is 10 minutes to complete a phone call to, perhaps, a building inspector. On other days, such as Friday or Saturday nights, no work will be done on problem orientated policing (POP). POP projects have no due dates, therefore, problem solving efforts might be best thought of as being accomplished in bits and pieces, not over the course of a day but over the course of a longer period of time. Departments, however, should be striving to find uninterrupted time for officers so that officers can increase their proactive responsibilities.)

The average time between calls is 21 minutes. Officers believe they are going from call to call with no time for anything else because of the relatively short periods of time between calls.

Of course, not all units or shifts will have the same experience as in this example. Time between calls varies considerably depending on the number of calls for a particular shift, the types of calls, and how much time they require. One or two fewer calls can make a big difference in whether there will be stretches of uninterrupted time.

Obviously, citizen calls are important and cannot be ignored. But the aim should be to handle citizen calls in an efficient and expedient manner. The

TABLE 7.2 **Example of a Unit's Workload during a Shift**

Activity	Time Dispatched	Time Cleared	Time on Call	Time to Next Call
Start of shift	4:00 P.M.			14 minutes
Accident	4:14	4:44 P.M.	30 minutes	18
Robbery	5:02	5:18	16	17
Suspicious activity	5:35	6:38	63	32
Family problem	7:10	7:40	30	28
Theft	8:08	8:26	18	10
Alarm	8:36	8:46	10	47
Emotionally disturbed person	9:33	11:21	108	17
Unwanted person	11:38	11:49	11	11
End of Shift	12:00 A.M.			
Total			286 minutes	194 minutes

following four methods can be used to overcome the problem of finding time for problem solving while still handling calls effectively.

1. *Allow units to perform problem solving assignments as self-initiated activities.* Under this approach, a unit would contact the dispatcher and go out of service for a problem solving assignment. The unit would be interrupted only for an emergency call in its area of responsibility. Otherwise, the dispatcher would hold nonemergency calls until the unit becomes available or send a unit from an adjacent area after holding the call for a predetermined amount of time. This approach obviously requires call codes for problem solving activities and a procedure in the communications center for delaying calls.

2. *Schedule one or two units to devote a predetermined part of their shift to problem solving.* As an example, a supervisor could designate one or two units each day to devote the first half of their shift or even only one hour to problem solving. Their calls would be handled by other units so that they have an uninterrupted block of time for problems. Of course, this approach means that the other units will be busier. The trade-off is that problem solving gets done and the supervisor can rotate the units designated for these activities.

3. *Take more reports over the telephone.* Many departments take certain non-emergency complaints by telephone rather than dispatching a patrol unit. The information about the incident is recorded on a department report form and entered in the department's information system as an incident or crime. The average telephone report taker can process four times as many report calls per hour compared to a field unit. It may be possible for the department to increase the types of calls handled by telephone, or the staffing for a telephone report unit can be increased to cover more hours of the day.

4. *Review the department policy on "assist" units.* In some departments, several units show up at the scene of a call even though they are not needed. Some units assist out of boredom or curiosity. The units may initiate themselves out of service to assist or the dispatcher may send several units to the scene. This problem is particularly acute with alarm calls. Many departments have a policy of dispatching two or more units to alarms, even when the source has a long history of false alarms. A department should undergo a detailed study on the types of calls for which assist units are actually appearing, with the aim of reducing the number of assists. In addition, officers should be discouraged from assisting other units unless it is necessary.

As a more general approach, a department should review its patrol plan to determine whether units are fielded in proportion to workload. Time between calls is a function not only of the number of incoming calls but also of the number of units in the field. More units result in more time between calls.

Indeed, we can calculate the number of units needed to assure that the time between calls averages, for example, 35 minutes. A department may also want to consider changes in officer schedules to facilitate overlapping during busy times of the day; however, adjustments within a shift may be the more effective approach.

Delaying response time to calls for service can also provide more time for officers. For example, by refining the manner in which 911 calls were dispatched in non–lifethreatening cases that did not require police presence, former New York City Commissioner Lee Brown reduced 911 responses by an estimated 450,000 radio runs annually. That was the equivalent of 752 police officers.[44]

Response time research implied that rapid responses were not needed for most calls. Furthermore, dispatchers can advise citizens of an officer's arrival time. Slower police responses to nonemergency calls has been found satisfactory to citizens if dispatchers tell citizens an officer might not arrive right away. Managers have also garnered more time for officers by having nonsworn employees handle noncrime incidents.[45]

Even after implementing all the specific changes mentioned, a review of the patrol plan may indicate that more officers are needed. A department may already need additional officers before entering into problem solving. Each police department needs to consider its own situation and set realistic objectives for patrol operations. These objectives could include the amount of time devoted to calls for service, average time between calls, average travel time to emergency calls, and many other items.

The number of units needed to accomplish these objectives can be calculated, and a determination can be made as to whether additional officers will be required. Departments are encouraged, however, to try to realign internal resources to find time for problem solving before seeking additional officers.

Time between calls is an important, but frequently overlooked, element of any problem solving strategy. The overall aim should be to provide officers with uninterrupted amounts of time for problem solving assignments. There are many ways to accomplish this aim, but they require a concerted planning effort by the department.

Figure 7.1 shows the 15-step exercise developed for police managers to recapture officers' time while working in a problem solving framework. If, during the "recapturing time" exercise a police manager finds potential ways to effectively solve problems and recapture time lost to repetitive incidents, then problem oriented policing may be a smart approach.

---

1. Assemble a group of patrol officers and emergency communications center personnel representing each shift.
2. Have each of them write down three to five locations where the police respond regularly to deal with the same general problem and people repeatedly.
3. Determine the average number of responses to those locations per month and approximately how long the problem has existed.
4. Determine the average number of officers who respond each time to those incidents.
5. Determine the average length of time involved in handling the incidents.
6. Using the information from 3, 4, and 5, determine the total number of staff hours devoted to each of these problem locations. Do this for the week, month, and year.
7. Identify all the key players that either participate in or are affected by the problem—all direct and indirect participants and groups such as the complaining parties, victims, witnesses, property owners and managers, and bystanders.
8. Through a roundtable discussion, decide what it is about the particular location that allows or encourages the problem to exist and continue.
9. Develop a list of things that have been done in the past to try to deal with the problem, and a candid assessment of why each has not worked.
10. In a free-flowing brainstorming session, develop as many traditional and non-traditional solutions to the problem as possible. Try to include alternative sources like other government and private agencies that could be involved in the solution. Encourage creative thinking and risk taking.
11. After you have completed the brainstorming session, consider which of those solutions are: (a) illegal, (b) immoral, (c) impractical, (d) unrealistic, or (e) not affordable.
12. Eliminate all those that fall in categories a and b.
13. For those that fall in categories c, d, and e, figure out if those reasons are because you are thinking in conventional terms like "We've never done it this way," "It won't work," "It can't be done." If you are satisfied that those solutions truly are impractical, unrealistic, or not affordable, then eliminate them, too. If there is a glimmer of hope that some may have merit with just a little different thinking or approach, then leave them.
14. For each remaining possible solution, list what would have to be done and who would have to be involved to make it happen. Which of those solutions and actions could be implemented relatively soon and with a minimum of difficulty?
15. If the solution were successful, consider the productive things officers could do with the time that would be recaptured from not having to deal with the problem anymore.

FIGURE 7.1 A 15-Step Exercise for Recapturing Officers' Time. [*Source:* Jerald R. Vaughn, *Community Oriented Policing: You Can Make It Happen* (Clearwater, Fla.: National Law Enforcement Leadership Institute, no date), pp. 6–7. Used with permission.]

ROLE OF THE RANK-AND-FILE OFFICERS

All experts on the subject of police innovation and change emphasize the importance of empowering and using the input from the street officers. Next we discuss these key personnel, including the unique nature of their recruitment, the need to give them a sense of ownership in their work, and means by which they can progress.

Change Begins with Recruitment

Selecting Problem Solvers

In the not too distant past, the hiring of police officers in many of the country's 17,000 police agencies—particularly smaller agencies—was a fairly simple affair. An applicant—preferably one who was male and large in stature, and often with military background—would have a short interview with the chief executive or a designee, be given such pearls of wisdom as "police work is mostly common sense," and be sent forth to enforce the law without benefit of training (except that provided by a few shifts riding in a patrol car with a veteran officer). Often, state law required only that recruits attend an academy within a year of their hiring date; therefore, officers were basically forced to fend for themselves until being formally trained.

A recruitment poster illustrates the department's diversity, values, and belief that one person can make a difference. (*Courtesy* Broken Arrow, Oklahoma, Police Department)

Times have changed greatly in this regard. The specter of liability and the shift to COPPS have forced police agencies to revise the recruiting and training processes (COPPS training is examined in Chapter 8). The shift to community policing has important implications for how we select police recruits, requiring a reevaluation of past practices and the development of more positively oriented selection criteria and procedures.[46]

The shift is from viewing the police as part of a professional crime-fighting organization to seeing them as a community oriented group with a proactive, problem solving focus. With COPPS, the "screening out" model focuses on eliminating those police recruits who are perceived as being detrimental to the public and to the police organization.[47]

The patrol officer is now a *problem solver*. Selection would favor those who are interested in creating solutions rather than applying learned rules. Furthermore, there is an emphasis on practical intelligence—the ability to quickly analyze key elements of a situation and identify possible courses of action to reach logical conclusions. It is difficult to neatly delineate separate problem solving elements. A patrol officer might witness, for example, neighborhood youth painting graffiti on a wall. The officer has to analyze the situation and define the problem. Another scenario might be a patrol officer assigned to a beat in which automobiles are smashed and vandalized each night. In order to formulate a response, the officer must define the problem and address the motivations of the offenders.[48]

Under COPPS, the patrol officer is expected to recognize when old methods are inadequate and new and different solutions are needed. The officer is expected to display many of the skills demanded in higher-level personnel, such as detectives—being creative, flexible, and innovative; working independently; and maintaining self-discipline. Communication skills are also vital. The officer must possess the ability to work cooperatively with others to solve problems, and to listen.[49]

Many police agencies, such as the Redding, California, Police Department, inform their applicants on their Web page and other recruitment materials that they have implemented COPPS and are thus interested in hiring people who can perform under that philosophy.[50]

Ownership: A "Prescription for Change"

Ownership, whether it be of things, time, or destiny, is a powerful force among humans. Lack of it brought down communism and the Berlin Wall. And so it is with policing, where the vast majority of work that is done each workday is done by people.

W. Edwards Deming, the founder of the total quality management movement (discussed in Chapter 3), believed that "the quality of any product is primarily a function of human commitment."[51] People involved in COPPS, those who have gone beyond mere theorizing about the concept and have observed the methodology in the field, have observed that the rank-and-file working under this new mode are highly enthusiastic. Officers acting in this capacity seem to flourish when they are "cut loose" and assigned to a specific neighborhood. They solve problems, motivate citizens to join together to do things for themselves, and create a feeling of security and goodwill. Equally important, they find their work rewarding and very satisfying. In the rank-and-file, one finds enormous talent, energy, and commitment that, under equally enthusiastic leadership, could transform the character of American policing.[52]

Malcolm Sparrow, Mark Morrew, and David Kennedy listed several key elements concerning the street officer in their "prescription" for progress with COPPS:

1. *High status for patrol officers:* Departmental commitment to a new style of policing can be credible only if appropriate status is accorded to patrol officers. Rates of pay, benefits, degree of autonomy, level of training provided, and provision of resources are some status indicators and provide credible support to high-priority functions. Other needs include allowing officers flexibility in setting their hours, giving them business cards, making special training available, giving them small enough beats to make an impact, discontinuing the current practice of regarding officers as "available" for any other task, and giving officers primary responsibility for investigating crime in their area.

2. *Master patrol officers:* Many departments have no means for officers to gain status or recognition other than promotion. Thus, there is no way a good patrol officer can be rewarded or recognized without being removed from patrol. There needs to be some career structure for patrol officers, which would carry substantial pay increases, and, most important, would keep successful beat officers on their beats without slowing their career progress.

3. *Relevant performance measures:* A meaningful monitoring and appraisal system for beat officers could include such measures as their knowledge about their area and its residents, officer initiative, community satisfaction with the officer's work (using some kind of public canvassing, either random or representative), and the process of problem solving using the S.A.R.A. model (discussed in Chapter 4).

4. *Learning from street officers:* Police executives must realize that they have much to learn from street officers. Those executives must remember that there are, in their own departments, officers who—through experience and creativity—have already developed images that differ significantly from the established norm. Their ideas should be unleashed and used to provide more effective policing and to garner community support.[53]

CASE STUDIES

Following are examples of how three police organizations approached some aspects of change needed with the COPPS philosophy.

Camden, New Jersey: Build a Blueprint

"The most successful police chiefs have demonstrated the ability to collect data, analyze the information, and instill enough flexibility into their traditional operations to accommodate change." That basic approach describes how the Camden, New Jersey, Police Department developed a comprehensive community policing strategy. Following are the steps of the planning process that was used to effect this change:

1. *Build a blueprint.* Officers required a needs assessment strategy and goals and objectives (all of which are discussed in Chapter 6).
2. *Develop innovative strategies.* This is the "creativity step." Examples include drug reversals, in which officers pose as drug dealers, and the team approach, in which officers work with other governmental officials to correct code and safety violations.
3. *Define roles.* When several governmental agencies are collaborating under COPPS, it is important to define roles for each agency, and each must demonstrate a commitment to that particular role.
4. *Establish timelines.* Time is money. It is good customer service to perform activities within a timeline, and as efficiently and cost effectively as possible.
5. *Provide training.* Orientation is key to supporting initiatives.
6. *Zero in on the problems.* Categorize problems first, then prioritize the list to address the most critical issues.
7. *Determine the resources that will be needed.* Identify sources of funding and agencies that will be able to offer financial assistance or other forms of support. Consider private and volunteer organizations, clubs, and youth-service programs.
8. *Evaluate your progress.* Be sure the results of whatever assessment tool you use can be supported by data.

With this blueprint to follow, an organization can move smoothly through the change process.[54]

Hayward, California: Hiring, Training, and Evaluating Personnel

After making the decision to change its policing philosophy, a systems change was required that would greatly impact personnel. Therefore, the initial focus was on personnel systems such as recruiting, hiring, training, performance appraisals, and promotability guidelines. To transform the recruiting and hiring processes, the city's personnel department and the police department began exploring the following questions:

1. Overall, what type of candidate, possessing what types of skills, should be recruited?

2. What specific knowledge, skills, and abilities reflect the COPPS philosophy—particularly problem solving abilities and sensitivity to the needs of the community?

3. How can these attributes best be identified through the initial screening process?[55]

The department also analyzed the city's demographics, finding that it had a diverse ethnic composition. To promote cultural diversity and sensitivity to the needs of the community, a psychologist was employed to develop a profile of an effective COPPS officer in Hayward. These considerations became an integral part of the department's hiring process.[56]

Next the training and performance evaluation systems were reappraised. All personnel—both sworn and civilian—had to receive COPPS training to provide a clear and thorough understanding of the history, philosophy, and transition to COPPS. The department's initial training was directed at management and supervisory personnel and was designed to assist these employees in accomplishing the department's goals of reinforcing COPPS values, modifying the existing police culture, strategically transitioning the organization from traditional policing to the new philosophy, and focusing on customer relations.[57] Rank-and-file officers were given 40-hour blocks of instruction.

Performance and reward practices for personnel were modified to reflect the new criteria. Emphasizing quality over quantity (e.g., arrest statistics, number of calls for service, response times), new criteria included an assessment of how well a call for service was handled and what type of problem solving approach was used to reach a solution for the problem.[58] Other mechanisms were developed to broadcast and communicate successes, including supervisors' logs, a COPPS newsletter, and citywide recognition of extraordinary customer service efforts.[59]

The department's promotional process was also retooled; a new phase was added to the department's promotional test—the "promotability" phase—to evaluate the candidate's decision-making abilities, analytical skills, communication skills, interpersonal skills, and professional contributions.[60]

Broken Arrow, Oklahoma: Beat a Path toward Change

An article entitled "Broken Arrow Beats a Path toward Change" describes how an Oklahoma agency defined where it was going, obtained the needed skills to get there, and organized to provide opportunities to practice those skills and to celebrate its successes:

- *Define where you are going:* Broken Arrow's command staff attended a management retreat with its new chief to determine "guideposts" for the transition to COPPS, including the development of vision, mission, and values statements.

- *Obtain needed skills:* Believing that training "is the backbone of any change process," all department personnel were trained in the concepts of COPPS to ensure that the department shifted its focus within every division at the same time.
- *Organize to promote use of skills:* The agency committed to an aggressive recruitment campaign and realigned its 8-hour shifts to 10-hours shifts to allow officers the opportunity to work on problem solving projects.
- *Promote the successes:* Complaints were documented, committees were formed, information was gathered, funding was obtained, and successes were achieved for addressing problems. With all of this, a federal grant was obtained to further teach the problem solving process to high school students, to help reduce violence in schools.[61]

SUMMARY

This chapter has been about change: how it can be quite difficult in organizations—especially those police agencies with the traditional, entrenched culture and management styles—as well as the roles of key police leaders and rank-and-file officers in effecting change.

The chapter underscores the importance and means of changing the culture of the police agency—from recruit to chief—to accommodate the new philosophy and the operation of COPPS. Also called for is a requisite, radical change in the way the police organization views itself, hones its values, and conducts its affairs. The chief executive must be a risk taker and all employees—sworn and civilian—must believe that change is a prerequisite within the organization if COPPS is to succeed. This modified approach to policing is also required in the view and latitude given the middle managers as well as first-line supervisors and especially the very important problem solving street officer. We also emphasized the need to examine—and probably shift—the organization's means for recruiting people as police problem solvers.

NOTES

1. Herman Goldstein, *Problem Oriented Policing* (New York: McGraw-Hill, 1990), p. 29.
2. J. L. Pierce and A. L. Delbecq, "Organization Structure, Individual Attitudes and Innovation." *Academy of Management Review* 2 (1977):27–37.
3. Community Policing Consortium, *Curricula. Module Four: Managing Organizational Change* (Washington, D.C.: Author, August 2000), pp. 4–5.
4. *Ibid.*, p. 6.
5. *Ibid.*, pp. 6–7.
6. Roy R. Roberg and Jack Kuykendall, *Police Management*, 2d ed. (Los Angeles: Roxbury, 1997), p. 370.
7. *Ibid.*, pp. 370–71.

8. *Ibid.*, pp. 375–76.

9. *Ibid.*, p. 376.

10. Charles R. Swanson, Leonard Territo, and Robert W. Taylor, *Police Administration: Structures, Processes, and Behavior*, 3rd ed. (New York: Macmillan, 1993), p. 668.

11. *Ibid.*, pp. 668–69.

12. L. E. Greiner, "Patterns of Organization Change," *Harvard Business Review* 45 (1967):124–25.

13. Malcolm K. Sparrow, "Implementing Community Policing" (Washington, D.C.: U.S. Department of Justice: National Institute of Justice, "Perspectives on Policing," no. 9 November 1988), pp. 1–2.

14. Thomas J. Peters and Robert H. Waterman Jr., *In Search of Excellence* (New York: Harper & Row, 1983), p. 15.

15. Robert Wasserman and Mark H. Moore, "Values in Policing" (Washington, D.C.: U.S. Department of Justice, National Institute of Justice, November 1988), pp. 6–7.

16. Malcolm K. Sparrow, Mark H. Moore, and David M. Kennedy, *Beyond 911: A New Era for Policing* (New York: Basic Books, 1990), p. 50.

17. *Ibid.*, pp. 51–53.

18. Andra J. (Katz) Bannister and David L. Carter, "Concerns and Roadblocks in the Evolution of Community Policing: A Pragmatic Perspective" (paper presented at the annual meeting of the Academy of Criminal Justice Sciences, Orlando, Fla., March 1999), p. 8.

19. Personal communication to Malcolm K. Sparrow, quoted in Sparrow, Moore, and Kennedy, *Beyond 911*, p. 55.

20. *Ibid.*, pp. 56–57.

21. *Ibid.*, p. 57.

22. California Department of Justice, Attorney General's Office, Crime Prevention Center, *COPPS: Community Oriented Policing and Problem Solving* (Sacramento, Calif.: Author, November 1992), pp. 67–68.

23. Mark H. Moore and Darrel W. Stephens, *Beyond Command and Control: The Strategic Management of Police Departments* (Washington, D.C.: Police Executive Research Forum, 1991), pp. 1, 3–4.

24. Gordon Witkin and Dan McGraw, "Beyond `Just the Facts, Ma'am'," *U.S.News and World Report* (August 2, 1993):29.

25. Sparrow, Moore, and Kennedy, *Beyond 911*, p. 149.

26. Lunell Haught, "Meaning, Resistance, and Sabotage—Elements of a Police Culture," *Community Policing Exchange* (May/June 1998):7.

27. William A. Geller and Guy Swanger, *Managing Innovation in Policing: The Untapped Potential of the Middle Manager* (Washington, D.C.: Police Executive Research Forum, 1995), p. 41.

28. Price Pritchett and Ron Pound, *A Survival Guide to the Stress of Organizational Change* (Dallas: Pritchett and Associates, 1995), p. 12.

29. Warren Friedman, "The Community Role in Community Policing," in *The Challenge of Community Policing: Testing the Promises*, ed. Dennis P. Rosenbaum (Thousand Oaks, Calif.: Sage, 1994), p. 268.

30. Quoted in William A. Geller and Guy Swanger, *Managing Innovation in Policing*, p. 48.

31. D. D. McNally, "Community Based Policing: Organizational Review Recommendations," in *By the Way . . . : A Bi-weekly Publication from the Chief of Police* (Edmonton, Alberta, Canada, 1991), p. 1.

32. Goldstein, *Problem Oriented Policing*, p. 35.

33. Mike Tharp and Dorian Friedman, "New Cops on the Block," *U.S.News and World Report* (August 2, 1993):23.

34. John Eck, quoted in *ibid.*, p. 24.

35. James Q. Wilson, "Six Things Police Leaders Can Do About Juvenile Crime," in *Subject to Debate* (newsletter of the Police Executive Research Forum, September/October 1997), p. 1.

36. Geller and Swanger, *Managing Innovation in Policing,* p. 105.
37. *Ibid.,* p. 131.
38. *Ibid.,* p. 109.
39. *Ibid.,* p. 112.
40. *Ibid.,* pp. 137–38.
41. George L. Kelling and William J. Bratton, *Implementing Community Policing: The Administrative Problem* (Washington, D.C.: National Institute of Justice, "Perspectives on Policing" no. 17, 1993), p. 11.
42. Goldstein, *Problem Oriented Policing,* p. 29.
43. Tom McEwen, "Finding Time for Problem Solving," *Problem Solving Quarterly* 5 (Spring 1992):1, 4.
44. Lee P. Brown, "Community Policing: Bring the Community into the Battle against Crime" (speech before the 19th Annual Lehman Lecture Series, Long Island University, New York, March 11, 1992).
45. John Eck and William Spelman, "A Problem-Oriented Approach to Police Service Delivery," in *Police and Policing: Contemporary Issues,* ed. Dennis Jay Kenney (New York: Praeger, 1989), pp. 95–111.
46. Eric Metchik and Ann Winton, "Community Policing and Its Implications for Alternative Models of Police Officer Selection," in *Issues in Community Policing,* eds. Peter C. Kratcoski and Duane Dukes (Cincinnati: Anderson, 1995), pp. 107–23.
47. *Ibid.,* pp. 112, 115–16.
48. *Ibid.,* p. 116.
49. *Ibid.,* p. 119–20.
50. See the Redding Police Department's Web site: http://ci.redding.ca.us/personel/porec.htm.
51. Quoted in Chris Braiden, "Policing Principles: Who Washes a Rented Car," *Blue Line Magazine* (February 1992):25.
52. Herman Goldstein, "The New Policing: Confronting Complexity" (paper presented at the Conference on Community Policing, U.S. Department of Justice, National Institute of Justice, Washington, D.C., August 24, 1993), p. 11.
53. Adapted from Sparrow, Moore, and Kennedy, *Beyond 911,* pp. 224–29.
54. Adapted from Charles J. Kocher, "A Blueprint for Developing Responsible Change," *Community Policing Exchange* (November/December 1998):6.
55. Joseph E. Brann and Suzanne Whalley, "COPPS: The Transformation of Police Organizations," in California Department of Justice, Attorney General's Office, Crime Prevention Center, *COPPS: Community Oriented Policing and Problem Solving,* p. 72.
56. *Ibid.,* p. 73.
57. *Ibid.*
58. *Ibid.,* pp. 74–75.
59. *Ibid.*
60. *Ibid.*
61. Brandon Berryhill, "Broken Arrow Beats a Path toward Change," *Community Policing Exchange* (July/August 1999):5.

TRAINING FOR COPPS
Approaches and Challenges

> A man can seldom—very, very seldom—fight a winning fight against his training: the odds are too heavy.
>
> —Mark Twain

INTRODUCTION

This observation by Mark Twain is made more eloquent, powerful, and lucid when reviewing some definitions of *training*, which include: (1) developing or forming the habits, thoughts, or behavior of [another person] by discipline and instruction; (2) making proficient by instruction and practice, as in some art, profession, or work;[1] and (3) imparting specific and immediately usable skills.[2]

As we have noted in previous chapters, the movement toward community oriented policing and problem solving (COPPS) involves a change in the philosophy and the organizational structure of the police agency. A philosophical shift is critical to the development of new skills, knowledge, and abilities, as well as to a reorientation of perceptions and a refining of current skills. This is a difficult challenge for those involved in the training and education of police officers.

This challenge is greatly enhanced because the successful implementation of COPPS requires the training of every employee inside the agency, as well as an orientation for a number of people and organizations outside the police department. Indeed, police administrators, federal and state criminal justice planning officials, and criminal justice policy advisory groups have rated training as the primary need in order for COPPS to reach its fullest potential.[3] Furthermore, it is important that the police educate the public and other public and private agencies and organizations in the concept, because they will be required, at times, to help carry out the COPPS effort. This chapter analyzes COPPS training from these disparate, yet related, perspectives.

Much has been written, and could be written in this chapter, about how people best learn and train others, and the various approaches for doing both. Given the present purposes and constraints, however, we begin this chapter with only a brief look at COPPS training nationally and why police officers are a challenging (and often difficult) learning audience. Then we remain focused on the best means and approaches for accomplishing COPPS training, discussing the need for and means of performing a training needs assessment. We discuss some places and means (such as in the academy or with field training officers) for conducting training. Following is a review of some technologies that are available for training. After examining in detail what a COPPS training program should minimally include and discussing the various audiences that should be exposed to COPPS training (such as business leaders, other government agencies, social service organizations, elected officials, and the media), the chapter concludes with a sample training program. Exhibits containing examples of police training initiatives are provided throughout the chapter.

COPPS TRAINING NATIONALLY

COPPS training is expanding as rapidly as the philosophy itself. Chapter 4 discussed findings from a national survey by the federal Bureau of Justice Studies[4] concerning community policing activities in more than 700 state and local law enforcement agencies, each employing 100 or more full-time sworn officers. The survey queried those agencies about their community policing training activities. Figure 8.1 shows findings for both 1997 and 1999.

The survey found that overall, 93 percent of the agencies had full-time community policing officers. All new officer recruits received community policing training in more than four-fifths of the county (87 percent) and municipal (81 percent) police agencies (84 percent of the agencies provided recruit training overall). Furthermore, a large majority of the municipal police (92 percent), sheriffs (82 percent), and county police (79 percent) departments trained at least some of their full-time sworn officers in community policing, and 64 percent actively encouraged their officers to engage in problem solving projects. Also, nearly three-fourths (72 percent) of these agencies trained citizens in community policing.

TRAINING POLICE OFFICERS, GENERALLY

Anyone who undertakes to train police officers must be mindful of the challenge at hand. First, new officers and recruits often expect to do law enforcement, not

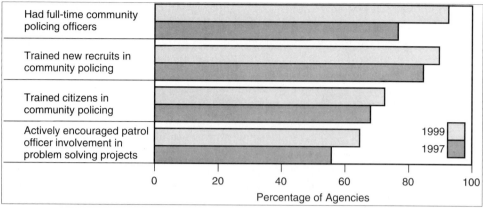

FIGURE 8.1 Community policing activities of local police agencies with 100 or more full-time sworn personnel, 1997 and 1999. [*Source:* Brian A. Reaves and Timothy C. Hart, *Law Enforcement Management and Administrative Statistics, 1999: Data for Individual State and Local Agencies with 100 or More Officers* (Washington, D.C.: U.S. Department of Justice, Bureau of Justice Statistics, November 2000), p. v.]

community service or social work. Michael E. Buerger provides other blunt food for thought concerning police training:

> Training is usually discussed in terms of a benefit provided to the rank-and-file. From the perspective of those receiving it, however, training is easily divided into two main categories: the kind officers like, and the kind they despise. What they like fits into their world view; what they despise is "training" that attempts to change that view.[5]

Community policing, being widely promoted as a "philosophy," can represent for some officers an attempt to change their belief system, raising the question, "Was the old way of doing things getting the job done?" And what is promoted at the top levels of the organization as an attitude, Buerger stated, can get translated and revised as it works its way down through the chain of command.[6] Police executives must obviously attempt to ensure that the vision they have for the department is accurately and appropriately communicated to, and understood and applied by, the line officers.

Because policing often attracts action-oriented individuals, police officers tend to be more receptive to hands-on skills training, such as arrest methods, weaponless defense, pursuit driving, firearms proficiency, baton usage, and so on. Certainly, these measures are needed from time to time, and for that reason (and because of the specter of liability) police personnel must receive training in those areas. As many studies have demonstrated, however, only a small fraction of the typical officers' work routine involves the use of weapons, defensive tactics, high-speed chases, and so forth. If training is to help officers do their jobs better, it must focus on what they need to know in order to do their job well. It should also be driven by the mission of the agency.

Training in COPPS must not, however, be presented merely as justification for adopting a new philosophy. As noted in following sections setting forth the objectives and components of a COPPS training curriculum, officers should be shown the "big picture," so they understand the history and mission of the organization and have basic and advanced problem solving skills.

It must also be remembered that police training is best conducted—and is better received by the officers—when it reflects skills with immediately recognizable application to the job and when that message is constantly reinforced throughout training. Thus, it is not surprising that officers prefer to be instructed by persons who both possess expertise in the activity and have "walked the walk" of police patrol, that is, other police officers.[7] It is also worthwhile to remember that an *environment* that is conducive to learning, with a clearly stated *outcome*, inspiring learners' *physical and mental engagement*, and activities that precipitate *critical thinking and problem solving* are important training processes as well. Dialogue with learners is important; instructors should "draw," not "dump" information, serving as facilitators for cognitive thinking and long-lasting learning.

DETERMINING TRAINING NEEDS

A needs assessment provides the trainer with vital information about the officers, how they view their daily work, and what obstacles exist that may prevent them from using COPPS training. It can also provide important information for changing officer performance evaluation systems, which rarely extend beyond simplistic assessments, such as tickets and number of arrests made. The assessment is a tool to establish departmentwide training needs and can be used for various purposes—academy training, in-service training, supervisory and nonsupervisory training, and so on—in order to survey trainees prior to their receiving instruction. The information obtained from such a survey can prove useful to the instructor in constructing a lesson plan that meets the specific needs of participants.

Exhibit 8.1 provides a preliminary COPPS training needs assessment questionnaire developed recently for Kansas and Nebraska by the Regional Community Policing Training Institute at Wichita State University (funded by the federal Office of Community Oriented Policing Services); the exhibit shows the types of questions that could be used by a police agency to do a preliminary survey of its training needs. Obviously, question 3 of the survey is critical and will require considerable deliberation.

It is also important for COPPS curriculum development that (1) the trainees be determined, (2) a task analysis be conducted, (3) tasks be selected that will be incorporated into the learning process, (4) performance measures be constructed by which trainees can be evaluated (to determine successful or unsuccessful course completion), (5) existing courses be identified that might address needs, and (6) the appropriate environment for the training be selected.[8]

It should be emphasized that there is no one best way or curriculum that will work for every agency. A needs assessment survey similar to that shown in Exhibit 8.1, however, can help agency administrators and instructors to develop a curriculum that best meets the needs of the agency and its employees.

DUE 4-16

EXHIBIT 8.1   Needs Assessment Survey

1. Does our department *currently* have a community policing strategy or plan?
2. Which of the following best describes our department's community policing practice?
   a. All *uniformed* officers are/will be actively involved in community policing.
   b. All *sworn* officers are/will be actively involved in community policing.
   c. Only specifically assigned officers are/will be involved in community policing.
   d. The department does not use community policing.
3. What are our *primary training needs* related to community policing? [Responses might be wide ranging, from community engagement issues to knowledge about crime prevention, the S.A.R.A. process generally, managing patrol time, resources and referrals, organizational change, responsibilities of administrators and supervisors, and so on.]
4. Have any of our officers received community policing training?
   a. Who presented/provided the training?
   b. What percentage of our officers received the training?
5. Does our department have at least one computer with a modem? Access to the Internet?
6. Does our department currently have an Internet Web page?
7. Does our agency currently have e-mail external to the department?
8. Have our officers had any Internet training?
9. Which programs does our department currently have? [Responses might include DARE (Drug Abuse Resistance Education), neighborhood or business watch, ride-along, GREAT (Gang Resistance Education and Training), and so on.]

Source: Adapted from Andra J. Katz, *The Community Policing Needs Assessment in Kansas and Nebraska: Final Report* (Wichita, Kans.: Regional Community Policing Training Institute, December 1997).

IMPARTING NEW KNOWLEDGE AND RETAINING LEARNED SKILLS

Training can be categorized into five primary areas: academy, field training officer, in-service, roll call, and specialized. Each is extremely important for imparting values and information concerning the COPPS philosophy. Thus, it is important that changes in training also be incorporated into recruitment, selection, and promotional practices.

The Recruit Academy

Academy training (the recruit or cadet phase) sets the tone for newly hired officers. It is at the academy that the recruits begin to develop a strong mind-set about their role as police officers.

Ideally, academy training will provide comprehensive instruction in the two primary elements of COPPS—community engagement and problem solving—if the proper philosophical mind-set for recruits is to be accomplished. In many cases, this will require that traditional courses, such as those in history, patrol procedures, police–community relations, and crime prevention, be revamped to include the topics and information recommended in this chapter; this information will teach officers to be more analytical and creative in their efforts to address community crime and disorder. A primary emphasis on the nature of crime and disorder and problem solving methods should be the foundation for this training. If police officers are to become problem solvers, they must hone their skills as street-level criminologists.

In the mid-1990s, the Boston Police Department created a new training curriculum called the Basic Course for the police. The curriculum presents a defined and structured environment and has four guiding principles: ethics (or officer character), the law (or the constitutional basis for law enforcement), fitness (both mental and physical), and community policing. The curriculum is founded on five fundamental objectives:

COPPS training should begin with new recruits in the academy. (*Courtesy* Arnold Brock)

1. Incorporate community policing throughout
2. Adopt a valued-driven model of police training
3. Integrate training and education
4. Train as a collaboration of police organizations (with the state police, the state office of public safety, and the chiefs of police association) with a shared history, a common body of knowledge, and an equal stake in self-evaluation
5. Enhance character by examining the complexities of society and the choices of police officers[9]

Figure 8.2 depicts the basic curriculum used by the Boston Police Department to effect these principles and objectives.

Field Training Officers

The next phase of training for newly hired officers is the *field training officer* (FTO) program, which is responsible for providing training to the recruit immediately on leaving the academy. This phase of the recruit's career can have a profound effect on later performance—reinforcing what was emphasized in the academy by putting the various methods and strategies to practice.

For this reason, the FTO has an enormous impact on how the trainee views policing and, as a result, how that officer will perform after completion of training. If a specially trained FTO, or other officers who assume the training of the new recruits, do not accept or espouse the COPPS philosophy, it will be virtually impossible for new officers—even those who are highly idealistic and enthusiastic—to put the strategy into practice. The goals and methods of the COPPS strategy will be lost on the new officers, and the chief executive's will to implement or maintain the concept will be undermined or even destroyed.

Many police agencies are now retooling their FTO programs to emphasize community policing. The Reno, Nevada, Police Department, for example, is now being assisted by the Police Executive Research Forum with funding by the federal Office of Community Oriented Policing Services to develop a model FTO program that fully integrates COPPS concepts and skills. Exhibit 8.2 describes how the Savannah, Georgia, Police Department uses the FTO under COPPS.

In-Service

In-service training provides an opportunity to impart information and to reinforce new skills learned in the academy and FTO program. In-service classes are useful for sharing officers' experiences in applying COPPS to a variety of problems, as well as their collaboration with other city agencies, social service organizations, or the community.

In-service training is one of the primary means of changing the culture and attitudes of persons trained and experienced in reactive policing. The entire department must be knowledgeable of what COPPS is and is not, and training

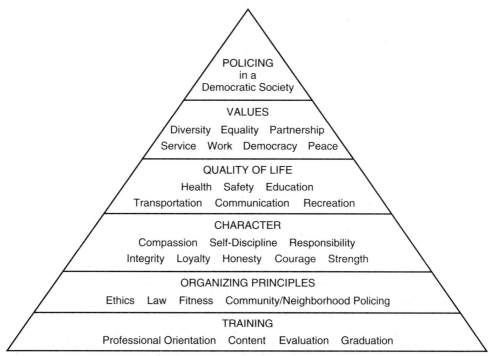

FIGURE 8.2 Massachusetts' values-driven educational model of police training: Basic course for police. [*Source:* Howard Lebowitz, "Academy Training Curriculum Minimizes the Physical Factor, Emphasizes Moral Decision Making," *Community Policing Exchange* (March/April 1997), p. 2. Used with permission.]

must target some of the common misperceptions about this strategy (for example, that it is soft on crime, will contribute to corruption, and is nothing more than social work).[10]

Obviously, a tremendous challenge for large police departments is providing COPPS training for all of the many hundreds or even thousands of officers and civilians. Some large agencies have used videotaped or computer-assisted training. Many departments, using drug-forfeiture funds, have also purchased high-technology equipment for use with training. To maximize the effect of COPPS training and to ensure that the proper message gets across, however, police executives should ensure that these methods are supplemental only and that instructors are physically present to facilitate training and answer questions. In addition to COPPS courses and orientations, departmental newsletters can disseminate information to personnel on a regular basis.

Roll Call

Roll call training is that period of time—from 15 to 30 minutes prior to the beginning of a tour of duty—in which supervisors prepare officers for patrol. Roll call sessions usually begin with a supervisor assigning the officers to their respective

Exhibit 8.2 Savannah, Georgia: Enhanced Field Training under COPPS

According to the Savannah Police Department, the ideal time to expose recruits to community policing is while they are open minded and, therefore, more impressionable.

Where to begin: The first challenge is in finding the right people, looking at the department's hiring process, recruiting and hiring officers for the future, looking for prospective employees who are analytical and motivated, and finding people who can work without being scrutinized. Then, the recruits' first introduction to community policing should be in the academy, focusing on its theory. Should the academy not teach community policing, the subject must be introduced during the departmental training phase.

In the field: Once the recruits begin the field training phase, the FTO should present COPPS in a positive light. Show recruits neighborhoods that have made a positive transformation under COPPS, and introduce them to neighborhood leaders and residents who can attest to its successes.

Making it hands-on: Recruits should be encouraged to help the FTO with a small-scale community problem solving project. Take recruits to community meetings and let them observe the police and citizens working out problems together.

Providing guidance in the field: The community policing coordinator of the department, precinct, or bureau should make follow-up contact with recruits. Recruits can be easily swayed, so it is suggested that FTOs intervene to prevent these young, impressionable minds from being negatively influenced by any cynical veterans.

Source: Adapted from Bill Harvey, "Getting Recruits on Board through Enhanced Field Training," *Community Policing Exchange* (March/April 1999), pp. 1, 4.

beats. Information about wanted and dangerous persons and major incidents on previous shifts is usually disseminated. Other matters may also be addressed, such as issuing officers court subpoenas, explaining new departmental policies and procedures, and discussing shift and beat-related matters.

Roll call meetings afford an excellent opportunity for supervisors to update officers' knowledge and to present new ideas and techniques. This is particularly advantageous for small police agencies that have limited training staff and resources. For example, videotapes or problem solving case studies can be used at briefing sessions to provide relevant information.

Specialized Training

Specialized training involves issues presented at conferences dedicated solely to COPPS. Such conferences have been conducted in San Diego, California (in 2000 San Diego hosted its 11th annual International Problem-Oriented Policing Conference, which attracted more than 1,500 participants from around the world; at this conference the prestigious Herman Goldstein Award for Excellence in Problem-Oriented Policing awards are presented); Newport News, Virginia; Portland, Oregon; Reno, Nevada; and elsewhere throughout the United States. Specialized training is also provided by the federal Office of Community Oriented Policing Services, the Police Executive Research Forum, the International Association of Chiefs of Police, the Community Policing Consortium (composed of the International Association of Chiefs of Police, the National Organization of Black Law Enforcement Executives, the National Sheriffs Association, the Police Executive Research Forum, and the Police Foundation), and many other such entities. Exhibit 8.3 shows what the federal Office of Community Oriented Policing Services has done to disseminate training across the country, with its Regional Community Policing Institute concept.

It should also be emphasized that with the spread of the COPPS concept across the United States, many public and private universities and colleges (including community colleges) are now retooling their old patrol procedures, police in America, and community relations courses and are offering courses specifically

The 11th Annual International Problem-Oriented Policing Conference in San Diego, California, drew more than 1,500 participants worldwide. (*Courtesy* Police Executive Research Forum)

The federal Office of Community Oriented Policing Services (COPS) envisions community policing as a philosophy that promotes and supports organizational strategies to address the causes and reduce the fears of crime and social disorder through problem solving tactics and community–police partnerships. The COPS Office recognized that this philosophy brings about unique challenges and changes in the way the police are trained. In fiscal year 1999, the COPS Office awarded more than $23 million to 28 Regional Community Policing Institutes (RCPI) across the United States to provide comprehensive and innovative training and education for police agencies (http://www.usdoj.gov/cops/gpa/grant_prog/ca/ca_rcpi.htm). Integral to this training is a national cadre of trainers, electronic dissemination of training sessions and content, and the use of multimedia approaches. By late 2000, these RCPI sites had trained 77,000 private citizens and individuals from police and local government agencies. The 28 RCPI sites are in the following locations:

Arizona:	Arizona RCPI
	Navajo Nation RCPI
California:	California RCPI at LA
	California RCPI at San Diego
	Sacramento RCPI
Colorado:	Colorado Community Policing Institute
Florida:	St. Petersburg Junior College RCPI
Illinois:	Institute for Public Safety Partnerships, University of Illinois, Chicago
Indiana:	Fort Wayne Police Department RCPI
Kansas:	Wichita State University RCPI
Kentucky:	RCPI at Eastern Kentucky University
Louisiana:	Louisiana Community Policing Institute
Massachusetts:	RCPI for New England
Maryland:	Mid-Atlantic RCPI
Michigan:	Michigan State University RCPI
Minnesota:	Upper Midwest Community Policing Institute
Missouri:	Missouri Western State College RCPI
North Carolina:	Carolina's Institute for Community Policing
New Jersey:	New Jersey RCPI
New York:	New York State RCPI

Ohio:	Tri-State RCPI
Oklahoma:	Oklahoma RCPI
Oregon:	Western Community Policing Center
Tennessee:	Knoxville Police Department RCPI
Texas:	Texas RCPI at the University of Texas at Austin
	Texas RCPI at the Sam Houston State University
Washington:	Washington Western Regional Institute for
	Community Oriented Public Safety
West Virginia:	West Virginia RCPI

Source: Office of Community Oriented Policing Services, *Grants, Programs, and Activities: Training and Technical Assistance* (Washington, D.C.: Author, September 2000).

on community oriented policing and problem solving (see Exhibit 8.4). These postsecondary courses will become increasingly available and significant as the concept continues to expand.

TRAINING TECHNOLOGIES

Today most police administrators recognize the importance of education and training for their employees. Many, however—particularly those in small agencies—are faced with limited resources and can never or only occasionally afford to bring in instructors from other agencies. It is also difficult for them to send employees for training beyond the minimum number of hours mandated by their state's regulatory agency; in addition to costs related to course registration, travel, meals, and lodging, they must also endure the loss of the employees while they attend the training sessions.

As technology progresses, however, new and better methods of instruction and delivery of material continue to evolve. Such technologies for administrators who have limited resources include distance learning, interactive computer disks, satellite television, and even correspondence courses. On-demand learning allows students to receive their training without placing too great a burden on their personal or professional lives.[11] On-line training can be self-paced, around-the-clock, and interactive and can contain one-on-one coaching and mentoring. Private individuals as well as corporations, colleges, and universities[12] now offer COPPS courses on-line.

Instructor-based training will always exist in some form, but it appears that the instructor may soon augment interactive training rather than vice-versa. For example, CD-ROM training may require a live instructor via telephone, video, or in person to assist the student in order for the training to be effective.[13] Nearly every state is changing its training curriculums to reflect some form of interactive

---

Exhibit 8.4   Baccalaureate Degree Programs in COPPS

An emerging movement is the study of community policing philosophy, in which students explore, analyze, and develop a variety of strategies and skills required to effectively understand and implement COPPS. For example, in 1997 the Department of Criminal Justice (CJ) at the University of Nevada, Reno, launched a new Bachelor of Arts degree in COPPS. Course requirements are basically the same as the conventional CJ degree with 128 credits, except that majors must complete courses in several COPPS areas. Courses are generally offered in the evenings, and area police practitioners with strong COPPS as well as other academic credentials instruct in the program, which is open to anyone but is geared for nontraditional, in-service students.

Furthermore, graduate students at a number of colleges and universities—such as those at St. Cloud State University in Minnesota—can take community policing courses as well.

Finally, some schools (such as the University of Delaware, Division of Continuing Education) offer a Certificate in Community Policing with courses that include the basic elements of COPPS: problem solving, strategic planning, ethics, and diversity.

---

learning. Training in the future may be a combination of classroom, interactive, and hands-on practical learning.[14]

Exhibit 8.5 provides informational and training resources that are available on the Internet. Do not overlook training that may be available via e-mail, audio- and videocassettes, teleconferencing, and television programming.

THE TRAINING PROGRAM

Purpose, Objectives, Components

The purpose of COPPS training is to provide officers with a level of understanding that allows them to effectively apply problem solving and community engagement techniques to their daily work. The objectives of such a training curriculum include the following:

- Providing participants with an overview of the history of policing and research that serves as the foundation for the COPPS approach
- Providing participants with basic problem solving skills and knowledge of the elements of community engagement
- Sharing with participants examples of case studies in jurisdictions where COPPS has been successful

Exhibit 8.5 Using the Internet for COPPS

For a very low cost, the Internet allows police officers and trainers to communicate with their colleagues across the nation or abroad about policies and programs, and to exchange ideas and information. Following are some Internet addresses where trainers can conduct research and gain information concerning virtually anything about law enforcement.

www.usdoj.gov	U.S. Department of Justice link to all DOJ agencies; includes information about a wide range of research, training, and grants
www.officer.com	Directory related to law enforcement issues
www.census.gov/	U.S. Census Bureau; provides demographic information by jurisdiction
www.ssc.msu.edu/~people.cp/	National Center for Community Policing; center at Michigan State University providing research, training, and information concerning community policing nationwide
www.communitypolicing.org/	Community Policing Consortium; community policing topics are updated monthly and include an array of information such as training sessions and curricula
www.usdoj.gov/cops/	COPS Office; promotes policing strategies and offers a variety of grants, training, and education to state agencies and local communities nationwide; created under the 1994 Violent Crime Control and Law Enforcement Act, with $8.8 billion over six years

www.ncjrs.org	National Criminal Justice Reference Service; clearinghouse of publications and on-line reference service about a broad range of criminal justice issues
www.nlectc.org	National Law Enforcement and Corrections Technology Center; provides information about new equipment and technologies to federal, state, and local law enforcement and corrections officials
www.ojp.usdoj.gov/bjs	Bureau of Justice Statistics; includes a variety of information about criminal justice statistics and provides links to other research Web sites
www.ih2000.net/ira/ira.htm	Law Enforcement Sites on the Web; lists all federal, state, and local agencies on the Web
www.policing.com/course1/	Representative of the kinds of on-line private training courses that are now provided
police.sas.ab.ca/	COPNET; myriad information about police training, job opportunities, links to other agencies, and chat rooms to various subjects

Also, the Police Executive Research Forum (PERF) (1120 Connecticut Avenue, Suite 930, Washington, D.C. 20036) manages an on-line resource known as POPNet that facilitates information sharing among problem solving officers and agencies across the country. POPNet provides a library of successful problem solving examples, and a bulletin board is in the planning stages. PERF also has literally dozens of COPPS publications that can assist trainers. The Community Policing Consortium (1726 M St. N.W., Suite 801, Washington, D.C. 20036; e-mail: look@aspensys.com), furthermore, publishes the *Information Access Guide,* a compilation of community policing practitioners, community organizers, and volunteers, updated and released the first week of every month.

- Providing participants with the opportunity to demonstrate the application of the problem solving model to local problems
- Sharing with participants the benefits of collaborating with other government agencies, businesses, social service organizations, and the community in a COPPS approach
- Exploring with participants the changes in leadership, management, and supervision styles required to develop an environment conducive to the implementation of COPPS
- Helping participants identify the internal and external organizational barriers to COPPS and to implementing problem oriented policing in their respective agencies
- Identifying other external individuals and groups that lend support to COPPS, such as business leaders, other government agencies, social service organizations, and the media

These objectives are discussed in detail in the next sections, following which we examine some sample training curricula that are in use around the country.

The University of Delaware offers a "Certificate in Community Policing." Courses include the basic elements of COPPS: problem solving, strategic planning, ethics, and diversity. (*Courtesy* University of Delaware)

Generally, problem solving requires that officers possess research skills, analytical abilities, and communications skills (including skills in public presentation; conflict resolution, including diffusing hostile situations and mediation; and group process, such as running public meetings and working with teams).[15] It also requires a more in-depth understanding of CPTED (discussed in Chapter 4).[16]

The Evolution of Policing

As indicated in Chapter 1, the evolution of policing toward COPPS has followed a logical progression. Policing, like other government organizations and private businesses, has simply developed new models for providing service based on past experiences and wisdom. Change has not been easy, however, nor has it been readily accepted by police officers. They often pose the following concerns and criticisms when new training or ideas are proposed: "Isn't this just a rehash of new methods that failed?" "It's just reinventing the wheel." "The way we're doing it works fine—my evaluations prove it." It is important, therefore, that trainers begin their instruction on COPPS with an overview of the history and evolution of policing.

This aspect of training should begin by describing the evolution of policing toward a COPPS approach. Chapter 1 provides an outline for this task. It is important to include in this history a discussion of how our society is changing and what the police must do to confront these challenges. Chapter 2, furthermore, includes an overview of what has occurred and what is expected to occur in the areas of demographics and crime, including discussion of the elderly, juvenile crime, violence, high technology, drugs, and fear of crime. This section of training should end by providing participants with clear definitions of the separate but complementary notions of community oriented and problem oriented policing.

Beginning COPPS training in this manner allows the trainer to answer questions most often posed and provide participants with a better understanding of the benefits as well as the necessity of a COPPS approach. It will be difficult for the trainer to gain the trainees' attention and participation until these questions are addressed. As indicated previously, the key to convincing officers that change is necessary is to show them how the training directly relates to their day-to-day work.

Community Engagement

As we have noted, providing service to the community is the very nature of police work. Unfortunately, most academy and in-service officer training limits discussions of the role of the community to police–community relations and crime prevention.

In this phase of the training program, participants should be introduced to the concept of community policing and its primary components. This segment also provides an opportunity for the participants to interact with one another in examining why their agency is moving into such a method of policing and what changes are likely to occur by doing so. The desired outcomes for this part of the training are for the participants to be able to

- Define what is meant by "community" and the concept of "community policing" and its components
- Identify why police have a difficult time dealing with crime alone and how a collaborative approach to problem solving can lead to more effective crime control
- Know how to develop a community profile that analyzes its problems and identifies its leaders and available resources
- Know how to communicate and mobilize the community using approaches such as public meetings; newsletters; and contact with leaders, groups, and organizations representing the community
- Understand a community's cultural, ethnic, and racial diversity
- Discuss the concepts of a "total quality" or "customer service" orientation in policing
- Identify the changes that may arise, both for their agency and for themselves

Diversity Training

COPPS training should include, and provides an excellent opportunity for, a training strategy for policing in a multicultural society (for an example see Exhibit 8.6). As Chapter 2 described, we live in an increasingly diverse society with many new cultural mores and languages that pose new challenges for police. Policing these new communities requires understanding and new skills.

Few people in policing today would dispute the important role that training must play in improving the relationship between police and the ethnocultural and visible minorities in communities. As former Los Angeles and Philadelphia police chief Willie Williams stated, police and people in general often do not like discussing the topic of police–minority relations because "you step on somebody's toes or it's embarrassing." Williams added that COPPS is "an issue whose time has come so we can stop tap-dancing" around racial and ethnic conflicts.[17]

At the same time, there appears to be increasing disagreement about which approaches are most effective as well as whether some approaches are counterproductive. In attempting to determine the role of training in promoting policing in a manner that is culturally sensitive and responsive, and an approach to training that will yield the greatest success, police agencies must remember the following six principles:

1. Respect for and sensitivity to the diverse communities served is essential for effective policing.
2. Respect for and sensitivity to ethnocultural communities can best be achieved through a broad-based multicultural strategy.

EXHIBIT 8.6   Diversity Training in Rockland County, New York

An example of diversity training is evident in Rockland County, New York. With a population of only 265,000 and a close proximity to New York City, it has attracted people from 15 different cultures. Settled in groups throughout the county are people of Jamaican, Korean, Hasidic, Filipino, Cambodian, Haitian, Chinese, and Ramapough Mountain Indian origins. Thus, the police must learn and be sensitive to the various cultures, customs, and religions of the citizens they serve.

The Rockland County sheriff's office has developed a police sensitivity training manual, targeted to police officers ranking from top brass to rookies and auxiliary personnel to judges. The 200-page manual's purpose is to break down the barriers between police and citizens. Contained in the manual is material describing each culture's religion, language, characteristics, and community dynamics (female officers, for example, learn that touching a Hasidic male is considered offensive). A 15-member group representing the various cultures in the county serves as a liaison council with the sheriff's office, to facilitate communication among officers and citizens. The training manual is also an integral part of the county police academy.

Source: Marie Merla, "Fair Treatment for All: Equal Opportunity Police Training" (Washington, D.C.: Community Policing Consortium, *Community Policing Exchange*, March/April 1996), p. 2.

---

3. Training must be an essential element of such a strategy.
4. Training must be ongoing and built into the experience of policing; that is, it must be more than a course or two on multiculturalism.
5. A multicultural strategy and the training that supports it will be most effective if they are perceived as integrated aspects of the philosophy and operations of policing.
6. A multicultural strategy and training program must be created in consultation with the ethnocultural communities served by the police.[18]

Although it is difficult to imagine how one could teach officers about the values and customs of all the communities they might encounter, training must attempt to overcome stereotyping if the officers' contact with the community is to be largely proactive and in response to perceived problems. Officers must understand that policing in a pluralistic society is challenging and that respect for and sensitivity to diversity are essential for effective policing.[19]

Problem Solving: Basics and Exercises

The problem solving session of training entails teaching officers the basics of conflict resolution, which is the focus of COPPS; it puts philosophy into practice, or "walks the talk" of COPPS. The analysis of problems is the most important component of problem solving. In-depth analysis provides the information necessary for officers to develop effective responses. The S.A.R.A. problem solving model (scanning, analysis, response, and assessment, which was discussed in detail in Chapter 4) is presented through an interactive lecture and use of case studies. The desired outcomes for this segment include the following:

- Identifying each component and principal elements of the S.A.R.A. process
- Learning the importance of in-depth analysis in the complete identification of a problem
- Learning to identify and apply a variety of responses to a problem
- Discussing the application of situational crime prevention and CPTED concepts on the environmental influences on crime and disorder
- Discussing the importance of both quantitative and qualitative evaluation measures of problem solving efforts

The California Attorney General's Office offers a clearinghouse of COPPS resources for agencies, including videos, curricula, Internet sources and links, and trainers and technical assistance.

- Discussing how accountability, empowerment, service orientation, and partnership fit into problem solving

Regarding the use of problem solving exercises, participants should identify current problems in their assigned areas. Facilitators should divide the classes into small work groups and ask them to examine each problem, developing strategies for analyzing, responding to, and assessing the effectiveness of their problem solving efforts. Figures and tables throughout Chapter 4 can be used to lead officers through the process. Brainstorming should be discussed and used as an appropriate tool to foster innovative and creative thinking in the work groups.[20] The desired outcomes for this segment include the participants' ability to

- Identify problems on the officer's beat
- Demonstrate an understanding of the problem analysis triangle
- Identify the diversity of resources available, variety of strategies to address the problem, and crime prevention techniques
- Evaluate the results using methods similar to those used in the analysis of the problem
- Discuss the advantages and disadvantages of the methods used

Once completed, each group will have the opportunity to present its problem to the entire class and explain each step of the S.A.R.A. model. Through these presentations, the participants will be exposed to the problem solving efforts of the other groups. This method of instruction not only provides officers with a practical exercise but also gives them the opportunity to work through an actual problem on their beat. Their efforts in the classroom can easily be repeated in the field, providing them with their first COPPS projects.

Case Studies

The case studies session provides the trainer with an opportunity to use the S.A.R.A. model of problem solving in addressing an actual situation. Case studies are an excellent training mechanism because they allow the instructor to put the theory (or, as in this case, a problem solving model) into practice. They also allow the trainer to demonstrate the flexibility of the model as well as emphasize important steps, such as analysis. The desired outcomes of this training segment include the participants' ability to

- Demonstrate the steps of S.A.R.A.
- Illustrate the importance of thoroughly analyzing a problem using a variety of informational resources and using the problem analysis triangle
- Discuss the methods and resources involved in problem solving
- Discuss the benefit of the problem solving model over traditional incident-driven responses

There are several resources from which to obtain and use case studies of successful problem solving initiatives, including the anthology *Problem Oriented Policing: Crime-Specific Problems, Critical Issues, and Making POP Work* by the Police Executive Research Forum,[21] and newspapers, such as the free *Community Policing Exchange,* published by the Community Policing Consortium.

Appendix A provides several case studies of problem solving efforts by police agencies across the United States. These examples show how the S.A.R.A. process was applied to a variety of problems to formulate effective responses.

Leadership and Middle Managers

Executive leadership and middle managers' support are critical to implementing the organizational changes required by the transition to COPPS. Chapters 6 and 7 discussed the role of leadership and management as they relate to the implementation and cultural change of an organization adopting COPPS. Police executives and managers face the same challenges as their counterparts in other organizations:

> Like most large, public service agencies, the requirements for innovation in policing include: changing the formal corporate values as well as the subculture of "front-line" policing; having an inspired chief executive who is committed to the new approach; having a motivated and experienced level of middle management which can implement the new approach in operational terms; recognizing innovations that come from the street level of policing; and obtaining support for the new approach and the risks that it runs from the police governing authorities and from the local community.[22]

In many instances, the ultimate challenge to a police organization is to change its hierarchical, paramilitary structure. Supervisors, managers, and executives working within a flattened, COPPS oriented organization would require new skills to ensure the successful adaptation and functioning of the police organization.[23] Exhibit 8.7 is an example of one attempt to support leadership in its transition to COPPS.

The Sergeant as Coach and Manager

As we pointed out in previous chapters, the successful implementation of a strategy such as COPPS requires the support of the first-line supervisor. One of the most difficult hurdles for supervisors to overcome is the idea that giving officers the opportunity to be creative and take risks does not diminish the role or authority of the supervisor. Risk taking and innovation require mutual trust between supervisors and line officers.

Supervising in a COPPS environment means a change from being a "controller," primarily concerned with rules, to being a "facilitator" and "coach" for officers involved in problem solving. Supervisors must learn to encourage innovation

---

EXHIBIT 8.7   Ambitious in Seattle: Leadership Conferencing and Tool Kits

The Seattle, Washington, Police Department (SPD), in collaboration with the Police Executive Research Forum, has offered a three-day conference entitled "Leadership Sessions to Support Problem Oriented Policing." The purpose of the conference is to "provide a forum for inspiration, motivation, guidance, and practical tools to leaders who are committed to supporting problem solving in their agencies." Invitees included police supervisors and managers and researchers. Topics included ethical challenges for leaders, politics inside and outside the organization, examining the organization from top to bottom to see how every system and structure supported problem oriented policing, and leadership.

The SPD also developed a "tool kit" of community policing training opportunities for department employees, other city employees, and community members. "Essentials of Problem Solving" is a one-day workshop covering the S.A.R.A. process, the agency's mission and values, and problem solving case studies. "Leadership Skills" is a three-day course for field training officers, supervisors, and managers that includes discussions on coaching, feedback, facilitation, leadership, and cultural competency. Also, a "Training of Trainers" for police and community academies was developed to assist community and police instructors to incorporate the mission and values of the organization into every phase of academy training. The course also includes adult learning theory, gender inclusiveness, and facilitation skills.

Source: Norm Stamper, "A Training Menu to Support Problem Oriented Policing" (Seattle, Wash.: Seattle Police Department, 1997).

---

and risk taking among their officers. Supervisors must be well skilled in problem solving, especially in the analysis of problems and evaluation of efforts. Conducting workload analyses and finding the time for officers to problem solve and engage with the community (discussed in Chapter 4) is an important aspect of supervision. A supervisor must also be prepared to intercede and remove any obstacles to officers' problem solving efforts. Supervisors must be able to respond to the following questions when officers are confused or resistant to the implementation of COPPS:

- What are the advantages and disadvantages of the traditional form of police supervision?
- What are officers' complaints about management?
- What are officers' complaints about their work?

- What kinds of objections does the supervisor anticipate from officers and detectives when they are told about COPPS?
- How will you respond to such statements as, "This is social work and we're not social workers," "We don't have the skills or training to do all this," or "Other cops won't see us as real cops"?[24]

COPPS supervisors should also understand that not all patrol officers or detectives will like this kind of work or be good at it. However, some officers will work on their own unpaid time to solve problems. Furthermore, subordinates will occasionally want to work on problems that really should not be police business and do not deserve a high priority. Supervisors also need to be informed that they must avoid isolating the problem solving function from the rest of the department. This could create the illusion that problem solving is composed of "privileged prima donnas" who get benefits that other officers do not. Also, supervisors should not allow the COPPS initiative to become a mere public relations campaign; the emphasis is always on results.[25]

The St. Petersburg, Florida, Police Department identified the characteristics of the "ideal" sergeant under the COPPS philosophy:

Availability	Leader
Flexibility	Champion
Innovative	Trustworthy
Widely experienced	Good speaker
Facilitator	Respected
Open minded	Risk taker
Humorous	Coach
Supportive	Dependable [26]
Buffer	

Finding the time for officers to engage in problem solving and tracking their efforts are also challenges for first-line supervisors. Chapter 4 includes a section on recapturing officers' time.

Barriers and Benefits

A large group discussion may also be facilitated in which participants are asked to identify the internal and external organizational barriers to COPPS and to implementing problem oriented policing in their respective agencies. Following the identification of all barriers, strategies are discussed for removing or dealing with the barriers. This discussion helps prepare the trainers for the questions and concerns of the officers in attendance. It also gives the trainers the opportunity to recognize the many benefits of a COPPS approach to policing.

One method of accomplishing this is to divide the class into small groups of 5 to 10 participants. Each group is then asked to identify 10 internal barriers to implementing COPPS (e.g., mind-set of officers, supervisory or management practices, time availability, lack of crime analysis, prohibition against officers contacting outside agencies, and so on), 10 external barriers (e.g., lack of support from city council, limited coordination with other city agencies, unrealistic expectations from citizens), and 10 benefits (e.g., reduction in calls for service, improved officer morale, improved police–community relations, increased officer performance). The groups should be given 30 to 45 minutes for this portion of the exercise and instructed not to debate the issues. Each member should participate and the group should prioritize the 10 most important items in each category.

Another commonly used method for initiating and teaching COPPS is for the trainer to lead the discussion on barriers. The key is for the trainer to facilitate an open discussion of the underlying concerns of the participants and to lead them toward discovering options to overcoming the barriers. The session should end with the trainer leading a discussion on the benefits.

The desired outcomes for this session include providing the trainer with a gauge as to how receptive the participants were to the training; allowing participants to voice their concerns and fears about the agency's transition to new methods of policing; providing command staff with a list of concerns that are most pressing and will need their attention; helping the trainer determine what additional training may be needed; and, finally, allowing the trainer to end the training on a high note by discussing the benefits.

Other Training Considerations

The curriculum discussed provides a basic foundation for COPPS. What has not been discussed are the special considerations for those individuals and groups occupying positions both within and outside the police agency that lend support to COPPS. These groups and individuals include

- Support personnel (police)
- The community
- Business leaders
- Other government agencies
- Social service organizations
- Elected officials
- The media

Support Personnel

Support personnel provide officers with information that is vital to the success of COPPS. For example, it would be difficult for officers to engage in problem solving if the dispatcher, unaware of the COPPS philosophy, was concerned only

It is important to educate the public about community policing. (*Courtesy Kris Solow, City of Charlotte, North Carolina*)

with eliminating pending calls and continued to dispatch officers to low-priority calls. The desired outcomes for training support personnel include the ability to

- Support and promote the COPPS concept within their agency and community
- Consider COPPS as a team approach
- Adopt a service and customer oriented approach
- Know the resources within their agency and the community
- Work with all employees and citizens to solve community problems
- Share information with other agency members
- Identify, analyze, and develop strategies to address problems encountered in their working environment
- Locate and organize resources required to implement solutions
- Employ other police officers as well as public and private agencies in problem solving strategies
- Use problem solving techniques to create innovative solutions
- Monitor involvement by nonpolice agency resources and follow up to ensure satisfactory results
- Make the first referral the correct referral
- Be willing to evaluate and improve their performance

The Community

As we discussed at length in Chapter 4, the community plays a vital role in COPPS. There are a number of ways in which the department and officers can educate citizens about COPPS, including newsletters, public service announcements, neighborhood meetings, and citizens' academies such as the one presented in Exhibit 8.8.

Business Leaders

It is important that community and business leaders are oriented in the operation of COPPS. Experience has shown that involving the business community can contribute to the success of the COPPS approach. Police executives must never underestimate the level of influence and concern possessed by the business community. Business and industrial leaders can be valuable allies, even with respect to providing financial support in causes they believe will help the community. Involving them can foster a cooperative relationship and can have any number of possible beneficial outcomes. Businesspeople might donate time and equipment or provide valuable information for problem solving efforts. Apartment owners should be informed of the wide array of services officers can provide under a COPPS philosophy, from screening potential tenants to keeping the area free of abandoned vehicles and trash. And business owners who apply CPTED principles may realize significant reductions in crime.

Other Government Agencies

Previous chapters have discussed how problem solving necessarily includes the involvement of agencies other than the police or sheriff's departments. A large percentage of calls for service handled by the police involve noncriminal matters that can be better handled by other city or county agencies. Furthermore, there is considerable overlap between agencies; a deteriorating neighborhood might implicate the health, fire, zoning, prosecutor's, street, social services, or other agencies in addition to the police department. Thus, it is imperative that key persons in those organizations—active partners in problem solving—be trained in the philosophy and workings of COPPS and CPTED, as shown, for example, in Exhibit 8.9. This is community oriented government, which is discussed thoroughly in Chapter 3.

Social Service Organizations

With respect to social service agencies, it is not uncommon for these organizations and police agencies to "fire cannon shots across the bows" of one another. When problems arise involving deteriorating neighborhoods and concomitant problems (such as child abuse), which involve both social service and police practitioners, it is particularly important that communication be given top

---

EXHIBIT 8.8   The Citizens' Police Academy and COPPS

The citizens' police academy concept appeared in the 1980s to create, through education, better understanding and communication among citizens and the police. Citizens can learn about the police role in the community as well as their views, methods, and functions, whereas the police can find out how and why citizens feel as they do about issues. These academies can also serve as a vehicle for imparting knowledge about community policing and problem solving to citizens.

Both the Arlington County, Virginia, and Santa Barbara, California, police departments offer 12-week citizens' police academies. Both provide citizens with an overview of their agency's history and mission, policies and procedures, as well as training in the use of firearms, police ethics, discipline policy and philosophy, communication, drug enforcement and education, and criminal and traffic law. Both agencies also provide introductory and applied COPPS instruction and include crime prevention through environmental design (CPTED, discussed thoroughly in Chapter 5) classes. The classes are taught by agency executives and veteran officers.

Sources: Arlington County, Virginia, Police Department, Web page: www.co.arlington.va.us/pol/comm.htm (12 February 2001); Santa Barbara, California, Police Department, Community Relations Unit, Web page: www. sbpd.com (21 February 2001).

---

priority. Social service workers must also understand the philosophy and operation of COPPS, because they can serve as a valuable resource and can also provide referrals to the police for solving problems. People who are homeless, mentally ill, survivors of domestic violence, and survivors of schoolyard violence are examples of the people whose calls for service account for a high volume of police responses. Working together, the police and other social service agencies can apply principles of problem solving.

Elected Officials

Politicians must be involved and educated early in the planning of COPPS. They often have the final word on whether new ideas or programs will be implemented. Failure to involve the mayor, city or county manager, and city or county commissioner can be like "shooting oneself in the foot." Not only is it bad for maintaining close interpersonal relationships with the mayor or manager and the governing board but it may also come to pass that these same people, also wishing to curry political favor with their constituents, may strongly disagree with the concept and openly reject the department and officers' COPPS efforts.

EXHIBIT 8.9   City Employee Training in Richmond, Virginia

The Richmond, Virginia, city employee police academy training session consists of a 14-week course that is similar to the city's citizen police academy. The city employee academy educates attendees in COPPS. The training forum helps police and other city employees identify one another. It teaches the latter about all sorts of crimes and police issues, as well as how such things as inadequate lighting, graffiti, and condemned buildings can foster crime. City employees are also encouraged to engage in ride-alongs with police and to serve as the "eyes and ears" of crime prevention as they go out in the neighborhoods each day.

Source: Adapted from Jerry A. Oliver, "City Employees Get Trained in Police Services" (Washington, D.C.: Community Policing Consortium, *Community Policing Exchange,* March/April 1996), p. 6.

The education of politicians regarding COPPS is also important in other respects. They need to understand that this philosophy is unique. A police chief may be horrified to hear the mayor announce, in response to a recent tragedy, that henceforth the police would make every effort to arrive no later than 15 minutes after any call for service was received. They must be taught that rapid response to calls is less effective at catching criminals than educating the public to call the police sooner after a crime is committed.[27] Police executives must inform politicians that police response time is largely unrelated to the probability of making an arrest or locating a witness.[28] Politicians must also understand that personnel evaluations are to be conducted differently under this strategy and that reported crimes may well increase as the partnership between the police and the public grows; in other words, under a COPPS approach the FBI's *Uniform Crime Reports* must cease to be the only or principal "yardstick" of police effectiveness.

In short, police executives must not assume that local politicians are well versed in the who, what, why, and how of COPPS. Elected officials must be educated in order to understand and support the concept. The police executive must decide when to bring the politicians on board, and deciding on a plan to approach and train them should be done early in the planning stage.

The Media

The police often overlook opportunities provided by the media. First, the local media provide an excellent forum for the police department to publicly announce its implementation of COPPS and its goals and objectives. To assist in this endeavor many departments have designated a public information officer (PIO). Large departments treat the PIO as the principal spokesperson for the organization, whereas others use the office simply as a facilitator of information. In smaller departments, where a PIO would be superfluous, the chief or sheriff must master the skills of public relations without the advantage of a PIO buffer.[29]

The most significant facets of effective media relations are truthfulness and reasonable accessibility. Another good tip for the chief executive is to "never alienate anyone who buys ink by the barrel." Of course, this caveat applies to the electronic media as well as the print media.

The chief executive who is attempting to implement COPPS will want and need to market the concept. After the strategy is implemented, COPPS successes should be reported to the community. The media can be of tremendous assistance in these regards, and they can present a police force with interests and abilities beyond the traditional, reactive, and incident-driven officers. Media accounts of COPPS and other activities can directly assist the police in obtaining resources. More than one department has passed a bond issue during difficult fiscal times for more personnel or newer facilities, because of favorable news accounts of police activities.[30]

A SAMPLE TRAINING PROGRAM

Next we look at a sample training program for preparing police personnel for their COPPS duties in Savannah, Georgia (also see Exhibit 8.10). The Savannah Police Department uses eight training modules, 38 hours in duration, for community oriented policing (COP). *Module I*, "Participatory Decisionmaking and Leadership Techniques for Management, Supervision, and Street Officers," is six hours long and is for upper-level supervisors. A professional facilitator presents this orientation, which is based largely on the concept of total quality management (discussed in Chapter 3).

Module II, "Community-Oriented Policing," is an overview that lasts four hours. It begins with the distribution of an in-depth study of crime in Savannah and exacerbating conditions that are found in the same high crime areas.

Module III explores "Problem-Oriented Policing" (POP) (four hours). POP is viewed by the department as a major component of COP. Themes and advantages are discussed, as are the means by which certain problems can be identified and solved through a structured process (the S.A.R.A. process, discussed in Chapter 4). The resources of the entire community are considered in relation to solving recurring problems. Also discussed are the report forms involved in POP for the officers to use in their duties.

Module IV, "Referral System, Materials, City Ordinances" (eight hours), examines the use of referrals and the specific agencies available to help in problem solving. Relevant city codes are reviewed with officers. This block of instruction includes discussions of the several benefits of a good referral system, the key elements of a "good" referral, sources for obtaining materials that explain referral services, and a crime victim brochure.

Module V, "Developing Sources of Human Information," focuses on communicating with citizens in a way that maximizes trust. Four hours in length, it

---

Exhibit 8.10   Practical Problem Solving Training in Charlotte-Mecklenburg

Members of the Charlotte-Mecklenburg, North Carolina, Police Department noticed that officers seemed to be underutilizing the agency's crime analysis capabilities. Indeed, it was determined that officers' training was all lecture-based and lacked a practical exercise component. The command staff believed this situation could be improved if officers were offered practical problem solving training sessions that introduced officers to the increased capacity of the Strategic Planning and Analysis Section (SP&A). A new problem solving course was developed that incorporated SP&A crime analysts as coinstructors with problem solving trainers and included practical exercises (officers prioritize a set of community problems, select a well-defined problem, analyze the problem, and make a presentation to command staff).

Source: John O'Hare and Marc DeLuca, workshop presentation at the 8th annual International Problem Oriented Policing Conference: Problem Oriented Policing 1997, November 17, 1997, San Diego, California.

---

focuses on problematic areas of field interviews and investigative detentions. Included are six barriers to effective communication, seven ways to enhance active listening, and a "citizen's internal checklist after a police–citizen contact." Reasons for conducting a field interview and the means for managing informant information are also included.

Module VI, "Neighborhood Meetings, Survey of Citizen Needs, Tactical Crime Analysis" (four hours), discusses how to organize and conduct neighborhood meetings and community surveys. Topics include identifying groups, formulating questions, pretesting, and gathering and analyzing data.

Module VII is "Crime Prevention Home and Business Surveys" (four hours). Crime prevention is examined in the context of community policing, and officers are trained to conduct security surveys of homes and businesses.

Finally, *Module VIII* explores tactical crime analysis; it entails organizing and interpreting crime data, identifying crime trends, and disseminating data in a timely manner (four hours).

Summary

This chapter has presented some of the obstacles to learning, an overview of those persons and groups needing to receive COPPS training, and types and component parts of a COPPS training program.

COPPS must become a philosophy before it can become a practice. This change in thinking is the major challenge facing those involved in the training and education of police officers and the public. This challenge is enhanced because large numbers of police officers and citizens require orientation and training in COPPS.

Police executives who have implemented the COPPS strategy must give due consideration to the training issue—a major aspect of COPPS that is a *sine qua non* of this strategy. Without training, there is nothing.

NOTES

1. P. B. Gove (ed.), *Webster's Encyclopedic Unabridged Dictionary of the English Language* (Springfield, Mass.: Merriam-Webster), pp. 1502–1503.
2. Larry K. Gaines, Victor E. Kappeler, and Jerald B. Vaughn, Policing in America (Cincinnati, Ohio: Anderson, 1994), pp. 88–89.
3. See, for example, Virginia Community Policing Institute, *Report on the Colloquium on the Future of Community Policing* (Richmond, Va.: Author, 1998), p. 1.
4. Brian A. Reaves and Timothy C. Hart, *Law Enforcement Management and Administrative Statistics, 1999: Data for Individual State and Local Agencies with 100 or More Officers* (Washington, D.C.: U.S. Department of Justice, Bureau of Justice Statistics, November 2000), p. v.
5. Michael E. Buerger, "Police Training as a Pentecost: Using Tools Singularly Ill-Suited to the Purpose of Reform," *Police Quarterly* 1 (1998):32.
6. *Ibid.*, p. 51.
7. *Ibid.*, p. 39.
8. Laurie Austen-Kern, "Training Needs Assessments," *The Law Enforcement Trainer* (November/December 1999):22.
9. Howard Lebowitz, "Academy Training Curriculum Minimizes the Physical Factor, Emphasizes Moral Decision Making" (Washington, D.C.: Community Policing Consortium, *Community Policing Exchange*, March/April 1997), p. 2.
10. Quoted in *ibid.*
11. Thomas Dempsey, "Cyberschool: Online Law Enforcement Classes," *FBI Law Enforcement Bulletin* (February 1998):10.
12. See, for example, the John Jay College of Criminal Justice School Safety and Security Professional Development course, "Community Policing in Schools," at www.jjay.cuny.edu/conference/teleconf/.
13. Richard D. Morrison, "Interactive Training," *Law Enforcement Technology* (January 2000):97.
14. Gregory May, quoted in *ibid.*
15. Province of British Columbia, Ministry of Attorney General, Police Services Branch, *Community Policing Advisory Committee Report* (Victoria, British Columbia, Canada: Author, 1993), pp. 54–55.
16. *Ibid.*, p. 55.
17. Quoted in P. A. Parker, "Tackling Unfinished Business," *Police* (December 1991):19.
18. Frum Himelfarb, "A Training Strategy for Policing in a Multicultural Society," *The Police Chief* (November 1991): 53–55.
19. *Ibid.*, pp. 53–54.
20. Nancy McPherson, "Problem Oriented Policing" (San Diego, Calif.: San Diego Police Department Training Outline, 1992), p. 2.
21. Tara O'Connor Shelley and Anne C. Grant (eds.), *Problem Oriented Policing: Crime-Specific Problems, Critical Issues, and Making POP Work* (Washington, D.C.: Police

Executive Research Forum, 1999).

22. Andre Normandeau and Barry Leighton, *A Vision of the Future of Policing in Canada: Police-Challenge 2000, Background Document* (Ottawa: Solicitor General Canada, Police and Security Branch, October 1990), p. 49.

23. Province of British Columbia, Ministry of Attorney General, Police Services Branch, *Community Policing Advisory Committee Report* (Victoria, British Columbia, Canada: Author, 1993), p. 56.

24. Police Executive Research Forum, "Supervising Problem-Solving" (Washington, D.C.: Author, training outline, 1990).

25. *Ibid.*, pp. 5–9.

26. Donald S. Quire, "Officers Select 'Ideal' Supervisors" (Washington, D.C.: Community Policing Consortium, *Community Policing Exchange* March/April 1996), p. 8.

27. George L. Kelling, Anthony Pate, Duane Dieckman, and Charles E. Brown, *The Kansas City Preventive Patrol Experiment: A Summary Report* (Washington, D.C.: The Police Foundation, 1974).

28. Joan Petersilia, "The Influence of Research on Policing," in *Critical Issues in Policing: Contemporary Readings*, eds. Roger C. Dunham and Geoffrey P. Alpert (Prospect Heights, Ill.: Waveland Press, 1989), pp. 230–47.

29. Arthur F. Nehrbass, "Promoting Effective Media Relations," *The Police Chief* (January 1989):40, 42–44.

30. See Ken Peak, Robert V. Bradshaw, and Ronald W. Glensor, "Improving Citizen Perceptions of the Police: `Back to the Basics' with a Community Policing Strategy," *Journal of Criminal Justice* 20 (1992):25–40.

handwritten note: ✓ Due 4-16 – major Topics – my Input –

POLICE IN A DIVERSE SOCIETY

> No man will treat with indifference the principle of race. It is the key of history.
>
> —Disraeli
>
> I believe we are most likely to mistrust people we don't know, most likely to hate someone we can't relate to, and most likely to not understand someone we don't communicate with.
>
> —Richard Myers, Chief of Police, Appleton, Wisconsin

INTRODUCTION

A minority group is a group or category of people who can be distinguished by special physical or cultural traits that can used to single them out for differential and unequal treatment. We observed in Chapter 1 that U.S. society is rapidly becoming more diverse; it is a cornucopia of multicultural, multiracial, and ethnically rich people with different and competing norms, mores, values, languages, experiences, and expectations. This increase in cultural diversity and languages poses new challenges for the police—who must learn about the diverse cultures if they are to be successful in their objective of providing aid and assistance to all people.

This is not strictly a black and white issue; Latino/Hispanic Americans, Asian/Pacific Americans, and other ethnic minorities have also had difficult relations with the police. Tensions have arisen because many racial and ethnic minorities, homosexuals, and women believed they had been prevented from entering the police field. The most serious problems in police–minority relations, however, have involved African Americans. We, therefore, devote a preponderance of this chapter's discussion to examining race relations between African Americans and police.

We begin this chapter with a brief history of police–minority conflict and contemporary views of police and minorities toward one another. Next we consider whether criminal justice in the United States systematically discriminates against minorities, including the sources of tensions wrought by police field practices. Then we consider some means by which police–minority relations can be enhanced, focusing on what community oriented policing and problem solving (COPPS) can do to facilitate that endeavor, including an understanding of cultural customs, differences, and problems.

Following a discussion of the need for diversity in police organizations, we examine "what works": innovative programs in several cities that have built bridges to their minorities communities. After considering police responses to hate crimes, we conclude the chapter with some scenarios involving ethnic customs that police officers might confront.

POLICE AND MINORITIES: A HISTORY OF CONFLICT

Changing Laws and Civil Unrest

In 1900 the African American scholar and activist W. E. B. DuBois said the problem of the twentieth century is the problem of the color line. More than 100 years later we are still proving him right. In the past four decades many changes in society have influenced the nature of police–minority relations:

- The 1954 *Brown v. Topeka Board of Education*[1] decision of the U.S. Supreme Court declared that separate educational facilities were inherently unequal.
- The use of civil disobedience and nonviolent resistance increased in the 1950s and 1960s and the Civil Rights Act was passed in 1964. Almost all of the riots in the 1960s were sparked by incidents involving the police.[2]
- The Equal Employment Opportunity Commission was established and the 1972 Amendment to the Civil Rights Act became law.[3]

Collectively, these actions prohibited discrimination in education, hiring and promotion, voting, and use of public accommodations, among other things.

Of particular importance in the history of U.S. race relations are the events that occurred between 1960 and 1970, when police–minority encounters frequently precipitated racial outbursts. Specifically, Harlem, Watts, Newark, and Detroit all were scenes of major race riots during the 1960s. There were 75 civil

A scene from the Walker Report of the 1968 Democratic National Convention in Chicago.

disorders involving African Americans and the police in 1967 alone, with at least 83 people killed, mostly African Americans. In addition, many police officers and firefighters were killed or injured. Property damage in these riots totaled hundreds of millions of dollars.[4] The 1970s busing programs introduced to integrate schools resulted in white "backlash" and more interracial conflict.

In the late 1980s police–community relations appeared to worsen, with a major riot in Miami, Florida, in 1989. Also in the 1980s, affirmative action programs led to charges of reverse discrimination and more dominant-group backlash.[5] More recently, of course, there has been burning and looting in Miami, Los Angeles, Atlanta, Las Vegas, Washington, D.C., St. Petersburg (Florida), and other cities. These incidents have demonstrated that the same tensions that found temporary release on the streets of African American communities in the past still remain with us.

The police were involved in all of the social changes described. At times police have been used to prevent minority group members from demonstrating on behalf of civil rights and on occasion police have had to use force against protesting groups. At other times the police have been required to protect those same protesting minorities from the wrath of the dominant group and others who opposed peaceful demonstrations. Over time, alienation has developed from these contacts. Thus, members of both groups today have an uneasy coexistence with a good deal of "baggage" based on what they have seen, heard, or been told of their interactions throughout history. The phrase *police–community relations*, as Samuel Walker wrote, is really a euphemism for *police–race relations*:

The police have not had the same kinds of conflicts with the white majority community as they do with racial minorities. The most serious aspect of the . . . problem involves *black Americans.* Similar problems exist with respect to other racial-minority groups. In areas with large numbers of *Hispanic Americans* . . . there are also serious conflicts with the police. *Native Americans* . . . have also had conflict with the police. Similar problems exist in cities with large *Asian-American* communities (emphases in original).[6]

Police–community problems are part of a larger problem of racism in our society. The highly respected National Academy of Sciences concluded more than a decade ago that "black crime and the position of blacks within the nation's system of criminal justice administration are related to past and present social opportunities and disadvantages and can be best understood through consideration of blacks' overall social status."[7] Recent mass gatherings in Washington, D.C., engendered by such groups as the Southern Christian Leadership Conference and the Rainbow Coalition, have involved protests against racial profiling (discussed later), police brutality, and other perceived prejudices toward people of color; such assemblies would indicate that the Academy's statement is still valid today. Minority group members remain frustrated because the pace of gains in our society has not kept pace with their expectations.

Police–Public Views toward Each Other

Interestingly, national surveys have found that an overwhelming majority of Americans are satisfied with the police in their community. One writer stated that, "On the whole, the public is modestly positive in its perceptions of the police."[8] Similar responses have been obtained in local surveys. Research has shown consistently, however, that from at least as early as 1968 to the present nonwhites—especially African Americans—express less favorable attitudes toward the police than do whites.[9]

The attitudes of minorities, however, do not necessarily reflect personal experience with the police. One survey found that twice as many African Americans as whites agreed with the statement that the police did not respond quickly to calls for service in their neighborhoods; only 25 percent of African Americans reported that it happened to them.[10]

To many minorities the police are an "occupying force," more concerned with restricting their freedom than providing service to their community. From the police's point of view, minority neighborhoods have not always been supportive of their efforts to combat crime.[11] Which perspective is more accurate? Perhaps that question cannot be answered. However, a key element in police–community relations—and one that is often overlooked—is how the police perceive the public.

Generally, studies have indicated that the police do not have an accurate perception of public attitudes, consistently viewing the public as hostile. As early as 1950, William Westley's pioneering work on the police subculture demonstrated that the majority (73 percent) of police officers thought the public was "against the police, [or] hates the police."[12] In 1967 Jerome Skolnick determined that suspicion of and hostility toward the public were among the key ingredients of the police officer's "working personality."[13] One year later the Kerner Commission found that about one-third of police officers surveyed in 13 large cities believed that "most" blacks "regard the police as enemies."[14] James Q. Wilson also concluded that police officers "probably exaggerate the extent of public hostility."[15]

Some police officers develop misperceptions of public attitudes because of selective contacts with the public. Not having regular contact with a cross-section of the community, and dealing in large measure with those who bend or blatantly break the laws, they become calloused and cynical toward the public. Dealing so often with lawbreakers, they sometimes forget that only a small fraction of the public choose to earn a living via illegal means. Furthermore, they often deal with the young and the lower-class male population, which is disproportionately involved in crime. Many of these contacts are negative and necessarily involve force and challenges to police authority. As a result, the attitudes of police officers change significantly during their career, especially during the early stages.

MINORITIES AND THE CRIMINAL JUSTICE SYSTEM

Sources of Tension: Racial Profiling and Other Field Tactics

Is the criminal justice system biased in its treatment of minorities? Many people remain convinced that the justice system unfairly draws minorities into its web, that police methods are at the forefront of this practice, and, therefore, that the answer to that question is a resounding yes. This has been and continues to be one of the most sensitive charges against the criminal justice system throughout its history, and it is our next topic of discussion.

In racial profiling—also known as "driving while black or brown" (DWBB)—a police officer stops a vehicle simply because the driver is of a certain race, acting on a personal bias.[16] This issue has driven a deep wedge between the police and minorities, many of whom claim to be victims of this practice. Indeed, the New Jersey state police superintendent was fired by that state's governor in March 1999 for statements that were perceived as racially insensitive concerning racial profiling. The police argue that the drivers they pull over (often, the police argue, in response to a bulletin or to suspicious behavior) or where the traffic stop occurs (for example, in an area with a large number of drug offenders) is police work that is standard, long-standing, and proper.

Anecdotal evidence of racial profiling has been accumulating for years, and now many people and groups (such as the American Civil Liberties Union's Police Practices Project) believe that all "pretext" traffic stops are wrong, because the chance that racism and racial profiling will creep into such stops is very high. In short, the ACLU objects to all traffic stops for nontraffic purposes when the goal of the stop has nothing to do with the underlying traffic stop or safety. As one ACLU official argued, "Police can find an excuse to stop virtually anyone for anything.

A scene from the Walker Report of the 1968 Democratic National Convention in Chicago.

'Out of place' stops are the most blatant example. It's also about officers who are a product of a society that is infected with conscious and unconscious racism."[17]

It is very difficult for the police to combat the public's perception that traffic stops of minorities simply on the basis of race is widespread and prejudicial in nature. It follows that when large numbers of people of color believe that the police will treat them unfairly, a serious erosion of trust occurs. Some police agencies, including those in San Diego and San Jose, California, voluntarily collect data to determine whether racial profiling exists. Many police executives, however, fear that the federal government will step in with legislation requiring that much more information be collected during traffic stops. (Indeed, Congressman John Conyers recently introduced a bill, the Traffic Stop Statistics Study Act, that would require police to collect racial data on subjects stopped for traffic infractions.) Because of the often contentious nature of traffic stops, police are concerned that having to collect additional information will only exacerbate an already tense situation.

Whatever approach is taken, this is an area in which the police are in a state of evolution. Traditional practices are being examined and redressed. Steven J. Hill, of the New York state attorney general's office, put it this way, "Racially motivated behavior in general is losing its hold throughout our society. Law enforcement should be a beacon of propriety in this respect."[18]

Other police field practices are another source of tensions between the police and racial minorities. The most important kinds of police actions contributing to these tensions are as follows:

1. *Delay in responding to calls for service.* Several studies of police work have found that patrol officers would often deliberately delay responding to calls for service, especially in cases of family disturbances.[19] Although this delay may be justified on grounds of officer safety (i.e., awaiting backup) and although these studies did not demonstrate any pattern of racial bias, it does not help perceptions of the police. Some research has found that African Americans perceived greater delays than did whites.

2. *Verbal abuse, including the use of racially offensive epithets or other forms of disrespect.* Offensive labels for people are a regular aspect of the "working language" of some police officers. One study found that 75 percent of all officers used some racially offensive words, most of which were not uttered in the presence of citizens. It was also found, however, that verbal expressions of disrespect did not necessarily translate into discriminatory behavior.[20] In fact, police have been found to openly ridicule and belittle citizens in only 5 percent of all encounters.[21] Derogatory terms are often an expression of the general alienation the police feel from the public. In some situations, the police use them as a "control" technique, in an attempt to establish their authority.[22] Nonetheless, they should be avoided at all times.

3. *Excessive questioning and frisking of African American citizens.* Allegations of harassment by police are often raised by racial minorities who believe they have been unnecessarily subjected to "field interrogations." Indeed, the President's Crime Commission observed nearly three decades ago that such field interrogations were "universally resented" by minorities.[23] Many officers, trained to be suspicious and often confronting individuals in questionable circumstances, regard such activities as legitimate and effective crime-fighting tactics. Because many law-abiding citizens may be treated in this manner, however, this approach can have quite negative effects on COPPS.

4. *Discriminatory patterns of arrest and traffic citations.* This is a particularly difficult and complex issue of police–minority relations. Although the RAND Corporation found that minorities are not overrepresented in the arrest population relative to the number of crimes they actually commit (discussed more later), African Americans are arrested more often than whites relative to their numbers in the population.[24] African American complainants request arrests more often than whites. Because most incidents were intraracial, this resulted in more arrests of African Americans.[25] Another study found that the police were more likely to comply with the wishes of white victims complaining against African American suspects than African American victims complaining against African American suspects, particularly in property crimes.[26] "Characteristics of the neighborhood" as a factor has particularly important implications. Like crime and punishment generally, police and minority relations cannot be properly analyzed apart from the broader social, political, and economic situations from which they emerge. Police have been found to be more likely to arrest both white and African American suspects in low-income areas. Insofar as African Americans are disproportionately represented among the poor, however, this factor is likely to result in a disproportionate rate of African American arrests.[27]

5. *Excessive use of physical force.* Police have been found to use force in about 5 percent of all encounters involving offenders. In about two-thirds of the incidents involving force, its application was judged as reasonable. Regardless of race, nearly all of the victims of excessive force were lower-class males. White and African American officers used excessive force at nearly the same rate. Excessive force appears to be used less frequently by "mixed" patrol teams of white and African American officers. Also, police were more likely to use excessive force when other citizens or officers were present, apparently reflecting officers' concern about maintaining their authority in the eyes of other people.[28] Studies are inconclusive, however. Whereas one researcher may find that white and African American officers were most likely to use force against members of their own race, other studies reveal different outcomes. Nonetheless, it is known that "a sizable minority of citizens experience police misconduct at one time or another."[29] The result, of course, is that many racial minorities *perceive* that their race is being unduly brutalized. And, to them, perception is reality.

6. *Excessive use of deadly force.* One study concluded unequivocally that "blacks and Hispanics are everywhere overrepresented among those on the other side of police guns."[30] A later study of police shootings in Memphis also found a pattern of extreme racial disparity, particularly with respect to unarmed citizens. In fact, of the 26 African Americans shot and killed in a five-year period there, half were nonassaultive and unarmed. The data suggested that the Memphis police were much readier to shoot unarmed African Americans than whites.[31]

Minority community members often believe they are unnecessarily detained and interviewed by police. (*Courtesy* Washoe County, Nevada, Sheriff's Office)

7. *Systematic underenforcement of the law and the failure to protect law-abiding citizens.* This is another complicated area of police–minority relations: Although the police are often criticized for being too aggressive with minorities and their neighborhoods, when asked to suggest improvements in policing, African Americans have been nearly as likely as whites to ask for more, not less, police protection.[32] This apparent contradiction can be explained by the diversity of racial–minority communities themselves. Complaints about police harassment are likely to come from young males who have a high level of contact with the police. Most members of a minority area or neighborhood, however, are law-abiding citizens who desire more, not less, police protection.[33]

Is There Systematic Discrimination against Minorities?

One of the most respected studies attempting to address whether the justice system is discriminatory against minorities involved the RAND Corporation; a number of major findings came out of the study.

First, RAND found no consistent, statistically significant, racial differences in the probability of arrest, given that an offender had committed a crime. Second, although case processing generally treated offenders similarly, racial differences were found at two key points: Minority suspects were more likely than whites to be given longer sentences and to be put in prison instead of jail. Because minorities were not found to have a higher probability of arrest, it was concluded that higher release rates might be explained by evidentiary problems. Research indicates that prosecutors do have greater problems making minority cases "stick" because victims often have difficulty identifying minority suspects. Moreover, minority victims and witnesses often refuse or fail to cooperate after an arrest is made.[34]

There were several explanations for why minorities received harsher sentences and served longer terms in prison. Plea bargaining resolved a higher percentage of felony cases involving white defendants, and jury trials resolved a higher percentage of minority cases. Conviction by jury usually results in more severe sentencing. Recidivism variables contained in the presentence investigation (PSI) concerning personal and social information may also contribute to longer sentences. Minorities often do not fare well in PSI indicators of recidivism, such as family stability and unemployment. As a result, judges and probation officers are often impelled to identify minorities as higher risks.[35] Significantly, the study noted that, "If recidivism indicators are valid and explain racial disparities in sentencing and time served, the system is not discriminating. It is simply reflecting the larger racial problems of society, and it can do little about the overrepresentation of minorities in prison."[36]

Regarding disparities in case processing, the study found that at most major decision points, the criminal justice system does not discriminate against minorities; they are not overrepresented in the arrest population, *relative to the number of crimes they actually commit* (emphasis in original), nor are they more likely than whites to be arrested for those crimes.[37] It was also discovered that African Americans and Latino/Hispanics were less likely to be given probation, more likely to receive prison sentences, and more likely to serve longer sentences. With respect to property crimes, the disparity between whites' and African Americans' proportions of arrest and prison populations widened considerably. The same held true for Latino/Hispanics, who served even longer time than African Americans.[38] The RAND investigation is perhaps summarized best in the following statements:

> Although this study shows that minorities are treated differently at a few points in the criminal justice system, it has not found evidence that this results from widespread and consistent racial prejudice in the system. Instead, what racial disparities we found seem to be due to the system's adopting procedures without analyzing their possible effects on different racial groups. Criminal justice research and policy . . . need to focus on the key actors and their decision making: what information they use, how accurate it is, and whether its imposition affects particular racial groups unfairly.[39]

Finally, if the *belief* that the system is racist leads to criminality, research should attempt to learn why African Americans and whites differ so sharply on the discrimination thesis, and the consequences in terms of behavior.[40]

IMPROVING POLICE–MINORITY RELATIONS

Complicating Factors, Possible Solutions

Given its history and all of the previously mentioned exacerbating factors, we are left to wonder whether police–minority relations can ever be improved.

Without question, some members of society believe the police have no redeeming qualities. To these people, police officers are, and will always be, symbolic agents of an entire system of injustice, never to be trusted under any circumstances. As long as the police have the duty to enforce the laws and the power to arrest and control the behavior of their fellows, there will be inherent problems in obtaining complete public support. "The most difficult of all police problems [is] how to make more palatable the basic regulatory nature of police work."[41] James Baldwin's classic and powerful description of how the police are viewed in the ghetto illustrates the point:

> The only way to police a ghetto is to be oppressive. None of the Police Commissioner's men, even with the best will in the world, have any way of understanding the lives led by the people they swagger about in twos and threes controlling. Their very presence is an insult, and it would be, even if they spent their entire day feeding gumdrops to children. They represent the force of the white world, and that world's criminal profit and ease, to keep the black man corralled up here, in his place. The badge, the gun in the holster, and the swinging club make vivid what will happen should his

rebellion become overt. He moves through Harlem, therefore, like an occupying soldier in a bitterly hostile country, which is precisely what and where he is, and is the reason he walks in twos and threes.[42]

WHAT COPPS CAN DO

Next we consider what COPPS can do in improving police–minority relations by being put into action in minority neighborhoods. A focal point of this section is the need for police officers to learn and understand different cultural beliefs and practices.

Confronting the Issues

One of the problems with addressing police–minority relations issues is that police and people in general do not like to discuss the topic because "you step on somebody's toes or it's embarrassing."[43]

The COPPS philosophy helps address this complex issue. In addition to getting the two groups talking with each other and, therefore, thwarting conflict, it enables police to pinpoint racial tension in their city. COPPS, by its very nature,

Lasting improvements between the police and minorities require that both groups make necessary changes. (*Courtesy* Kris Solow, City of Charlotte, North Carolina)

encourages officers to find out exactly what is occurring in neighborhoods, including who is involved and what their motives are.

As we've discussed in earlier chapters, supervisors must support officers in this endeavor. Officers must be allowed to interact with different people rather than functioning as mere report-takers. Through this interaction, officers begin to learn the cultural diversities of various racial, ethnic, and religious groups.

What can COPPS do to improve relations between the police and minorities? To begin with, at its most fundamental level, COPPS tries to emphasize the interrelationship between the police and the community. COPPS dictates that officers understand their unique, problem solving relationship with the community as they execute the law. There is no denying that this is at times a huge task, given the history of problems between the two groups.

Indeed, notwithstanding the RAND findings, many people remain convinced that the U.S. criminal justice system is racist. Another often-cited Georgia study found that killers of whites are 4.3 times more likely to receive death sentences than murderers of African Americans.[44] Although COPPS cannot change these statistics, it can humanize the justice system, showing a side of the police that is in stark contrast to these figures.

The acceptance and management of diversity, like the implementation of COPPS, cannot be simply a "program" or strategy. For either to succeed, there must be major personal, personnel, and policy changes from the top to the bottom of the organization.

The key to managing diversity and celebrating cultural differences is training and education. But training in both COPPS and diversity, if not conducted correctly and supported by changes in the organization, is better left undone. As Gayle Fisher-Stewart has noted, too often both COPPS and the management of diversity are introduced

> with a "shot in the arm." A curriculum is developed, and the entire staff of the department is marched through for their inoculation. After the first dose, there are no boosters. The curriculum is not modified on the basis of rank . . . officers are often viewed as the only ones who need training, because they are viewed as the ones causing problems in the community.[45]

In a related vein, Exhibit 9.1 contains 15 appropriate, pointed questions compiled by Minneapolis, Minnesota, Chief of Police Robert K. Olson, to be considered by police agencies that are attempting to engage in "balancing crime strategies and democratic principles."

Understanding Cultural Customs, Differences, Problems

This section discusses the negative consequences of police not understanding the cultural differences of the people they confront. Indeed, actions that are common in mainstream American culture can result in miscommunication and have dire consequences if the police do not recognize cultural nuances. As a fundamental

Exhibit 9.1   Self-Evaluation: Balancing Crime Strategies and Democratic Principles

1. Is your department really doing community-oriented policing: a continual discussion of implementation of crime control strategies involving the direct input of the citizens affected by police action?

2. Does your department routinely give detailed cultural awareness/diversity training to recruits, with follow-up in-services yearly to the rest of the police department?

3. Does your police department have a reputation in the minority community for taking swift internal discipline when serious police misconduct occurs?

4. Have you developed true school liaison and additional police interaction—other than enforcement—with young people?

5. Are there incentives or requirements for the chief and upper staff and/or other members of the department to reside in the city in which they are responsible for policing?

6. Has your department established strong community ties, particularly with the leadership of all relevant organizations representing people of color, so that when crisis happens—and it will—the department will have immediate access and assistance in dealing with it?

7. Has the department and its political leadership made clear to all its employees that racial intolerance will not be permitted, crushed at the slightest hint of its appearance, and that the public, particularly people of color, feel confident that their city will address those issues?

8. Who polices the police or chief in your community? Is there an alternative to internal affairs? Is the police chief held accountable by the appropriate elected body for insuring a corruption-free police department?

9. Is the chief executive clearly supported by mayor and council in their community policing and other activities designed to include, rather than exclude, all their constituents?

10. Does your department have a hiring process that will not only [e]nsure diversity within the ranks, but is fair and does not exclude people, and is designed to bring in candidates who wish to join for the spirit of service and not the spirit of adventure? Has your department created an internal atmosphere where people of color would want to become a member and have a rewarding, 20-year career?

11. Does each department offer internal promotional and assignment opportunities equally to all? Do the promoted ranks clearly reflect the diversity of the whole organization and the community that it serves?

12. Is the community routinely involved in the discussion of all issues that affect policing within their neighborhoods?

13. Is your police organization structured to ensure there is accountability at every level for the performance and actions of each and every officer who encounters citizens in their daily work?

14. Does your department have consistent institutionalized citizen communication instruments that allow the department to not only keep the citizens informed of police activity, but to receive citizen input on a regular basis on a wide variety of issues?

15. Does your police department have a reasonable standard of behavior and protocol for the stopping of citizens, particularly in high crime areas? Are persons being stopped and clearly being advised of the reason for the stop? Are they being told exactly what the police are doing? Most particularly, does your police training include disengagement techniques—how to get out of a situation where, in fact, the officer may well have been wrong in their assumption, and must appropriately explain and apologize to the citizen for their inconvenience?

Source: List compiled by Chief Robert K. Olson of Minneapolis, Minnesota. Police Executive Research Forum, *Subject to Debate,* 13(6) (June 1999):5. Used with permission.

example, it is not uncommon for an officer to get someone's attention by beckoning with a crooked index finger, repeatedly moving it back and forth; although this is an innocuous gesture to Americans, it is an insult to an Ethiopian man, who uses it to call a person a dog.[46]

A more serious example would be the custom of certain Asian cultures to exchange gifts at initial meetings. On meeting with members of such a culture, the COPPS officer can be placed in an uncomfortable position at having to offend those persons whom he or she is there to serve either by not offering a gift or by refusing to accept a gift.[47] These are true ethical if not legal dilemmas that today's police officer—and his or her administrators and supervisors—must address. It has been stated that "law enforcement professionals need to develop cultural empathy."[48]

There are other cultural customs and problems about which the police should be cognizant. For example, during an argument it would not be uncommon for a Mexican American to shout to his friend, "I'm going to kill you if you do that again." In the Anglo culture, this statement would clearly signal one's intent to do harm. However, in the context of the Latino/Hispanic culture, this simply conveys anger. Therefore, the Spanish word *matar* (to kill) is often used to show feelings, not intent. Another example is that Anglo Americans tend to assume that there is a short distance between an emotional, verbal expression of disagreement and a full-blown conflict. For African Americans, though, stating a position with feeling shows sincerity. For most African Americans, threatening movements, not angry words, indicate the start of a fight. In fact, some would argue that fights do not begin when people are talking or arguing, but rather, when they stop talking.

Many possible breakdowns in verbal communication can cause difficulties for police officers and those of different cultures.[49] For example, for many Tongans, being handcuffed when arrested for minor crimes is a cultural taboo; that treatment is reserved for only the very worst offenders in their culture. To many Southeast Asians, being asked by an officer to assume a kneeling position with fingers interlocked behind the head is cause for rebellion; to them, this posture is a prelude to being assassinated. For the Chinese, causing someone to lose face through disrespect—such as not being able to use both hands to convey an object—is one of the worst things one person can do to another.[50]

For Latino/Hispanics, the concept of masculine superiority is important, as are dominance of the father in the family, division of labor according to sex, and the belief that the family is more important than the individual. Arguing politics on street corners is an old tradition which, in its frenzy, might appear to be assaultive behavior. It is culturally taboo for a stranger to touch a small Hispanic girl. The use of surnames and last names may be confusing to some police officers. Latin custom dictates the use of the father's and the mother's last name (e.g., Jose Jesus Leon Flores). The legal name is the surname (Leon); the maternal name is the last name in the series (Flores).[51]

Native Americans, unfortunately, suffer severe social problems. Alcohol has been found to be a factor in 80 percent of all Native American suicides and in 90 percent of all homicides. Alcohol has also been found to play a part in the social, physical, psychological, economic, and cultural disruption experienced by Native Americans.[52]

In addition to these traits, other cultural differences that might be observed by the police include the following:

- *Body position:* A police sergeant relaxing at a desk with feet up, baring the soles of the feet, would likely offend a Saudi Arabian or Thai, because the foot is considered the dirtiest part of the body.
- *Facial expressions and expressiveness:* A smile is a source of confusion for police officers when encountering Asian cultures. A smile or giggle can cover up pain, humiliation, or embarrassment; on hearing something sad, they may smile appearing to be a "smart aleck." And, whereas Latin Americans, Mediterranean, Arab, Israeli, and African Americans tend to show emotions facially, other groups tend to be less facially expressive; and officers may assume that these persons are not being cooperative.

Preservice and in-service police training should cover these cultural differences. At the very least, police officers should know what terms are the least offensive when referring to ethnic or racial groups. For example, most Asians prefer not to be called Orientals; they prefer their nationality of origin, such as

Korean American. Many American Indians resent the term "Native American" because it was invented by the U.S. government. They prefer being called American Indian or to be known by their tribal ancestry (e.g., Crow, Winnebago). The terms *black American* and *African American* can usually be used interchangeably; however, the latter is more commonly used among younger people. Mexican Americans usually refer to themselves as *Chicanos*, whereas the term *Latino* is preferred by those from Central America.[53]

EMPLOYING A DIVERSE POLICE DEPARTMENT

Women and minorities are underrepresented in policing. The organizational culture of policing has been noticeably slow to change in this regard. Female officers may help improve the tarnished image of policing; improve community relations; and foster a more flexible, less violent, approach to keeping the peace. Former Houston, Texas, Police Chief Elizabeth Watson stated that, "Women tend to rely more on intellectual than physical prowess. From that standpoint, policing is a natural match for them."[54]

The recruitment of minority officers remains a difficult task. Probably the single most difficult barrier has to do with the image that police officers have among these groups. Unfortunately, for many African Americans and Latino/Hispanics, police officers are symbols of oppression and have been charged with using excessive brutality; they are often seen as an army of occupation. Meanwhile, many women are reluctant to try to enter what they perceive as a male-dominated, sexist occupation. They may also be aware of high turnover rates of female police officers and the glass ceiling that militates against promotion of women.

The hiring of minority group officers, however, should not mean that only African Americans patrol in black neighborhoods, Latino/Hispanic officers in those neighborhoods, and so on. In fact, there is evidence that police–minority relations suffer because of such practices, because minority officers are often more severe in dealing with members of their own group. Moreover, minority officers are frequently regarded as traitors by members of their own group.[55] For a COPPS oriented department, however, it is significant that one study found that African American officers who knew their neighborhood (i.e., had grown up on their beat) were more markedly at ease and accepted than were their fellow African American officers from outside the neighborhood. Being indigenous to the neighborhood seems almost more important than the color of their skin.[56]

Having a department that is representative of the community, however, does not guarantee freedom from cultural conflict. The police organizational culture, reinforced through its policies, practices, and informal norms, can foster a bias against those who are different and can have serious ramifications in the treatment of minority and female segments of society, within both the police department and the community.[57]

Until more minority and female officers are promoted to administrative levels and can affect policy and serve as role models, there is a higher risk of their being treated unequally and having difficulty being promoted—a classic catch-22

Communities are seeking to employ a police force that is representative of the community. (*Courtesy* NYPD Photo Unit)

situation. Nonetheless, as the United States generally becomes more diverse, police organizations must take measures to reflect the larger society.

WHAT WORKS: SUCCESSFUL INITIATIVES

Following are some examples of how cities have helped bring about unity among their diverse people and problems. Note the unique role played by criminal justice practitioners in each.

Chelsea, Massachusetts, and Conflict Intervention

A small, crowded city two miles north of downtown Boston, Massachusetts, Chelsea is populated by 36,000 people and is one of the state's poorest cities. Nearly half of Chelsea's children under the age of 14 live in poverty, and an estimated 10,000 undocumented Hispanic and Southeast Asian immigrants reside in the city's three-square-mile area as well.[58]

At the beginning of the 1990s, the city was completely mired in conflict. Problems ran the gamut from neighborhood crime and disorder to a demoralized police department and a corrupt mayor's office. The city's severe financial and political hardships prompted the Massachusetts legislature to place Chelsea into receivership in 1991—the first such occurrence for a city since the depression. Conflicts were fueled by ethnic tensions that began flaring in the 1970s when waves of immigrants changed the city's ethnic makeup.[59]

This receivership and the possibility of annexation to Boston forced Chelsea's residents to become more involved in finding solutions to the city's crime, poverty, education, and housing problems. The police initiated the COPPS strategy, Neighborhood Watch groups were organized, bilingual officers were hired, a local youth center was opened, and a partnership was formed with Boston University to help manage Chelsea's public schools. In September 1997 the city police received a $75,000 federal grant to start a Conflict Intervention Unit (CIU), which was designed to address noncriminal disputes; it began accepting referrals in May 1998. The first important test for the CIU was whether it would be accepted by the Chelsea police officers and the housing authority. Indeed, many officers were skeptical, concerned that CIU was not "real police work."

Now, however, about 80 percent of the department's officers refer disputes to the unit. Interpersonal problems, such as neighbor-to-neighbor disputes that often escalate into violence or litigation, are brought to CIU. The program employs specially trained staff who have developed rapport with the community, who have independence from the police and courts, and who engage in follow-up.

It is estimated that the CIU has saved the Chelsea Police Department thousands of dollars and hundreds of patrol hours. The CIU staff has reduced crime and racial tension in minority communities by giving residents a peaceful way to settle disputes without involving the police.[60]

Serving Immigrant Victims: Philadelphia and Jackson Heights

Research has shown that immigrant populations in the United States are victimized at rates similar to the general population, but their rates of reporting crimes are lower. Reasons for this underreporting include language barriers, cultural differences, and ignorance of the U.S. justice system.[61]

Two cities with well-established programs that provide services to immigrants are Philadelphia and Jackson Heights, New York. Philadelphia, although not known as a city with large immigrant populations, nevertheless is a national leader in criminal justice programs that serve immigrants. Both the district attorney's office and the police department have outreach programs to Southeast Asian immigrants. In the district attorney's office, Vietnamese and Cambodian caseworkers screen arrest reports citywide for victims with Southeast Asian surnames and attempt to contact these individuals by telephone or letter. Brochures describing the court process are provided in Cambodian, Vietnamese, and Korean.[62]

Caseworkers communicate with victims in their native languages, answering questions about the justice process, notifying them of court dates, and encouraging them to go to court. They also arrange for interpreters to go to court with victims, help victims complete a victim impact statement, and assist with preparing for testimony. One police ministation serves as a home base for a Vietnamese police liaison staff person, and a similar liaison for Cambodians is based in a ministation near the University of Pennsylvania.[63]

Jackson Heights offers services to immigrant victims that include lock replacement, shelter referral, and multilinqual counseling for both individual and group support. Staff help immigrants determine eligibility for various social services. This program also provides legal counseling on such issues as applications for visas or for citizenship, petitions for relatives to join the family, or deportation hearings. An immigration hotline program offers information on relevant laws and procedures, employment, and housing from counselors fluent in 14 languages. English classes are offered, and police have Spanish-speaking receptionists on duty at all times.[64]

Other Approaches: A Museum Tour, a Unique Citizens' Academy, a Helping Hand with Naturalization

There are other innovative and unique initiatives in progress that help to build bridges between law enforcement and minority communities. For example, the Washington, D.C., Metropolitan Police Department has embarked on a training program for recruits that examines the issue of protecting individual rights through a new project: the U.S. Holocaust Memorial Museum. The program mandates that all police recruits attend a tour of the museum as part of the hate-crimes component of their training. They learn about the role of the German municipal police in carrying out repressive Nazi orders and explore such issues as immigration restrictions and efforts to define groups along racial lines.[65]

In Corcoran, California, with a Hispanic population near 80 percent, the police department knew that a lack of communication with the Spanish-speaking residents created an obstacle to effective community policing. Enlisting the help of several bilingual employees, the department created the "Amigos de la Comunidad" ("Friends of the Community") program, a Spanish-speaking citizen police academy. Of the first 25 academy graduates, six moved on to form a Spanish-language unit of the police department's all-volunteer community patrol. Residents who were once fearful and resentful of the police now busily patrol the city's streets.[66]

Realizing that people from other countries wanting to become U.S. citizens frequently turn to special programs to help them prepare for the test and other naturalization requirements, the Dallas, Texas, Police Department launched a unique way to build bridges with immigrants. What better way to reach out to the different cultures of Dallas and build relationships than by helping residents become citizens? The department's Office of Community Affairs and Employee Communications developed the program, targeting the Asian community—specifically, Cambodians, Koreans, Laotians, Thai, and the Vietnamese. During a five-week program, police employees who are certified as "citizenship facilitators" teach American history and other appropriate lessons in the students' native languages. It is also hoped that the program will lead to an increase in Asian applicants for sworn and nonsworn positions in the police department.[67]

RESPONDING TO HATE CRIMES

In recent years the United States has become more outraged by hate- or bias-motivated crimes—criminal offenses against persons, property, or society that are motivated by an offender's bias against an individual's or group's race, religion, ethnic/national origin, gender, age, disability, or sexual orientation.[68]

Such crimes can have a special emotional and psychological impact on the victim and the community. Hate violence can exacerbate racial, religious, or ethnic tensions in a community and lead to a cycle of escalating reprisals. Police executives must demonstrate a commitment to be both tough on hate-crime perpetrators and sensitive to the impact of hate violence on the community.[69]

As the new millennium arrived, 40 states and the District of Columbia had enacted laws enhancing the penalties for hate crimes and addressing hate violence. The 1990 Hate Crime Statistics Act requires the Department of Justice to collect and publish data on bias-motivated crimes across the United States. In 1998, 7,775 bias-motivated crimes were reported, 4,321 (54 percent) of which were motivated by racial bias, 1,390 (18 percent) by religious bias, 1,260 (16 percent) by sexual orientation bias, and 754 (10 percent) by ethnic/national origin bias. Of the incidents that were motivated by religious bias, 1,082 (about 77 percent) were directed against Jews and Jewish institutions.[70]

The Justice Department has developed a new hate-crime training curriculum for police officers, and the Anti-Defamation League has also produced a number of hate-crime resources and prevention initiatives. See Exhibit 9.2, also.

ON THE STREET: SOME PERPLEXING SCENARIOS

Following are five scenarios that are based on actual events and demonstrate some of the situations that might be confronted by COPPS officers. For each scenario we have provided some of the cultural beliefs and practices that might come into play. Try to consider how police officers might best handle each situation and the possible repercussions if they fail to recognize the nonverbal communication and beliefs and practices that are at work in each. Also consider the need for cultural diversity to be incorporated into basic police academy training curricula.

Scenario 1: You witness a traffic violation and when you stop the driver of the vehicle, you notice two things. First, he speaks with a heavy Spanish accent; second, he appears very nervous. You ask for his license and registration. When he gives them to you, you find that he has also enclosed a $100 bill. The traffic offense carries a fine of $25, but now you also have the offense of bribery. How would you handle this situation?[71]

EXHIBIT 9.2   Tear-Out Pocket Guide

Definition of a Hate Crime

A hate crime is a criminal offense committed against persons, property or society that is motivated, in whole or in part, by an offender's bias against an individual's or a group's perceived race, religion, ethnic/national origin, gender, age, disability or sexual orientation. Legal definitions of hate crimes vary. Check your state statutes for the definition of hate crime in your jurisdiction.

Hate incidents are those actions by an individual or group that, while motivated by bias, do not rise to the level of a criminal offense.

Community Trauma

Hate crimes victimize the entire community and may involve

- Victimization projected to all community members
- Sense of group vulnerability
- Community fear/tension
- Possibility of reactive crimes or copycat incidents
- Community polarization
- Redirection of law enforcement resources
- Loss of trust in criminal justice institutions
- Public damage (i.e., buildings such as churches)

Victim Trauma

Because the basis for the attack is the victim's identity, victim(s) may suffer

- Deep personal crisis
- Increased vulnerability to repeat attack
- Sense of community/system betrayal
- Acute shock and disbelief
- Extreme fear of certain groups
- Hopelessness
- Anger/desire for revenge
- Shame and humiliation

Action to Be Taken at the Scene:

- Explain to the victim(s) and witnesses the likely progression of the investigation
- Report the suspected hate crime to the supervisor on duty
- Refer media representatives to the public information officer or supervisor on duty
- Document the incident thoroughly on the department report forms, noting any particular hate crime indicators and quoting exact wording of statements made by perpetrators

Source: L. E. Technology, "Healing the Hate," p. 58; adapted as "Tear-Out Pocket Guide" by IACP, 515 N. Washington Street, Alexandria, Virginia 22314 (800 The-IACP; www.theiacp.org).

Here, the officer might consider the fact that in some Latin American countries, the way to do business with any public official—especially the police—is to offer money. It is expected, and there are severe penalties for noncompliance. The offense of bribery has been committed and the officer would be well within the law to arrest the driver. After further questioning the driver regarding his country of origin, the officer could explain that the exchange of money is a punishable offense in the United States and charge him only for the traffic offense.

> *Scenario 2:* You are summoned to a local school by the principal, who has been informed of a case of child abuse by a sixth-grade teacher. On arriving at the principal's office, you are shown a Vietnamese girl who had been absent from school for several days with a high fever. The girl has heavy bruising on the left side of her neck. You go to the child's home and question her father, who admits in broken English that he caused the bruising on the girl's neck. What is your reaction?

In parts of Asia, a medical practice called "coining" involves rubbing the skin with a heated coin, leaving highly visible marks on the neck or back. This practice, intended to heal the child, may easily be misinterpreted as child abuse by police, school, or social service agencies. This is a good example of why police officers must avoid being ethnocentric or interpreting what they see through their own cultural "filters."

> *Scenario 3:* You are summoned to a murder scene involving a family picnic in a neighborhood park. On arriving you learn that a Mexican woman had been involved in an extramarital affair and had been bragging about her activities in front of many extended family members in the park. The woman also made comments about her new lover's sexual prowess and her

husband's inability to satisfy her. Her husband then left the park. Returning shortly thereafter with a shotgun, he shot and killed his wife. He gives himself up to you. For what criminal charge should the defendant be convicted?

In probably all states, a case such as this would result in a minimum charge of second-degree murder against the defendant. However, in this actual case (in California), because the jury took into consideration the cultural background of this couple, the husband was convicted of a lesser charge of manslaughter. It was argued that the wife's boasting about her lover and the emasculation of her husband created a passion and emotion that completely undermined his "machismo," pride, and honor—what it means to be humiliated in the context of the Latin culture in front of one's family.[72]

> *Scenario 4:* While on foot patrol, a COPPS officer responds to neighbors' complaints. The scene is a brawl at a barbecue party in the backyard of a home where Samoans reside. How should the officer proceed?

The officer could immediately summon backup assistance, and together the officers could make a show of force, breaking up the fighting but also acquiring the undying disrespect of the Samoan community and widening the gap between the two groups. Alternatively, the police could locate the "chief" of this group and let that person deal with the problem in a manner in which he would handle it in Samoa. The chief has a prominent role to play and can serve as a bridge between the police and the community (and keep the matter out of court).[73]

> *Scenario 5:* A police officer stops a Nigerian cabdriver, who moves close to the officer and ignores the officer's command to "step back." He also averts his eyes from the officer, and begins defiantly "babbling to the ground" in a high-pitched tone of voice while making gestures. The officer believes that the cabdriver is out of control, unstable, and possibly dangerous. How should the officer perceive this individual?

In Nigeria, the social distance for conversation is much closer than in the United States; it may be less than 15 inches. Furthermore, Nigerian people often show respect and humility by averting their eyes. What is perceived by the officer as "babbling" is actually the cabdriver's way of sending a message of respect and humility. Most likely, the cabdriver is not even aware that he is perceived as out of control, unstable, and dangerous.

These case studies are not presented to question the rightness or wrongness of any group's values, beliefs, or practices; nor should they be interpreted to mean that serious crimes should be excused on cultural grounds. Rather, the point is to illustrate to the COPPS officer the importance of understanding cultural differences and individual backgrounds.

Obviously the police must take differences in nonverbal communication into account when dealing with people of different cultures. These case studies also reveal that discretion at the police level is much more important than that practiced at the courts level.

It would be unrealistic to expect all police officers to be aware of every possibility for miscommunication or cultural insult. Policing in a multicultural society, however, requires a humanistic approach through which differences are understood and celebrated rather than viewed as cause for conflict. Opponents of COPPS may believe that adding a multicultural focus will soften an allegedly already soft approach to crime prevention; however, not understanding cultural differences can and does result in officer or citizen injury and death and disorder.[74]

SUMMARY

This chapter focused on the often-fractured relations that have historically come between the police and the minority communities they serve.

Ours is not a perfect world. The Constitution notwithstanding, people are *not* created equal, at least with respect to legal, social, political, and economic opportunities. This disparity creates confrontations, mistrust, and enmity between many citizens and the police.

Although studies may indicate that there is no systematic racism within our criminal justice system, minorities often believe strongly that biases are, nonetheless, deeply entrenched within it. And, as one author noted, "A little bias goes a long way."[75]

We must work to improve this situation. And we must acknowledge that many police field tactics (such as racial profiling) have exacerbated the problem. We also need more minorities who are willing to assist as citizens or as police officers to join the cause, as well as more culturally informed police training.

For these reasons, COPPS offers hope for improvement, as this strategy fosters a partnership that is based on trust, communication, and understanding.

NOTES

1. 347 U.S. 483 (1954).
2. Anthony M. Platt (ed.), *The Politics of Riot Commissions* (New York: Collier Books, 1971).
3. *Ibid.*, Chapter 8.
4. See, for example, Allen D. Grimshaw, *Racial Violence in the United States* (Chicago: Aldine, 1969), pp. 269–98; *Report of the National Advisory Commission on Civil Disorders Report* (New York: Bantam Books, 1968).
5. Steven M. Cox and Jack D. Fitzgerald, *Police in Community Relations: Critical Issues*, 2nd ed. (Dubuque, Iowa: William C. Brown, 1992), p. 129.
6. Samuel Walker, *The Police in America: An Introduction*, 2nd ed. (New York: McGraw-Hill, 1993), p. 224.
7. National Research Council, *A Common Destiny: Blacks and American Society* (Washington, D.C.: National Academy Press, 1989), p. 453.

8. Scott Decker, "Citizen Attitudes Toward the Police: A Review of Past Findings and Suggestions for Future Policy," *Journal of Police Science and Administration* 9 (1981):81.

9. James Frank, Steven G. Brandl, Francis T. Cullen, and Amy Stichman, "Reassessing Attitudes Toward the Police: A Research Note," *Justice Quarterly* 13 (June 1996):320.

10. Walker, *The Police in America*, p. 227.

11. Louis A. Radelet, *The Police and the Community*, 4th ed. (New York: Macmillan, 1986).

12. William A. Westley, *Violence and the Police: A Sociological Study of Law, Custom, and Morality* (Cambridge, Mass.: MIT Press, 1977), p. 93. Based on the author's research in 1950 as part of the requirements for a doctorate, this book is now considered a classic and a pioneer in the study of police violence.

13. Jerome Skolnick, *Justice without Trial* (New York: Wiley, 1967), pp. 42–70.

14. W. Eugene Groves and Peter H. Rossi, "Police Perceptions of a Hostile Ghetto: Realism or Projection?" in *Police in Urban Society*, ed. Harlan H. Hahn (Beverly Hills, Calif.: Sage, 1971), pp. 175–91.

15. James Q. Wilson, *Varieties of Police Behavior* (New York: Atheneum, 1973), p. 28.

16. Ron Neubauer, quoted in Keith W. Strandberg, "Racial Profiling," *Law Enforcement Technology* (June 1999):62.

17. John Crew, quoted in *ibid.*

18. Steven J. Hill, "Racial Profiling: A Challenge for American Policing," *Law and Order* (November 1999):94.

19. Donald Black, *Manners and Customs of the Police* (New York: Academic Press, 1980), p. 117; Richard J. Lundman, "Domestic Police-Citizen Encounters," *Journal of Police Science and Administration* 2 (March 1974):25.

20. Albert J. Reiss Jr., *The Police and the Public* (New Haven, Conn.: Yale University Press, 1971), p. 142.

21. Jerome Skolnick, *The Police and the Urban Ghetto* (Chicago: American Bar Foundation, 1968).

22. Walker, *The Police in America*, p. 234.

23. President's Commission on Law Enforcement and Administration of Justice, *Field Studies, IV*, "The Police and the Community," Vol. 1 (Washington, D.C.: U.S. Government Printing Office, 1967), pp. 66, 85.

24. Walker, *The Police in America*, p. 235.

25. Robert Friedrich, "Racial Prejudice and Police Treatment of Blacks," in *Evaluating Alternative Law Enforcement Policies*, eds. Ralph Baker and Fred A. Meyers (Lexington, Mass.: Lexington Books, 1979), pp. 160–61.

26. Douglas A. Smith and Christy A. Visher, and Laura A. Davidson, "Equity and Discretionary Justice: The Influence of Race on Police Discretion," *Journal of Criminal Law and Criminology* 15 (January 1978):74–91.

27. Douglas A. Smith and Christy A. Visher, "Street-Level Justice: Situational Determinants of Police Arrest Decisions," *Social Problems* 29 (December 1981):167–77.

28. Robert J. Friedrich, "Police Use of Force: Individuals, Situations, and Organizations," *Annals of the American Academy of Political and Social Science* 452 (November 1980):82–97; see also Albert J. Reiss, "Police Brutality—Answers to Key Questions," *Transaction* 5 (July/August 1968):10–19.

29. Reiss, *The Police and the Public*, p. 151.

30. James J. Fyfe, "Reducing the Use of Deadly Force: The New York Experience," in U.S. Department of Justice, *Police Use of Deadly Force* (Washington, D.C.: U.S. Government Printing Office, 1978), p. 29.

31. James J. Fyfe, "Blind Justice: Police Shootings in Memphis," *Journal of Criminal Law and Criminology* 73 (1982):707–722.

32. U.S. Department of Justice, *The Police and Public Opinion* (Washington, D.C.: Author, 1987), pp. 39–40.

33. Walker, *The Police in America*, p. 241.

34. Joan Petersilia, "Racial Disparities in the Criminal Justice System: Executive Summary of RAND Institute Study, 1983," in *The Criminal Justice System and Blacks*, ed. Daniel Georges-Abeyle (New York: Clark Boardman, 1984), pp. 225–58.
35. *Ibid.*, p. 243.
36. *Ibid.*, p. 230.
37. *Ibid.*, pp. 240–41.
38. *Ibid.*, pp. 241–42.
39. *Ibid.*, pp. 231, 249.
40. William Wilbanks, *The Myth of a Racist Criminal Justice System* (Monterey, Calif.: Brooks/Cole, 1987), pp. 147–48.
41. A. C. Germann, Frank D. Day, and Robert R. J. Gallati, *Introduction to Law Enforcement and Criminal Justice* (Springfield, Ill.: Charles C. Thomas, 1976), p. 241.
42. James Baldwin, *Nobody Knows My Name* (New York: Dial Press, 1961), p. 65.
43. Willie Williams, quoted in Patricia A. Parker, "Tackling Unfinished Business," *Police* (December 1991):19, 84.
44. Ted Gest, "Crime's Bias Problem," *U.S. News and World Report* (July 25, 1994):31–32.
45. Gayle Fisher-Stewart, "Multicultural Training for Police," *MIS Report* 26(9) (September 1994):7.
46. *Ibid.*, p. 4.
47. *Ibid.*, p. 5.
48. Gary Weaver, "Law Enforcement in a Culturally Diverse Society," *FBI Law Enforcement Bulletin* 61 (September 1992):1–7.
49. *Ibid.*
50. Pamela D. Mayhall, *Police–Community Relations and the Administration of Justice*, 3rd ed. (Englewood Cliffs, N.J.: Prentice Hall, 1985), pp. 308–309.
51. *Ibid.*, pp. 312–13.
52. Ken Peak and Jack Spencer, "Crime in Indian Country: Another 'Trail of Tears.'" *Journal of Criminal Justice* 15 (1987):485–94.
53. Mayhall, *Police-Community Relations*, p. 6.
54. Jeanne McDowell, "Are Women Better Cops?" *Time* (February 17, 1992):70.
55. See, for example, Nicholas Alex, *Black in Blue* (New York: Appleton-Century-Crofts, 1969).
56. Jesse G. Rubin, "Police Identity and the Police Role," in *The Police Community*, eds. Jack Goldsmith and Sharon S. Goldsmith (Pacific Palisades, Calif.: Palisades, 1974), p. 143.
57. *Ibid.*, p. 5.
58. Chadwick Bash, Maria Amato, and Michele Sacks, *Chelsea, Massachusetts: A City Helps Its Diverse People Get Along* (Washington, D.C.: Bureau of Justice Assistance, January 2000), p. 1.
59. *Ibid.*, p. 2.
60. *Ibid.*, pp. 3–5.
61. Robert C. Davis and Edna Erez, *Immigrant Populations as Victims: Toward a Multicultural Criminal Justice System* (Washington, D.C.: National Institute of Justice Research in Brief, May 1998), pp. 1–2.
62. *Ibid.*, p. 3.
63. *Ibid.*
64. *Ibid.*
65. Alison Milofsky, "Examining Police Behavior under Nazi Rule Offers Contemporary Lessons on Moral Responsibility and Civil Liberties," *Community Policing Exchange* (Washington, D.C.: Community Policing Consortium, January/February 2000), p. 3.
66. Stephanie Hard, in *ibid.*, p. 6.
67. Jennifer I. Ward, in *ibid.*, p. 7.
68. International Association of Chiefs of Police, *Responding to Hate Crimes: A Police Officers Guide to Investigation and Prevention* (Arlington, Va.: Author, 2000), p. 27.

69. Michael Lieberman, "Responding to Hate Crimes," *Community Policing Exchange* (Washington, D.C.: Community Policing Consortium, January/February 2000), p. 3.
70. *Ibid.*
71. Fisher-Stewart, "Multicultural Training for Police," p. 8.
72. Adapted from Robert M. Shusta, Deena R. Levine, Philip R. Harris, and Herbert Z. Wong, *Multicultural Law Enforcement: Strategies for Peacekeeping in a Diverse Society* (Englewood Cliffs, N.J.: Prentice Hall, 1995), pp. 21–22.
73. *Ibid.*, p. 22.
74. Fisher-Stewart, "Multicultural Training for Police," p. 4.
75. Harold E. Pepinsky, "Better Living through Police Discretion," *Law and Contemporary Problems* 47 (Autumn 1984):255.

NEW STRATEGIES FOR OLD PROBLEMS
COPPS on the Beat

> The time's come: there's a terrific thunder-cloud advancing upon us . . . it's going to blow away all this idleness . . . I'm going to work.
>
> —Anton Chekhov

INTRODUCTION

As Chekhov indicated, there comes a time when preliminary preparations must cease, and action must be substituted in its place—in the present context, applying community oriented policing and problem solving (COPPS) on the street. Indeed, the litmus test for COPPS is the degree to which it succeeds in addressing crime and disorder in communities and neighborhoods.

This chapter demonstrates that COPPS can be highly effective. Perhaps its focal point is the several examples of COPPS's accomplishments that are provided in the chapter's exhibits, revealing how COPPS has prevailed over crime and disorder. The success of this strategy, however, remains predicated on the police having laid the groundwork well and knowing what is going on in their neighborhoods and beats by using the S.A.R.A. process (discussed in Chapter 4). As Zachary Tumin put it,

> The role of the professional police officer as a professional is . . . to know the status of his local institutions; to understand how, when, and why they work; to understand their strengths and their vulnerabilities; to know their members or users, that is, to know the people whose relationships comprise the institutions, and why they participate or don't.[1]

This chapter examines several types of problems the police can confront with the problem solving process. Specifically, it includes the application of COPPS to drug violations, gangs, special populations and problems (the mentally ill, the homeless, and alcohol-related crimes), domestic violence, school violence, rental properties and neighborhood disorder, prostitution, and other selected problems (cruising, false alarms, and teen hangouts in video arcades). The essence of the chapter lies in the case studies, which deal with each type of problem; 11 exhibits as well as numerous examples demonstrate police agencies and other stakeholders collaborating to implement the COPPS strategy.

DRUG VIOLATIONS

That the United States is in the throes of a grave drug problem is no secret. More than 1.5 million U.S. citizens are arrested for drug abuse violations per year; about one-fifth of those arrests are for the sale or manufacturing of drugs.[2] And this is only the tip of the iceberg in comparison with the actual level of manufacturing, use, and trafficking.

The U.S. drug problem—including ubiquitous methamphetamine labs, where a $100 investment can yield $2,000 worth of meth[3]—poses an organizational challenge that now requires new skills, long-range strategies, and coordinated responses of police. Although the potency, cost, and types of drugs that are in high demand might fluctuate, the threat caused by drug abuse—and the seeming inability to get the problem under control—does not. Whereas billions of dollars have been spent in enforcement, treatment, and education at all levels of government, drug problems show little sign of abatement. Drug buying and selling have eroded the environment, created undesirable role models for many youth, given rise to a wide variety of related criminal acts, and resulted in innumerable gun-wielding gang members across the United States who are fighting to expand their turf.

COPPS has wide applications to the problem of drugs. As will be seen in the following examples, this strategy presents a unique opportunity for police agencies to address the street-level drug dealing that has made urban life a nightmare for many residents in major cities.

A traditional police approach to a citizen's call concerning drug activity involved the officer's arrival and a quick response, often resulting in a misdemeanor arrest. Little analysis or measurement of results occurred. Conversely,

Operation Seaload, a joint effort of the NYPD, FBI, and U.S. Customs, ended with the seizure of 9.5 tons of marijuana and numerous arrests. (*Courtesy* NYPD Photo Unit)

although a COPPS officer's arrival might also involve a short-term response (an arrest), there would most likely be an analytical assessment of the situation to determine why the area was the scene of almost constant drug activity: What is the calls for service (CFS) pattern for the location? Are the arrestees youths who are truant from school? When is the activity occurring? Is lighting inadequate? Are grounds littered and vandalized? Are vacant apartments available to foster drug activity? Do abandoned vehicles provide convenient places for drug stashes? The S.A.R.A. process would likely be applied, with follow-up monitoring of the situation. This chapter section examines some COPPS initiatives in cities that were not content with the traditional approach.

COPPS officers are being challenged to use their creative abilities and to do anything legally possible to attack and harass drug trafficking. Officers are parking their patrol vehicles and eating their lunch in front of known dope houses, repeatedly knocking on dealers' doors, or simply standing outside their homes. Officers and citizens brazenly photograph open drug deals and write down license plate numbers of dealers and sellers. These officers, emphasizing a new partnership with the community, gather tremendous amounts of information from citizens and even carry beepers to enhance public contact. Public chats with citizens are so commonplace that individuals seen talking with officers are not targeted for attack as snitches. Officers meet regularly with Neighborhood Watch and other groups to exchange intelligence information. Preliminary results of applying the COPPS approach are promising.

Delray Beach, Florida, recently experienced a drug problem that involved a variety of police tactics for resolution. A convenience store (Mario's Market) had been a problem for 20 years, generating hundreds of calls for service for robberies and drug dealing because 30 to 40 drug dealers, users, and robbers hung around the neighborhood. A nearby drug house contributed to the problem, and a T-shaped alley behind the store provided easy ingress and egress for buyers, both on foot and in vehicles. The lighting was poor, and pay phones in the store's front area were constantly used by traffickers.

Officers began walking a beat in the area, made videos of the dealing, and made drug buys in the market. They contacted the owner of the drug house near Mario's, but the owner cared little about the problem—even after officers bought drugs in the house. Officers initiated a nuisance-abatement suit against the house. They asked the utility company to install bulletproof security lights around and behind the market, and they erected barriers to prevent vehicles from entering and exiting the alleys.

Mario agreed to install a chain-link fence behind the property. The drug dealing decreased because several dealers were sent to prison and others moved out because the location was no longer convenient. When dealers began scaling the chain-link fence, officers smeared axle grease on it ("Even drug dealers don't want to get their clothes dirty," an officer commented), slowing drug activity even further. Next, wanting Mario to succeed, officers offered to paint the market, using paint purchased by Mario and the assistance of probationers. To ward off any remaining dealers, the officers installed a fake video camera at the market's entryway. Annual calls for service declined from more than 100 to 10. Clearly, removing some of the drug dealers' "amenities" had much to do with changing this 20-year-old problem.[4] Exhibit 10.1 provides another example of COPPS strategies against drug dealing, in Portland, Oregon.

GANGS

Today, gangs remain a substantial problem in the United States—even in many middle-size and smaller cities and suburban communities—and their members are becoming younger. The typical age range of gang members has been approximately 14 to 24; youngsters generally begin hanging out with gangs at 12 or 13 years of age, join the gang at 13 or 14, and are first arrested at 14.[5]

The challenge of responding to today's gang problem is indeed great. According to Justice Department estimates,[6] there are more than 16,000 gangs and more than half a million gang members in the United States.[7] Nearly half of all gang members (48 percent) are African American youth, whereas Hispanic youngsters account for 43 percent and Asians total 5 percent. "Gang-banging" can be quite lucrative. An ethnographic study of street gangs found that one large, now defunct gang that consisted of several hundred gang members realized more than 70 percent of its total annual revenue of approximately $280,000 from the sale of crack cocaine. The gang operated in a neighborhood of roughly four city blocks.[8]

EXHIBIT 10.1   A Drug Problem in Portland, Oregon

Different types of drug markets involve different types of strategies for closing them. In Portland, the corner of Mississippi and Shaver had posed a problem for decades. Arrests at the intersection provided only temporary results, and when two officers began focusing their efforts there, dealers learned their duty shifts and simply modified their trafficking to occur when the officers were off duty. The corner even attracted national attention, being spotlighted on ABC's *World News Tonight.* In one of the corner buildings, addicts used the second floor to shoot up. The owner put a pit bull inside, ending that problem. The first floor housed a pool hall where drug sales were common; within a year, the building was condemned and leveled. Near the corner was a vacant lot with high weeds that buyers and dealers used as an escape route; city crews leveled the vegetation. Abandoned vehicles littered area streets and alleys, providing convenient shooting galleries for addicts. Officers tagged and towed the vehicles as hazards. A nearby water fountain was used by dealers for "refreshment" and by buyers to use their drugs. The fountain was shut off. Red traffic lights provided convenient traffic stops for buyers, making it unnecessary for them to exit their vehicles; the transportation department recommended changing the lights to flashing— red one way and yellow the other. Eventually, the dealers cleared out, no longer being comfortably ensconced at the location; calls for service dropped from nearly 100 per year to the low teens. This case study shows the kinds of environmental conditions that can make locations more attractive to drug dealers and what the police can do to eradicate them.

Source: Rana Sampson and Michael S. Scott, *Tackling Crime and Other Public Safety Problems: Case Studies in Problem Solving* (Washington, D.C.: U.S. Department of Justice, Office of Community Policing Services, 2000), pp. 29–30.

Boston, Massachusetts, recently suffered from a youth homicide problem, with 155 young people being either shot or stabbed in three neighborhoods in a four-year period; 60 percent of the homicides were gang related. An interagency group was created, consisting of local, state, and federal law enforcement officers; researchers; probation officers; and gang-intervention street workers. Their responses to the problem focused on both the supply of and demand for guns among the gangs.[9] The guns used in the youth homicides were typically manufactured less than two years before the crimes. This suggested a strategy to the group: identifying and arresting gun traffickers who were supplying guns to the gangs. On the demand side of the problem (why young people carried guns and shot one another), the group identified 61 Boston gangs, with about 1,300 members, representing only about 3 percent of the youth in the affected neighborhoods. Youth homicides, it was determined, were committed by a few gang members who committed many crimes. Enhanced penalties—ranging from strict curfew checks by probation officers to federal prosecutions for street crimes—were enforced against gang members for violent behavior; extraordinary crimes brought extraordinary punishment. The threat of these penalties was communicated to members firsthand. Homicides of young people dropped 67 percent from the mean of the previous seven years.[10]

When gang violence spread in San Mateo, California, primarily because of seven-year warfare between two opposing gangs—involving shootings, stabbings, car bombings, and murder—a street detective requested and received a transfer to the police department's community policing unit. After receiving training in problem solving, he enlisted the support of a local volunteer mediation agency as well as that of the probation department, because of its court-ordered guardianship over many of the seasoned gang members. He also requested a juvenile court judge to waive the nonassociation clause that was a term of most of the gang members' probation, so that they could meet without fear of court-ordered sanctions.[11]

The mediation service arranged for separate meetings with the two rival gangs to be held in a neutral place. Three mediators, two probation officers, and one police officer (the detective) also attended. The groups talked about respect, community racism, the police, and the need to try something new. The idea of a truce was raised, but the two gangs' leaders laughed at the idea. The mediators met individually with each gang four more times; both sides remained curious about the other's commitment, and both seemed tired of the ongoing violence. The gangs finally agreed to meet together. Each gang selected five members as spokespeople who brought a list of items to be addressed; respect was at the top of both lists.[12] An agreement for peace was eventually reached and handshakes were exchanged; all agreed to a follow-up meeting, where 41 gang members agreed to a truce and no more violence. They agreed to respect each other, and if a confrontation arose, they would try to talk through it rather than use weapons.[13] In the four years since this problem solving effort began, there have been no reports of violence between the two gangs.

Finally, another promising strategy, "designing out" gang homicides and street assaults, has been successful in Los Angeles. When a systematic pattern of opportunity was found—that the majority of drive-by shootings and violent gang encounters occurred in clusters on the periphery of neighborhoods linked to major thoroughfares—police closed all major roads leading to and from the identified hot spots by placing cement freeway dividers at the end of streets that led directly to these roads. An evaluation determined that blocking opportunities reduced homicides and street assaults significantly, and that crime was not displaced to other areas.[14]

Another problem arising from teen gangs involves graffiti, which is another "harm" that is associated with gangs (harms were discussed in Chapter 4). Reducing the harm can help to reduce the larger problem. The style and quality

Youths remove graffiti from a public building. (*Courtesy* Sgt. Dominic Licavoli, LAPD)

of graffiti can create and enhance the gang's image; graffiti is even used to advertise those rival gang members they are going to kill. Graffiti also serves to mark the gang's turf; police and neighborhoods have become frustrated with the "tagging" of walls and objects with paint. Graffiti depreciates property values, adds to the deterioration of neighborhoods, and contributes to economic and urban blight.

To combat the problem, some cities have enacted ordinances that require property owners to remove graffiti within a specified period of time; in other areas the city will paint over the graffiti for a set fee, usually $50 to $75. (Table 10.1 shows an example of a graffiti ordinance.)

Nonetheless, the problem persists, and the police are working to eradicate the problem in order to diminish the gangs' sense of territory, improve the appearance of the neighborhoods, and make a community statement that gang-type activities will not be tolerated. Youths on probation work on graffiti removal programs. Police and citizens are organizing "paint-out" parties on specified days of the month. Chambers of commerce and other civic groups often contribute paint, and some cities have a full-time antigraffiti coordinator on the payroll. In addition, graffiti hot lines have been established in some cities, enabling citizens to call the police or other city offices to report problems and collect information.

SPECIAL POPULATIONS AND PROBLEMS

Next we examine how COPPS can assist the police in dealing with persons who are mentally ill or homeless, and offenders who are heavily involved with alcohol. Discussed in Chapter 4 (and illustrated in Figure 4.8) was the fact that police

TABLE 10.1 Example of a Municipal Antigraffiti Ordinance

WHEREAS, property defaced by gang members is an act of vandalism and is against the law; and

WHEREAS, gang members frequently deface property by painting, drawing, writing, etching, or carving gang graffiti; and

WHEREAS, gang graffiti is the first indication of gang activity; and

WHEREAS, gang graffiti constitutes a public nuisance which causes depreciation of the value of the defaced property, the surrounding property, and contributes to the deterioration of the neighborhood and the City in general; and

WHEREAS, depreciation of property values and deterioration of neighborhoods leads to economic blight, an increase in criminal activity, and is injurious to the public health, safety, morals, and general welfare of the residents of the City,

NOW, THEREFORE, BE IT ORDAINED BY THE CITY COUNCIL OF THE CITY OF LAKEWOOD, COLORADO, THAT:

9.85.060 NOTIFICATION OF NUISANCE. (a) The owner of any property defaced by gang graffiti shall be given written notice to abate the public nuisance on his property by removal within five (5) days after service of the notice. Such notice shall be by personal service to the owner, or by posting the notice on the defaced property together with written notice mailed to the owner by first-class mail. The notice to the property owner shall contain:

(1) The location of and a description of the violation;

(2) A demand that the owner remove or eradicate the gang graffiti from the property within five (5) days after service of the notice;

(3) A statement that the owner's failure or refusal to remove or eradicate the gang graffiti may result in abatement by the City;

(4) A statement that if the costs of abatement plus the $75 fee for inspection and incidental costs is not paid to the City within 30 days after notice, an additional $75 will be assessed for administrative and other incidental costs.

Source: Adapted from the Antigraffiti Ordinance of Lakewood, Colorado, 0-91-29, Title 9, Article 85, Chapter 9.85.

need to concentrate efforts on helping or addressing those individuals who account for a disproportionate share of community problems. The mentally ill, homeless, and alcohol-abuser populations would fall into that category.

The Mentally Ill

One of the saddest aspects of police work involves trying to help people who are mentally ill or unstable, many of whom frequently act incoherently or illegally and are addicted to alcohol or drugs. Many such people are also homeless. It is estimated that 200,000 people with mental illness are jailed or imprisoned in the United States every day.[15] A related problem has arisen recently in which individuals who are mentally unstable and who want to die employ a technique that has been termed "suicide by cop"—engaging in a shoot-out with and being killed by the police.

Funding cutbacks and changing laws and policies (such as the deinstitutionalization policies of the 1980s) have concurrently made it more difficult for the police and relatives of the mentally ill to have them committed to institutions; these factors have left many disturbed people—including families—in the streets and alleys and on the riverbanks to fend for themselves. Limited bed space and selective admission practices at detoxification and other alcoholism facilities have also curtailed the ability of the police to transport public inebriates to health care facilities.

How can the COPPS strategy work with these special populations? One way of expanding the options for handling these populations is to share responsibility for dealing with them with the social service system. The networks have three common objectives: (1) to relieve police officers from having to deal with individuals whose problems are primarily psychiatric, medical, or economic; (2) to ensure that police officers refer only those special populations that facilities are mandated to assist; (3) to provide the assistance these populations need to prevent their coming to the attention of the criminal justice system again.[16]

As an example of a problem solving approach to helping people who are mentally ill, in New Orleans, Louisiana, the police and the state's mental health services have established a mobile crisis service using trained, nonsworn volunteers to respond to psychiatric emergencies and to provide crisis intervention and mental health assessments. If determining at the scene that an individual is gravely disabled in judgment and poses a threat to self or others, the volunteers have a limited commission that empowers them to compel the ill person to enter an appropriate mental health facility.

Every day, between noon and midnight, these volunteers provide crisis intervention and mental health evaluations at the scenes of psychiatric emergencies to which the police department has responded. In more than 85 percent of the calls the service answers, the volunteers successfully intervene and defuse the subjects by the time they reach the mental health facility. This crisis service has allowed police officers to concentrate on their policing duties and reduced the number of lawsuits filed against police by individuals who are mentally ill or their advocates.[17]

Exhibit 10.2 provides another look at how the police are dealing with the mentally ill under COPPS, with a special training program in St. Petersburg, Florida. Similar programs are under way in Albuquerque, New Mexico; Portland, Oregon; and Tampa, Florida.[18]

The Homeless

The homeless—estimates of whom range from 300,000 to three million—often panhandle, use intimidation, and generally are a problem for businesses and citizens using parks and public sidewalks. Most studies indicate that although the homeless have higher overall arrest rates than the general population, the vast majority of their offenses do not involve violence. Rather, the police most

---

Exhibit 10.2   Police Training in St. Petersburg, Florida: Reaching Out to the Mentally Ill

After mental health advocates began to complain that the police did not understand mental illness and the interventions they should take when encountering such individuals, the police chief instituted a mandatory eight-hour curriculum for all of the agency's 550 officers—the first such training curriculum in the United States. The heart of the course is a four-step approach called CIAF—*calming the subject, investigating* and *assessing* the situation, and *facilitating* a situation. The training, developed by mental health professionals, teaches officers how to look at behavior, intellectual state, attitude, verbal indicators, and environmental factors to optimize the outcome for both the officer and the individual. Instructors emphasize that officers must treat individuals who are mentally ill or unstable with respect, understanding, and compassion—but always have the situation under control. As one observer stated about the program, the police are in effect "untrained mental health counselors. They're problem solvers for people with nowhere else to turn." Officer feedback concerning the training has been positive, and success stories from using the training are beginning to mount, which underscores its effectiveness.

Source: Ronald J. Getz, "Reaching Out to the Mentally Ill," *Law and Order*, May 1999, p. 51.

---

often arrest the homeless for public intoxication, theft or shoplifting, and burglary.[19] One study also found that an average of 29 percent of people who are homeless suffer from severe mental disorders. A surprising number of the homeless are military veterans; runaways comprise another sizable category. Many, however, have experienced economic hard times or cannot afford their own housing.[20]

As with the mentally ill population, police officers dealing with the homeless often have few options; not only is shelter space limited, but most shelters refuse to admit the large percentage of homeless who are also mentally ill or alcoholic.

Clearwater, Florida, a community of 100,000 residents that regularly draws another 20,000 tourists during the beach season, recently experienced an upsurge in problems related to street people—thefts, drugs, prostitution, and vandalism. Additionally, these people were sleeping on private property; defecating and urinating on public streets; and engaging in public drunkenness, graffiti, and littering.[21]

The police department, which entered into community policing in 1983 and takes nontraditional approaches to tough problems, decided to get into the housing business. First, the city opened a homeless shelter that included a police substation; virtually every area organization and agency working with the homeless has a presence at the shelter, dealing with everything from mental problems to substance abuse and job placement. Everyone living in the shelter is required to enroll in the Salvation Army Intervention Program, follow strict rules, attend Alcoholics Anonymous meetings regardless of whether they are addicted, participate in counseling, and abide by a curfew. The department used money seized from drug operations to purchase a single-family home, which it in turn leases to a social service agency; the home is used to provide transitional living units for people leaving the shelter, thus facilitating their return back into their own living quarters. Dedicated phone lines allow each homeless person to get calls from prospective employers and set up interviews.[22]

The city has seen a turnaround with its homeless problems. Businesses that once fought the shelters are now allies, and investors are putting money into nearby properties for new construction and to rehabilitate existing buildings. For another example of the homelessness problem, see Exhibit 10.3.

Alcohol-Related Crimes

Many of the problems that are discussed in this chapter involve alcohol abuse. Given the extent of this problem, however, it will be treated separately (alcohol abuse was also discussed as being a crime accelerator in Chapter 2).

More than 7 percent of the population age 18 and older—nearly 13.8 million U.S. citizens—have problems with alcohol, including 8.1 million people who are alcoholic; furthermore, alcohol contributes to 100,000 deaths annually.[23] The problem of alcohol in the United States is even more serious when viewed in terms of underage drinking, and where it leads—many youthful problem drinkers will eventually become adult alcoholics and commit crimes. Approximately 9.5 million drinkers are young, between the ages of 12 and 20; of this number, 4.4 million are binge drinkers, including 1.9 million heavy drinkers. Young people who begin drinking before age 15 are four times more likely to develop alcohol addiction than those who begin drinking at age 21. Alcohol is a factor in 35 percent of traffic fatalities involving persons age 15 to 20.[24]

Portland, Oregon, police were recently compelled to focus on a specific type of beverage. Large (32- and 40-ounce) containers of fortified wine, each containing the alcohol equivalent of up to six drinks, contributed to problem street drinking in the Old Town/Chinatown district, causing many acts of fighting, disorderly conduct, harassment, littering, panhandling, and public urination and defecation. Four neighborhood convenience stores and four large chain stores—each selling from 60 to 100 cases of the wine per week—contributed to the area's problems by serving several hundred street drinkers. The police believed that restricting the drinkers' access to megasize beverages would reduce the problem.

EXHIBIT 10.3 Addressing Homeless-Related Crimes in San Diego, California

California's Otay River Valley is a massive tract of undeveloped land covering 8,000 acres. It is bordered by the cities of San Diego, Chula Visa, and Imperial Beach. Businesses surrounding the river valley suffered from burglary, panhandling, theft, and vandalism. People often illegally dumped trash and debris in the valley. Transients, perhaps as many as 300, lived at campsites in the valley in bamboo, metal, plywood, and tarpaulin huts. Many of the transients booby trapped their campsites to ward off intruders. A large number of them also suffered from infectious diseases, such as AIDS and sexual and skin diseases, and some were mentally ill. Police response was reactive until an increase in crime was noted; transients were becoming more aggressive, and two young boys were found murdered in the area. After political pressure began to mount to remove the transients, a three-phase effort was developed, including the enforcement of trespassing laws, the cleanup of the property, and the restoration of the land that would discourage illegal camping. In addition to the cities that were stakeholders, the state of California, San Diego County, the U.S. Fish and Wildlife Service, and the Army Corps of Engineers joined in the massive project. A prosecutor was assigned as legal counsel as well. Police issued trespassing warnings to transients, provided them with information about area homeless shelters and other services, and photographed the transients in case it became necessary to arrest them. Police also made three sweeps through the area to ensure that all trespassers had been warned—making nearly 100 arrests in the process for outstanding warrants and other offenses. Approximately 200 volunteers collected refuse from the area, a private waste-hauling company removed 31 tons of trash (with the use of donated trash containers), and a private landfill company agreed to waive $1,500 in dumping fees. Burglaries and related crimes dropped 80 percent after the evictions and cleanups. Before the project, San Diego police were spending about 3,000 hours per year on valley-related crimes; since the project's completion, that number has dropped to between 500 and 800 hours.

Source: Rana Sampson and Michael S. Scott, *Tackling Crime and Other Public Safety Problems: Case Studies in Problem Solving* (Washington, D.C.: U.S. Department of Justice, Office of Community Policing Services, 2000), pp. 109–10.

Eventually, more than 100 retailers throughout the city volunteered to remove 16-ounce (or larger) beverages from their shelves. The impact in the neighborhood was huge: There was a 50 percent reduction in the number of detoxification holds and drinking-in-public incidents, and disorderly conduct

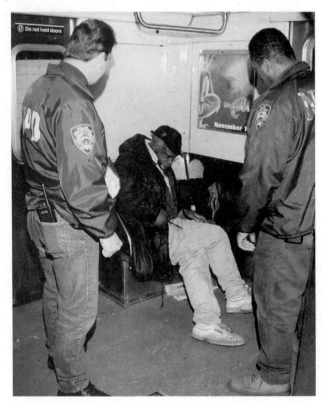

NYPD officers attend to a
transient person found sleeping
in the city's subway system.
(*Courtesy* NYPD Photo Unit)

incidents decreased 25 percent. Citizens reported that the neighborhood felt safer
and looked better, and few people are now observed in the area with open containers.[25] See Exhibit 10.4 for a discussion of alcohol problems in the Arctic.

DOMESTIC VIOLENCE

Domestic violence concerns one person dominating and controlling another by
force, threats, or physical violence. Traditionally, much of society and many
police agencies turned their backs on the problem, refusing to become involved
in "family quarrels." Accordingly, police rarely made arrests. Studies in the mid-
1980s, however, found that arrests served as an independent deterrent to future
violence, labeled the assailant's actions as criminal, and punished the attacker for
his or her actions.[26] Communities with low unemployment rates were recommended to use a mandatory arrest policy; conversely, communities with high
unemployment rates were urged to develop some alternative policies and rely
very little on arrest.[27] Today nearly all states have legislation mandating police
officers to effect warrantless arrests where evidence of spousal assault is present.

EXHIBIT 10.4 Alcohol Problems in the Arctic

With the arrival of oil workers in the 1970s, alcohol consumption became a significant part of local culture in Barrow, Alaska. Two studies linked much of Barrow's premature deaths, violence, disease, and social disorder to alcohol abuse. Alaska state law provides for a local option on the sale of liquor, but mere prohibitions on alcohol sales had little impact on the problem. Data analysis revealed that in this small community of about 5,000 residents, there were 87 rapes by drunk men, 675 drunken assaults, 503 domestic disputes involving drunk spouses, 388 arrests for drunk driving, 229 arrests of drunk children, and 2,057 incidents in which people were taken into protective custody because of alcohol-induced incapacitation. Most problems were related to alcohol illegally imported and consumed by citizens who were binge drinkers. Police concluded that a total ban on alcohol was the only viable response. Such a ban was passed by city voters in October 1994. Fetal alcohol exposure in pregnant women dropped from 45 percent to less than 10 percent, and alcohol-related calls for service to police declined by 81 percent. But the story does not end there on a happy note. The community then legalized alcohol in 1995, making the city "wet" again. The same alcohol-related problems recurred, at levels that were even higher than those preceding the ban. Furthermore, a proalcohol administration was elected into office, leading to a change in police administration as well. Police officers were ordered not to officially support the alcohol ban or release information about alcohol-related matters. Nonetheless, this problem solving effort demonstrates a uniquely comprehensive and detailed analysis of the harm caused by alcohol, as well as an ambitious response strategy that might be unthinkable in many jurisdictions.

Source: Rana Sampson and Michael S. Scott, *Tackling Crime and Other Public Safety Problems: Case Studies in Problem Solving* (Washington, D.C.: U.S. Department of Justice, Office of Community Policing Services, 2000), pp. 53–55.

Unfortunately, however, domestic violence remains the most prevalent form of violence confronting our society today.

Domestic violence, like the other problems discussed in this chapter, must be viewed as a communitywide problem. Police can collect and analyze information about domestic violence and assist the community in becoming aware of its magnitude. Officers can also solicit community support in developing alternative strategies for combating it. Police must work closely with victims' advocates, social service agencies, and the judiciary (injunctive relief can be used to bar an abusive spouse from returning to the family residence). This is a quality-of-life issue, and—like problems such as drugs, gangs, or prostitution—if left unchecked it will fester and grow.

What can be done proactively about this problem? (See Exhibit 10.5 for one solution.) A growing number of promising COPPS practices have been identified. One Georgia police department, for example, trained county process servers to work with domestic violence survivors. Because many domestic violence incidents go unreported to the police, the person serving a restraining order is often the first authority to learn of a domestic violence situation. Officers can also encourage neighbors to anonymously report disturbances or signs of abuse. Religious organizations can be encouraged to reach out to members who are victims. Substance abuse treatment can be arranged for abusers when alcohol and other drugs play a role in the violence.[28]

The Lapeer County, Michigan, sheriff's department reacted to a rise in domestic violence calls by using a unique approach. The department, in conjunction with a regional hospital, a citizens' group, and 17 other county agencies, formed a coalition that created a list of goals and objectives that serve as a foundation for reducing domestic violence in the county:

- Reduce to 10 percent or less the number of battered women and children turned away from emergency housing because of a lack of space.
- Reduce physical abuse directed at women by male partners to no more than 27 out of 1,000 couples.
- Ensure that a crisis intervention shelter and support resources are accessible to all, regardless of ability to pay.
- Increase the number of physicians, nurses, social workers, teachers, and criminal justice professionals who receive training in identifying and referring victims.
- Establish a tracking mechanism to record the rate of assault injuries.[29]

SCHOOL VIOLENCE

The recent increase in shootings on school campuses has all of America wondering what has happened to its children. In one six-year period, from July 1992 to June 1998, there were 225 school-associated violent deaths[30] (this figure excludes the April 1999 massacre of 13 people at Columbine High School in Littleton, Colorado). Common traits among the perpetrators of school violence include an orientation toward violent TV shows, videos, and music; a feeling of inferiority or being teased, and having a grudge against some student or teacher; easy access to weapons; suicidal tendencies and above-average intelligence; and the presence of ample warning signs, either in writing or talking about killing others.[31]

There is no single cause for the increase in school shootings. Even with the zero-tolerance laws concerning the carrying of weapons to school, students say they carry weapons for self-protection or to maintain an image. Several strategies have been suggested for police and citizens to help prevent school violence:

EXHIBIT 10.5 Addressing Domestic Violence in Largo, Florida

Recently the Largo, Florida, Police Department realized that its domestic violence (DV) efforts were of little avail; the community of 75,000 was receiving about 1,000 such calls per year, with only about 16 percent of them resulting in a prosecution. The department formed a partnership with a wide array of governmental agencies, private organizations, and citizen groups, with the goals of getting perpetrators into the justice or social services systems, providing survivor assistance, and finding ways to break the cycle and reduce the violence. Prosecution rates immediately increased to 85 percent. Following are other approaches used by the partnership:

- A DV Web site was established—the first of its kind in the United States.
- A mandatory arrest policy was initiated for DV perpetrators.
- A team of DV intervention specialists was established whose first priorities are the survivors and their families.
- A cellular phone program was begun to safeguard victims.
- A partnering among organizations from every spectrum of the community was begun to provide long-term solutions to reduce the number of incidents.

Although acknowledging the difficulty of obtaining measurable statistics on DV (long-term recidivism data are not yet available), the police department points to the permanent partnership it has formed with most of the stakeholders in DV issues.

Source: Adapted from Ronald J. Getz, "Largo Police Attack Domestic Violence," *Law and Order*, November 1998, pp. 44–45.

- Publicizing the philosophy that a gang presence will not be tolerated, and institutionalizing a code of conduct
- Alerting students and parents about school rules and punishments for infractions
- Creating alternative schools for those students who cannot function in a regular classroom
- Training teachers, parents, and school staff to identify children who are most at risk for violent behavior
- Developing community initiatives focused on breaking family cycles of violence, and providing programs on parenting, conflict resolution, anger management, and recovery from substance abuse

- Establishing peer counseling in schools to give troubled youths the opportunity to talk to someone their own age
- Teaching children that it is not "tattling" to go to a school teacher or staff member if they know someone who is discussing "killing"[32]

Recently the National Institute of Justice sponsored a research project on school safety, incorporating the program into a social studies class curriculum in a high school in Charlotte, North Carolina. The program had three major components: regular meetings among faculty, administrators, and the police; problem solving classes for the students; and regular reviews by the police and teachers to identify problem students. The curriculum was based on the S.A.R.A. problem solving process and was to be student-driven, with teachers acting as mentors and facilitators. Students identified fighting and disorder in the lunchroom as a major issue. The root of the problem was that the entire school population—as many as 1,500 students—was released for lunch at the same time. Students proposed several solutions (an open campus policy was rejected by the administration) and met with lunchroom workers, who agreed to open additional lines and improve the food serving system. Police calls for service at the school, fear levels of students, and actual incidents of violence declined, as did vandalism, theft, and obscene threats and gestures.[33]

It is also recommended that representatives from the police, the schools, and the community come together to sign memorandums of understanding that clearly define what each organization or agency will do from the beginning if a school-violence crisis occurs.[34] Furthermore, basic crime prevention techniques such as the following may be employed to create safer schools: Have all school visitors check in at the office; monitor campus perimeters and hallways; make certain that area police agencies have maps or site plans of schools, as well as master keys to all school classrooms and offices; have a warning signal when a school encounters a threat or emergency; and ensure that police and school personnel remain in constant contact during a crisis.[35] Exhibit 10.6 describes a multistate program against youth violence.

Rental Properties and Neighborhood Disorder

Neighborhoods deteriorate one home at a time. This deterioration can have many root causes and be accelerated when drug houses, gangs, prostitutes, graffiti, abandoned houses and vehicles, and general neighborhood decay become commonplace. Public housing areas are particularly susceptible to such problems. The police must work in partnership with citizens, tailoring tactics to specific neighborhoods and assisting in their defense against crime and disorder.

A wide range of activities may be undertaken to attack neighborhood crime and deterioration. Herman Goldstein described some of the measures that police may undertake when, for example, a public housing project is suffering from a rash of burglaries:

EXHIBIT 10.6   Preventing Youth Violence: A Multistate Program Unites Communities

The Southeastern Community Oriented Policing Education Institute (SCOPE), a partnership of the Knoxville, Tennessee, Police Department, the Metropolitan Drug Commission, and the University of Tennessee's Institute for Public Service, has provided a plan of action known as "Challenge to Change" to bring together stakeholders and take aim at youth violence. In December 1998 SCOPE held a teleconference to present the eight-month, step-by-step approach to the five communities chosen to participate in Challenge to Change: Jonesboro, Arkansas; Hartsville, South Carolina; Chattanooga, Tennessee; Wilson, North Carolina; and Vicksburg, Mississippi. SCOPE staff visited each city to help leaders conduct a community policing assessment of their city and to offer specialized training. Each city then formed a leadership team and began developing strategies to bring their communities and police agencies closer together. Activities in the five cities varied but included, among others, developing a violence prevention curriculum, a music video about peace, and a youth panel (Jonesboro); creating a mentoring program to match at-risk students with mentors and establishing a roundtable of students, police, school teachers, and officials (Hartsville); organizing a block party and releasing hundreds of balloons in memory of the people killed at Columbine High School in Colorado (Chattanooga); developing after-school and summer recreational activities (Wilson); and organizing a youth violence awareness project (Vicksburg).

Source: Adapted from Mike Hill, "Youth Violence Prevention Becomes a Vehicle for Uniting Communities," *Community Policing Exchange* (Community Policing Consortium), September/October 1999, pp. 1–2.

- Make efforts to apprehend those responsible for the burglaries.
- Counsel management regarding lighting, lock systems, landscaping that provides hiding places for burglars, fencing, appearance of buildings and grounds, and so forth.
- Refer uncorrected conditions that are in violation of the law to building inspectors, zoning authorities, or health authorities.
- Work with tenants, informing them of their rights vis-a-vis management, of various government services available to them, and of measures they can take to prevent crimes.
- Work with school authorities regarding any problem of truancy that may be related to burglaries, and with recreation and park authorities regarding any problem of idle youth.[36]

Crime, drugs, and violence often plague public housing neighborhoods. (*Courtesy* Sgt. Dominic Licavoli, LAPD)

This list demonstrates what Goldstein observed: Once the police break out of the mold of looking only within the criminal justice system for solutions, "large vistas are opened to exploration" and the police can engage in a "far-reaching and imaginative search for alternative ways" to deal with recurring problems.[37] Exhibit 10.7 describes a problem of horrendous proportions in Santa Barbara, California, underscoring what can happen when landlords and management companies ignore their legal and moral responsibilities to their tenants.

As Goldstein mentioned, it is essential that property owners and landlords know their rights with respect to tenants. Because most drug activity occurs on rental property, prevention efforts must involve the property management community. Landlord–tenant training programs are being undertaken by a number of police departments to help owners and managers keep drugs and other criminal activities off their property.

Such a situation occurred in 1989 in Portland, Oregon, when John Campbell, a resident of a quiet neighborhood, woke up one morning to find a crack house on his block. Campbell's frustration with the drug problem led him to investigate how landlords and neighbors could better detect and stem crime at rental properties. With the Portland Police Bureau's support—and after researching state and local laws and interviewing more than 40 people—Campbell developed an eight-hour training course for landlords and property managers. Since 1989 Campbell's crusade has resulted in more than 6,000 Portland-area landlords and property managers receiving this training. Furthermore, communities in other states have modified his approach to meet their particular needs.[38] Although such training programs vary, most include the following topics:

- An overview of what landlords and managers can do to keep neighborhoods healthy

---

Exhibit 10.7 Apartment Complex Crime in Santa Barbara, California

Police officers began looking into problems involving a local apartment complex, where tenants had complained about disturbances, an illegal auto repair shop, littering, and illegally built dwellings. The owner—who had 34 other properties in the city—resisted taking any corrective action and had never hired a property manager; as a result, nearly all of his properties were in disrepair and causing a tremendous drain on police resources. Health and safety codes were ignored, and apartments were overrun with cockroaches and rats. A number were also illegally subdivided, with up to 10 people living in a two-bedroom unit. Fire and building codes were also ignored, and there were excessive noise complaints and litter coming from the complexes. Children used abandoned vehicles in the parking lots as playgrounds. Officers found that 758 arrestees and 121 people with outstanding misdemeanor bench warrants listed the properties as their residences. Officers asked neighbors to keep logs of the problems at the properties for two months; officers also photographed the worst conditions and documented the rubble and running sewage. They suggested prosecuting the slumlord with an "unfair competition" charge, because his unlawful neglect of the properties gave him an unfair advantage over legitimately run properties. Officers enlisted the aid of a deputy from the district attorney's fraud unit and organized a task force that included representatives from several city and county prosecutor's, fire, and community development offices. Inspection teams took cameras and camcorders to the site, documenting 750 code violations. Media coverage focused community awareness on the site as well. With this evidence, a criminal court judge convicted the owner and ordered that, as a condition of his probation, he comply with all building codes and regulations; management by a management company was also ordered.

Source: Rana Sampson and Michael S. Scott, *Tackling Crime and Other Public Safety Problems: Case Studies in Problem Solving* (Washington, D.C.: U.S. Department of Justice, Office of Community Policing Services, 2000), pp. 14–18.

- How to screen out dishonest applicants, while assuring that honest applicants are encouraged to apply
- Rental agreements and approaches that will strengthen the ability to evict tenants who are drug users or dealers
- Warning signs of drug and other criminal activity, the drugs involved, and the behavior associated with growing, dealing, selling
- What to do if a clandestine drug lab is discovered

- The options and process of eviction
- How to work with the police
- Rights and responsibilities under Section 8 (subsidized) housing[39]

For many poor, urban families, public housing represents the only hope for housing of any kind. Disadvantaged by lack of education, skills, and health, the urban poor pass on public housing dependency from generation to generation. For young, single-parent families who cannot find decent, safe, and affordable temporary housing, severely distressed public housing becomes the permanent housing of last resort.

In most cases these young residents have the greatest need for affordable housing; they are also the most vulnerable, the most difficult to manage, and the most difficult for whom to provide security. Public housing residents ask that the police clear the hallways, stairways, lobbies, and streets of open-air drug sales. The police recognize that distressed housing can be difficult to patrol. Community policing offers the best hope for successful order maintenance in public housing. Sooner or later, a housing authority police force will encounter problems. The conflict usually centers on crime problems, maintenance and repair issues, or such turf issues as who should enforce conduct provisions of the lease.[40]

PROSTITUTION

Street prostitution constitutes an offense to the moral standards of the community. It creates a nuisance to passersby and nearby residents and merchants, and parking and traffic problems develop; the behavior may also foment other more serious crimes as well as the spread of sexually transmitted diseases, including AIDS. Street criminals such as prostitutes may also gather juveniles into their web.

Prostitutes often become brazen, know the law, and develop ways to avoid arrest and conviction. Therefore, police who undertake to address this problem need to perform a systematic inquiry into the extent and nature of the problem: How often are juveniles involved? How much crime (such as robberies of "johns") is related to prostitution? Is organized crime involved? Are prostitutes injuring others or being injured themselves? Answers to these and other related questions will help bring the problem into focus. Officers must also consider alternative strategies to thwarting problems. For example, New York City police officers enforced the mandatory safety belt law disproportionately against drivers in areas frequented by street prostitutes. "We use whatever tools we can," stated the officer in charge.[41] Some jurisdictions now publish the names of johns in local newspapers and send letters to homes of registered owners of vehicles, warning the resident(s) that their vehicle was seen loitering in an area frequented by prostitutes.

At times the officers must also gather information from prostitutes themselves to bring a greater degree of order to the situation. The most severe problems associated with street prostitution can be reduced if prostitutes can be encouraged to bring juvenile prostitutes to police attention, expose those who rob their customers, and respect each other's turf. See Exhibit 10.8 for an example of how one community handled its prostitution situation.

An example of ways to address illicit sexual pandering can be seen in Nassau County, New York, where 31 massage parlors in seven communities advertised in local newspapers and magazines. They were unlicensed to do so and actually offered sexual services. A survey of citizens, vice squad members, and patrol officers determined that most parlor employees were Korean or Hispanic. COPPS officers, using records from the county clerk's office, located the building owners in which the massage parlors were operating. Interviews with owners revealed that lease agreements had typically been executed under false pretenses by parlor operators (most had told building owners that they were operating physical therapy centers or legitimate massage therapy clinics).[42]

The COPPS officers decided that the best strategy was to force the property owners to help them shut down the businesses. Officers notified the owners about building and fire code violations and fraudulent lease agreements that had been detected. The officers informed the owners that the absence of appropriate professional licenses and the fraudulent nature of the leases were sufficient grounds to evict the massage parlor tenants. When property owners did not cooperate, police, fire marshals, and building inspectors reinspected the massage parlors and cited the owners, putting as much pressure as possible on them to evict the unlawful tenants. The building violations could cost them from $200 to $1,000 per day; fire code violations could reach $5,000 per day. The district attorney's office also threatened to file criminal charges for criminal nuisance against owners who refused to evict, and police notified the properties' mortgage holders of the illegal activity, suggesting to them that the prostitution and consequent arrests could result in adverse publicity for them.[43]

The result of these efforts was that all of the county's illegal massage parlors were closed or vacated. Soon the police were working with attorneys to draft local legislation that would strengthen the county's authority to close down businesses that failed to meet all occupational and building requirements.

OTHER SELECTED PROBLEMS

Next we look briefly at COPPS responses to three other kinds of public safety problems: cruising, false alarms, and teen hangouts in video arcades.

Cruising

Cruising may be loosely defined as repeatedly driving a motor vehicle in or near a congested area, within (and often during) a specified time period. What is meant by "repeatedly" and "specified period of time" is determined by each municipality.

EXHIBIT 10.8   Addressing Prostitution in Champaign, Illinois

Champaign, Illinois, had a chronic prostitution problem in its downtown area. Arrests provided only temporary relief, and the prostitutes were rarely convicted. Collateral crimes (theft, robbery, assaults, and "john rolling") caused a significant drain on police resources. Citizens complained that prostitutes used apartment building foyers, church parking lots, driveways, and private alleys to have sex. Ninety percent of the prostitutes were repeat offenders; 15 of them held the majority of all convictions. The city's antisolicitation ordinance, merely resulting in a fine, offered no long-term solution. Female officers dressed as prostitutes arrested johns for attempted patronizing, but the state attorney's office typically dismissed these cases, because entrapment defenses were difficult to refute without evidence of the john's predisposition. The state legislature made a third prostitution conviction a felony, but often many years would pass before an offender would amass a criminal history that made her or him eligible for the enhanced felony sentencing. Finally, court-imposed travel restrictions were investigated. The police crime analysis unit found that 92 percent of 321 prostitution arrests over five years occurred in a 12-block downtown area. Armed with a pin map, police requested that the court impose travel restrictions on one chronic prostitute, thus keeping her away from the downtown area and potential customers. The judge agreed, and within two months Champaign courts imposed such restrictions on 13 chronic prostitutes, taking care of the recidivistic offenders; a state appeals court upheld the restrictions. The following year, the state legislature codified travel restrictions. Over the next year and a half, the city's street prostitution dropped by 90 percent. Limiting access to the area disrupted the market and separated prostitutes from their customers.

Source: Rana Sampson and Michael S. Scott, *Tackling Crime and Other Public Safety Problems: Case Studies in Problem Solving* (Washington, D.C.: U.S. Department of Justice, Office of Community Policing Services, 2000), pp. 14–18.

Cruising may seem on the surface to be a relatively harmless activity, and indeed people like to cruise for several reasons: socializing with friends, displaying driving ability, lack of other activities, and showing off cars.[44] But cruising has become intolerable in some communities, resulting in citizen harassment, vandalism, underage drinking, littering, urinating in public, trashing of parking lots, excessive noise, and general disorderly behavior. Police often have to devote large amounts of time to areas congested with cruisers and the attendant problems that arise.

Communities have responded with cruising ordinances, using citations and fines for cruising past a control or checkpoint more than a certain number of times during a specified time period. Some departments even enter license plate numbers into a computer, which "alerts" officers on seeing the same license plate a second or third time. Other communities have only aggravated the problem with their cruising ordinances, raising the ire of young and old alike who enjoy this activity. Therefore, some alternative measures have been used with greater success.

Arlington, Texas, rented a parking lot and posted a 10-mile-per-hour speed limit and two officers to patrol the area. Portland, Oregon, published a brochure on cruising and distributed it to cruisers in the affected areas. Topeka, Kansas, police located a "cruising zone" close enough to downtown to be acceptable to cruisers but not a nuisance to the community. Other communities have formed a Teen Court or some form of youth council to handle the violations that arise in the cruise area.[45] See Exhibit 10.9 for another example of how a community dealt with the problem of cruising.

False Alarms

The proliferation of electronic security systems for both commercial and residential use—although expanding crime-prevention efforts—has brought with it a serious problem for police officers nationwide. On average, 98 percent of all activations prove to be false alarms, set off by weather conditions, a moving rodent, or an errant store owner. False alarms—which now range from 5 to 30 percent of all calls for police service—cost police departments about $1.4 billion each year.[46] Recent financial difficulties in some jurisdictions have forced police executives to reassess alarm responses—formerly provided free of charge.

Faced with budget cuts, an increasing number of police executives are charging business and residential owners for police responses to false alarms that are, in effect, wasted effort. A strategy of assessing fines for false alarms and termination of alarm use, now beginning to spread across the United States, obviously represents a major break with traditional police practices. A COPPS response can be helpful here, and Exhibit 10.10 shows how one police department addressed this problem.

Teen Hangouts in Video Arcades

The local teen hangout is not a new phenomenon; video arcades provide entertainment for today's youth. Some arcades are relatively problem free, whereas others attract drugs, gangs, and runaways. One that became quite crime prone was in Delta, British Columbia, near Vancouver, Canada.[47] Beginning in 1988 an arcade located in a mall suddenly began to attract crime and impact surrounding businesses and the community. Police received an increasing number of calls for service for vandalism, litter, graffiti, theft, and other criminal behavior. Indeed, CFS increased by 47 percent in one year alone, and soon area residents were signing a petition for the city council and police to do something. Two enforcement

---

Exhibit 10.9   Cruising Trouble in Santa Ana, California

The street cruising problem in Santa Ana, California, became uncontrollable in the 1990s. On Sunday evenings 1,000 carloads of youths brought one six-block-long area in the community to a point of gridlock; this situation created a heightened sense of fear in the city because of associated criminal activity and rival gang violence (with 16 related homicides and more than 100 aggravated assaults in a two-and-a-half-year period). Traditional police responses failed and were expensive. Officers in the district formed a problem solving team and developed a series of operation plans to address the issues. Police devised a traffic control scheme and used their legal authority to stop all traffic, identify drivers, and provide information on cruising violations. They entered driver and vehicle information in a computer database at the traffic control points and sent follow-up letters to registered vehicle owners, to reinforce their warnings and to ensure that parents were informed of young drivers' activities. They also erected warning signs along the highways. On the first night of the operation, police stopped 70 percent of the cruising vehicles at checkpoints; during the next two nights, 83 percent were stopped. The number of returning cruisers diminished so much by the fourth night that the police suspended the checkpoints in favor of traffic stops. Cruising eventually ceased altogether. During the program, the police issued more than 2,000 personal warnings and sent more than 1,700 follow-up letters. The warning-and-education campaign turned out to be at least as effective as enforcement, and more efficient. Ninety percent of the cruisers warned on the first night did not return. There have been no cruising related calls during the past two years, and crime associated with it has disappeared.

Source: Rana Sampson and Michael S. Scott, *Tackling Crime and Other Public Safety Problems: Case Studies in Problem Solving* (Washington, D.C.: U.S. Department of Justice, Office of Community Policing Services, 2000), pp. 14–18.

---

strategies—increased surveillance and saturation patrol—were largely unsuccessful; a long-term approach was needed.

A constable began by analyzing the crime statistics and police reports; conducting on-site interviews; and meeting with mall, arcade, and community groups. He found that although there were originally 25 video machines at the arcade, the owner had recently doubled the number of machines and made design changes inside the arcade, reducing vision and making it impossible for staff to monitor patrons. Using CPTED (crime prevention through environmental design) principles, the constable found numerous problems, including poor management, lack of proper natural surveillance, and no control of interior spaces.

EXHIBIT 10.10   Alarm Problems in Charlotte-Mecklenburg

Alarm calls for service increased from 48,643 to 94,417 in five years (a 94 percent increase) and constituted 18 percent of all police calls for service to the Charlotte-Mecklenburg, North Carolina, Police Department. More than 98 percent of these calls were false alarms, caused by improper installation and maintenance and owner/operator error. A false alarm task force was formed, which contacted other cities regarding solutions and provided copies of relevant ordinances. Ordinances were passed providing for the registration of all alarms (at no fee), with an escalating scale of fines for repeat false alarms and indicating that police would not respond to future alarms if fines were unpaid. A media campaign began educating citizens. During the first year after the alarm ordinances went into effect, there was a 30 percent reduction in alarm calls; actual response to calls was reduced 42 percent.

Source: Workshop presentation, Gary Whitt, Charlotte-Mecklenburg, North Carolina, Police Department, "The 8th Annual International Problem Oriented Policing Conference: Problem Oriented Policing 1997," November 15, 1997, San Diego, California.

The arcade was also a crime generator for the entire mall, with conflicts between different groups of youths spilling into surrounding businesses and the parking lot area. Drug transactions and sales of stolen property began to occur, and stores around the arcade began closing as a result of losses in revenue. A security guard service also became necessary.

First, the officer concluded that CPTED changes would be a good start; the arcade owner, however, refused to remove the extra 25 video machines or to return the lighting to original levels; he took a "show me" stance, wanting proof that such changes would succeed. The constable contacted the mall's original architects, and together they decided to conduct a full study of arcade crime in the city; this study found that certain designs accompany low-problem video arcades throughout the city. The problem arcade owner was then summoned to city hall to hear the study results; he finally agreed to make the changes. Machines were set up only around the periphery, and a clear and open view to the exterior was made available; ample lighting was provided as well. A parking-stall-to-patron ratio (2:20) was implemented to help limit the number of arcade users, and hours of operation were restricted. In-house security staff were hired, and age restrictions were enforced. Access was controlled to washrooms, and the city drafted new ordinances for future arcades. CFS were reduced by about 150 percent during the first year following these problem solving activities.

Exhibit 10.11 discusses another problem for police: 911 calls.

Exhibit 10.11   Addressing the Dominance of 911

Today's 911 system is a pervasive example of technology driving police departments. With an estimated 268,000 911 calls per day—90 percent of which are for nonemergencies—the system is a major criticism among police practitioners. Departments must also find ways to free officers from what has been called the "tyranny of 911": nonstop calls that send officers bouncing from one nonemergency call for service to the next. To relieve the burden on 911, in August 1996 the federal Office of Community Policing Services asked the Federal Communications Commission to reserve 311 for national nonemergency use. A one-year experiment with 311 in the Baltimore Police Department—involving an aggressive public education campaign—revealed "spectacular" results, with the city reporting a 25 percent decrease in 911 calls for service. Meanwhile, the public's use of 311 allowed Baltimore police to engage and expand their COPPS efforts. The 311 system would appear to hold much promise for the future, alleviating the burden on officers and 911.

Source: U.S. Department of Justice, Office of Community Oriented Policing Services, "COPS Facts: 3-1-1 National Non-Emergency Number," October/November 1996, p. 1.

SUMMARY

This chapter has applied COPPS to the street, demonstrating how it works with specific crimes. The efficacy of COPPS in dealing with these problems was convincingly demonstrated. The police agencies described in this chapter and their peers across the United States are realizing many successes, breaking with tradition and attacking the contributing or underlying problems, while empowering neighborhoods to defend themselves against crime and deterioration.

NOTES

1. Zachary Tumin, "Managing Relations with the Community" (working paper 86–05–06, Program in Criminal Justice Policy and Management, John F. Kennedy School of Government, Harvard University, Cambridge, Massachusetts, November 1986), final page.
2. U.S. Department of Justice, Federal Bureau of Investigation, *Uniform Crime Reports: Crime in the United States—1998* (Washington, D.C.: Author, 1999), pp. 209–10.
3. Ellen Perlman, "The Meth Monster," *Governing* (January 2000):22.

Gasoline station drive-offs (leaving without paying for gas) can account
for a high number of calls for service. A prepay policy is one simple
method for reducing this problem.

4. Rana Sampson and Michael S. Scott, *Tackling Crime and Other Public Safety Problems:
   Case Studies in Problem Solving* (Washington, D.C.: U.S. Department of Justice, Office
   of Community Policing Services, 2000), pp. 23–26.
5. C. Ronald Huff, *Comparing the Criminal Behavior of Youth Gangs and At-Risk Youths*
   (Washington, D.C.: National Institute of Justice Research in Brief, 1998).
6. G. David Curry, Richard A. Ball, and Scott H. Decker, *Estimating the National Scope of
   Gang Crime from Law Enforcement Data* (Washington, D.C.: National Institute of Justice Research in Brief, 1996).
7. Scott H. Decker and G. David Curry, "Responding to Gangs: Comparing Gang
   Member, Police, and Task Force Perspectives," *Journal of Criminal Justice* 28
   (2000):129–37.
8. S. Vantakesh, "The Financial Activity of a Modern American Street Gang," in *Looking at Crime from the Street Level: Plenary Papers of the 1999 Conference on Criminal
   Justice Research and Evaluation—Enhancing Policing and Practice through Research, Volume 1* (Washington, D.C.: U.S. Department of Justice, Office of Justice Programs,
   National Institute of Justice, 1999).
9. Sampson and Scott, *Tackling Crime and Other Public Safety Problems*, p. 63.
10. *Ibid.*, p. 64.
11. *Ibid.*, p. 67.
12. *Ibid.*, p. 68.
13. *Ibid.*

14. James Lasley, *"Designing Out" Gang Homicides and Street Assaults* (Washington, D.C.: U.S. Department of Justice, National Institute of Justice Research in Brief, November 1998), pp. 1–4.

15. Ronald J. Getz, "Reaching Out to the Mentally Ill," *Law and Order* (May 1999):51.

16. Peter E. Finn and Monique Sullivan, *Police Response to Special Populations* (Washington, D.C.: U.S. Department of Justice, National Institute of Justice, 1988), p. 139.

17. Jeff Wellborn, "Responding to Individuals with Mental Illness," *FBI Law Enforcement Bulletin* (November 1999):6–7.

18. Donald G. Turnbaugh, "Curing Police Problems with the Mentally Ill," *The Police Chief* (February 1999):52.

19. David L. Carter and Allen D. Sapp, "Police Response to Street People: A Survey of Perspectives and Practices," *FBI Law Enforcement Bulletin* (March 1993):5–10.

20. Peter Finn, *Street People*. United States Department of Justice, National Institute of Justice, Crime File Study Guide (Washington, D.C.: USGPO, 1988), p. 1.

21. Ronald J. Getz, "A Positive Police Program for the Homeless," *Law and Order* (May 1999):93–96.

22. *Ibid.*

23. National Council on Alcohol and Drug Dependence, *Alcoholism and Alcohol-Related Problems: A Sobering Look* (Washington, D.C.: Author, 2000).

24. U.S. Department of Justice, Office of Juvenile Justice and Delinquency Prevention, OJJDP Fact Sheet, *Combating Underage Drinking* (Washington, D.C.: Author, February 1998), p. 1.

25. Sampson and Scott, *Tackling Crime and Other Public Safety Problems*, pp. 57–59.

26. Lawrence Sherman and Robert A. Berk, "The Specific Deterrent Effects of Arrest for Domestic Assault," *American Sociological Review* 49 (1984):261–71.

27. Jacob R. Clark, "Where to Now on Domestic-Violence? Studies Offer Mixed Policy Guidance," *Law Enforcement News* (April 30, 1993):1.

28. "Taking a Problem-Solving Approach to Domestic Violence," in *Domestic Violence: 1995–1998 Edition* (Washington, D.C.: Community Policing Consortium, 1998), p. 4.

29. Ronald J. Kalanquin, "Coalition Works to Curb Rising Rate of Domestic Violence in Lapeer County," in *ibid.*, p. 5.

30. Gene Marlin and Barbara Vogt, "Violence in the Schools," *The Police Chief* (April 1999):169.

31. Timothy Egan, "Killing Sprees at Nation's Schools Share Number of Common Traits," *The Springfield State–Journal Register*, June 14, 1998, p. 9.

32. Marlin and Vogt, "Violence in the Schools," p. 169.

33. Dennis Kenney, *Crime in the Schools: A Problem-Solving Approach* (Washington, D.C.: National Institute of Justice Research Preview, August 1998), pp. 1–3.

34. Stephen R. Band and Joseph A. Harpold, "School Violence: Lessons Learned," *FBI Law Enforcement Bulletin*, September 1999, p. 10.

35. Dennis Bridges, "Safeguarding Our Schools," *FBI Law Enforcement Bulletin* (September 1999):21–23.

36. Herman Goldstein, *Problem-Oriented Policing* (New York: McGraw-Hill, 1990), pp. 44–45.

37. *Ibid.*, p. 44. See also *Keeping Illegal Activity out of Rental Property: A Police Guide for Establishing Landlord Training Programs* (Washington, D.C.: U.S. Department of Justice, Bureau of Justice Assistance, March 2000).

38. Sampson and Scott, *Tackling Crime and Other Public Safety Problems*, pp. 13–14.

39. See, for example, Campbell Resources, Inc., *The Landlord Training Program: Keeping Illegal Activity out of Rental Property* (Portland, Ore.: Author, 1992), p. 2.

40. W. H. Matthews, *Policing Distressed Public Housing Developments: Community Policing Could Be the Answer* (Washington, D.C.: U.S. Department of Housing and Urban Development, Crime Prevention and Security Division, no date).

41. *New York Times* (March 8, 1985) as cited in Goldstein, *Problem-Oriented Policing*, p. 44.

42. Sampson and Scott, *Tackling Crime and Other Public Safety Problems*, pp. 157–59.
43. *Ibid.*
44. Boise Police Department Planning Unit, *Downtown "Cruising" in Major U.S. Cities and One City's Response to the Problem* (Boise, Id.: Author, 1990), pp. 1–2.
45. *Ibid.*, pp. 1–21.
46. Anya Sostek, "Alarm Aggravation," *Governing* (October 1998):34.
47. Delta, British Columbia, Canada, Police Department, *The Elite Arcade: Taming a Crime Generator* (Delta, British Columbia: Author, 1997).

The "Devil's Advocate"
Addressing Concerns with COPPS

> Pessimism, when you get used to it, is just as agreeable as optimism.
>
> —Arnold Bennett

INTRODUCTION

Some writers have manifested concerns with and criticisms of community oriented policing and problem solving (COPPS). This chapter examines these concerns—we have termed them the "devil's advocate" positions toward COPPS. Although several reservations were lodged against COPPS in the early stages of its development, they have probably been reduced or eliminated during the intervening years; however, we believe it is important for these concerns to be considered and addressed.

This chapter addresses nine concerns that have appeared in the literature. The concern is first described, then it is followed by a response, with some impressions of how COPPS—when implemented and practiced in a thoughtful and appropriate manner—addresses each stated concern.

THE ISSUES

Following are the nine general concerns and criticisms about COPPS:

1. Is there a true "community"?
2. Is this a proper role for police?
3. Does the concept violate the political neutrality of police?
4. Can COPPS work when it cannot cure the underlying societal problems of crime and disorder?
5. Does the concept require too much officer discretion?
6. Is this simply a faddish, costly gimmick?
7. Do officers possess the intellectual capacity and temperament to sustain the concept?
8. Can police departments change from within?
9. Will adequate evaluations be done of COPPS?

Some of these concerns overlap in varying degrees. Two more concerns are addressed at the chapter's end, including the recent phenomenon in policing termed "zero tolerance," and whether COPPS will continue to exist when federal funds are no longer available to assist in providing such initiatives.

Concern and Response 1: Is There a True "Community"?

The community organizing role of the police in community policing tends to assume there is a viable "community" to organize. Some writers, however, question the ability of the police to create a feeling of community where none exists.[1] Legitimate concerns have also been lodged about the ability of COPPS to work in neighborhoods that are severely crime ridden and occupied with more reticent and fearful citizens. As stated by James Q. Wilson and John J. DiIulio,

> Much is made these days of "community oriented" policing. Both of us have written favorably about it and the problem solving, police–neighborhood collaboration that lies at its heart. But the success stories are always in communities in which the people are willing to step forward and the police are willing to meet them halfway. Where open-air drug markets operate every night, where Uzi-toting thugs shoot rivals and bystanders alike, it is a brave or foolhardy resident who will even testify against a criminal, much less lead an anticrime crusade.[2]

A related concern is that community organizing efforts may help organize only the middle class. Early COPPS experiments in Houston, Chicago, and Minneapolis found they were more successful among middle-income people, homeowners, and whites than among the poor, renters, and racial minorities.[3]

Block parties help establish a "sense of community" by providing an opportunity for neighbors to get acquainted. (*Courtesy* Minneapolis, Minnesota, Police Department)

The question is whether the police will be able to organize communities that have disintegrated. Extremely poor neighborhoods may lack any organized community life, have an extremely transient population, and contain powerless people who do not have the ability to work with the police. As Samuel Walker put it, this may be "the *paradox* of community policing: The communities that need it most are least able to take advantage of it" (emphasis in original).[4] Another argument is that there are many groups in society who do not want a continued police presence.

Response

Neighborhoods do exist where there is very little sense of "community," particularly in highly transient areas or multicultural areas where language or police–community relations are problematic. In these areas, people may be extremely reluctant to step forward, to attend neighborhood meetings, or to assist the police in other ways to address problems. These people may also, for various reasons, hold their police in low regard.

Such situations will require that the police and other governmental agencies shoulder a much larger brunt of the responsibility for neighborhood problem solving. The police must hope that, over time, citizens assume some civic responsibility to and engage in the "communitarianism" spirit, which was discussed in Chapter 3.

Furthermore, some cities—especially relatively young cities that have grown rapidly in recent years—may not have communities or neighborhoods in the traditional sense, or a long-term identification with the neighborhood or community institutions. It has been shown, however, in examples presented in earlier chapters, that COPPS can function in the most dismal of neighborhoods. Granted, these neighborhoods are a greater challenge than those with fewer "broken windows," but COPPS can function in any locale where citizens are tired of problems going unsolved. Programs such as Secret Witness and police storefronts can help reduce citizens' anxiety about working with the police to curb disorder.

Is the "community" a city, a block, a neighborhood? Can police and citizens share decision making and power in the community? What happens when community interest in solving problems fades?[5] These are questions that sociologists could debate indefinitely. This question/concern did not originate, however, with attempts to implement COPPS. A lack of a sense of community, anonymity, a mixture of lifestyles, and tensions have existed ever since people began living in groups. Still, despite strained relationships, people have always looked for order and to the police for solutions to their most troublesome problems.

Furthermore, as noted in Chapter 4, the community remains a largely untapped resource for identifying and reducing problems. Eliciting the help of the community should be a major objective in police efforts to identify and solve problems. Community surveys and other interactions by the police help to focus COPPS's efforts and empower communities to learn to police themselves.

Concern and Response 2: Is This a Proper Role for the Police?

Another issue in the community policing debate involves the proper role of police: *Should* police officers function as community organizers, working on community problems that do not directly involve crime (such as garbage, graffiti, and abandoned vehicles)? Is this the proper function for a police officer? Some believe there are serious dangers in the community policing expansion of the police role, given our Anglo American heritage of limits on police power. Some critics ask whether police officers should be going door to door, calling on law-abiding citizens who have not summoned the police. They worry that they will turn into political advocacy groups who will lobby for candidates or issues that the police support.[6]

There are also reservations about the potential for community policing to "weaken the rule of law" in the sense of equal protection and evenhanded enforcement, which "may lessen the protection afforded by law to unpopular persons."[7] The requirement that police become more decentralized is seen as a threat to the rule of law.

Another concern has been whether public safety will decline under community policing. Naysayers contend that the efficacy of using the public in the battle for crime control is untested. Of a related nature is the argument that the concept is "soft" on crime because of its very nature, because the police fear using any forceful action that would anger the community and jeopardize the gains from community policing. They ask, "Can the police put on a velvet glove and keep their iron hand in shape?"[8]

At the same time, there is concern with what is perceived as the "big brother" nature of community policing—the increased use of close circuit television, police coming into homes to make security inspections, and police asking about neighborhood problems. Skeptics also worry about the ease with which computer-stored information could be obtained.

Response

These concerns are, to a degree, a matter of policy choice for each community. A community may choose the COPPS model or subscribe to the traditional crime-fighting role of policing. COPPS advocates, however, believe that the police *should* take the initiative to identify emerging problems and offer solutions. They are in a unique position to collect and analyze data and quickly attempt to deal with problems rather than waiting until problems become ominous in nature. The police should be more vocal in addressing problems and in presenting options to, and being advocates for, the community.

Also, as noted in Chapter 2, COPPS is simply a response to the major concerns and fears of Americans, most of whom do not fear being a victim of a major crime, but of the lesser crimes involving neighborhood disorder: drug violations, gang activities, noise, strangers, fighting, physical disorder (such as litter, graffiti, junk cars), and so on. Here the police are analogous to the medical profession: Whereas physicians treat people who are in *physical* disorder, police have opportunities to assist people who are in *social* disorder, often in fear of the problems surrounding them. The police, like physicians, are in a unique position to intervene when peoples' lives are in disarray and to work with them to solve personal crises.

Some writers suggest that not all members of society want the same level of police service or visibility. This begs the questions: "But don't *all* citizens want neighborhood disorder eliminated? To have the freedom to leave their homes at night believing they are secure? To not have to douse the lights early to avoid becoming targets of area shootings? To be able to use the parks and streets instead of turning them over to gangs and drug dealers?" The answers to these questions override the concern by some that not all individuals want the same police service or visibility. COPPS offers the hope for a better quality of life.

In response to the concern or criticism that COPPS is "soft" on crime, *no one* recommends that crime be ignored under COPPS; the laws must still be enforced, and COPPS is not soft on crime. This concept is founded on prevention and control.

Another concern with COPPS follows the old expression, "Why aren't you chasing bank robbers instead of writing me a traffic ticket?" Critics claim that although community policing calls for foot patrols and neighborhood newsletters, there are international drug dealers and a globalization of crime and policing. They add that this concept "needs re-thinking when the broken windows in your neighborhood result from actions of drug lords in the Andes."[9]

To assume that neighborhood newsletters and foot patrols fail to deal with important issuess, such as major crime, misses the point. Police do not exist in a vacuum; information is—and has always been—the lifeblood of policing, and it is critical to its success. Furthermore, the police belong in America's neighborhoods as much as they belong in the poppy fields of Turkey or on boats and planes watching our borders. Officers patrolling neighborhoods and business districts on foot are not on public relations excursions; they are seeking to maintain order and provide public safety. Indeed, these officers often glean important information that assists them in eradicating crimes and arresting criminals. The police cannot chase major drug lords and ignore neighborhoods any more than they can ignore drug lords and concentrate only on neighborhood order maintenance.

Finally, computerized data is the wave of the future; we bank, buy, research, and initiate personal relationships on the World Wide Web. Access, security, and privacy are major concerns, and police and other governmental agencies need to ensure that individual rights are not violated.

Concern and Response 3: Does the Concept Violate the Political Neutrality of Police?

Should the police be used to define and shape community norms? Should police officers be used as agents of informal social control? Some writers believe that this violates the political neutrality of the police and that it would be dangerous to give those with the power to enforce laws the additional authority to enforce norms.[10] Pessimists assert that "there is great potential for troublesome political entanglements, particularly when police are asked to take sides in battles between interest groups, neighbors, or racial bigots."[11] They also note that police traditionally arrested, constrained, warned, and deterred; now, however, under the COPPS philosophy, the police "advise, mediate, lecture, organize, participate, cooperate, communicate, reach out, solicit, and encourage."[12]

Other writers worry that some community policing programs will give influential citizens control over the police. They believe the objectives of improved community relations, creative problem solving, and crime prevention are the greatest threat to this neutrality. And, the argument goes, because the police must focus not only on the symptoms of crime but also on its root causes, the police have become politically involved in various agencies.[13] This concern includes the possibility that police will be led more and more to behave like politicians, developing powers of patronage and even advising how grant and local monies should be distributed.

Response

Regarding the concerns that COPPS will allow the police to become politically involved in various agencies, and be led more and more to behave like politicians, this is precisely the kind of ingenuous and innovative work we would hope to see from our police officers.

COPPS critics are concerned that establishing a close relationship with neighborhood residents will violate police neutrality and allow citizens to control police. (*Courtesy* Ft. Pierce, Florida, Police Department)

Does society expect police to be apolitical? The police are not, nor have they ever been, politically neutral, at least in a partisan sense. Nor does society appear to want them to be neutral. They are decidedly *not* neutral when they form coalitions and work with prosecutors and political bodies (city councils, county commissions, state legislatures), or in lobbying efforts for new laws. They also lead drives for bond issues for more personnel and new stationhouses and represent neighborhoods in parking, traffic control, and other projects.

What we *do* ask of our police, however, is that they be equitable and fair to the public. It is also important that agencies proactively enact disciplinary policies that are based on standards of fairness, consistency, and equity so that the organization, the involved officer, and the public's interest are protected.

Concern and Response 4: Can COPPS Work When It Cannot Cure the Underlying Societal Problems of Crime and Disorder?

Those who raise this issue obviously believe that because COPPS can neither eliminate crime nor attack its underlying causes (such as poverty, prejudice, broken homes, peer influences), it is a doomed undertaking. Some even question whether, for this reason, the police are the proper agency to fulfill the goals of community policing. For them, the questions are whether the police should be working to solve *any* nonlegal problems (and should instead strictly be law enforcers) and whether social service functions should be removed from the police function.[14]

Response

This concern is particularly vexing. Is it implying that the United States should abandon its attempts to curb drug dealers and addicts, arrest serial murderers, or provide for the homeless because these groups represent social problems beyond control? The deep-seated problem with drugs may never be resolved; yet there are many neighborhoods in which the police and the community have worked together to rid the area of drug dealers and significantly improve living conditions.

No one has suggested that COPPS is a panacea to all our social ills. No modern police Moseses are going to lead society to the Promised Land, nor can our police achieve world peace. COPPS does offer, though, our best hope for dealing efficiently and effectively with a variety of conditions that plague our neighborhoods and cause people to live in fear. Bright police leaders are willing to reengineer their agencies to provide better service and a more representative government. And young, educated, and energetic officers possess the skills to mobilize communities and coordinate the efforts of the police, other agencies, and the community in identifying and eradicating problems. Agencies across the nation are providing examples of their successes with COPPS.

As we noted in Chapter 4, it is important that the police pursue the resolution of major problems in the context of "small wins," rather than attempting to address problems on a massive scale. Some problems are too deeply ingrained, or too rooted in other complex social problems, to be eliminated. Some community problems must be broken down into smaller, more controllable problems.[15]

Concern and Response 5: Does the Concept Require Too Much Officer Discretion?

Some police executives are concerned with the increased use of discretionary authority of patrol officers and that greater intimacy with the public may threaten officer accountability (in other words, lead to graft).[16] Concern is also apparent that under community policing, officers may be encouraged to use any method at all to "handle" a neighborhood problem. Certain tactics could violate the rights of individual citizens (especially members of groups whom community residents do not like).[17]

Pessimists also emphasize that the police have traditionally not been in a policy making position—a responsibility reserved for the legislatures and governing bodies. Thus, another worry is that community policing will "weaken" the rule of law. By expanding the use of discretion, community policing "can easily be read as bending the law so as not to offend. Local commanders may begin to think it is more important not to alienate loud voices than to protect quiet ones."[18]

Response

The police have always been disseminated in the field without being subject to direct supervision, while wielding tremendous authority and making difficult decisions that affect the lives of others. This is now assumed to be a necessary aspect of their job. No one expects the police to work without discretion and totally within the letter of the law—for example, to cite all traffic violators for driving a few miles per hour over the speed limit. As noted previously, we do require that they use discretion in a professional, fair, and equitable manner. We know that police have used informal means of problem solving for centuries.

Much of the reserve of knowledge possessed by the patrol officer has gone untapped. We hire the best persons we can for the job and then ask them, as Herman Goldstein put it, to behave like "automatons" when they arrive at work—following orders and regulations blindly and generally being treated like children.[19] Indeed, the many applications of the COPPS philosophy have shown that patrol officers can and do implement informal commonsense solutions to problems that work.

The job of the patrol officer has become much broader than it was in the past, and officers must use a greater range of discretion to deal with community problems and a wider range of community resources in responding to incidents. The time has come to release their creativity and allow their problem solving skills to unfold.

Finally, in this era of increased use of citizen review boards, the specter of civil liability, and judicial review, police officers have become more accountable with their discretionary authority than ever before. The COPPS approach encourages and facilitates even greater accountability on the part of the police. Officers are forced to think through how they respond to problems and to be prepared to justify their decisions to higher authorities within the department. This reduces the risk of arbitrariness and value judgments that may be illegal or improper.[20]

Concern and Response 6: Is This Simply a Faddish, Costly Gimmick?

Some critics have wondered whether this concept is nothing more than "putting old wine in new bottles," arguing that it is a set of aspirations wrapped in a slogan, or a "trendy phrase spread thinly over customary reality."[21]

In the same vein, some have described the community oriented approach as simply "fuzzy feel good politics" that has not been effectively implemented, with too much of it transpiring in "the boardroom and not on the boardwalk."[22] For others, community policing is akin to learning that the "emperor has no clothes."[23] And, for still others, it is merely "helping little old ladies across the street." In sum, for many persons COPPS is little more than a public relations gimmick.

Another concern is that community policing will squander community resources if police are spread too thinly, attempting to provide services for which other social agencies are statutorily responsible. To address this problem, several departments are increasingly using civilians as police assistants, performing a variety of jobs once performed by more costly, sworn personnel.

Response

To disregard COPPS as a "trendy phrase spread thinly over customary reality"[24] is to ignore the efforts of numerous agencies that have successfully implemented COPPS and co-opted partnerships with the community to identify and resolve neighborhood problems. It also ignores the following facts: The federal government invested nearly $9 billion in community policing; scholarly publications abound on the subject, and college degrees are now being offered in the discipline; police academy and in-service curriculums have changed significantly to include COPPS instruction; many agencies have changed their entire organization's strategic plans and methods of recruiting, hiring, and promoting to include the principles of COPPS; and, as detailed in Chapter 14, agencies worldwide have followed very similar paths to changing their strategies toward COPPS.

Also ignored is the degree to which the implementation of COPPS has transformed these agencies. In many cases it involved major internal changes, including the creation of new mission statements and department values, organizational restructuring, geographic reorganization, realignment of ranks, changes in promotional policies and operational policies, developing new recruiting practices, and providing new training programs. It also required the development of partnerships with the community, other government agencies, private business, and other police agencies. No past efforts at new programs in policing have had such significant impacts on agencies.

Concerning the costs associated with community policing, it is not the objective of COPPS to further obligate officers to issues that are better handled by other agencies. In fact, the opposite is true. The objective of COPPS is for officers to enlist the cooperation of agencies to handle the problems for which they are better equipped and more responsible. A problem oriented approach also provides officers with the tools to reduce calls for service and crime—a further example of fiscal accountability and efficiency.

Concern and Response 7: Do Officers Possess the Intellectual Capacity and Temperament to Sustain the Concept?

Some authors have maintained that care should be given in considering whether police personnel are "ready to fulfill the demands of such a role."[25] Community and problem solving policing, it has been noted, requires line officers to

> alleviate specific problems, which they have helped to identify by orienting themselves to the needs of the community, with *creative* and *innovative solutions* in a fair, just, and legal manner. This requires certain skills, including problem conceptualization, synthesis and analysis of information, action plans, program evaluation, and communication of evaluation results and

policy implications. . . . [S]uffice it to say that the sensitivity and demands of the role of community policing require an individual with a high degree of intelligence, open-mindedness, and nonprejudicial attitudes (emphasis in original).[26]

Response

Many of the skills required of line officers do involve a certain degree of cognitive and logical ability. Police chief executives must endeavor to explore ways to tap the inventive nature of the rank-and-file.

Patrol officers have always possessed tremendous amounts of information concerning what is occurring in their communities—information about people (law-abiding and otherwise) and their streets and neighborhoods. According to Herman Goldstein, the street cop

should have a detailed understanding of such varied problems as homicides involving teenage victims; drive-by shootings; and carjacking; and . . . at the micro level, a beat officer should have in depth knowledge about the corner drug house; the rowdy teenage gang that assembles at the convenience store each Friday night; and the panhandler who harasses passersby on a given street corner.[27]

To not attempt to utilize this resource to the fullest extent possible seems irrational.

A police officer's job requires a high level of education and specialized technical training. (*Courtesy* NYPD Photo Unit)

We now have a better educated assemblage of police personnel than ever before. To intimate that police officers do not have the cognitive capacities to work within or carry the mandate of COPPS is nonsensical and insulting. The task of training officers on the problem solving process (S.A.R.A.), and to facilitate neighborhood meetings and to mobilize community efforts is no more difficult than many of the other technical skills for which we hold police accountable. Chris Braiden, former superintendent of the Edmonton, Alberta, Police Department in Canada, complained that police live in cognitive prisons and are controlled by convention. He suggests that a "bureaucratic garage sale" is needed to correct this problem.[28]

For all of these reasons, to intimate that police are not educationally sophisticated enough to implement and evaluate this approach is groundless and unsupported.

Concern and Response 8: Can Police Departments Change from Within?

Some authors have asserted that the current movement toward community policing attempts to change old policing philosophies, organizational designs, and management practices. This is a significant development, because it means that those agencies truly interested in adopting community policing must abandon long-standing traditional methods. It has been suggested that COPPS might eventually be seen as another "failed attempt at reform, much like team policing."[29] Problems are also anticipated with getting midlevel police managers to accept significant changes to the status quo. They maintain that if team policing was any indication, the answer will likely be less than favorable. Under this view, for community policing to work, there will have to be changes in organizational structure, management style, and personnel.

Skeptics worry that community policing makes supervision within police organizations ends- rather than means-based, that executives rate officers by their ability to achieve general objectives—management by objective, which now, in their view, permeates community policing. They believe that we will see "work schedules become more flexible, paperwork less detailed, dress more casual, contacts with citizens more offhand, supervision more collegial, and working behavior less rule-oriented."[30] According to this view, this "negotiated" policing may undermine professionalism, substituting responsiveness to community opinion with exogenous standards.

Response

We dealt with the subject of changing the culture of the police department in Chapter 7. There is a need, however, to respond here to the concern that old policing philosophies, organizational designs, and management practices may be too well entrenched to change.

COPPS requires a fundamental change in the way police view their mission. As long as the agency's traditionalists understand that the department is serious about community policing—and the message is constantly reinforced from the top—they can become an integral part of making the concept work.[31] As one writer observed, "Moving ahead doesn't mean forgetting where you've been. It means acknowledging that where you've been is not the only place you can go."[32]

Policing needs chief executives who are willing to do things that have not been done before, or, as another writer put it, "risk takers and boat rockers within a culture [policing] where daily exposure to life-or-death situations makes officers natural conservators of the status quo."[33] Departments must also find ways to free officers from the "tyranny of 911."

Changing an agency from the reactive, incident-driven mode to COPPS is a complex endeavor. As we noted in Chapter 6, four principal components of implementation profoundly affect the way agencies do business: leadership and administration (which includes roles of the chief executive, middle managers, and first-line supervisors), human resources (recruiting and training in particular, as well as the issue of labor relations), field operations (including decentralization and the roles of detectives and patrol personnel), and external relations (such as the community, local government agencies, service providers, business, and the media).

Concern and Response 9: Will Adequate Evaluations Be Done of COPPS?

A caveat for many observers of community policing lies in the manner in which its work is to be evaluated. (Note that Chapter 12 deals entirely with the evaluation of COPPS strategies.) They note that if the police attempt to implement community policing while primarily using traditional "quantity-based evaluation criteria," the program will not be successful. Quality- and community-based criteria, they argue, including citizen attitudes and fear of crime issues (measured, at least in part, by community surveys), will need to become an integral part of how police effectiveness is measured.[34] Robert Friedmann added that perhaps

> the biggest drawback of the concept of community policing lies in impreciseness or overreach. It seems to include anything that has to do with the "community." What, after all, is community policing? Is it public policing? Is it a strategy? How does it blend with other strategies or other orientations? What is to be changed? Crime rates, fear of crime, attitudes of citizens toward police? Or cooperation with the police? What are acceptable levels of crime? and for what types of crime? How, and by whom, are they defined? Who is to do what? Does the rookie or the experienced police officer do "community work"?[35]

Chris Offer also faulted the evaluations that have been done of community policing, saying there is no evidence that no other variables caused the change, that the change is long term, and that there even has been change.[36]

Response

For the first time in the history of modern policing, agencies are seriously considering the importance of qualitative assessments, and more evaluation is now being done than ever before—indeed, evaluation is highly encouraged. For example, the Department of Justice, Office of Community Oriented Policing Services (COPS), requires that 10 percent of every problem solving grant be devoted to project evaluation, and the National Institute of Justice has been given funds by the COPS office to conduct evaluations of problem solving initiatives across the United States. Through this process a lot of information is being collected and much is being learned—both scientifically and anecdotally.

Some would go further and argue that data concerning crime statistics, clearance rates, and calls for service are unnecessary. The problem with traditional policing was that these "boilerplate" measurements were the *only* data gathered and were the sole basis for performance measurements. Research has shown that the majority of a police officer's activity (roughly 80 percent) involves nonpolicing activities. Therefore, it is important that systems are developed to shift evaluative efforts to better assess both the individual officer and agency. The police have already begun evaluating themselves differently.

As will be seen in Chapter 12, efforts are also being made to include COPPS efforts in evaluations of officers' performance. The S.A.R.A. process guides officers through problem solving and helps them to identify and evaluate the underlying conditions contributing to crime and disorder. With this information, officers are better prepared to consider their responses. In some cases, arrests may be required; however, in other matters, simply improving the environmental factors contributing to crime may be the best response. Officers also learn what agencies both inside and outside their own jurisdiction or government can assist them with a problem. Officers engaged in COPPS efforts learn how important other agencies and the community are in addressing crime and disorder.

Other Concerns: Zero Tolerance and Existing without Federal Funds

Following are discussions of two associated concerns that do not necessarily fit into the previous categories: zero tolerance and whether COPPS can exist without the availability of federal funding to assist with such services.

Zero-Tolerance Movement

Recently, some agencies have adopted "zero tolerance"—the back-to-basics, hard-nosed, "get tough" approach to crime by the police. The best-known and most frequently cited example of this approach is the recent experience in the New York City Police Department (NYPD). The primary lesson from the NYPD's approach to disorder type crimes in downtown Manhattan was that a sustained and aggressive crackdown on disorder and minor crime will result in tremendous crime decreases.[37] According to the NYPD, significant improvements in crime control were realized as a result.

As Gary Cordner observed, however, this phenomenon "may pose the biggest threat of all to problem-oriented policing."[38] Cordner believes that zero tolerance represents a perversion of problem oriented policing, because it is usually employed without the benefit of careful problem identification or analysis, without any effort to identify underlying conditions and causes, and without careful consideration of possible alternatives. It returns policing to an overreliance on law enforcement.

Several points should be made about the NYPD's recent successes with the city's crime rate. First, several other initiatives were simultaneously undertaken by the department, including the CompStat meetings at which commanders were held more accountable for reviewing crime statistics in their precincts and making disorder type crimes their priority, and the addition of more than 10,000 officers during the 1990s (some of whom were a result of amalgamations with other special police agencies, but many of whom were simply new personnel). Furthermore, it is possible that zero tolerance had an impact in New York City because prior enforcement levels were quite low.[39]

It is also notable that San Diego, California, experienced almost exactly the same crime decrease as New York City, without adding substantially more officers. Indeed, whereas New York achieved 25 fewer reported Part I crimes for

COPPS office funding assisted many agencies in taking the first step toward implementing COPPS. The future success of those agencies will be determined by their ability to implement COPPS agencywide. (*Courtesy* U.S. Department of Justice)

each additional officer hired, San Diego achieved 322 fewer Part I crimes reported per new officer—a return on its investment that was 13 times better than New York's. San Diego operates on a skeleton crew compared with New York, has about the same crime rate, and is one of the nation's primary devotees of COPPS. As Gary Cordner noted,

> It is tempting to assert, therefore, that [problem oriented policing] is at least as successful as zero tolerance, and that it is much less costly. It would appear that problem-oriented policing requires fewer officers than traditional, enforcement-oriented policing. Fiscal conservatives should be flocking to it.[40]

Life Beyond the Office of Community Oriented Policing Services

Recent COPPS literature often presents questions and concerns about the fate of COPPS once federal funding expires for the Office of Community Oriented Policing Services. The question surfaces as to whether COPPS is sufficiently entrenched to sustain itself or, alternatively, whether the strategy will be cast aside. To borrow from Gregory Berg, many people are concerned that policing might revert to its old ways:

> We will muddle through, crisis to crisis, forever attempting to circle the wagons. We will lose our talented people to attrition or the dulling of their spirit. We will lose the faith and respect of those we are sworn to serve.[41]

It is probably true that COPPS initiatives in many jurisdictions will not realize the attention they received during the life of federal funding. In most cases, this is because those initiatives were never properly or earnestly implemented in the first place. Catchy COPPS acronyms may have been coined that were merely intended as window dressing. Indeed, some COPPS initiatives were probably undertaken in name only, involving the assignment of a few specialist officers or bicycle patrols with a misguided emphasis on community relations rather than collaborative problem solving partnerships. Such "false advertising" and cosmetic changes will result only in short-lived successes. In addition, those agencies that attempted to implement COPPS with limited support of leadership and without substantive changes in the organization as noted in Chapter 6 will also find long-term success to be difficult.

If COPPS is to continue into the future, police executives must be determined to keep COPPS functional and must believe that COPPS works—with or without federal monies. Furthermore, they should take into consideration the capabilities and potential achievements of the problem solving officers. As Aurora, Illinois, Police Commander Michael J. Nila stated, many officers have been "rescued" by COPPS:

We now have police officers interacting with the citizens, and because they are able to do more long-term problem solving and see the results of their labors, the officers' job satisfaction is much higher than under traditional policing.[42]

SUMMARY

This chapter set out nine concerns with the COPPS concept and presented for each concern what we believe are countervailing responses. Even the most cautious scholars, such as David Bayley, who wrote that community oriented policing was "more rhetoric than reality,"[43] have considerable optimism. Bayley wrote, "I do not believe that community policing should be abandoned. Its goals are worthwhile and its practice responsive to defects in current police performance."[44]

Some pessimism will always remain with the COPPS concept as there was with the policing innovations of Robert Peel and August Vollmer. We believe, however, that this skepticism is healthy and establishes increased police effectiveness, accountability, and professionalism as policing enters a new era in problem solving and partnership with the community and other organizations.

NOTES

1. Samuel Walker, *The Police in America: An Introduction*, 2nd ed. (New York: McGraw-Hill, 1992), p. 189.
2. James Q. Wilson and John J. DiIulio, "Crackdown," *The New Republic* 201 (July 10, 1989):21–25.
3. See Wesley G. Skogan, *Disorder and Decline: Crime and the Spiral of Decay in American Neighborhoods* (New York: Free Press, 1990), p. 95.
4. Walker, *The Police in America*, p. 190.
5. Herman Goldstein, *Problem Oriented Policing* (New York: McGraw-Hill, 1990), p. 25.
6. David Bayley, "Community Policing: A Report from the Devil's Advocate," in *Community Policing: Rhetoric or Reality?*, eds. Jack R. Greene and Stephen D. Mastrofski (New York: Praeger, 1988), pp. 225–37.
7. *Ibid.*, pp. 231–32.
8. *Ibid.*, p. 228.
9. William F. McDonald, "Police and Community: In Search of a New Relationship," *The World and I* (March 1992):463.
10. Lisa M. Riechers and Roy R. Roberg, "Community Policing: A Critical Review of Underlying Assumptions," *Journal of Police Science and Administration* 17 (1990):109.
11. McDonald, "Police and Community," p. 457.
12. Bayley, p. 231.
13. C. Short, "Community Policing—Beyond Slogans," in *The Future of Policing*, ed. T. Bennet (Cambridge, England: Institute of Criminology, 1983).
14. See *ibid.*, p. 112.
15. Karl E. Weick, "Small Wins: Redefining the Scale of Social Problems," *American Psychologist* 39 (January 1984):40–49.
16. George L. Kelling, Robert Wasserman, and Hubert Williams, *Police Accountability and Community Policing* (Washington, D.C.: National Institute of Justice, 1988).

17. Bayley, "Community Policing," pp. 225–37.
18. *Ibid.*, p. 232.
19. Goldstein, *Problem Oriented Policing*, p. 27.
20. *Ibid.*, pp. 43, 47.
21. David Bayley, "Community Policing as Reform: A Cautionary Tale," in *Community Policing*, eds. Greene and Mastrofski, pp. 47–67.
22. Jack Greene, quoted in "Community Policing Six Years Later: What Have We Learned?" *Law and Order* (May 1991):53.
23. Chris Offer, "C-OP Fads and Emperor without Clothes," *Law Enforcement News* (March 15, 1993): 8.
24. Bayley, "Community Policing," pp. 225–26.
25. See Riechers and Roberg, "Community Policing," pp. 105–14.
26. *Ibid.*, p. 111.
27. Herman Goldstein, "The New Policing: Confronting Complexity" (paper presented at the Conference on Community Policing, U.S. Department of Justice, National Institute of Justice, Washington, D.C., August 24, 1993).
28. Chris Braiden, "Community Policing: Nothing New under the Sun," in *Community Oriented Policing and Problem Solving* (Sacramento, Calif.: California Department of Justice, 1992), p. 21.
29. Roy R. Roberg and Jack Kuykendall, *Police and Society* (Belmont, Calif.: Wadsworth, 1993), p. 443.
30. Bayley, "Community Policing," p. 234.
31. Robert Trojanowicz and Bonnie Bucqueroux, "The Community Policing Challenge," *PTM* (November 1990):40–44, 51.
32. Jerald R. Vaughn, *Community-Oriented Policing: You Can Make It Happen* (Clearwater, Fla.: National Law Enforcement Leadership Institute, no date), p. 8.
33. Mike Tharp and Dorian Friedman, "New Cops on the Block," *U.S. News and World Report* (August 2, 1993):23.
34. See A. Lurigio and D. Rosenbaum, "Evaluation Research in Community Crime Prevention: A Critical Look at the Field," in *Community Crime Prevention*, ed. D. Rosenbaum (Beverly Hills, Calif.: Sage Publishers, 1986), pp. 19–44.
35. Robert R. Friedman, "Community Policing: Promises and Challenges," *Journal of Contemporary Justice* 6 (May 1990):84.
36. Chris Offer, "C-OP Fads," p. 8.
37. Gary Cordner, "Problem-Oriented Policing versus Zero Tolerance," in *Problem Oriented Policing: Crime-Specific Problems, Critical Issues, and Making POP Work*, eds. Tara O'Connor and Anne C. Grant (Washington, D.C.: Police Executive Research Forum, 1998), pp. 303–13.
38. *Ibid.*, p. 304.
39. *Ibid.*
40. *Ibid.*, p. 312.
41. Gregory R. Berg, "Promises versus Reality in Community Policing," *Law and Order* (September 1995):148.
42. Quoted in Keith W. Strandberg, "The State of Community Policing," *Law Enforcement Technology* (October 1997): 45.
43. Bayley, "Community Policing," p. 225.
44. *Ibid.*, p. 236.

EVALUATING **COPPS** INITIATIVES

> Not everything that counts can be counted; and not everything
> that can be counted counts.
>
> —Albert Einstein

INTRODUCTION

A 75-year-old woman rose to her feet at a town meeting in a midwestern city to offer a suggestion on how an open-air drug market problem might be addressed. "You know," she said, "if you add one more street light per block, you might just get rid of these thugs selling drugs. They're like rats. They prefer the dark." The city manager's office and the police department designated the 16-block neighborhood as a test zone, used Community Development Block Grant money to purchase three new street lights per block for the high-crime area, and gathered data on reported crimes and drug trafficking. After three months (and still a year later), there were significant decreases in all monitored crimes for the area. The desired outcomes were achieved.[1]

This case study shows that the police, citizens, community leaders, and evaluators, working together—with community oriented policing and problem solving (COPPS) strategies—can create and evaluate change. With sound techniques and measurable results, communities can solve problems and demonstrate that the solutions employed were effective.

Although there are many evaluations of COPPS initiatives being performed, the lack of a formal evaluation of outcomes remains one of the most prevalent and enduring criticisms of those strategies; furthermore, few police agencies employ personnel who are adequately trained and educated to conduct program evaluations. Thus, this is one area that sorely needs "shoring up." This chapter explains how to perform evaluations and to acquire the assistance of a trained evaluator.

We begin by discussing rationales for evaluating COPPS generally and some of the questions that might be asked prior to commencing this task. Next we review some important issues for an agency to consider in selecting an outside evaluator, and then we examine the kinds of criteria to be used in evaluating COPPS, including several types of measures to be used. Then we review the kinds of criteria that might be employed for assessing the individual officer's problem solving skills, and we include a rating scale. Following is the use of surveys—community, neighborhood, and individual patrol officers—to obtain input for evaluative purposes. We conclude the chapter with two case studies of COPPS evaluations (other examples of evaluative efforts are provided throughout the chapter as well).

It should be noted that the evaluation of outcomes of problem solving projects is not the same as the assessment stage of the S.A.R.A. problem solving process (discussed thoroughly in Chapter 4). Evaluation is the more overarching concept, and it involves large projects—surveys, performance evaluations, and so on. Also, most evaluations discussed in this chapter are not highly structured or based on any scientific design; they are, again, mostly outcome measures.

An officer's efforts to improve overall safety in a shopping mall may decrease crime and increase safety and profits for merchants. (*Courtesy* Community Policing Consortium)

BEFORE ASSESSING COPPS: RATIONALE AND PRELIMINARY QUESTIONS

Efforts to evaluate crime control, community collaboration, and crime prevention are relatively new. Program evaluation differs from research-style evaluations that use "scientific" hypothesis testing and controlled experimental designs. Program evaluation is used to inform decision makers, clarify options, reduce uncertainties, and provide feedback to decision makers and stakeholders about the program being evaluated. It is, therefore, more decision oriented than research oriented. It focuses more on what is intended and accomplished than on control groups and experimental or quasi-experimental treatment groups.[2]

A COPPS initiative that is not reinforced by an evaluation process may have difficulty justifying its survival and continuing to receive resources. (Indeed, local grants funded by the federal Office of Community Oriented Policing Services have required grantees to complete evaluations of the outcomes; therefore, grantees were compelled to follow the S.A.R.A. problem solving process very carefully.) Rigorous evaluation is an essential component of the COPPS initiative.

Furthermore, evaluations provide knowledge; key decision makers in the jurisdiction need a gauge of the strategy's impact and cost effectiveness. (See Exhibit 12.1). Assessing progress will inform top management whether necessary changes in the culture and in support systems are indeed taking place.[3] Until rigorous evaluations are completed, there will be no clear verdict on whether the COPPS approach makes a difference in controlling crime and disorder. An evaluation also helps ascertain whether a crime prevention initiative has achieved such goals as reducing crime and the fear of crime, raising the community's quality of life, and determining whether it is worthy of continued funding.

Broken down into simplified steps, evaluation asks some or all of the following questions:

- What is the problem (defined by such measures as community indicators, police data, public surveys, and so on)?
- How does the project intend to address the problem? (Look at the project's goal statements.)
- What does the project do to resolve the problem? (Look at the project's objectives.)
- How does the project carry out its objectives? (Look, for example, at collaborative efforts among the police, other governmental agencies, private businesses, and so on.)
- What (over time) impact does the prevention project have on the problem? (For example, over a specified time period, by what percentage have reported crimes increased or decreased?)[4]

Evaluation should also be linked to the agency's strategic plan (discussed in Chapter 6), which includes the vision or mission statements, goals and objectives, strategies, and tactics.

Exhibit 12.1   Obtaining a Snapshot of the Police, the Public, and Neighborhood Quality of Life

Recently the National Institute of Justice and the Office of Community Oriented Policing Services funded a study of policing in two cities—Indianapolis, Indiana, and St. Petersburg, Florida—to determine whether community policing encouraged local police agencies to increase cooperation with the citizens they serve. First, researchers were able to discern how officers' time was distributed among encounters with the public, paperwork, problem-directed activities, and other tasks. As part of this evaluation, researchers were also able to expand officers' free time per shift, allowing more time for proactive, self-directed activities. The amount and levels of cooperation between officers and citizens were also obtained, and through interviews with officers the observers were able to ascertain officers' perceptions of problem solving, law enforcement, and call-handling priorities. Citizen interviews, however, provided insight into how residents rated their work with the police, their satisfaction with police services, and feelings of fear. This exhibit shows the kinds of information that can be obtained through such an approach. It provides a snapshot of the police, the public, and neighborhood quality of life.

Sources: Stephen D. Mastrofski, Roger B. Parks, Albert J. Reiss Jr., and Robert E. Worden, *Policing Neighborhoods: A Report from Indianapolis* (Washington, D.C.: U.S. Department of Justice, National Institute of Justice Research Preview, July 1998); Stephen D. Mastrofski, Roger B. Parks, Albert J. Reiss Jr., and Robert E. Worden, *Policing Neighborhoods: A Report From St. Petersburg* (Washington, D.C.: U.S. Department of Justice, National Institute of Justice Research Preview, July 1999).

DOING THE JOB RIGHT: SELECTING AN OUTSIDE EVALUATOR

As mentioned previously, few police agencies possess adequately trained and educated persons for conducting program evaluations. Furthermore, for purposes of subjectivity and credibility, it is probably far better to go outside the police agency to obtain the services of an evaluator—one who understands the complexity of the task, often someone with an academic orientation. Gloria Laycock of the United Kingdom, an International Visiting Fellow with the National Institute of Justice, recently discussed the rift that often exists between practitioners and academics:

> Police practitioners and researchers have operated in different universes for a long time. Researchers study police practices and criticize what they find; that is what researchers are trained to do. The police complain and ignore the research, feeling that they do not need the problems research fosters and

that they can perform their functions without any help from academics. But some fundamental changes are now under way, with research becoming far more central to policing than ever before.[5]

The police need good research. There is a demand for outcomes. It is no longer good enough for the police to say they made X number of arrests or wrote thousands of tickets. The public expects crime to decline—and to continue doing so. Laycock noted that many police chief executives think they know how to reduce crime. In New York, crime is believed to have been reduced because of CompStat (discussed in Chapter 4) and zero tolerance, whereas crime reductions in Chicago and San Diego were said to have been the result of community policing and problem oriented policing, respectively. As Laycock observed, this means that either what the police do is irrelevant and crime was going down anyway, or what they do does matter, and there are lots of ways of reducing crime:

> The sad fact is we don't know, and the researchers and police have spent years arguing about it. There is no published knowledge base on what works and what doesn't work in the profession. The only way to establish a real body of knowledge is through systematic and prolonged investment in research.[6]

There are thus occasions when the police agency should acquire the services of one who is well grounded in research methodology.

Using the Proper Criteria

The Old versus the New

The evaluative criteria employed in the professional policing model, such as crime rates, clearance rates, and response times, have been problematic when applied to the professional model itself and are even less appropriate for the COPPS model. These measures do not gauge the effect of crime prevention efforts. A decrease in the reliance on these quantitative measures of police success is also important, because communities differ in the services they desire, depending on the particular characteristics of individual communities.[7]

These current measurements of police effectiveness and efficiency are of serious concern to police managers. Such measures do not capture much of the work that police do or how they do it. Evaluating COPPS requires measurements that better reflect the objectives of this strategy. As one writer put it, "New measures of police service effectiveness or performance must be developed that stress its impact rather than the processes and structures for accomplishing community policing."[8]

Some new indicators for success include identifying and solving local crime and disorder problems through a police–community consultation process; higher reporting rates for both traditional crime categories and for nontraditional crime and disorder problems; reducing the number of repeat calls for service from repeat addresses; improving the satisfaction with police services by public users of those services, particularly with victims of crime; increasing the job satisfaction of police officers; increasing the reporting of information of local crime and disorder problems by community residents and increasing the knowledge of the community and its problems by local beat officers; and decreasing the fear of personal victimization.[9]

Three General Criteria

According to the Community Policing Consortium, three major criteria can assist in assessing the success of a COPPS effort. These criteria—effectiveness, efficiency, and equity—offer a sound foundation for developing quantitative and qualitative measures of progress.

Effectiveness

An effective COPPS strategy has a positive impact on reducing neighborhood crime, allays citizen fear of crime, and enhances the quality of life in the community. It accomplishes this by combining the efforts and resources of the police, local government, and the community.[10] Assessing the effectiveness of COPPS efforts includes determining whether problems have indeed been solved and how well the managers and patrol officers have used the community partnership and problem solving components of COPPS.

Assessment should not only focus on whether the problem has been effectively eradicated or reduced but also on the manner in which this was accomplished. Solving problems does not always involve making arrests.[11] Improved quality of life is difficult to measure (and define), but it is an important goal of COPPS. Everyone desires a safe environment in which families can live and work. COPPS helps identify the fears, concerns, and needs at the neighborhood level. The factors that may determine "quality of life" may differ from neighborhood to neighborhood; removing signs of disorder—drunks, panhandlers, prostitutes, gang members—will enhance the quality of life. The absence of previous signs of neglect—abandoned vehicles, derelict buildings, garbage and debris— offers a tangible indication that COPPS is working.[12]

Efficiency

Efficiency means getting the most impact from available resources. Evaluation measures determine whether available resources—including the police agency, local government and private agencies, citizen groups, and the business community—are being used to their fullest to solve any given problem.[13]

Two major shifts must occur within the police organization if COPPS is to be successful. The first shift, as mentioned previously, involves establishing staunch partnerships and collaborative efforts within the community. The second

The closure of a home can impact residents' feelings about safety and their overall quality of life.

shift involves moving from a centralized to a decentralized command structure in which problem solving, decision making, and accountability are spread downward to all levels of the organization. This "pride of ownership" offers a strong and common motivation to solve the problems that affect the security and harmony of the neighborhood.[14]

Employee job satisfaction takes on a new significance in a COPPS organization. Patrol officers function more efficiently and effectively as catalysts and mobilizers of community support if they are highly motivated, given the necessary support, and appropriately rewarded for their efforts.[15] The need to survey the officers becomes evident in an organization where employee morale and satisfaction take on a greater level of meaning and importance.

Controlling calls for service is also central to achieving efficiency in time and dollars. Sophisticated technology advances can help prioritize calls and facilitate communication within the police organization and among the COPPS partners.

Equity

Equity, the third major criterion for judging progress, has the most comprehensive impact on the success of COPPS. Equity is especially important because officers work closely with the community and may be increasingly confronted with moral and ethical dilemmas.[16]

Equity has three separate dimensions in COPPS: (1) equal access to police service by all citizens; (2) equal treatment of all individuals according to the Constitution; "respect for dignity is incompatible with needless confrontation, excessive force, or discrimination;"[17] and (3) equal distribution of police services and resources among communities (it is critical that one community not be given preference over another).[18]

Evaluation Measures

Measures used in evaluations include process measures, outcome measures, and impact measures.

> *Process measures:* Process measures are used to track organizational progress (such as whether a strategic plan has been developed, an evaluator has been employed, meetings held, and so on).
>
> *Outcome measures:* Outcome measures can include the following:
> - Control of crime—Compare, for example, the present rates of serious and violent crimes with those of an earlier time. Included in this category are behavioral changes, such as increased use of the once drug-infested park or increases in students attending drug education programs.
> - Citizen satisfaction with police services and fear levels of crime—Basic survey techniques (discussed later) measure citizen satisfaction and fear levels. Media content analysis, analysis of letters from citizens, and citizen complaints can also be used to evaluate citizen satisfaction with police services.[19] Outcome measures can also reflect environmental changes (such as the number of street lights installed, traffic patterns altered, or graffiti removed).
>
> *Impact measures:* Impact measures describe and monitor changes in community indicators (such as community efforts to prevent or deal with crime and violence, community perception of quality of life, level of business, and other activity in the area).[20]

Exhibit 12.2 provides a discussion of one program.

OFFICER PERFORMANCE EVALUATIONS

A major need of police agencies that have adopted COPPS is a performance evaluation system that is specifically intended for the street officer who is applying COPPS skills to crime and disorder issues. Exhibit 12.3 shows six steps for revising a police performance evaluation system.

EXHIBIT 12.2   A National Evaluation of "Operation Weed and Seed"

Background, Sites, and Definitions

Operation Weed and Seed was an ambitious federal, state, and local effort, begun in 1991, that originally was intended to control violent crime, drug trafficking, and drug-related crime in three cities: Kansas City, Missouri; Trenton, New Jersey; and Omaha, Nebraska. Eventually the strategy grew to include 200 sites nationwide. "Weeding" strategies included concentrated and enhanced police efforts to identify, arrest, and prosecute violent offenders and drug traffickers; "seeding" included human activities, such as after-school and summer school activities, adult literacy classes, parental counseling, and neighborhood revitalization efforts. Proactive community policing and problem solving served as the bridge between weeding and seeding.

Cities were funded either as demonstration sites (receiving between $500,000 and $750,000 each for four consecutive years) or officially recognized sites, which received much smaller amounts ($35,000 in some cases). As of 1999, most sites were receiving about $225,000 annually. Eight sites—Hartford, Connecticut; Manatee and Sarasota Counties, Florida; Shreveport, Louisiana; Las Vegas, Nevada; Akron, Ohio; Pittsburgh, Pennsylvania; Salt Lake City, Utah; and Seattle, Washington—were selected by the National Institute of Justice for an evaluation of their implementation and measurable effects on crime and public safety.

Evaluation Components and Findings

The evaluation of each site included a variety of activities, including a review of funding applications, interviews with key program personnel and service providers, analysis of crime and arrest records, group interviews with seeding program participants, and resident surveys. The evaluation found significant favorable effects of Weed and Seed on key outcome measures for some sites. The most effective implementation strategies were those that relied on bottom-up participatory decision-making approaches, especially when combined with efforts to build partnerships among local organizations. Preexisting community features were also found to make Weed and Seed easier or more difficult to operate effectively. Important factors included the strength of community-based organizations and community leaders, the severity of crime problems, geographical advantages favoring economic development, and transiency of the community population. Sites also seemed to have greater success if they concentrated their program resources on smaller population groups. At the same time, the evaluation uncovered a number of weak links in the operation, most noticeably the limited and tenuous role that many local prosecutors played in the weeding process.

Source: Terence Dunworth and Gregory Mills, *National Evaluation of Weed and Seed* (Washington, D.C.: U.S. Department of Justice, National Institute of Justice Research in Brief, 1999).

Next we discuss 10 performance criteria for rating officers' skills and a rating scale that might be used to evaluate their efforts.

COPPS Skills, Knowledge, and Abilities

Supervisors must measure how well officers perform COPPS during the course of their tour of duty. If officers are not familiar with the problem solving process, their performance will be deficient. Supervisors should work with officers to correct any deficiencies regarding the following performance criteria:

- *Time management:* using uncommitted time to scan neighborhoods and identify problems; balancing problem solving efforts with other responsibilities
- *Awareness:* knowledge of problems in assigned areas, and taking steps to stay informed via citizen contact, familiarity with current events, reviewing departmental information, and sharing information with colleagues
- *Communication:* eliciting information from colleagues, supervisors, and citizens to facilitate problem solving; conveying information in a clear, concise manner
- *Analysis:* ability to relate symptoms to underlying circumstances; identifying factors that cause incidents to occur and knowing what questions to ask
- *Judgment:* identifying legitimate alternatives that can be used as responses in addressing problems; selecting the best alternative based on resource availability, ease of implementation, and perceived effectiveness of response
- *Goal setting:* distinguishing between short- and long-term goals of response; identifying goals that are measurable; relating the goal to the problem
- *Planning:* preparing a legitimate action plan to implement a response; identifying responsibilities of participants, appropriate procedures, and a timetable
- *Coordination:* demonstrating competency in organizing efforts of participants involved in implementing responses

Exhibit 12.3   Steps for Revising Police Performance Evaluation Systems

Step 1: *Decide on the purpose(s) of the evaluation.* The purpose(s) to be served by an evaluation system will dictate both what and how officer behavior is measured.

Step 2: *Identify performance criteria.* Traditional measures of police performance do not capture the entirety of the community policing officer's role. New performance evaluations must reflect the work that administration desires. A job analysis, identifying tasks typically performed by an employee (such as learning about beat problems and area residents, and developing means of problem solving), might be included. Related activities (such as conducting neighborhood meetings or analyzing crime data) might also be performed.

Step 3: *Define effective behavior.* Each police agency must define effectiveness individually as it relates to its own vision, mission, values, goals, and objectives. Input from officers, supervisors, and citizens may be required to determine what effective policing is, depending on realistic expectations of what they can accomplish.

Step 4: *Decide who should be evaluated.* Several officers and supervisors may be jointly responsible for a certain geographic area or beat, working as a team to solve problems therein. The extent to which officers are working in teams or groups must be considered for evaluation.

Step 5: *Decide who will participate in the evaluation process.* Many different constituencies may provide input to the evaluation of community policing officers, with supervisors being the primary source of evaluation. Other officers who are equal to, above, or below in rank from the officer to be evaluated may also provide input. Citizen feedback should also be considered.

Step 6: *Develop or revise instrumentation and rating scales.* Remember that much of the community policing officer's work is of a qualitative nature, therefore, not easily reduced to numbers. As performance criteria change, and community policing "behaviors," such as communication and innovation, are modified, so should the performance evaluation instrument and the rating scales.

Source: Adapted from Meghan S. Chandek, "Meaningful and Effective Performance Evaluations in a Time of Community Policing," *The Journal of Community Policing* 2 (Spring 2000):7–24. This article includes examples of sample tasks and activities, definitions of effectiveness, quantifiable community policing activities, and an officer performance evaluation scale.

- *Initiative:* self-motivation for engaging in the problem solving process and identifying and addressing problems; helping others when appropriate
- *Assessment:* properly identifying variables to assess; knowing the types of information to collect to assess results; describing implications of results attained[21]

The Rating Scale

The supervisor's rating of subordinates' COPPS efforts must be accurately reflected on a rating scale. Five value descriptions have been developed to help establish reliability in this regard, as follows:

SUPERIOR skill performance: The officer's skill performance is consistently excellent as to quality, accuracy, thoroughness, and technical excellence. The

PERSONNEL PERFORMANCE EVALUATIONS IN THE COMMUNITY POLICING CONTEXT

TIM OETTMEIER
MARY ANN WYCOFF

A guide for evaluating COPPS officers' performance was developed by the Community Policing Consortium in Washington, D.C. (*Courtesy* Police Executive Research Forum)

officer has a superior understanding of what skills to use to accomplish assigned responsibilities. Officer initiates and completes responsibilities without prompting from the supervisor, and there is no doubt as to officer's exercise of sound judgment. Supervisor and officer work in consultation with each other when appropriate.

STRONG skill performance: Performance exhibited is above average. Work performed and skills displayed regularly exceed basic requirements. Officer demonstrates an advanced ability to apply skills to various responsibilities and projects and makes conscientious effort to adhere to procedures and standards. Sound judgment is always exercised, and officer is always willing to perform the skills to do the work—without instructions or directions from supervisor.

EFFECTIVE skill performance: Performance in response to each skill is acceptable. Officer has demonstrated the ability to perform problem skills effectively and efficiently in a consistent manner. Officer applies knowledge and skills while using sound judgment and is usually desirous and willing to perform skills with minimum instructions and directions from the supervisor.

MARGINAL skill performance: Performance is barely satisfactory, and skill performance is marginal. There is limited ability to perform the skill in association with appropriate activities. Officer frequently disregards performing the skill properly or does not adhere to standards governing the skill and occasionally exercises sound judgment in skill performance. Supervisor is often required to observe the officer performing the skill; instructions are usually needed. Performance is sufficient, inconsistent, occasionally effective, but only to a minimally acceptable degree.

POOR skill performance: Officer's skill performance causes supervisor great concern about officer's capabilities. Demonstration of skill is weak, leading one to question officer's understanding of what is expected and his or her ability to perform with consistent competency. Officer demonstrates signs of "going through the motions" and tends to act quickly, without regard to effects or consequences of actions. Supervisor spends an inordinate amount of time correcting officer's actions or telling officer what must be done.[22]

Figure 12.1 shows the Columbia, South Carolina, Police Department's monthly performance evaluation report form based on the preceding criteria.

USE OF SURVEYS

Social scientists and political pollsters survey the public to learn about social relations and predict future events. Government agencies use surveys to learn how people will react to new policies. In criminal justice, researchers use surveys to get a better understanding of crime and the fear of crime.[23]

COLUMBIA POLICE DEPARTMENT
MONTHLY PERFORMANCE EVALUATION REPORT

Supervisor's Name: _____   Time/Date: _____

Officer's Name: _____   Assignment/Shift: _____

Use the following criteria to assess an officer's ability to perform problem solving skills to address crime and disorder within assigned neighborhoods.

A B I L I T Y

	Poor		Marginal		Effective		Strong		Superior	
Time Management	1	2	3	4	5	6	7	8	9	10
Awareness	1	2	3	4	5	6	7	8	9	10
Communication	1	2	3	4	5	6	7	8	9	10
Analysis	1	2	3	4	5	6	7	8	9	10
Judgment	1	2	3	4	5	6	7	8	9	10
Goal Seeking	1	2	3	4	5	6	7	8	9	10
Planning	1	2	3	4	5	6	7	8	9	10
Coordination	1	2	3	4	5	6	7	8	9	10
Initiative	1	2	3	4	5	6	7	8	9	10
Assessment	1	2	3	4	5	6	7	8	9	10

Grand Total: _____

Final Classification

Check:

_____ Category 1: Poor .... 10 - 19
_____ Category 2: Marginal .... 20 - 49
_____ Category 3: Effective .... 50 - 69
_____ Category 4: Strong .... 70 - 89
_____ Category 5: Superior .... 90 - 100

_____   _____   _____   _____
Supervisor's Signature   *Date*   *Officer Signature*   *Date*

FIGURE 12.1 Columbia Police Department Monthly Performance Evaluation
Report (*Source:* Columbia, South Carolina, Police Department.)

This section discusses three types of surveys that police managers find increasingly useful: surveys of the community, of the physical environment, and of the street officers who are engaged in the work of COPPS. We do not include an in-depth discussion of survey research methodology; instead, we provide citations of some helpful resources in the Notes section at the end of the chapter.

Polling the Community

Why the Effort?

The public's perception of crime in the community should be an important part of any measurement of community life—and of police performance within a given community.[24] And no other sector of government in our society has more frequent and direct contact with the public than the police. It has been noted that

> Whatever the citizen thinks of the police, they can hardly be ignored. Whereas other public bureaucrats are often lost from the public's view, locked in rooms filled with typewriters and anonymity, police officers are out in the world—on the sidewalks and in the streets and shopping malls, cruising, strolling, watching, as both state protectors and state repressors.[25]

Surveys can be a vital part of a COPPS strategy. Given their position, role, and function in the community, it is all the more important that police agencies attempt to "feel the pulse" of their communities. The importance of surveying community needs cannot be overstated. Public opinion surveys provide vital information and feedback in the matter of the public's perception of officer performance and can assess the effectiveness of police department communication with the public. The mood of the public should be a vital consideration when police make public policy decisions.[26]

Police agencies have long used citizen surveys to measure performance and assess the quality of their work. Surveys have been used to evaluate random patrolling, rapid response to calls for service, patrol deployment schemes, and community policing strategies. Thus, although direct police use of surveys is relatively new, the application of survey research to management and policy questions is quite extensive.[27] In recent years, carefully developed surveys have been used to great advantage for measuring citizen attitudes toward police and citizen satisfaction with police services.

Methods and Issues

Those persons who are about to conduct community surveys will find a very valuable resource in a joint publication by the federal Bureau of Justice Statistics and the Office of Community Oriented Policing Services' *Conducting Community Surveys: A Practical Guide for Law Enforcement Agencies*.[28] This is a very good

Many agencies use neighborhood meetings as a method to evaluate their performance and to identify residents' needs and priorities. (*Courtesy Arlington County, Virginia, Police Department*)

primer on the use of surveys by police agencies, discussing survey development and administration and ways to analyze and interpret survey results. Many other books have been written that are devoted exclusively to the subject of evaluation.[29] Individuals who are contemplating COPPS evaluations can review these texts to determine the best method to use given the nature of their operation. There are several key issues to resolve before developing a questionnaire:

- *What are the specific purposes of the survey and what kinds of questions are most likely to yield responses that are consistent with those purposes?* It is important to clarify the goals of the survey project to minimize the number of questions asked. Without clear goals the number of questions tends to mushroom. This increases the amount of time required to administer each survey, which is a burden on both interviewer and interviewee. In short, fight the temptation to include everyone's "pet" question.

- *How will the survey be administered—by mail, telephone, or in person?* There are three basic types of strategies: A questionnaire can be mailed to everyone in the sample to complete and return; the sampled respondents can be interviewed by telephone; or they can be interviewed in person (at home, in the office, on the bus, or wherever they are). Mail surveys are an inexpensive method of obtaining large sample sizes.[30] There are advantages and disadvantages to each type of survey that should be explored prior to determining which type is to be used.

   ▪ *How much time will it take to complete the survey, and is this a reasonable amount of time to impose on respondents?* Remember that completion of a survey is an intrusion on the time of others. Most people will allow such intrusion if the cause is worthwhile and the time burden is not too onerous. About 10 to 15 minutes to complete a questionnaire is reasonable; but if examining, say, problems involving drugs and violence, 30 to 40 minutes might be reasonable. The key is to be considerate about demands on others.[31]

Neighborhood Surveys

Neighborhood surveys are often employed by police officers in problem solving; usually such surveys are informal, but they can provide large amounts of information that is not available in crime statistics. Some evidence even suggests that door-to-door surveys by officers are enough to reduce crime and fear and enhance citizen attitudes toward police, independent of any information they gain or what police do with it. Surveys can also help measure the characteristics of neighborhood residents, the background of crime victims, or the background of offenders. Surveys also seek information on the "mental state" of the community, and they frequently address such issues as

   ▪ Attitudes toward police performance
   ▪ Fear of crime
   ▪ Future plans and intentions
   ▪ Concerns about specific problems
   ▪ Suggestions for police actions

   Surveys are also useful for gathering data on individuals' behaviors and experiences. Common topics addressed in surveys of this type include

   ▪ Crime-prevention actions taken
   ▪ Experiences as victims of crime
   ▪ Experiences with the police
   ▪ Experiences with problems[32]

   Surveys are useful in revealing characteristics of groups of people, such as

   ▪ The characteristics of people living in a neighborhood
   ▪ The background of victims of crimes
   ▪ The personal history of offenders[33]

   In short, surveys can be used to achieve four goals:

- To gather information on the public's attitudes toward police and neighborhood priorities
- To detect and analyze problems in neighborhoods or among special population groups
- To evaluate problem solving efforts and other programs
- To control crime and reduce fear of crime[34]

There are many alternative sources of information as well. For example, census data provide a great deal of information about neighborhoods. Characteristics of victims can be obtained from offense reports. Offender background information can be obtained from arrest reports.

Surveying Officers

Under COPPS, patrol officers become key decision makers and catalysts. And, as we commented earlier, employee morale and job satisfaction take on a new significance in a COPPS organization. Patrol officers function more efficiently and effectively as catalysts and mobilizers of community support if they are highly motivated, given the necessary support, and appropriately rewarded for their efforts. Job satisfaction will both affect and result from the success of the COPPS philosophy. As Montgomery County, Maryland (and former Portland, Oregon), Police Chief Charles A. Moose and his coauthors noted,

> With added responsibilities for police officers, job satisfaction becomes critical. If they are satisfied, they perform better and are able to support their agency's mission. Employee job satisfaction is not simply an indicator of success in community policing—it is a goal of community policing.[35]

Therefore, intraagency surveys can be invaluable for providing a look at the big picture of a COPPS initiative: the attitudes, opinions, and impressions of officers toward their jobs, the department, and the COPPS philosophy.

Officers can be asked a wide variety of questions concerning their knowledge and application of community oriented and problem solving policing. Following is a sample of the subjects and questions that might be posed to officers.[36] Note that these items are only a sample of general and topical questions that might be considered. Actual questions should be carefully written for use in a survey and for the particular venue, and some sort of Likert Scale is needed to assess the direction and strength of feeling for each question.

The Role of the Police

- What is the role of the police in a community?
- Do you believe the increase in administrative responsibilities and paperwork has stripped you of your ability to expand COPPS initiatives? If yes, how?

Proactive Action

- In what ways does your department emphasize proactive action, reactive action, or a blend of the two?

Public Expectations

- In what manner does your community want its police force, first and foremost, to focus on reactive tasks? To respond rapidly to all calls for service? To reduce the fear of crime? Does the public want to be educated on crime prevention? To work with the police to solve problems of crime and disorder? (Note: This subject area has any number of possible items that could be included.)

Work Activities

- How much of your duty time is spent conducting administrative or paperwork functions? Responding to calls for service? Explaining crime-prevention techniques to citizens? Working with citizens to solve underlying causes of crime? Coordinating with other governmental agencies to improve police service or solve problems? (This subject area also has a wide range of possible questions.)

Perceptions of COPPS

- What have you been told about the purpose of COPPS (or, how valuable was the academy training in this regard)?
- What have you been told concerning the implementation of COPPS?
- How would you rate the quality of your department's in-service training concerning COPPS?

Co-Workers' Attitudes

- How do your co-workers feel about COPPS? About working with citizens to solve crimes? Crime prevention? Reducing the fear of crime? Sharing information with the community regarding police activities? The proactive style of policing?

Selected Issues

- To what extent do your citizens understand the problems of police?
- Describe the kinds of discretion you are given to carry out COPPS initiatives.
- Explain why you believe the investigative division or other specialized units are or are not more "elite" than the patrol division.
- Are COPPS activities given equal weight with conventional policing activities?
- How have the performance appraisal and promotional processes of your department been appropriate for a COPPS philosophy?

Analyzing the Data

To handle large sets of survey data—many questions answered by many respondents—a computer will probably be needed. Today computers are inexpensive, and user-friendly software programs are available for analyses. Also, police agencies can partner with local colleges and universities for assistance with data analysis. Someone will have to read each questionnaire, note how each question was answered, determine the code for each answer, and enter the codes into a data file. This must be done with care to minimize data entry errors.[37] Once the data have been entered, there are four types of analyses to be performed:

1. *The characteristics of the sample must be determined.* During this most basic stage of data analysis, the frequency, central tendency (the average, or typical responses to a question; includes the mean, median, and mode), and dispersion of responses (i.e., standard deviation or variance) to each question is calculated.

2. *A determination is needed of how representative the sample really is of the population being studied.* The principal method for checking representativeness is by comparing answers to a few of the questions with information known about the population. If there are no substantial differences, the sample is likely representative of the entire population under study. It may not always be possible to make such a comparison, however.

3. *An investigator may want to make inferences from the sample to the population it represents.* There are two types of inferences that can be made about the population based on sample data. First, characteristics of the population can be determined from what is learned from the sample. Second, one can determine whether there are relationships among the characteristics of members of the population (for example, whether the age and sex of a person have an influence on fear of crime).

4. *The investigator may want to determine whether there are relationships between or among the attitudes, behaviors, and characteristics identified in the sample population.* When analyzing relationships, social scientists usually talk about variables. Two variables can be causally or noncausally related. A noncausal relationship means that neither variable causes the other; they merely happen to be associated, perhaps because a third variable is causing both of them. In a causal relationship, one variable is causing the other. In statistical analysis, the causes are called *independent* variables, and the effects are the *dependent* variables.[38]

CASE STUDIES

The following two case studies provide views of COPPS evaluations for Chicago, Illinois, and Lawrence, Massachusetts.

Chicago, Illinois

The Chicago Alternative Policing Strategy (CAPS) initiative was field tested in 1993 in five selected districts (and later implemented on a citywide basis) to cultivate problem solving and to reorganize policing around the city's 279 police beats. In 1995 researchers found that perceived crime problems had decreased significantly in all five districts; furthermore, physical decay had declined in three districts, and citizen assessments of police had improved significantly.[39]

A more recent evaluation of CAPS was conducted in 1999 with funding by the U.S. Department of Justice and the Illinois Criminal Justice Information Authority. Some of the findings were as follows:

- Since 1996 recognition of CAPS had grown from 53 percent to 79 percent; awareness of the strategy had increased the most among young adults. The greatest source of information was television, with nearly 40 percent of Chicagoans recalling hearing about CAPS via that media outlet.
- Involvement continued to be strong among some of the city's poorest and most crime-ridden communities. Attendance at beat meetings was highest in predominately African American areas. Overall, 14 percent of Chicagoans said they had attended a beat meeting in the past year. The meetings, however, were weak at finding solutions to problems. Most actions were proposed by the police rather than residents, and residents were particularly ineffective at reporting back to the group about their recent problem solving efforts.
- Police officers who attended beat community meetings reported satisfaction with the effectiveness of the meetings. More than three-quarters were happy with levels of attendance.
- Community policing had become a routine aspect of the city's life. Within the police department, the strategy was no longer described as "just smoke and mirrors."[40]

Lawrence, Massachusetts

Lawrence, Massachusetts, is a dense, urban center of 70,000 people, 28 miles north of Boston, whose residents live in an area of only seven miles. In the 1980s the Massachusetts Criminal Justice Training Council submitted a critical report concerning the operations of the Lawrence Police Department. A wide gap existed between the police and the public. The department's budget was cut as well. The department began to explore new philosophies for delivering police service and to generally reform its operations.

The police chief and a nine-member management team began rethinking their basic strategies. First, the police chief adopted total quality management (TQM, discussed in Chapter 3). Then a bilingual community questionnaire was designed to identify crime and disorder issues important to citizens. Next, a citizen advisory committee was established to get more direct input about the needs of the customers.[41] The management team then began to develop a "vision" for the department; from this process, new mission and values statements were written.

The department began to explore how to strategically address problems. The team chose the Arlington neighborhood, a 45-square-block area consisting mostly of multiple-family, residential units and little single-family housing. A team of six community police officers (CPOs) was assigned to Arlington to seek citizen input, analyze problems, and develop intervention strategies. Questionnaires were again used to identify problems and concerns in the area. Returns of these questionnaires produced a lot of valuable information on drug dealers' operations and also raised the fear levels of dealers. A public education campaign was launched in the area, and police activity was enhanced.

The department believed it was important to develop an objective means of evaluating whether the strategy was worth the effort. A pre–post citizen survey approach was adopted with a random sample of households, using a 60-item questionnaire distributed to 3,676 households (with a 30.3 percent response rate). Responses to each question were given a numerical weight and an average score was computed. The following formula was developed and helped obtain a fear index for the neighborhood:[42]

$$\frac{(\# \text{ increased} \times 5) + (\# \text{ same} \times 3) + (\# \text{ decreased} \times 0)}{\text{Total responses}}$$

A disorder index was developed from the survey, based on the following formula:

$$\frac{(\# \text{ big problem} \times 5) + (\# \text{ problem} \times 3) + (\# \text{ no problem} \times 0)}{\text{Total responses}}$$

Using this procedure, a summary measure of disorder for each neighborhood was obtained.

The findings indicated that Arlington residents experienced substantial reductions in their fear and perceptions of crime and disorder. The close attention to both involvement of staff and managers in the organizational change process and the carefully planned community intervention strategy make Lawrence an important case study in the systematic implementation of COPPS in a medium-size city.[43]

SUMMARY

This chapter emphasized the fact that the evaluation of the impact of COPPS is critical; without such scrutiny this initiative may be jeopardized in the long term.

Although there is no one evaluation process that will work for all communities, this chapter offered some reasons, methods, and criteria for evaluating such a social intervention. The chapter also provided several examples of successful evaluations.

The philosophy and methods under COPPS are quite different than traditional policing and obviously require different measurements of performance.

NOTES

1. Adapted from the National Crime Prevention Council, *How Are We Doing? A Guide to Local Program Evaluation* (Washington, D.C.: Author, 1998), p. 5. This is a valuable resource for COPPS evaluations, including many examples of forms that may be used in the evaluation process (see, for example, Chapter II, "A Toolkit for Evaluation Design") and other types of information not commonly found in evaluation textbooks (such as communicating findings and results for maximum results).
2. *Ibid.*, p. 3.
3. U.S. Department of Justice, Bureau of Justice Assistance, The Community Policing Consortium, *Understanding Community Policing: A Framework for Action* (Washington, D.C.: Author, 1993), p. 82.
4. Adapted from *ibid.*, p. 4.
5. Gloria Laycock, "Becoming More Assertive about Good Research," *Subject to Debate* (Police Executive Research Forum newsletter) 14 (July 2000), p. 1.
6. *Ibid.*, p. 3.
7. Community Policing Advisory Committee, *Community Policing Advisory Committee Report*, p. 61.
8. Barry Leighton, "Visions of Community Policing: Rhetoric and Reality in Canada," *Canadian Journal of Criminology* (July/October 1991):75–87.
9. *Ibid.*
10. U.S. Department of Justice, Bureau of Justice Assistance, The Community Policing Consortium, *Understanding Community Policing: A Framework for Action* (Washington, D.C.: Author, 1993), p. 86.
11. *Ibid.*, pp. 87–89.
12. *Ibid.*, p. 90.
13. *Ibid.*, p. 91.
14. *Ibid.*, pp. 92–93.
15. *Ibid.*, p. 93.
16. *Ibid.*, p. 97.
17. Edwin Delattre and Cornelius Behan, quoted in *ibid.*, p. 99.
18. *Ibid.*, pp. 101–102.
19. California Department of Justice, Attorney General's Office, Crime Prevention Center, *COPPS: Community Oriented Policing and Problem Solving* (Sacramento, Calif.: Author, November 1992), pp. 90–91.
20. *Ibid.*, pp. 4–5.
21. Adapted from Columbia, South Carolina, Police Department, *Columbia Patrol Officer Performance Evaluation Workbook* (Columbia, S.C.: Author, March 1997), pp. 6–7; also see Timothy N. Oettmeier and Mary Ann Wycoff, Personnel Performance Evaluations in the Community Policing Context (Washington, D.C.: Community Policing Consortium, 1997).
22. *Ibid.*, pp. 8–9.
23. Police Executive Research Forum, *A Police Practitioner's Guide to Surveying Citizens and Their Environment: Monograph* (Washington, D.C.: U.S. Department of Justice, Bureau of Justice Assistance, 1993), p. 1.
24. Richard D. Morrison, "What Effect Is Community Policing Having on Crime Statistics," *Law Enforcement Technology* (October 1998):26.

25. N. D. Walker and R. J. Richardson, *Public Attitudes toward the Police* (Chapel Hill, N.C.: Institute for Research in Social Science, 1974), p. 1.

26. Mervin F. White and Ben A. Menke, "A Critical Analysis on Public Opinions toward Police Agencies," *Journal of Police Science and Administration* 6 (1978):204–18.

27. *Ibid.*, p. 1.

28. Deborah Weisel, *Conducting Community Surveys: A Practical Guide for Law Enforcement Agencies* (Washington, D.C.: U.S. Department of Justice, Bureau of Justice Statistics and the Office of Community Oriented Policing Services, 1999).

29. See, for example, Carl A. Bennett and Arthur A. Lumsdaine, *Evaluation and Experiment* (New York: Academic Press, 1975); Ronald Roesch and Raymond R. Corrado (eds.) *Evaluation and Criminal Justice Policy* (Beverly Hills, Calif.: Sage, 1981); Malcolm W. Klein and Katherine Teilmann Van Dusen, *Handbook of Criminal Justice Evaluation* (Beverly Hills, Calif.: Sage, 1980); and Richard H. Price and Peter E. Politser, *Evaluation and Action in the Social Science Environment* (New York: Academic Press, 1980).

30. See, for example, Ken Peak, "On Successful Criminal Justice Survey Research: A 'Personal Touch' Model for Enhancing Rates of Return," *Criminal Justice Policy Review* 4, no. 3:268–77 (Spring 1992); Don A. Dillman, *Mail and Telephone Surveys: The Total Design Method* (New York: Wiley, 1978); Arlene Fink and Jacqueline Kosecoff, *How to Conduct Surveys: A Step-by-Step Guide* (Beverly Hills, Calif.: Sage, 1985); Floyd J. Fowler, *Survey Research Methods* (Newbury Park, Calif.: Sage, 1988); Abraham Nastali Oppenheim, *Questionnaire Design, Interviewing, and Attitude Measurement* (New York: St. Martin's Press, 1992); Charles H. Backstrom and Gerald Hursh-Cesar, *Survey Research*, 2nd ed. (New York: Macmillan, 1981).

31. Police Executive Research Forum, *A Police Practitioner's Guide*, p. 22.

32. *Ibid.*, p. 8.

33. *Ibid.*, pp. 8–9.

34. *Ibid.*

35. Charles A. Moose, Wendy Lin-Kelly, Steve Beedle, and Brian Stipak, "Evaluating Community Policing with Employee Surveys," *The Police Chief* (March 2000):44.

36. Adapted from the Royal Canadian Mounted Police, Community Policing Branch, *R.C.M.P. Community Policing: Blending Tradition with Innovation* (Ottawa, Ontario, Canada: Author, 1992).

37. For a more detailed introduction to analyzing data in policing, see John Eck, *Using Research: A Primer for Law Enforcement* (Washington, D.C.: Police Executive Research Forum, 1984).

38. Adapted from Police Executive Research Forum, *A Police Practitioners Guide*, pp. 31–34.

39. U.S. Department of Justice, National Institute of Justice Research Preview, "Community Policing in Chicago: Year Two" (October 1995): 1–2.

40. Institute for Policy Research, *Northwestern Study Shows Great Strides in Community Policing Program* (Evanston, Ill.: IPR News, May 1999, pp. 1–2. A 120-page report on Years Five–Six of CAPS is available at: http://www.new.edu/IPR/news/CAPS99release.html.

41. Allen W. Cole and Gordon Bazemore, "Police and the 'Laboratory' of the Neighborhood: Evaluating Problem-Oriented Strategies in a Medium Sized City," *American Journal of Police*, forthcoming.

42. *Ibid.*, p. 24.

43. *Ibid.*, p. 31.

SELECTED AMERICAN APPROACHES

Example moves the world more than doctrine.

—Henry Miller

INTRODUCTION

Henry Miller is correct: Example is an efficacious means by which to disseminate information and move the world. This chapter provides case studies of community oriented policing and problem solving (COPPS) initiatives. Featured are case studies of COPPS activities in 21 jurisdictions: seven "large" (more than 250,000 population), nine "medium-size" (between 50,000 and 250,000 population), and five "small" (less than 50,000 population). Also discussed in lesser detail are COPPS initiatives in federal and state agencies.

LARGE COMMUNITIES

Austin, Texas

Austin, located in central Texas, has about 465,000 residents; the city's police department (APD) consists of approximately 900 sworn officers. The APD began reviewing the COPPS philosophy and designed a strategy to incorporate the concept throughout the entire organization. A five-year transition was developed and submitted to the city council, and implementation was soon under way.

A sergeant selected to serve as the community policing coordinator designated a task force of APD personnel to promote, encourage, and oversee the implementation. This task force also addressed issues such as changing the mission statement, training, tracking officers' problem solving efforts, media involvement, an officer reward system, and changes to the departmental manual.

The coordinator conducted a three-hour, in-service orientation on community policing; both sworn and civilian supervisors received an eight-hour orientation. A problem solving component was developed, and soon 109 problem oriented policing (POP) projects were actively working. The APD has nine neighborhood centers (storefronts); each is staffed with a full-time officer. Each center has an advisory council comprised of citizens. The task force forged a relationship with the media and the "Partners against Crime" campaign was born. A local television station had a weekly "Partners against Crime" segment, featuring COPPS projects, success stories from citizens, or crime prevention information.

Furthermore, a new chief was hired who continued the transition with the concept of Achieving Self-Reliant Neighborhoods through Community Policing. The patrol division was restructured to enhance accountability and responsiveness to the community. A lieutenant was put in charge in each of the city's six sectors; they are responsible for their sector 24 hours a day. Other programs either implemented or in the developmental stages include

- A leadership academy for citizens
- A landlord training program
- A citizen patrol program, including classroom instruction and radios
- A children-at-risk grant with a major COPPS component that designated Drug Free School Zones and safe houses for youth
- Texas Cities Action Plan (TCAP)—part of the National Crime Prevention Council's pilot program in Texas
- A community policing grant
- POP projects for cadets at the academy and after graduation
- A neighborhood cleanup program in conjunction with the Community Justice Council
- Strategies to incorporate the juvenile justice system into COPPS[1]

See Exhibit 13.1 for a discussion of San Antonio's program.

Chicago, Illinois

Although we discussed the Chicago Police Department's (CPD) mapping system in Chapter 4, as well as the CPD's crime-prevention strategies in Chapter 5 and its COPPS evaluation in Chapter 12, here we discuss more comprehensively the organization's COPPS efforts with its 13,500 sworn personnel.

Exhibit 13.1 COPPS in San Antonio, Texas

The San Antonio, Texas, Police Department has embraced COPPS for many decades through its Community Services, School Services, and Crime Prevention programs; store fronts; decentralized patrol substations; and downtown foot and bicycle patrol units. In 1995 the department went a step further, creating a special community policing unit called San Antonio Fear Free Environment (SAFFE), which is linked closely with community involvement programs. First established in 1995 with 60 officers, and enlarged to 100 officers in 1996, the SAFFE unit focuses on identifying, evaluating, and resolving community crime problems with the cooperation and participation of community residents. Beginning in 2000 an additional 10 officers are being added to the unit each year for five years. SAFFE officers are not tied to radio calls but, instead, are able to establish and maintain day-to-day interaction with residents and businesses within their assigned beats to prevent crimes before they occur. SAFFE officers also act as liaisons with other city agencies, work closely with schools and youth programs, coordinate graffiti-removal activities, and serve as resources to residents.

Source: San Antonio Police Department Web page: http://www.sannet.gov/police/crime-prevention/np.shtml, October 20, 2000.

Because of soaring crime rates in the early 1990s, the city wanted a "smarter" approach to policing—one that mobilized residents, police officers, and other city workers around a problem solving approach. Initiated at the highest levels, the Chicago Alternative Policing Strategy (CAPS) was planned for more than a year before it was officially instituted in April 1993 in 5 of the city's 25 police districts. Patrol officers were permanently assigned to fixed beats and trained in problem solving strategies. Neighborhood meetings between officers and area residents were held, and citizen committees were formed to advise district commanders. In the fall of 1994 elements of CAPS began to be introduced in Chicago's other districts; citywide involvement in the strategy began in the spring of 1995.[2]

A long-term evaluation has found evidence of CAPS-related success with physical decay problems in three of the five initial experimental districts, as well as a decline in gang and drug problems in two districts and a decline in major crimes in two districts. Many other positive changes have been recorded, but they could not be directly linked to CAPS. When the program expanded to encompass the entire city, the evaluation team began tracking parallel citywide measures over time. Reported crime has been declining at a steady rate. Although this decline began before CAPS, analysis of the strategy suggests that community policing may be helping with the trend. Furthermore, since CAPS went citywide, surveys of all major groups indicate steady increases in satisfaction with the quality of police service.

The police department promotes citizen participation through an aggressive advertising campaign that publicizes CAPS and encourages people to participate in beat meetings and activities. A recent survey found that nearly 80 percent of Chicagoans knew of CAPS, more than 60 percent knew of beat meetings in their neighborhood, and, of the latter group, 31 percent had attended at least one meeting.

Thousands of officers are assigned to teams dedicated to working in small beats. The department's dispatch policy was revised to enable officers to remain on their assigned beats for most of their duty shift. All of the city's sworn officers and their supervisors have been trained in problem solving. Surveys have found that officers are generally optimistic about the impact of CAPS on their work and on the community, about their own ability to engage in problem solving, and about the viability of community policing and problem solving.

CAPS has been recognized as one of the most ambitious COPPS initiatives in the United States; it has been cited as a model by numerous police experts and the federal government. One unique feature of the Chicago COPPS strategy is a

St. Petersburg, Florida, neighborhood police officers attempt to get to know residents and youths on their beat. (*Courtesy* St. Petersburg, Florida, Police Department)

special episode of the city's "Chicago CrimeWatch" program: "Block by Block." Viewers are taken on a guided tour through the CAPS problem solving process, showing how effective problem solving can be when the police and citizens collaborate. The success of problem solving is told through the story of Gill Park, an area that was reclaimed from drug dealers and gangs.[3]

Fort Lauderdale, Florida

Fort Lauderdale is a community of about 150,000 residents in south Florida. In June 1995 the city's police department set out to develop a COPPS initiative that would be used to guide the future of the entire agency in terms of how it provided police services. This model was founded on principles that would

- Meaningfully represent the community in the development of COPPS
- Develop working relationships with all governmental and private entities
- Target a primary area of geographic responsibility that is stable, but threatened
- Foster conduct among personnel assigned to COPPS efforts that reflects a sense of ownership to the neighborhoods

The COPPS initiative aims to marshall community and governmental resources and, as problems are addressed, the community will be enlisted to develop a self-sustaining effort. Three teams operate under a captain and are assigned to one of three districts and staffed by one sergeant and six officers. A crime prevention unit is staffed by three detectives and assigned to provide expertise in the area of crime prevention through environmental design (CPTED, discussed in Chapter 5). They provide this service throughout the community. Furthermore, code enforcement officers (two permanent, two temporary) are assigned to work closely with the fire, building, and zoning departments. They provide inspections and subsequent enforcement of all city codes.

There have been several major accomplishments since the inception of COPPS, involving reclaiming neighborhoods and parks, initiating nuisance abatement proceedings against problem properties, and acquiring three dog drug teams.[4]

Fresno, California

Fresno's 402,000 residents are served by a police force of 471 sworn officers who adopted COPPS in 1992 as an operating philosophy. The department members believe strongly that—because of understaffing, inmate overcrowding, growing caseloads, and shrinking resources—police agencies can no longer rely on the criminal justice system for addressing drugs, crime, and violence; rather, police administrators should be encouraging their employees to seek unconventional solutions to problems.

In Fresno, officers routinely request the assistance of city building code officials to conduct inspections before a search warrant is executed at a residence likely to be in substandard condition. Irresponsible landlords are forced to make needed structural repairs and upgrades and remove trash and debris in yards. Occupants engaged in criminal activity and problem tenants are charged with violations.

Another effective tactic is to encourage nearby residents who are directly affected by problem tenants to seek small claims court actions against responsible persons. A civil suit may also be initiated against the property owner or manager if it can be shown that the person was aware of the problem but took no corrective action.[5]

Exhibit 13.2 shows how Fresno dealt with the problem of child custody.

St. Louis, Missouri

Since initiating a pilot COPPS project in a single neighborhood, a "chronology of significant events" undertaken by the St. Louis Police Department regarding this concept has grown to more than 10 pages in length. More than 600 officers, supervisors, and command staff received COPPS training as the concept expanded; nationally recognized experts have helped launch both the community oriented and problem solving efforts.

Perhaps the most notable undertaking has been the department's efforts with COPPS "on the beat"—efforts in specialized functions. Following is a brief description of how COPPS has been mainstreamed into various aspects of police work:

Narcotics section: All narcotics detectives have been assigned to specific neighborhoods and are responsible for coordinating all POP responses to narcotics problems with patrol officers. Narcotics detectives focus their work on community hot spots. An innovative computerized tracking system for citizen-generated calls to a hotline was recently developed.

Auto theft unit: The auto theft unit works with COPPS officers to target certain neighborhoods for theft prevention. The expertise of the auto theft detectives and the community contacts of the patrol officers is combined to enhance police response to the problem.

Juvenile division: The juvenile division helps coordinate the department's School Assistance Grant, placing 14 uniformed patrol officers in selected high schools and middle schools and their neighborhoods; the department participates in the Substance Abuse Prevention Partnership. A COPPS response to family violence has also been developed.

Gang unit: After conducting a thorough study of gang activity in St. Louis, this unit developed educational materials for parents and school officials and conducted gang awareness training for patrol officers.

Mobile reserve unit: The mobile reserve unit identifies persistent problems of crime and disorder throughout the city, ranging from narcotics sales to graffiti to fights and disturbances. It also provides patrol support while officers are attending COPPS training.

Exhibit 13.2   Addressing Child Custody Problems in Fresno

Fresno was one of the winners of the 1999 Herman Goldstein Award for Excellence in Problem-Oriented Policing for its approach to an overwhelming number of calls for service to assist with child custody disputes. After being shocked to learn that one single-family residence had generated 19 calls for service in one month for child custody–related matters, with each call averaging one hour in length, officers began wondering what was happening in this regard across the rest of the city. Officers discovered that the police department responded to more than 2,300 calls that concerned violations of child custody court orders and to assist with child custody exchanges in one year. And, of 1,400 police reports filed in those cases with the district attorney's office, fewer than 10 percent of the cases were prosecuted. Three officers were charged with coordinating a project to address the problem. They began by determining which other governmental agencies were affected by this problem and calling all major actors together to coordinate a strategy. Meetings were held and options were discussed for placing responsibility back on parents; judges were requested to issue necessary standing orders that would apply to all family court orders; and other countywide procedures were implemented. As a result, the police experienced a 56 percent reduction in the number of calls for service during the ensuing year. Furthermore, an initial investment of about 100 hours of time by the three project coordinators resulted in a savings of an estimated 3,100 officer hours over a year's time.

Source: "Stemming Calls for Service Related to Child Custody: A Multiagency Approach to a Countywide Problem," in U.S. Department of Justice, National Institute of Justice, *Best Practices in Problem-Oriented Policing: Winners of the 1999 Herman Goldstein Award for Excellence in Problem-Oriented Policing* (Washington, D.C.: Author, November 1999), pp. 12–15.

Legal division: In-house counsel assists officers with their COPPS efforts, hearings to enforce building code violations, and condemnation proceedings on problem property.

In addition, a CAD flagging system will notify officers of safety alerts, ongoing COPPS projects, and hot spots. An Implementation Advisory Group of 12 employees and citizens designed a computerized problem solving database, prepared a revised policy on awards and recognition, and oversaw publication of the department's monthly COPPS newsletter. An Information Division was created that includes the library, the TV Section (which produces videotapes of crime problems, for training), Computer Center, and Planning and Development. A Performance Appraisal Review Committee of eight officers and supervisors prepares recommendations to the chief for a new system that is consistent with COPPS. Plans also include redrawing district and beat boundaries so they are congruent with neighborhood boundaries, and a patrol plan review and work-load assessment to provide officers with more time for COPPS activities.[6]

St. Petersburg, Florida

The Community Policing Division was formed following a November 1990 reorganization of the department. Six primary goals were developed to guide COPPS efforts:

> *Goal 1—Partnership:* It was deemed necessary that internal and external partnerships (e.g., the community, city administration, other public and private agencies, the justice system) be developed.
>
> *Goal 2—Empowerment:* An organizational structure was needed that reflected and supported community values and facilitated joint citizen and employee empowerment.
>
> *Goal 3—Service Orientation:* A customer orientation had to be developed that would provide services to citizens and responsiveness to employees (e.g., training, reward and recognition systems, physical fitness and wellness programs, and career development).
>
> *Goal 4—Problem Solving:* Coactive, problem solving approaches were needed that enhanced community quality of life, reduced crime and fear of crime, and prevented crime.
>
> *Goal 5—Accountability:* Also essential was mutual accountability for public safety resources and strategies among police management and employees, the city manager, other city employees, the city council, and the community. (This goal included fiscal practices and policies, a new personnel appraisal system, and community input in all police operations.)
>
> *Goal 6—Project Management and Direction:* A process had to be developed for the overall management and evaluation of the transition to COPPS.

There are 48 community policing areas (CPAs) designed by a "Crime-Tract Analysis for Geo-Based Community Profile/Assessment." This approach used existing computer-aided dispatch information that was analyzed and applied in a new and creative way for new community-based patrol beats designed around neighborhoods. This enabled the department to reassign 48 officers to full-time COPPS endeavors without hiring additional personnel.

Community policing teams consist of full-time community police officers who serve as the core of a team that includes patrol officers, detectives, and supervisors. Patrol sergeants serve as team leaders, patrol lieutenants serve as sector leaders, and patrol majors have districtwide team responsibility.

Technology has been integrated in a creative and innovative way. A sophisticated computer system—the Community Problem Solving Policing Data-Base

Management System (DBMS)—assists in the automated analysis and evaluation of COPPS initiatives. The system captures information on geographic location of problems, nature of problems, and internal/external resources available to resolve the problems. DBMS flags repeated calls for service (five or more calls at one address in one month) and tracks officers' daily activities.[7]

San Diego, California

Like many other incident-driven police agencies, San Diego treated symptoms while the underlying problems continued to grow. Communication between the top and the bottom of the organization was not occurring in an effective and timely manner. The decision was made that officers could more effectively deal with underlying problems.

Since the early 1970s community policing has been San Diego's guiding philosophy.[8] The San Diego Police Department (SDPD) entered Neighborhood Policing in a major way by forming STOP (Selected Tactics of Policing). Ten patrol officers formed a team to combine traditional policing with COPPS to target crime. Neighborhoods on two beats in midcity were selected as target locations. SDPD also became involved in a Neighborhood Policing Restructuring Project to strengthen and expand neighborhood policing throughout the department by developing a plan to convert the police "beat" system from a census tract basis to a community-based format, and by incorporating problem solving into all department levels and functions.

To professionalize problem solving as an accepted policing strategy, the SDPD and the Police Executive Research Forum founded the annual National Problem Oriented Policing Conference. As many as 1,500 participants from around the world attend this conference, which has a rich blend of hands-on advice combined with the most recent research in the field.[9]

Recent examples of Neighborhood Policing in San Diego include

- A revitalized Neighborhood Watch program consisting of community coordinators, watch coordinators, and block captains all working toward a common goal
- Citizens' Patrol groups throughout the city, acting as eyes and ears to observe suspicious activities and report problems
- Safe Streets Now! working to get rid of nuisance properties through civil remedies
- The Drug Abatement Response Team, involving the city attorney, housing inspectors, and police in identifying properties that have a long history of ongoing narcotics activities (in a recent six-month period, more than 70 drug houses were targeted for abatement action)

Also, in February 1997, the SDPD adopted a strategic planning process as a means to improve organizational management. The process was opened to community members, other city employees, and police employees. In the first phase of developing a three- to five-year strategic plan, nearly 215 people had a voice in the goals and objectives the SDPD would pursue. In the second phase, begun in November 1997, plans were developed to put the overall strategies into action.[10]

Appendix A contains a description of a recent successful problem solving endeavor in San Diego concerning a school truancy problem.

MEDIUM-SIZE COUNTIES AND CITIES

Arlington County, Virginia

Arlington County, Virginia, is an urban community of approximately 26 square miles, located across the Potomac River from Washington, D.C. Being both a residential community and an employment center, its population swells from about 187,000 residents to about 265,000 each workday with the influx of commuters.

Using federal and state community policing grants, five community-based teams were deployed to diverse communities throughout the county. Teams, consisting of up to 24 officers and 3 supervisors, establish a cooperative relationship with the community and identify broad-based strategies to address crime problems. Additionally, Community Resource Officers in each of the county's schools act as a part of the faculty, serving as instructors (teaching antidrug and antigang classes), enhancing the schools' security efforts, and coordinating Neighborhood Watch programs.

Geographic accountability is a management and motivational tool to facilitate agencywide implementation of COPPS. Officers are responsible and accountable for specific "turf" rather than a particular shift. Four districts were created, and the department's 10 police beats follow the natural boundaries of its civic organizations. This design enhances departmentwide communications and encourages neighborhood focus. Officers are assigned to fixed areas for extended periods of time and are responsible for their specific areas 24 hours per day, seven days per week. In addition to responding to both emergency and nonemergency calls for service, they are responsible for preliminary criminal investigations, special event planning, and school liaisoning. The middle managers within the department have been identified as the key players to making COPPS work.

The department's COPPS efforts have resulted in a significant reduction in crime and calls for service. The department is also working aggressively to develop a technology strategy that will support its new geographic policing strategy. Through another recently funded grant, the department hopes to develop a technology infrastructure to support the requirements of beat officers engaged in problem solving.[11]

Eugene, Oregon

Eugene, Oregon, covers 36 square miles and, being home to more than 130,000 people, is Oregon's second-largest city. COPPS is now in development, and a number of related strategies or activities have been implemented during the past few years, including

- A Community Response Team (CRT) composed of six officers who are assigned to three sectors and work on community safety issues with social service providers and citizen groups
- Foot patrol, working closely with businesses, the local university, and residents to establish partnerships
- Public safety stations, which have citizens' advisory boards staffed by volunteers, provide police resources to individuals and businesses in the surrounding areas, and work closely with the CRTs
- The Safer Schools Program, with four officers working with school administrators and students to create a safer learning environment
- The Rapid Deployment Unit, a specialized team of officers focusing on improving neighborhood safety and quality of life through proactive enforcement; the unit is free from having to respond to dispatched calls and can focus on specific problems
- The Citizens' Police Academy, with 10-week programs meeting one evening each week and two Saturdays
- The Police Forum, a citizen policy advisory group, meeting once per month to assist the department with COPPS issues

Since 1995 the patrol division has been reorganized to carry out COPPS throughout the city, within three geographical areas and nine patrol beats. A police lieutenant and officers are given responsibility for each sector for an extended period of time. Reducing the geographical size of areas for which officers are responsible allows more time and opportunities for problem solving.

Hayward, California, police work closely with other city agencies to resolve neighborhood problems. (*Courtesy* Hayward, California, Police Department)

The department also conducts community workshops as well as community surveys to obtain feedback on its efforts; strategic planning documents have been developed as well.[12]

Grand Rapids, Michigan

Grand Rapids has the second-largest police department in the state of Michigan, with nearly 400 sworn officers to serve about 200,000 people. The city is composed of six service areas (residents can log on to the department's Web site to find out the service area in which they reside and to contact their team of officers). Each service area has a team of officers assigned to it, including a captain, a lieutenant, several sergeants, two detectives, and patrol officers. This team concept allows captains to run their particular service area as they see fit.

The department proclaims on its Web site that "Community policing works!" The department plans to take COPPS to a higher level, implementing it as part of community oriented government. A five-year strategic plan is guiding this goal, which includes the construction of a Neighborhood Police Service Center in each of the six new service areas. Another part of the plan is the vision statement, which reads in part

> The Grand Rapids Police Department shall lead in developing collaborative working partnerships with all of our community and service providers, so that each and every citizen may enjoy the highest quality of life. Through our leadership, courage, and relentless pursuit of service excellence, the City of Grand Rapids will lead American cities in the twenty-first century.

New community oriented job categories have been created as well: Community officers serve as generalists, are free from answering calls for service, and serve as the department's front-line ombudsman; community detectives are also generalists, providing investigative follow-up to the beat teams; and community resource specialists serve each of the new Neighborhood Police Service Centers.[13]

Hayward, California

Hayward has a population of about 120,000 and 160 sworn police officers. The 1990s were marked by increases in crime, drug trafficking, gangs, and traffic problems. Like other communities, Hayward's growing social ills contributed to the evolution of an incident-driven policing system in which "random patrol produces random results" and rapid response was a key priority. Realizing that the authority of the Hayward Police Department (HPD) was centralized and stifled the creativity of employees, the department began developing a new approach to policing, believing it was time for law enforcement to change.

The Hayward Plan—officially known as Community Oriented Policing and Problem Solving (COPPS)—was activated and incorporated into all routine police functions (HPD's methods for changing its culture and mission statement are described in Chapter 6). New means of responding to calls for service were developed to free up officer time for problem solving. Officers are "managers" of their beats, encouraged to engage in responsible, creative ways to bring about problem resolution. They meet and talk with residents to build and nurture partnership and commitment as well as to explore viable solutions and seek out available resources.

The Hayward model is intended to be flexible, effective, and responsive to the needs of that community, stressing the importance of partnerships, problem solving, and visionary leadership. The process, the department acknowledges, requires considerable time, planning, and cooperation by everyone concerned. Such a comprehensive change in philosophy dictates a new policing style and "ushers in an exciting era."[14]

Lincoln, Nebraska

The city of Lincoln has formed a Problem Resolution Team (PRT) composed of a group of representatives from key public agencies and neighborhood associations, including the city police department, victim and witness unit, attorney's office, building and safety department, housing authority, and urban development office, as well as the county health and social services departments. The team has several functions:

- Gathering information relevant to cases—the team assembles relevant documents that pertain to a complaint or problem, such as reports, correspondence, or other records.
- Sharing information among public agencies—at regular meetings cases are shared among the team.
- Developing action plans or strategies—team members discuss possible strategies for resolving problems, finalizing action plans, and making specific assignments by consensus. Each team member coordinates the activities of his or her own agency that are necessary to fulfill its portion of the action plan.
- Keeping citizens informed about the status of cases and outcomes of city actions.
- Making recommendations to city officials to improve city practices or policies.

The PRT is currently developing a computer program that will match the police computer-aided dispatching and other agency responses at specific locations to those that are flagged as public housing properties. Another program is being developed that will alert area police captains about excessive calls-for-service locations in order to identify problems before they become entrenched.

Perhaps the jewel in the crown of Lincoln's community policing efforts is the Quality Service Audit—a partnership between the Lincoln Police Department and the Gallup Organization. This audit is an ongoing, systematic survey of citizen perceptions regarding the quality of the city's police services; it seeks to provide officers with feedback about their contacts with citizens and to provide strategic information to police managers.[15]

Each year, student interns from the University of Nebraska and other area colleges, working at the police department, complete more than 6,000 telephone surveys with Lincoln residents who have recently received police services. Crime victims, drivers in traffic accidents, and even persons who have been arrested or ticketed by the police are surveyed using 10 questions developed by Gallup. The department requires all new officers to receive audit feedback as a condition of their employment; officers with more than three years of service are allowed to participate voluntarily. Only aggregate data are provided to managers, and narrative comments are provided to the officers on a monthly basis.[16]

Although surveying citizens is not a new approach under COPPS, this concept is given exceptional importance and sophistication in Lincoln. As the mayor and police chief state,

> The tendency to overvalue workload data and underutilize measures of quality service may result in an organizational milieu that rewards a sort of fast driving, rapid response policing which retards efforts to improve relationships with the public, build citizen trust, and implement or encourage a community based style of policing. Overemphasis on statistics can be detrimental if an agency does not make a concerted effort to also utilize data about the quality of services provided.[17]

The city received a $50,000 federal grant from the National Institute of Justice to study how its audit system affects officers' behavior.

Reno, Nevada

Reno is located in northwest Nevada on the eastern slopes of the Sierra Nevada. It is a 24-hour gaming community of 59 square miles and about 150,000 population (swelling to more than 250,000 people with the influx of tourists for gaming and during special events).

In 1987 the Reno Police Department (RPD) reorganized its entire agency toward a new community policing strategy. In June 1987 COPPS was initiated. The department decentralized its operational functions. Call methods and priorities were modified to allow officers more time to become involved in problem solving. The department opened two substations, staffed by civilian dispatchers and volunteers, to further facilitate telephone reporting and the delivery of information and programs to neighborhoods. The city was decentralized into three geographic areas of command. A captain was assigned to each area, with 24-hour responsibility for all operations and administration. Supervisors and officers worked in teams assigned to areas on a permanent basis to become more familiar with neighborhood problems and citizens and businesses.

Neighborhood Advisory Groups (NAGs) were formed in several city areas, meeting quarterly with their area captain and officers to discuss neighborhood problems and to explore solutions together. A newsletter provides residents with information about police department programs, crimes in their neighborhood, and problem solving efforts. NAGs were also established to represent the special interests of minority communities and to meet regularly. A Quality Assurance unit was formed to conduct semiannual community surveys to determine the efficacy of the agency's efforts. Using self-administered questionnaires, Quality Assurance also surveyed line and supervisory officers to assess their views of COPPS and its effects on the department and the community. The chief added three groups for feedback and guidance: a Media Advisory Group, Citizen's Advisory Group, and Technical Advisory Group.

All personnel attended a 40-hour orientation program. All officers received a resource manual regarding social service referral agencies, enabling them to provide that form of service as well. Annual refresher training is conducted with new courses to emphasize the role of the supervisor and problem oriented policing. Recruitment and selection were revamped to pursue applicants who best reflected the department's notion of community police officers. COPPS was included in the academy curriculum and became an area of evaluation in the 16-week Field Training Officer program. Policies concerning promotion, specialty assignments, annual performance evaluations, and awards programs were all modified to accommodate the new philosophy.[18]

Savannah, Georgia

In 1991 Savannah's police department began a plan of COPPS implementation that necessitated the hiring of 34 new officers and the reorganization from a centralized command to a system of precincts housed in four different locations. Several programs were then initiated under the COPPS umbrella:

1. *Showcase Neighborhood Program:* The city improved livability in depressed neighborhoods by becoming partners with area residents. Police worked with citizens to identify problems and establish priorities for eliminating them. For this effort, the city won an award from the U.S. Conference of Mayors.
2. *Horse and bicycle patrols:* Public interest led to the development of horse patrols in 1987 in the downtown area (later they were used in targeted problem neighborhoods). Bicycle patrols, also begun downtown, were eventually used successfully in a number of COPPS initiatives. The emphasis of the bicycle patrol is now on problem solving.
3. *Police ministations:* One officer was assigned to four public housing areas that experienced high crime rates. Each ministation sponsors a Boy Scout Troop and makes constant checks on shut-ins and the elderly.

Since the initiation of COPPS, other new programs have evolved. The Volunteer Program used 20 actively participating volunteers, and a Citizens Police Academy consists of a 10-week, one-day-per-week course on the operation of the Savannah Police Department. The department considers COPPS a continually

In the Kids Korner program in Reno, Nevada, beat officers and medical personnel visit low-income rental motels to identify children who are truant and in need of medical and social services. (*Courtesy* Reno, Nevada, Police Department)

evolving process of changing the way it does business, forcing officers to open their minds to new ideas and change attitudes concerning the delivery of services—all of which, it is hoped, will result in long-term benefits for the police and citizens alike.[19]

Spokane, Washington

Spokane is unique because of its geographic location and regional orientation. Although the current city population is about 185,000, the city is the urban center of the Spokane–Coeur d'Alene area, which has a combined population of more than 450,000. Many demands for city services are generated daily from a nonresident population base, which includes out-of-state workers, surrounding county residents, and Canadian visitors.

Like most police agencies dealing with increasing violent crimes, more drug-related offenses, and limited staff and resources, the Spokane Police Department (SPD) had fallen into the reactive, incident-driven, call-to-call policing model. Officers became seriously stressed, with as many as 40 officers at one time off work because of fatigue-related illnesses.

In late 1991 the department created a strategic planning team to mold its future and identify and remedy obstacles to change. Members met regularly to tackle separate issues; a monthly department newsletter was created as well. The department then teamed with the Washington State Institute for Community Oriented Policing (WSICOP) to focus on the COPPS philosophy, develop community partnerships, strengthen informal social control, expand police and community empowerment, and increase social and cultural awareness. Written surveys were distributed to police employees and 1,200 citizens.[20]

Also in late 1991, spurred by the tragic abduction of two local girls, citizens were sparked by their grief to form a task force to address neighborhood problems. They approached the city council and proposed to open a neighborhood police substation, staffed by community volunteers, as a central distribution point for information on crime and disorder, as well as problem solving. The city council and police chief supported the idea, and on May 1, 1992, the facility opened; four years later, there were nine "COPS Shops" in the city, with four more in planning stages. The volunteers take police reports, deal with nuisances, disseminate resource information, register bicycles, aid victims, and sponsor guest speakers and "get together" nights. Since the original COPS facilities opened, crime rates have declined significantly.[21]

Tempe, Arizona

Tempe is a growing suburb of Phoenix and the most densely populated city in the state, with about 156,000 residents in a 40-square-mile area. City departments have a reputation for interdepartmental cooperation and problem solving, and citizen surveys have repeatedly indicated the city has an excellent quality of life.

The Tempe Police Department (TPD) employs 256 sworn officers. In response to the changing public safety needs of the city, the TPD initially introduced COPPS in one beat to demonstrate how COPPS strategies could be used to reduce drug demand and overall crime and disorder. This Innovative Neighborhood Oriented Policing (INOP) project was eventually used as a model for citywide implementation of COPPS strategies.[22]

TPD first ensured that officers had the flexibility to solve problems (using the S.A.R.A. model). Patrol officers worked as a self-directed team, sharing information, problem solving, and scheduling with a COPPS philosophy. Officers were in the beat area for extended time periods.

TPD's first task was to perform a comprehensive and detailed profile of the target area using community and business surveys measuring demographic characteristics, fear of crime, perception of quality of life, and so on. Next, the department involved business owners, residents, neighborhood organizations, other city departments, and social service agencies in project coordination. The team of beat officers then used a variety of intelligence and information sources to support drug enforcement and demand reduction efforts. Newsletters, meetings, and a citizen hotline were used to disseminate information.

An evaluation component was developed by an independent consulting agency to assess INOP's implementation, process, and impact. Although the impact on the community has yet to be determined, the project's impact on the department has been significant. The agency believes that once it made the commitment to INOP, there was no turning back. Changes in organizational structure, management and supervisory roles, policies, goals, recruitment practices, evaluation and award systems, and COPPS information system are permanent.

A feature of COPPS in Tempe is the department's elaborate system for geographic deployment of patrol officers, allowing officers within a geographic area to have varying schedules. Such deployment provides officers with better information about their beats, increases officer job satisfaction as they take ownership of areas and solve problems, holds officers accountable for their geographic areas, and allows the community to become more involved in solving problems in their neighborhoods.[23] Tempe officers are scheduled individually, rather than by squads, to facilitate greater coverage during peak times. This system has been quantitatively shown to yield higher correlations between calls for service and available staffing.

SMALL COMMUNITIES

Abington, Virginia

The township of Abington is located in southeastern Virginia. It has a population of about 56,000 and 92 sworn officers; approximately 11 percent of Abington's residents are minority group members. In March 1992 the police department began the process of implementing community oriented policing to reduce crime, fear of crime, disorder, and decay and to improve the quality of life in the city's neighborhoods. All representatives of the community were invited to participate in reaching these goals. Beat officers attended town meetings and Neighborhood Watch meetings and participated in civic activities in their sectors.

Park & Walk was instituted to help officers get to know citizens better, gather information, and do proactive crime prevention. A two-year minimum beat assignment was also initiated. A citizen's advisory board was organized to open lines of communication and prioritize neighborhood problems. Community surveys were conducted as well.

Youth programs were introduced (trips to athletic events, the zoo, and so on), allowing the relationship between police and youth to become much less adversarial. A nonprofit corporation—Citizens and Police Together (C.A.P.T.)—was created to help purchase tickets and provide transportation and food for youth trips and educational activities. C.A.P.T. also solicits donations and holds fund-raisers (such as T-shirt sales, police auctions, charity ballgames, and golf tournaments). A bicycle patrol was instituted recently, with donated bikes and 24 officers assigned on a part-time basis. A mobile ministation vehicle was purchased with funding assistance from state and federal (HUD) grants to bring police, social, and health services to citizens. Free health screenings are provided through this vehicle by local hospitals. A new computer-aided dispatch system improved record keeping and information flow. This system allows the police to identify problems, track ongoing COPPS projects, and document successes.[24]

Arroyo Grande, California

With a complement of 29 staff members, the Arroyo Grande Police Department advertises the fact that should citizens visit their newly expanded police facility, they will not find COPPS written as a specific program, or a COPPS officer or unit; rather, their COPPS philosophy is based on a "Value Based Policing" philosophy that involves every member of the organization.

The agency has developed an organizational culture that seeks to form true partnerships with the community's various stakeholders in order to provide a better quality of life for all residents. The department's operations attempt to anticipate and solve problems before they erupt into major issues. Some examples of COPPS initiatives include

- Employee Participation Program
- Community Advisory Council
- Adopt-a-School Program
- Juvenile Diversion Program
- Bicycle Patrol Program
- Citizen Academy
- Crime Prevention/Neighborhood Watch
- Citizens Assisting Police (CAP) Volunteer Program

Huntington Beach, California, police found bicycle patrol to be an efficient and effective method of delivering services to beach recreation areas. (*Courtesy* Huntington Beach, California, Police Department)

- The Parent Project (for parents of high-risk children)
- Crime Prevention through Environmental Design (CPTED)
- DARE and Drug Free Zone
- Neighborhood Officer Program
- Community Services Program
- Foot Patrol Program
- Teen Citizen Academy

Several police agencies have visited or contacted the department concerning its COPPS initiative and these programs, and the California Peace Officer Standards and Training (POST) has used the department's programs as a resource for developing its training.

The Neighborhood Officer Program in Arroyo Grande is a major aspect of COPPS. This program is unique in that instead of assigning a few officers to cover districts or beats across the city as their primary assignment, each patrol officer is responsible for a particular neighborhood as an ancillary duty, thereby involving the entire uniformed division in the program. Patrol officers, while on duty, respond to calls for service but also pay attention to ongoing problems in their assigned neighborhoods. The officers act as liaisons between citizens and the department and coordinate problem solving projects in their areas. The neighborhood officer also meets with individuals and organizations regarding disturbances, juvenile problems, and a variety of civil problems and attempts to solve these problems with creativity or appropriate enforcement methods.[25]

Elmhurst, Illinois

Elmhurst is a city of 43,000 in the southern portion of Illinois, where the police attempt to provide citizens with "one-stop shopping" convenience. The police department has a cadre of officers who can handle the full range of citizens' needs, including noise complaints, broken street lamps, fallen trees, and other problems. When possible, officers handle problems themselves, or, if need be, the problem is communicated to an appropriate city agency. Steps have been taken to ensure that officers have a stake in the policing process. Each officer has policy- and procedure-making power. They even test and select department equipment and uniforms, and they have developed a new design for police vehicles.

Perhaps a unique aspect of Elmhurst's COPPS strategy lies in its approach to officer evaluation. Instead of relying on traditional quantitative criteria—such as number of arrests—the department uses what it calls "community sensing mechanisms." The chief actively seeks feedback from elected government officials and residents. Random callbacks are conducted to gauge citizen satisfaction with officers and calls for service. In addition to letters to the chief, other sources of input that are given weight include newspaper articles, editorials, and comments from the chamber of commerce.[26]

Gresham, Oregon

Gresham has seen dramatic growth, burgeoning housing and commercial development, and increasing demands for governmental services. With 72,000 residents, Gresham is the fourth-largest city in Oregon. Issues such as drug abuse, gang activity, theft, and violent crime forced a transition from the traditional policing model.[27]

The department became Oregon's first COPPS agency in 1992 as part of the department's five-year strategic plan.[28] A new mission was developed, along with the following activities: forming partnerships with many segments of the community; solving problems through a comprehensive process involving a chief's forum, zone advisory groups, and a neighborhood association; empowering citizens; and responding to underlying problems and conditions that cause crime. To design a foundation that would reflect the agency's values, the department conducted a public opinion survey; reconfigured its six patrol districts into three service delivery zones; assigned a lieutenant and team officers to each zone to further develop partnerships with neighborhood associations, schools, and businesses; and received donated office space, furnishings, and materials for zone offices. These efforts led to overall decentralization, greater initiative and empowerment among all levels of staff and officers, and heightened awareness of community concerns and priorities. Several "success stories" have resulted from Gresham's COPPS strategy:

- Establishment of a community services center
- Placement of a School Resource Officer, a DARE officer, and a Gang Enforcement Officer at each of the two Gresham-area school districts
- Implementation of the Desk Officer Program to reduce response time to lower-priority calls and enable more face-to-face contact between officers and citizens
- Eviction of drug dealers and overall cleanup of apartment complexes
- Voter approval of a three-year, $2 million levy that will, in part, allow for the hiring of nine new officers, three Community Resource Specialists, and one Community Policing Analyst[29]

Orange County, Florida

Tourists are an often-forgotten population in our communities. Orlando, Florida, is the number one tourist destination in the world, with a 78-square-mile tourist corridor. There is also a plethora of criminals seeking to take advantage of unsuspecting victims—many of whom experience armed robbery and theft when items are stolen from their automobiles and hotel rooms. The items most frequently stolen are expensive video cameras, foreign passports, and money.

The Orange County Sheriff's Office developed a Tourist Oriented Police Service (TOPS) program that offers tourists the same services that are available to locals: crisis intervention, assistance with crimes compensation, interaction with foreign consulates, language translation services, and accompaniment throughout the criminal justice system. A tourist advocate is assigned to the patrol unit, and deputies assigned to TOPS make themselves accessible to tourists, leaving their cars, horses, and motorcycles so that they can walk their beats and interact with visitors. The sheriff's office has also developed a training video to teach hotel and business employees how to prevent crimes against tourists.[30]

FED____ ___TE AGENCIES

_____ ncies are also engaged in COPPS. One example is the U.S. _____ ategic Problem Solving (SPS) initiative, which is composed _____ ents:

_____ lves determining and stating the goals, objec-
_____ rable terms)

_____ oblems through brainstorming

_____ using SPS in 1996, more than 350 projects have
_____ ted States. The Office of Strategic Problem Solving
_____ their successes in dealing with a wide range of prob-

_____ at land ports of entry

_____ cle exportations at major seaports

_____ smuggling conspiracies involving airlines, railroads, and shipping
_____ pany employees

_____ ug smuggling across land and via air travel

_____ S has proven to be an effective tool, because it brings together interdisciplinary teams of subject matter experts who are encouraged to be creative in developing solutions to problems.[31]

State Police and Universities

The Delaware State Police Rural Community Policing Unit has been in existence since mid-1994. Rural community policing is not common among state police

In many jurisdictions, partnerships and training between local and federal law enforcement agencies and private business have proved instrumental in combating crime. (*Courtesy* Community Policing Consortium)

agencies. The demographics of Delaware, however, make this an ideal venue for this concept. Sussex County, the most rural county in Delaware, has communities with high crime rates and few resources to assist the residents of these communities. The purpose and goal of the state police Rural Community Policing Unit is to reduce crime and provide resources to eight targeted communities in Sussex County. The unit is composed of four full-time troopers. The unit engages in activities such as conflict resolution, peer leadership, drug awareness, and Neighborhood Watch.

Calls for service in the targeted communities declined about 10 percent after the first year of the COPPS initiative, and other notable accomplishments include working with outside agencies to improve homes, streets, and water systems; obtaining a computerized information system from the department of health to locate available health resources and job information; giving bicycle helmets and infant or child car seats to parents; and joining with local physicians to provide free physicals for youths attending camps.[32]

State colleges and universities across the nation are also involved with COPPS, including Harvard University (see Exhibit 13.3). Many college and university police departments, such as those at Harvard, Northwestern University,[33] University of South Dakota,[34] and Eastern Connecticut State University[35] have their own Web pages for describing their COPPS approach to the public; such

---

Exhibit 13.3   A New Policing Model for Harvard University

Harvard University's decision to restructure resulted in a significant transformation of the Harvard University Police Department (HUPD). Begun in 1997 the HUPD revised its management structure to reflect the needs of the COPPS approach, emphasizing

- Familiarity with the community through a "neighborhood beat cop" system that builds on frequent, positive interactions with students, faculty, staff, and visitors
- A concentration on crime prevention
- A team approach to problem solving
- Increased training at all levels of the agency
- A unified management philosophy governing decision making at all levels of the department

Source: Harvard University Web page: http://www.news.harvard.edu/specials/policing/policing.html, October 20, 2000, p. 4.

Web sites also discuss such matters as the agency's history, philosophy, purpose, goals and objectives, and COPPS initiatives.

Some COPPS initiatives are instituted statewide (see Exhibit 13.4).

SUMMARY

A common thread running through most if not all of the COPPS approaches in this chapter is the realization by the police that new strategies were necessary for addressing crime and neighborhood disorder. The cities and counties discussed in this chapter have demonstrated that the path to attaining a full-fledged COPPS initiative involves a complete transformation in ideology and more than mere rhetoric or putting officers on footbeats or on bicycles. This path may not be an easy one, but it has been shown that the rewards can be substantial.

NOTES

1. Information provided by Sr./Sgt. Kim Nobles, Community Policing, Austin, Texas, Police Department, 17 January 1994.
2. Susan M. Hartnett and Wesley G. Skogan, *Community Policing: Chicago's Experience* (Washington, D.C.: National Institute of Justice Journal, April 1999), pp. 2–3.

Exhibit 13.4   COPPS at the Statewide Level: Problem Solving in Maryland

The ability of state government to integrate the problem solving philosophy throughout the state's entities is relatively new. State governments need to be able to communicate with local governments using similar resources for similar goals. Maryland needed a comprehensive statewide approach to pool resources and form partnerships among state and local governments along with business and community leaders. This approach considers a geographic focus on crime. Hot spots exist in urban, suburban, and rural parts of Maryland. To increase the quality of life for citizens, several inter-related statewide initiatives were developed, which included assistance from the State Multi-Agency Response Teams, HotSpot Communities and its component initiative Operation Spotlight, and statewide HotSpot Computer Mapping.

Source: Workshop presentation, Danny Shell, Maryland State Police, "The 8th Annual International Problem Oriented Policing Conference: Problem Oriented Policing 1997," November 16, 1997, San Diego, California.

---

3. Chicago, Illinois, Police Department Web page: http://www.ci.chi.il.us/Community Policing.htm, October 20, 2000.
4. Fort Lauderdale, Florida, Police Department Web page: http://ci.ftlaud.fl.us/police/cpipaul.html, October 20, 2000.
5. Marty West, "POP in Fresno: Effective Problem-Solving Techniques," *The Police Chief* (March 1995):37–43.
6. Information in this section was obtained from two progress reports on COPPS in St. Louis, Missouri, developed by Michael S. Scott, Special Assistant to the Chief of Police, December 23, 1993.
7. Information provided by Donald S. Quire, St. Petersburg, Florida, Police Department, January 31, 1994.
8. Bob Burgreen and Nancy McPherson, "Implementing POP: The San Diego Experience," *The Police Chief* (October 1990):50–56.
9. *Ibid.*, p. 17.
10. San Diego Police Department Web page: http://www.sannet.gov/police/sdpd, November 26, 1997.
11. Arlington County, Virginia, Web page: http://www.co.arlington.va.us/pol/comm/htm, October 20, 2000.
12. Eugene, Oregon, Police Department Web page: http://www.ci.eugene.or.us/DPS/police/copoov.htm, October 20, 2000.
13. Grand Rapids, Michigan, Police Department Web page: http:www.grpolice.grand-rapids.mi.us/default.htm, October 20, 2000.
14. California Department of Justice, Attorney General's Office, Crime Prevention Center, *COPPS: Community Oriented Policing and Problem Solving* (Sacramento, Calif.: Author, November 1992), pp. 43–46.
15. Mike Johanns and Tom Casady, "Quality Service Audit Improves Community-Based Policing," *U.S. Mayor*, April 7, 1997, p. 3.

16. *Community Policing Journal*, Fall 1996, p. 14.
17. Johanns and Casady, "Quality Service Audit Improves Community-Based Policing," p. 3.
18. For a more complete description of Reno's COPPS initiative, see Ken Peak, Robert V. Bradshaw, and Ronald Glensor, "Improving Citizen Perceptions of the Police: 'Back to the Basics' with a Community Policing Strategy," *Journal of Criminal Justice* 20 (1992):25–40.
19. Information provided by Dan Reynolds, Savannah, Georgia, Police Department, December 9, 1993.
20. Information provided by Robert C. Van Leuven, Spokane, Washington, Police Department, December 14, 1993.
21. Ellen Painter, "Tragedy Sparks Community Policing in Spokane, Washington," *Community Policing Exchange* (May/June 1995):5.
22. Tempe, Arizona, Police Department, Overview: http://www.tempe.gov, November 26, 1997.
23. Tempe, Arizona, Police Department, *Geographic Deployment of Patrol* (Tempe, Ariz.: Author, 1993).
24. Information provided by George M. Megelsh, Abingdon, Virginia, Police Department, December 20, 1993.
25. Community oriented policing in Arroyo Grande: http://www.thegrid.net/agpd/community.html, November 26, 1997.
26. Steve Anzaldi, "Adapting to Needs: Community Policing around the State," *The Compiler* (Chicago: Illinois Criminal Justice Information Authority, Fall 1993), p. 8.
27. Gresham, Oregon, Police Department, "A Call for Challenge: Community-Based Policing" (Gresham, Ore.: Author, no date), p. 1.
28. Gresham, Oregon, Police Department, "Community Policing: Vision, Mission, Values" (Gresham, Ore.: Author, no date), p. 2.
29. Information provided by Gerald Johnson, Acting Chief of Police, Gresham, Oregon, Police Department, October 27, 1993.
30. Greta Snitkin, "Tourist Victim Advocacy: Servicing Your Extended Community," *Sheriff Times* (Spring 1997):1, 8.
31. http://www.customs.treas.gov/enforcem/sps.htm.
32. http://www.state.de.us./dsp/rural/htm.
33. http://www.new.edu/up/community.html.
34. http://www.operations.und.nodak.edu/Op/police/CoP.htm.
35. http://www.ecsu.ctstateu.edu/depts/police/cops/html.

IN FOREIGN VENUES
COPPS Abroad

The world is but a school of inquiry.

—Michel de Montaigne

INTRODUCTION

The world has become a global village. Through technology, rapid intercontinental travel, and high-technology communications systems, we are virtual neighbors around the planet. Even very disparate countries can learn from, and have shared much with, one another.

It has been said that the comparative approach provides the opportunity to "search for order."[1] This chapter does so by comparing the work of community oriented policing and problem solving (COPPS) in foreign venues with that in the United States. It will be seen that COPPS has indeed gone international and is now the operational strategy of many police agencies around the globe.

First we "travel" to Canada, looking at the country generally, then viewing COPPS in Vancouver and with the Royal Canadian Mounted Police (problem solving efforts in Ontario and British Columbia are also discussed in exhibits). Next we look at some of the earliest community policing efforts in Japan, then move on to Australia, where COPPS is having a major effect across that country; our focus is on Queensland. Great Britain is our next stop. We conclude the chapter with a brief review of COPPS in some other venues, including Scotland, the

Isle of Man, Israel, Hong Kong, New Zealand, and the Scandinavian countries. Other venues are discussed in five exhibits spread throughout the chapter.

Much can be learned from examining the activities and approaches undertaken in each venue. The reader is encouraged to determine whether there are common elements of COPPS in these countries, and to compare each with the American strategy as it is described in earlier chapters. We discuss in the chapter summary whether common denominators exist and an international understanding and application of the concepts around the world.

CANADA

Canada stretches nearly 5,000 miles from east to west, touches both the Atlantic and Pacific Oceans, embraces four million square miles, covers six time zones, and has 10 provinces. More than 30 million people reside in Canada—90 percent of whom are within 100 miles of the southern border, near the United States. They speak more than 60 languages and are members of 70 ethnocultural groups.[2]

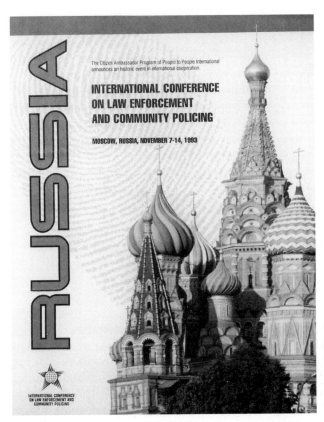

The fall of communism led Russia and other countries to explore more democratic forms of policing, as illustrated by this International Conference on Community Policing brochure.

More than 56,000 sworn officers work in about 400 independent police services in Canada, translating to about one officer for every 520 Canadians. Of the total number of officers, about one-quarter are members of the Royal Canadian Mounted Police (RCMP, discussed later), and 16 percent work for the three independent provincial police forces—the Ontario Provincial Police (see Exhibit 14.1), the Surete du Quebec, and the Royal Newfoundland Constabulary. More than half (56 percent) of Canada's police officers work in 361 independent municipal police services. But the average size of a Canadian police service is 141 sworn personnel.[3]

Community policing is now the official approach to policing across Canada, at all levels of government. The most widely recognized "police service of excellence" in Canada is the City of Edmonton Police Service, which pioneered a demonstration project on neighborhood foot patrol in 1993. Edmonton is considered by many to be the "Mayo Clinic of policing" and is perhaps the model of a very modern police service.[4]

But the question of whether community policing has succeeded in Canada is yet to be answered. Despite its widespread adoption, there has been little in the way of comprehensive, rigorous evaluations of community policing in Canada—which lacks a police research arm that would be equivalent to the U.S. Police Executive Research Forum, Police Foundation, or National Institute of Justice.[5] It is believed, however, that four challenges still confront community policing in Canada:

1. The police have yet to overcome the unrealistic expectations and demands placed on them by the public, that they provide rapid emergency response while providing order maintenance services—what one author described as demanding both a "Green Beret" and a "Peace Corps" role of the police.[6]
2. Community policing in Canada carries a bias toward dealing with local problems, at a time when drug, smuggling, money laundering, and other crimes demand national and international focuses.
3. The police are still challenged to move beyond the traditional criteria for police success: arrests, clearance rates, and response times.
4. Police need to take advantage of a brief window of opportunity to implement and prove the effectiveness of COPPS before a fiscal crisis of governments drives policing back to the reactive, incident-driven, traditional form of policing.[7]

Victory in Vancouver

During the summer months of late 1997 and 1998, the intersection at First Avenue and Commercial Drive became a focal point for complaints to the Grandview Woodland Community Policing Center in Vancouver, Canada. A community survey conducted in 1997, with studies by Simon Fraser University criminology students, determined that a multitude of disorder issues at this intersection were affecting the quality of life of the residents and local businesses. Citizens were fearful of using bank machines, shopping at the businesses, or walking or driving

---

EXHIBIT 14.1 Community Policing in Ontario

The Ontario Provincial Police (OPP) have created an impressive Web site that describes in detail (in both English and French) its Community Policing Development Centre. The site describes its community policing strategy (including the differences between COPPS and traditional policing); presents the agency's mission (including the use of police–community "prevention partnerships" and teams), objectives, and strategic implementation plan; provides a news bulletin; and presents a thorough explanation of the S.A.R.A. problem solving process. A "Just for Kids" page is available, as well as an "Honour Roll" of citizens and police, a slate of current programs, OPP recruitment information, wanted/missing persons information, and links to other governmental agencies.

Source: OPP Web site: http://www.gov.on.ca/opp/english/cpdc/index.htm (13 February 2001).

---

by the intersection; 911 calls indicated that patrol officers frequently went to the intersection to deal with aggressive panhandlers, intoxicated persons, and "squeegee" cases—young people who, with automobile window squeegees stolen from nearby service stations, were harassing people in vehicles at the intersection to "hire" them to clean their windshields.[8] The police were determined to reclaim the intersection and instill a sense of civility and ownership there.

Street interviews were conducted with all kinds of people at the intersection—including the squeegee people, panhandlers, drunks, and local business and home owners. The surveys revealed that citizens were generally tolerant of most street behaviors, but when the behaviors crossed a certain line, they expected the police to provide solutions. Indeed, the intersection was creating a variety of problems, including increased citizens' fear, disputes over territory, graffiti, thefts and assaults, traffic problems, and street people sleeping in nearby alcoves, parks, and businesses.[9]

The police initiated enforcement of traffic and criminal codes, developed a list of squeegee offenders, asked aggressive panhandlers to move on, and took intoxicated people to detoxification centers. The environment was also modified: Benches on which intoxicated persons slept were removed, and newspaper boxes in which the drunks hid their bottles and panhandlers rested were removed. A private firm was hired to remove the graffiti, and a mural was painted in its place (the mural being covered with an antigraffiti coating).[10]

There was a dramatic decline in calls for service to the intersection within three months of the project's initiation: Total calls were reduced by 54 percent, and calls for squeegee activity, public drunkenness, and aggressive panhandling dropped by 38 percent.[11]

The Royal Canadian Mounted Police

Community policing efforts of the Royal Canadian Mounted Police have been making significant strides in its smaller detachments, where COPPS has been operational for a long time. In September 1993 the RCMP resolved to pilot a detachmentwide COPPS initiative in one of its largest areas—Burnaby, British Columbia—with a population of about 150,000 and approximately 150 officers.[12]

The RCMP mission statement is shown in Figure 14.1. The official view is that the adoption of community policing allows the RCMP to become more responsive to the needs of the communities it serves.

The RCMP also believes that, "the open management style under this philosophy allows all officers to make appropriate informed decisions and take action, giving the RCMP [the] flexibility needed to provide completely responsive, integrated, and relevant police service."[13] The primary elements of the strategy include the following (note that there is a strong problem oriented policing flavor):

- *Direct service delivery*—working with the community to identify its problems; resolving the identified problems; empowering officers to make decisions and take action; and making patrol, enforcement, and investigative work effective and directed.
- *Changing the administrative organization*—decentralizing, using modern management concepts (such as problem solving, innovative resource deployment, risk management, flattening organizational hierarchy, and participatory management); creating an enhanced generalist career path; reducing the paper burden; and utilizing citizen satisfaction surveys.[14]

FIGURE 14.1 Mission Statement of the Royal Canadian Mounted Police

---

RCMP community policing is . . .

---

a partnership between the police and the community, sharing in the delivery of police services.

With this valuable community cooperation, the RCMP pledges to . . .

- Uphold the principles of the Canadian Charter of Rights and Freedoms.
- Provide a professional standard of service.
- Ensure all policing services are provided courteously and impartially.
- Work with the community and other agencies to prevent or resolve problems that affect the community's safety and quality of life.
- Act with the Canadian justice system to address community problems.
- Promote a creative and responsible environment to allow all RCMP members to deliver community services.

(*Source:* Vancouver, B.C., Royal Canadian Mounted Police, *RCMP Community Policing: Strategic Action Plan Update, 1992–1995* [June 1993], p. 9.)

EXHIBIT 14.2   Problem Solving in British Columbia

Mt. Pleasant, Vancouver, British Columbia, is located in southwest Canada and has about 26,000 residents. It was beset with problems at apartment buildings—major sources of complaints of heavy prostitution, drug activity, disturbances, and bribed building managers. Buildings were visited and property owners were informed of problems within their buildings. When owners failed to cooperate in rooting out problems, licensing and health agencies were contacted to assist in dealing with the problems. Local bars— sources of a variety of crimes and disturbances—were also addressed via heavy patrols and bar checks. The provincial liquor branch threatened to cancel liquor licenses and cut back the hours of sales, significantly reducing closing time problems and after hours parties. Juvenile prostitution—a serious problem, with an estimated 300 teenagers working the streets—was also addressed, with juvenile prostitutes identified by social service, police, or probation officers, who then successfully removed a significant number of these youths from the streets. Building managers were pressured to help clean up the area and keep out tenants with criminal records, or else have their license revoked. Aggressive patrols were adopted and empty patrol cars were parked at high-activity corners. Traffic stops and person checks were obvious, with red lights flashing on patrol cars to scare away prostitutes and customers. Arrests were prosecuted rapidly. The prostitution task force then began targeting drug dealers in the area. After three years, almost every prostitute had moved out of the residential areas and most of the known drug houses had shut down. Communication with, and support from, the community had significantly developed.

Source: Policing in British Columbia, Commission of Inquiry, *Interim Report* (February 1993), pp. 1–9.

COMMUNITY POLICING IN JAPAN

The Earliest Community-Based Approach

Japan—with its Showa Constitution containing many articles that are similar to those found in the Fourth, Fifth, Sixth, and Eighth Amendments to the U.S. Constitution[15]—can lay claim to possessing the oldest and best-established community policing system in the world. Japan initiated its system immediately after World War II out of a combination of traditional culture and American democratic ideals. According to Jerome Skolnick and David Bayley, four elements seem to be at the core of this philosophy: (1) community-based crime prevention, (2) reorientation of patrol activities to emphasize nonemergency servicing,

(3) increased accountability to the public, and (4) decentralization of command.[16] Next we briefly discuss these four elements.

Each of Japan's 47 prefectures has its own autonomous police force, and together they employ about 220,000 officers—on a densely populated island of about 144,000 square miles and 127 million people.[17] If community policing began with *community-based crime prevention*, the Japanese experience offers several valuable insights. One of the basic reasons Japanese policing works as well as it does is that the officers daily deal face-to-face with citizens and, therefore, have become a part of the community, rather than being separated from the people in a vehicle. Also, Japanese neighborhood crime-prevention associations (the Japanese tradition of the *gonin-gumi*—a group of five people in a neighborhood) have generally given Japanese culture a much closer relationship between people and their neighbors.

With regard to Japanese police *patrol activities*, people in Japan seem not to have the same "we versus they" perceptions about the police as Americans have.[18] Thus, the Japanese appear to be far more willing than Americans to accept police presence. As a result, Japanese police place heavy emphasis on order maintenance and crime prevention, aiding the community to resolve problems that could lead to disorder.[19] A major part of this effort includes the counseling services that are part of every Japanese police station. All police stations assign an experienced older officer, usually a sergeant, to provide a wide range of general counseling, ranging from family disputes to questions about contracts and indebtedness. Trained in dispute resolution, the police are able to provide a helpful, informal conciliation.[20]

If the police and the community are to become coproducers of an orderly society, police must have *closer accountability to the public* and begin to share power with the community they serve, beginning with closer relations with community groups, clubs, churches, and civic organizations to help obtain information, define priorities, and aid in planning effective strategies.[21]

If all of this is to be accomplished, however, the fourth major element in COPPS must be developed: *decentralization of command*. Providing neighborhood police centers and beat offices as well as giving officers greater discretion to develop responses to community problems form the nucleus of this strategy. This has been one of the strengths of the Japanese system.[22] Patrol officers in Japan are under even closer supervision than are rank-and-file officers in the United States. Yet the *kobun-oyabun* (a kind of student–mentor relationship) between the Japanese patrol officers and their superiors allows the officers a great deal of input into decisions about local problems.

The Koban

Like the *chusai-san* (a rural police officer, who is required to visit each household twice per year and works with citizens to solve area problems), the urban police officer in Japan visits neighborhood households and does police business in the koban. These police boxes are the foundation of the sense of security of the

Japanese officers perform their duties in a neighborhood koban. (*Courtesy* Office of International Criminal Justice)

people, and they function as the bases of police functions closest to the citizens. Officers prepare and disseminate crime bulletins and provide citizens with tips concerning crime prevention, stories of good deeds by children, and opinions of residents.[23] Exhibit 14.3 provides a case study of the work of koban police.

A koban may be found every few blocks; there are about 15,000 kobans across the country, 6,000 of which are residential in nature. There are also *mobile police-boxes* or wagons that assist the koban as needed, and temporary kobans are established at times as well.[24] The Japanese police try to keep the number of people for which a koban is responsible to less than 12,000, and the area less than four-tenths of a square mile. No koban may be less than six-tenths of a mile from another one. They are often put in areas with more than 320 criminal cases per year, more than 45 traffic accidents, and a high volume of pedestrian traffic.[25]

Kobans are usually storefront offices or tiny buildings resembling sentry stations. They consist of a reception room with a low counter or desk, telephone, radio, and wall maps; a resting room for personnel, often with a television set; a small kitchen or at least a hotplate and refrigerator; an interview room; a storeroom; and a toilet.[26] The officers' work shifts are long; they spend 24 hours at the

---

Exhibit 14.3 Work of the Japanese Koban

A police officer of the police box of the Sendai Higashi police station, Miyagi Prefecture, visited once a week and took care of a 75-year-old woman who had no relatives in the neighborhood, suffered from diabetes, and had problems with her legs. One day the officer called on the woman and got no answer. Knowing that this was unusual, and in view of her physical state, the officer entered the home to check on her welfare. He found the woman lying unconscious and assisted in hospitalizing her. Then the officer tried to find the woman's relatives and determined that she had a niece living in Sendai. As a result, the aged woman was able to obtain better care with the help of her niece.

---

koban every three days. From a tour of duty in a koban, officers move on to detective work, traffic patrol, riot police, and other specialized assignments.[27] The koban officer also

> has a wealth of . . . data on the jurisdiction . . . such as lists of people working late at night who might be of help as witnesses to crime, of people who are normally cooperative with the police, of people who own guns or swords, of all rented homes and apartments that might serve as hideouts for fugitives of people with criminal records, and of people with mental illness; organizational charts of gangs in the police station jurisdiction (sometimes with photographs of all the gangsters); lists of old people in the area living alone who should be visited periodically . . . and of all bars, restaurants, and amusement facilities in the jurisdiction; a short history of the koban; and a compilation of the total population, area, and number of households in the jurisdiction.[28]

Herein lies a fundamental difference between the Japanese and American police: Whereas American police come to the home only when called by citizens, their Japanese counterparts are constantly watchful of, informed about, and involved with the people in their neighborhoods.

Australia's Policing Strategy

"Stopbreak" in Queensland

Data analysis by Queensland, Australia, police in 1996 revealed that residential burglaries had increased 176 percent during the past 20 years, and 66 percent during one five-year period. Burglaries represented one in five of all criminal offenses. Analysis revealed two contributing factors to the burglary problem: a lack of proper security measures and the ease with which stolen goods could be "fenced" for profit. It was no wonder that many of the 3.4 million citizens of Queensland—Australia's second largest state—no longer felt safe in their homes.

Furthermore, there were disturbingly high rates of repeat victimization and low rates of offender apprehension. The police also concluded that "even if the number of police patrols were doubled, the typical dwelling or business would still only be under surveillance for an average of 60 seconds per day."[29]

A response—termed *Stopbreak*—was developed to address the primary contributing factors. A proactive COPPS philosophy was adopted on several levels. The police were trained in proper security audit techniques, and "hot spots" were examined to reduce repeat victimization and home burglaries in general. Citizens were advised concerning crime prevention and proper security measures they could take in their homes. Victims were referred to victim support organizations,

Australian police officer takes a crime report at a neighborhood station.

and homes and businesses that had been targets of repeat burglaries had temporary, portable silent burglary alarms installed. These alarms were linked to police headquarters.

An assessment found that officers and victims alike indicated that the strategies were substantially positive in nature, and a majority of victims implemented at least one of the security measures recommended by the police.[30]

A Pilot Project in Toowoomba

In May 1993 the Criminal Justice Commission and the Queensland Police Service established a two-year beat policing pilot project in the city of Toowoomba in southeastern Queensland. The impetus for the project was a governmental report that recommended the adoption of COPPS.

This project was designed to promote a community-based policing style, characterized by localized, problem oriented service delivery. The key features of the project were to be the following:

- Assignment of officers to two defined beat areas on a long-term basis; the officers were to reside in these beat areas as well
- Provision of most policing services by the locally based officers
- Use of foot patrols by the beat area officers
- Inclusion of proactive policing activities as part of the normal duties of the officers
- Introduction of a negotiated response strategy[31]

The pilot project was based on COPPS initiatives in the United States and Canada and was designed to incorporate a problem solving orientation into the normal duties of the police officers, so they could focus on the underlying conditions generating calls for service (CFS) and develop strategies to address those conditions. Management and beat officers provided strong support for the problem oriented approach.

After the two-year period ended, the Criminal Justice Commission in Brisbane determined that the number of CFS generated by the top 10 addresses in the beat areas decreased over the first 12 months of the project, that the problems handled by the beat officers ranged from prowlers and alcohol-related incidents to disputes between neighbors, and that the two most common strategies employed by the beat officers to resolve problems were "removing the problem" and preventive activities such as fixing street lighting. Table 14.1 presents other key findings of the Toowoomba evaluation.

Following are four brief case studies of problem solving by beat officers in the Toowoomba area. The first case study concerns police actions involving a mentally ill woman who lived alone and constantly reported "phantom" prowlers; police officers around the globe can relate similar stories of people who repeatedly contact the police about imagined aliens in their homes or other such "invasion." Using the problem solving process, the Toowoomba police were able to address this woman's psychological problems and CFS. The second case study

TABLE 14.1 Key Findings of the Toowoomba Evaluation

Key Evaluation Areas	Major Finding	Main Contributing Features	Future Action (if any)
Problem solving in the beat areas	Problem solving perspective developed and successful problem solving activities identified	▪ Long-term assignment of beat officers ▪ Work environment that encouraged problem solving ▪ Training in problem solving	▪ Provide accurate, timely, and interpretable information to beat officers ▪ Encourage sharing of information across beat projects ▪ Provide appropriate training support
Beat residents' satisfaction with police	Significant increase in levels of satisfaction	▪ Beat officers more accessible and visible ▪ Officers offer more personalized service ▪ More time to interact with the community and undertake proactive duties	▪ Greater use of negotiated response ▪ Reduce administrative burden on beat officers ▪ Conduct a further community awareness campaign
Levels of victimization in the beat areas	Appears to have led to some reduction in property-related crime and stealing offenses	▪ Use of problem solving strategies ▪ Increased community awareness ▪ Greater police visibility and targeted patrolling ▪ Improved flow of information to local police	▪ Treat crime reduction/control as an aspect of problem solving, rather than as a discrete objective
Beat residents' sense of safety	No overall effect on fear of crime (or perception of risk)	▪ Limited impact because of relatively low levels of fear in the beat areas, small scale of project, officers' activities possibly working at cross-purposes, many factors that affect fear outside police control	▪ Reduce emphasis on these issues; alternatively, introduce more targeted strategies
Beat officer job satisfaction	High levels of satisfaction reported	▪ Greater autonomy and discretion for beat officers ▪ Promotion of a sense of "ownership" ▪ Supportive work environment ▪ Positive feedback on job performance ▪ No significant threats to officer safety	▪ Ensure that features contributing to high levels of satisfaction are maintained
Overall assessment	Project substantially successful and should be continued	▪ Project carefully planned and appropriately resourced ▪ Quality of beat officers ▪ Beat policing given an operational focus ▪ Solid organizational support	▪ Make project objectives more focused ▪ Review beat boundaries and staffing levels ▪ Investigate ways of making project more information-driven

Source: Criminal Justice Commission, *Toowoomba Beat Policing Pilot Project: Main Evaluation Report* (Brisbane, Australia: Author, 1995), p. 97.

CASE STUDY 1

Background

Regular calls for assistance about prowlers or persons breaking into her house were made by a woman living alone in one of the beat areas. Police responding to the complaints would find no prowler and no visible signs of entry. The radio dispatcher identified this as a recurrent problem and asked the beat officer if he could "fix it."

Officer Response

The beat officer rang the complainant and arranged to come and see her.

Nature of Problem

While speaking with the complainant, the officer noticed that she showed several symptoms consistent with suffering from some mental illness. When asked who her doctor was, the woman volunteered that she was seeing a psychiatrist.

Strategy

1. The beat officer contacted the woman's doctors about his concerns, explaining that she had been regularly calling the police about "phantom prowlers." That afternoon, arrangements were made for her to return to the hospital to monitor her medication.
2. After the woman was discharged from the hospital, the officer asked one of her neighbors to "keep an eye on her." As the officer is concerned that his continuing presence could aggravate her condition, he keeps in contact with the neighbor.

Outcome

No further calls have been received from the complainant.

CASE STUDY 2

Background

In a relatively low-income area, there was a small, run-down shopping center complex. Several shopkeepers reported to the beat officer that they were regular victims of break-and-enter offenses and shoplifting. They were becoming quite disgruntled with the frequency of the incidents. Analysis of police records confirmed that police were regularly attending this shopping complex.

Officer Response

The beat officer patrolled the shopping center. This gave him the opportunity to observe the shopping center and the surrounding area.

Nature of Problem

The officer identified a number of problems: inadequate security and lighting, bad design of the complex, and the presence of a video store and a bottle shop open late at night.

Strategy

1. The officer negotiated with the video store to reduce their operating hours.
2. The officer discussed the possibility of jointly employing a private security guard with the owners of the video store and bottle shop.
3. The officer approached the owner of the shopping complex about implementing some design changes. The owners were not interested.
4. The officer discussed various strategies to improve security with the shop owners.
5. The beat officer increased his patrolling of the center for a limited period.

Outcome

Various security measures were taken by the stores. Shopkeepers reported that shoplifting and other stealing offenses declined.

CASE STUDY 3

Background

One beat had a significant proportion of elderly residents. One particular incident highlighted the concerns of the beat officer. An elderly woman lay helpless in her home for 36 hours after falling out of bed. The officer broke into her home after being contacted by concerned neighbors.

Nature of Problem

The officer wanted to better protect the health and safety of elderly people living in the beat area.

Strategy

1. The beat officer introduced an "Adopt-a-Neighbor" scheme. This involved residents introducing themselves to their elderly neighbors and becoming aware of their habits, such as picking up the paper each morning. Residents were encouraged to contact the beat officer if they thought a neighbor might be in distress. An "adoption form" was devised, containing details about key holders and contact numbers. This could be completed by elderly residents and sent to the police for use in emergencies.
2. A government welfare agency was provided with kits. There was also newspaper coverage of the scheme.

Outcome

The program was implemented in two beats. About 20 to 30 residents responded. Because of this low participation rate, the officers did not pursue the strategy.

CASE STUDY 4

Background

A family with young boys and a household of older women lived across the road from each other. The boys liked to play football and cricket, and often played in the street. Their balls frequently ended up in the other yard. The women refused to return the balls. This had been going on for some time. However, when [the women] heard there was a beat officer in the area, they contacted the officer.

Officer Response

The officer spoke to the young family about what the boys were doing and their problems. He discussed the problem with the women residents across the road. Their main concerns were the damage caused by the balls to their windows and garden, and the boys playing in the middle of the road.

Nature of Problem

Basically, there had been a lack of communication. Neither party had discussed its concerns with the other.

Strategy

The beat officer brought the two households together to talk through their problems. He decided that his presence was not needed to mediate the discussion.

Outcome

The two families decided that the boys would be more careful about where they played. The balls were returned, and the boys helped fix the garden and repair any damage that they caused. No further complaint about the matter has been made to the beat officer.

deals with another common problem—burglaries and shoplifting in a run-down shopping center. The third describes another ubiquitous police problem: elderly residents who at times fall down and are unable to obtain assistance. The final case study involves a problem that is also familiar and can easily escalate: a dispute between neighbors.[32]

COPPS IN GREAT BRITAIN

There are 41 police forces in England and Wales. There are 27 county police forces, 8 combined police areas (where 2 or 3 counties have been united for policing purposes), and 6 metropolitan forces.[33] Almost all police forces in this region are introducing or are actively considering the introduction of COPPS in some form.[34]

Indeed, COPPS has progressed to such a level in Great Britain that the Home Office in London has published dozens of mongraphs on the subject, including two that are highly significant in the field: the Police Research Group's *Problem-Oriented Policing: Brit POP*, 1996, which described the early stages of a development project implementing problem oriented policing in one division in Leicestershire, and *Brit POP II: Problem-Oriented Policing in Practice*, published in 1998, which highlighted "the lessons learned over the past two to three years for introducing and maximizing the benefits from POP."[35]

A Guiding Philosophy

The philosophy of community oriented policing in Britain, as well as several important aspects of its practice (such as neighborhood based patrols) can be traced to the formation of professional policing in the nineteenth century and the ways in which the police mandate was established and legitimated.[36]

Early architects of British policing established the idea that effective policing can be achieved only with the consent of the community.[37] From the 1970s onward, arguments in favor of greater use of foot patrol have assumed an increasingly important place in public debate about policing in Britain. Community surveys have found that more foot patrol is clearly what most people want. So there has been a return to the bobby on the beat—a virtually unanimously accepted goal of public policy.[38] Foot patrol remains a key feature of community oriented policing in Britain.

Exhibit 14.4 discusses one community's program.

Early Initiatives

Sir Kenneth Newman, who served as commissioner of Scotland Yard from 1982 to 1987, brought to the job a new intellectual dimension and a willingness to challenge existing police practices. He launched many planning initiatives, including the authorizing of his staff in 1983 "to evaluate the feasibility of adopting the 'Problem Oriented Approach' in the Metropolitan Police."[39]

Exhibit 14.4 West Mercia Constabulary's Four Tracks of Policing

West Mercia Constabulary serves 1.1 million people in Herfordshire, Worcestershire, and Shropshire Counties in England, which spread out over 2,868 miles. The constabulary has developed a policing model known as the "four tracks of policing," which sets out a strategic approach to implementing COPPS. The first track, local policing, stresses the constabulary's commitment to local policing and local partnerships to achieve effective solutions to local problems. The second track, responsive policing, focuses on the constabulary's duty to respond appropriately to requests for assistance and to provide adequate resources for emergency situations. The third track, targeted policing, concentrates on using intelligence-based policing operations to solve specific problems. Finally, the fourth track, policing partnerships, recognizes that no matter how effective the constabulary may be in the other three tracks, it is vitally important to work with communities to develop shared solutions.

Source: Workshop presentation, Constable David C. Blakely, The 8th Annual International Problem Oriented Policing Conference: Problem Oriented Policing 1997, November 15, 1997, San Diego, California.

Four problems were selected for study: Asian gangs, shopping victims (on a specific street), prostitutes (in a specified area), and motor vehicle crime. An evaluation of the studies found that COPPS had the potential to improve police performance.[40] The studies demonstrated that the potential for the implementation of COPPS was severely limited unless greater flexibility was introduced into the organization. The Metropolitan Police organization is centralized in its policy making, and management communications are designed by "line" or territory, not by problem. Newman stated in a letter to the force in 1984 that "the structure of our hierarchy [was] hindering more than helping the good work done on the ground." He concluded that "too much energy and effort are wasted in keeping the organization going instead of serving the mainline job of policing" and that "there is a tendency for our organization to try to cope with problems through superficial changes in the bureaucratic system, rather than looking for real solutions."[41] Thus, Newman sought to reduce the rigidity of the organization. In 1985 he wrote that

> The aim of the Metropolitan Police will . . . be to work with other agencies to develop . . . a "problem solving" approach to crime prevention, where, rather than merely dealing with individual acts of law-breaking, careful analysis is made of the total circumstances surrounding the commission of types of crime, taking account of wide-ranging social and environmental factors, in order better to understand—and counter—the causes of those acts.[42]

Today, undoubtedly the key issue concerning COPPS in Britain is accountability. Public opinion is especially intense in London, where no local control over the police exists, and there are about 30,000 sworn officers. Critics are calling for greater role definition for community constables and a greater permeation of the community philosophy throughout the police organization and in its operations. They also argue that if concrete progress is to be made, the mechanics of community policing need to be made visible and the principles they embody openly and skeptically debated. In short, for many to this point the community approach to policing in Britain has been more rhetoric than reality.

The Role of Constables

Britain's constables have a mandate to control crime. They are to "penetrate the community in a multitude of ways in order to influence its behavior for illegality and toward legality."[43] The officer's primary role is defined as being concerned with crime and criminals; and his or her effectiveness is to be judged by the amount of information passed on to colleagues. The emphasis is largely on crime fighting and law enforcement, and contact with the public is to be fostered mainly in terms of its contribution toward meeting these ends.[44]

Public input is growing concerning the police task, however. Almost all of the 41 police authorities in England and Wales now have established formal police–community consultative committees. Some of the issues addressed by the committees are maintaining mutual trust between the police and the public; maintaining community peacefulness and improving quality of life; promoting greater public understanding of policing issues, such as causes of crime and

A British constable provides a tourist with directions at Parliament Square in London.

police procedures and policies; examining patterns of complaints against officers; fostering links with local beat officers; and developing victim support services.[45]

For Britain's police, Neighborhood Watch forms the most common and popular form of community-based crime prevention. Neighborhood Watch programs have grown immensely in Britain. At the instigation of the Home Office, roughly 300 crime prevention advisory panels were established within Britain's 41 police force jurisdictions from 1985 to 1988. And, in terms of patrol deployment, referred to as "general duties," foot beats returned in large measure after being virtually eliminated in favor of motorized units in the early 1970s. By the late 1980s the London Metropolitan Police had assigned 5 percent of its officers to "home beats" as "community constables." These constables were charged with developing an intimate knowledge of their beats, encouraging crime prevention, patrolling on foot, and building closer rapport with the community.[46]

See Exhibit 14.5 for another example.

Contemporary Approaches

A number of recent attempts in Great Britain have introduced problem solving strategies in England and Wales. Following is an overview of past implementations of COPPS in five police forces. The lessons learned from these five locations were used to implement COPPS in Leicestershire.[47]

In London, the *Metropolitan Police* experiment involved the formation of a project team to define and diagnose specific problems, such as prostitution and motor vehicle crime, in four pilot sites. The problems were then addressed by dedicated teams that developed responses. Following riots in an area in *Northumbria* known for high crime and poor police–community relations, police established a dedicated COPPS unit to develop tactics; beat officers were given greater discretion and were encouraged to manage their time and think proactively to get to the root causes of the local problems. In *Thames Valley*, police graded call responses in order to "buy time" for COPPS, so that dedicated beat officers could identify problems. In *West Yorkshire*, COPPS was introduced in Killingbeck, Leeds, with the formation of two cohesive groups of beat officers who shared information and brainstormed local problems. The *Surrey Constabulary* has a long history of interest in COPPS.

Implementation of COPPS in *Leicestershire* and other subsequent venues was made difficult by the variations in the forms of COPPS adopted in the previously mentioned locations. Administrators had to decide between a wide or narrow geographical spread, a short- or long-term lifespan of the initiative, problem identification from the top down or bottom up, the introduction of problem solving teams or the adoption of COPPS by all officers, and the identification of problems by the police or by the community and external agencies. In relation to these questions and concerns, the following premises of successful COPPS implementation have become accepted in Great Britain:

- COPPS can create more time for officers, because the source of problems is dealt with and CFS reduced.

Exhibit 14.5   Problem Solving in Merseyside

The impetus to pursue a problem solving policing style in Merseyside, England, was stimulated by an operation to combat its increasing number of shootings. A project team was established in mid-1997 to consider how the problem solving approach could be adopted across the entire force. The team produced a clearly defined philosophy of problem solving policing; systems and structures that would support the adoption of problem solving policing; a clear definition of the skills needed to deliver this policing style, with subsequent training needs; and a plan (and its costs) for implementation of the approach. The first task was to visit police agencies that had publicly professed to be using problem solving policing to some degree. Next, a comprehensive internal consultation program was conducted to establish the current extent of problem solving activity within the force, introduce the concept of problem solving, identify potential issues that would need consideration in order to adopt effective problem solving, and identify peoples' views on possible solutions to these issues. One-to-one interviews were conducted with all officers and heads of other operational and support departments. A series of focus group meetings was held with a cross-section of front-line staff from each police district, as well as with other citizens and agency heads—a very lengthy process. There was widespread support for adopting a problem solving approach. Two areas appeared to be fundamental to the process: the identification of problems (including the provision of up-to-date information) and the need for training. Eventually the team produced recommendations in five broad areas: structure and organization of the force, systems and processes, information technology, human resources, and marketing. The adoption of COPPS as an "umbrella" philosophy in Merseyside represented a fundamental shift in policing.

Source: Adapted from Brian Gresty and Geoff Berry, "Problem-Solving Policing: The Merseyside Philosophy," in *Focus on Police Research and Development* (London: Home Office Police Research Group, 1998), pp. 12–13.

- Deliberately and systematically introduced, COPPS can build on existing partnership work and yield increased benefits from it.
- Humane and efficient responses to individual incidents can occur alongside COPPS.
- Regardless of COPPS, the police still have to provide a wide-ranging service to the public, for which they will have to maintain their response to non-crime-related incidents.
- Police officers will find COPPS rewarding, and gradually the police culture will accept the centrality of COPPS.[48]

Cleveland Police and Problem Youth

Cleveland Police is the smallest force in the United Kingdom, covering an area of about 24,000 acres in northeast England. The Cleveland force employs 1,500 officers. Hartlepool is the most northerly city in the force area, located on the northeast coast, with a population of 90,000. Cleveland, and Hartlepool in particular, is at the top of almost every poverty index in the country. Most of the problems, furthermore, are centered on the Raby Gardens Housing Estate.[49]

In the late 1990s the police began looking at school truancy rates in Hartlepool: Fifty percent of the youths were offenders (the highest in the United Kingdom). One-half of the youths involved in crime were regularly absent from schools, and 58 percent of the youths had behavioral problems. Specifically, the youths of the Raby Estates area had low self-esteem; there was also a huge schism between the younger and older residents of the area and a lack of parental interest and control. These problems had existed for a number of years, and the police had, by their own admission, been merely "papering over the cracks" where these problems were concerned. The formation of a community policing team was the first movement toward forging a partnership with the community.

First, officers interviewed citizens who had contacted the police concerning problems with youths of the area; it was emphasized that they needed to identify who the youth were and what they were doing. The police promised extra policing and to try to ascertain whether something could be done for the youths. Interviews with the youths determined that they were bored and disillusioned with life. The police approached several public and private agencies to obtain funding to change things. Second, police identified the potential ringleaders and troublemakers and invited them and their friends from the Estates to a series of meetings. Eventually, the "Raby Rebels" was formed; it was composed of and run, policed, and organized by the young people. The Rebels formulated a set of rules that included behavioral boundaries. Meanwhile, legal proceedings were commenced against families who would not take control of their youths.

The most significant breakthrough for the police came when, at one of the Raby Rebels' meetings, the main complainants arrived. The complainants spoke to the group, explaining their side of the matter in a calm, positive way. They offered their support for the youths in the form of fund-raising so the group could continue. This signaled the beginning of a new community spirit. After the meetings there were fewer calls per week pertaining to the youths.

COPPS IN OTHER VENUES

Scotland

Although overall crime had been decreasing in the Strathclyde region of Scotland, many of its 2.25 million citizens perceived that crime rates were increasing dramatically. Violent crimes, however, were increasing; and it became part of the culture of the west of Scotland to carry knives. The Strathclyde police—an amalgamation of six police forces in west central Scotland and the largest in the country—decided that it had to find a solution to the fear and violent crime problems.[50]

The Spotlight Initiative—the first program of its kind in the United Kingdom—was implemented with a "listening tour," as police sought to learn which types of crimes were of major concern to the public. The police learned that minor crimes—litter, graffiti, and disorderly gangs shouting obscenities, smashing bottles, carrying weapons—worried them the most. From this, four fundamental principles of the initiative developed: It must address public concerns, fully exploit corporate partnerships, address serious crimes through concentration on minor crimes, and feature maximum presence of officers on the beat. Eleven major crimes were spotlighted as well.

Division commanders were immediately instructed to seek improved environmental clean-up resources to rid their areas of litter and graffiti. A media coverage campaign was launched to boost the public's and police officers' confidence. To attack minor crimes, the department made greater use of intelligence and crime management systems, employed new technology (such as satellite tracking systems, telephone bugs, high-definition nighttime cameras), and worked with every group with a legitimate interest in reducing crime.

On the day the program was operationalized, officers arrested almost 400 men and women in a series of dawn raids, targeting people who had "forgotten" to appear in court or for whom bench warrants had been issued. Police searched 43,000 people for weapons in the first three months (with the number of people carrying weapons declining about 50 percent). Truancy rates at local schools declined dramatically. The department installed a series of closed-circuit cameras in high-crime areas. Crime declined as well, and more drugs were recovered than ever before. The department was quite pleased with its results.[51]

Isle of Man

Even very small countries have COPPS. One such example is the Isle of Man—part of the British Islands and situated midway between England, Scotland, Ireland, and Wales—which has a land mass of only 227 square miles, measures 33 miles by 13 miles, and is occupied by only 73,000 people.

The Isle of Man Constabulary has large aims, however. Its 2000/2001 Policing Plan reveals its vision:

> We will provide a world-class, community-based policing service to the whole of the Island's community. Cooperation, consultation, and a partnership approach will drive all that we do, helping to make the Island an even safer place in which to live. Our aim: to be a world-class police service. What we will offer: community-based policing excellence.

The constabulary's values statement is also brief but powerful:

A constable from the Isle of Man converses with a citizen while walking a footbeat in a city's business district. (*Courtesy* Isle of Man Police Department)

> Ours is an organization that is open, honest, and caring. The organization itself, and those who work for it, view integrity as being vital to our success.

And its policing style and philosophy are as follows:

> We aim to provide excellence in all that we do. Our policing style will be friendly, approachable, and neighborly, offering the best possible service to the whole of the Island's community. The main driver will be a problem solving approach, both internally and externally.[52]

These may seem to be ambitious statements, but when one views these words in conjunction with the total package of materials that the constabulary has developed and disseminated to its populace—as well as its *Strategic Plan, 2000–2003*—as part of an "extensive program of modernization underpinned by the philosophy of continuous improvement," there can be little doubt as to the sincerity of the organization's resolve.

Israel

In the mid-1990s the police in Israel—providing services to about 5.5 million people—decided to change from a basically reactive form of policing to COPPS, knowing it would not be easy. The national police force had been, for the previous 20 years, engulfed in security duties by virtue of terrorist and other emergency matters. Because of a shifting of police resources to antiterrorist and bomb-disposal units, efforts to reduce crime at the local station level had not been successful, and domestic violence and family abuse had become particularly problematic.[53]

A strategic plan was developed to implement COPPS. A new headquarters unit was established to implement the planned change—beginning with a "bottom-up" approach that would start with the station level and officers in the field, because they best knew the communities' problems. In phase one, the local police and mayors of many communities were approached and asked if they were willing to undertake the change to COPPS. Their enthusiasm was usually high. Then the officers and selected community leaders were trained in the working principles of COPPS. Such training included explanations of the need for the police and the public to collaborate, and the problem solving approach to analyzing and addressing problems.

A three-day planning workshop was then held with the police, community and local organizations and associations. The police station's mission statement was developed, and local problems and needs were scanned, prioritized, and analyzed. The strategic plan was then developed, including timetables, responsible persons, and needed resources. Each police station was to work on 10 objectives during a six-month period.[54]

By the second year of its implementation across Israel, more than 50 communities had undergone the shift to COPPS. Cities were "rewarded" by being allowed to send one person abroad to study COPPS in other countries. Furthermore, the shift to COPPS had advanced to such an extent that the decision was made to effect the shift at the senior management (police headquarters) level. The atmosphere there, however, was not so enthusiastic, being more of a "business as usual" attitude, while the local police stations went about their "quiet revolution." Planning workshops were provided and headquarters' objectives were developed, leading to greater acceptance of the new philosophy. Community Policing Centers were set up in neighborhoods to decentralize services, and a major organizational change occurred, resulting in a greater flattening of the force, to empower local levels and to provide more efficient and effective police services.[55]

Hong Kong

Hong Kong's population is about 6.4 million, making it one of the most densely populated places in the world—up to 25,000 people per square mile in the urban areas.[56]

Hong Kong began practicing some forms of COPPS in the 1960s, with its early policing style being typical of British colonial policing. The result was a series of police–community relations initiatives that were launched in the late 1960s, with a view to improving police–public relations, developing popular trust, and cultivating public support for crime control. During 40 years of evolution of community policing, the Hong Kong Police Force has undergone six stages, involving five major community policing schemes with different focuses:

1. The Police Community Relations Officer (PCRO), a community relations program, focusing on the promotion of police–public relations
2. The Neighbourhoods Police Unit (NPU), a crime control device with the objective of providing convenient locations for the public to report criminal activities to the police and offer support for combating crime
3. The Junior Police Call (JPC), centering on the control of juvenile delinquency and including a range of activities and programs for youth
4. The Police School Liaison (PSL), dealing with juvenile crimes in school by working with students, authorities, and teachers
5. The Neighbourhood Watch (NW), which organized local residents' efforts to control and prevent burglaries and sexual offenses[57]

The first stage of community policing for Hong Kong occurred from 1968 to 1973. With the relaxation of police–public tension as the theme, the police established the Police Public Information Bureau. The second stage was the adoption of a community orientation in crime control that signaled Hong Kong's entering the era of community policing. The focus was on two-way communication, and the PCRO marked the first major attempt by the police to reach community members and involve them in crime fighting.

The third stage was the rapid growth of community policing across Hong Kong. The PCRO was quickly expanded to cover every police district, and the JPC, the PSL, and the NPU concepts were launched. The fourth stage was the retrenchment of the police community relations effort briefly from 1983 to 1985. The focus was on the reorganization of tight police resources for effective crime control. NPUs were replaced by a small scale of Neighborhood Police Coordinators (NPCs)—viewed widely as a step backward from the force's previous police strategy.

The fifth stage involved reassessment, during which community policing was under a severe test in a tight resource situation. There was a lack of consensus among police administration concerning the proper role of community relations activities within the broader context of crime control. The introduction of NW and the restoration of PSL indicated, however, that community policing had remained a preferred strategy for policing the society. The sixth stage was reorientation, with community relations affirmed as the key aspect of the policing strategy. The focus of this stage has been the improvement of the police's public image and collaborative police–public working relationships for crime control.

Today, the PCROs have taken an active role in liaisoning with community leaders, and the NPC police have attempted to work with community members.

The JPC officers have devoted their full attention to approaching young people, and the PSLs have engaged most of their time in keeping close contact with schools and school children. The NW is probably the weakest among all of these programs in terms of communication with the community. Police officers seem more approachable through the NPU and NPC concepts, and the PCRO remains the backbone of the police dedication to COPPS.

Despite these favorable reports, however, there are problems. Although the force recognizes the need for harmony with the public, the organizational commitment to COPPS still appears to be limited because of the lack of a long-term vision for the strategy. There is a strong temporary outlook for the NPU, the PSL, and the NW concepts, and a shortage of well-thought-out action for the PSL and NW schemes. There has not been any rigorous evaluation of the effectiveness of any of these approaches. Furthermore, because of a lack of incentive measures to motivate police officers for COPPS work, they evidence a lack of knowledge and commitment.

Several lessons can be learned from this case study. Hong Kong entered into community policing nearly four decades ago for the primary purpose of obtaining public support for ordering the society. Five major policy schemes have evolved to translate this strategy into action, but they have met with limited success. This lack of progress in the force's COPPS strategy and the limited performance of its policy initiatives are mainly due to the force's pragmatic approach of using COPPS initiatives for the sole purpose of crime control and prevention. Without proper public support, consultation, and participation, COPPS will fall short in attempting to provide a mechanism for addressing crime and disorder.

New Zealand

COPPS has been designated as the principal operational strategy for the delivery of police services by the New Zealand police, as set forth in the organization's Corporate Plan of 1994–1995. The police mission statement is, "To serve the community by reducing the incidence and effects of crime, detecting and apprehending offenders, maintaining law and order and enhancing public safety."[58] Its values statement is to "Maintain the highest level of integrity and professionalism; respect individual rights and freedoms; consult with, and be responsive to, the needs of the community; uphold the rule of law; and be culturally sensitive."[59] Furthermore, its strategic goals for 1993 to 1998 included the implementation of community oriented policing and states that COPPS "will remain the primary policing strategy for service delivery . . . aimed at reversing the upward crime trends of the last three decades."[60]

Figure 14.2 shows the New Zealand strategic plan outline for 1993 to 1998. The New Zealand Police COPPS strategy includes the following:

- *Change style of policing:* Police as individuals and groups work to form a partnership with the community, identify issues and problems, innovate solutions, and share perspectives with the community.

- *Localize resources:* Establish smaller police stations in major areas and community policing centers in communities.
- *Enhance patrol and investigation strategies:* Determine and implement patrol objectives and strategies, adopt appropriate patrol assignments according to time of day and so on, and establish community-based investigators (who will focus on communities rather than type of crime).
- *Engage in problem solving:* Apply the S.A.R.A. model.
- *Adopt a new management style:* Managers are to have a commitment to COPPS, encourage bottom-up innovation, and attend COPPS training and education.[61]

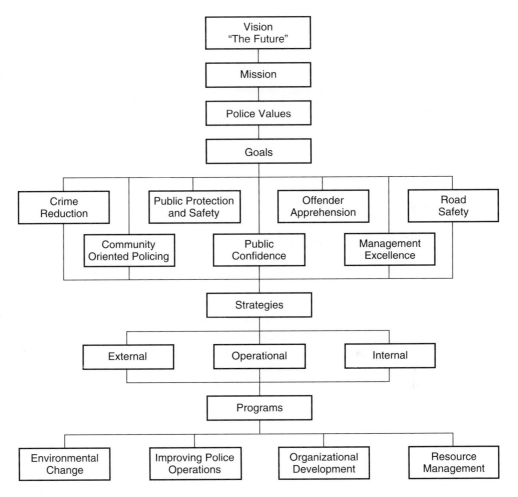

FIGURE 14.2 Strategic Plan Outline, 1993–1998 (*Source:* New Zealand Police, *Strategic Plan, 1993–1998*, Reference Version, December 1992, p. 4.)

Scandinavian Countries

Norway

Norway has produced the most influential report in Scandinavian policing today.[62] Its theory of the role of the police in society can be asserted in 10 principles that are an adequate prescription and philosophical foundation for the community oriented concept:

1. The police shall reflect the ideals of the society.
2. The police shall have a civilian profile.
3. The police must be "integrated" (as an organization).
4. The police must be decentralized.
5. The police officer should be a generalist.
6. The police shall function in interplay with the public.
7. The police shall be an integrated part of the local community.
8. There must be broad recruitment to the police.
9. The police must decide the priority of their different tasks and place the emphasis on preventive activity.
10. The police shall be subject to effective control by the society.[63]

Sweden

The rhetoric of official Sweden is comparable to that of official Norway. Positive relations between the police and the public are considered to be "a vital element in successful police work."[64] Constables in Stockholm work out of neighborhood police offices. The police are not decentralized, however; officers are paid by a National Police Board, and police training and assignment are also nationalized. This means that rookies out of the training academy are assigned to cities as they are needed or requested.

Many if not most of Stockholm's patrol officers are young and grew up in the countryside. Although they work in Stockholm, their spouses and children continue living in the country. Thus, Stockholm has a dominance of officers who would prefer to be assigned elsewhere, who would rather work in a patrol car with another officer, and who do not live in or identify with the city or its residents. As the officers mature, they request transfers to more rural posts to be closer to their families. The prevalence of this kind of officer thus impedes the implementation of a COPPS strategy, because there is little rank-and-file support for neighborhood police posts.[65]

Denmark

Danish police engage in three kinds of preventive policing, with some overlap. The officers teach courses in safety, crime prevention, and drug prevention to school children. Their main task is to develop a positive relationship between the police and the youngsters. These officers address the needs of schoolchildren who have not experienced difficulties with the law.

The city of Copenhagen also employs "SSP" officers—units coordinated and located within police stations to bring together *schools, social workers,* and *police.* Each unit has six to eight members. Basically SSP works with a sizable number of children who have spent a good deal of time on the streets, often come from broken homes, and have been arrested for minor crimes. SSP provides these youths with role models and a "big brother/sister" commitment by police. Denmark is a relatively homogeneous society in which the police can identify with wayward children. No formal evaluations have been done of SSP, but the police regard the program as positive and successful.

Neighborhood police houses are another aspect of COPPS in Denmark. Police there undertake foot patrol, hold meetings with neighborhood residents regarding crime control, teach children in the educational program, work with SSP, and so forth.[66]

Finland

Finnish police have to deal with a significant amount of alcohol abuse among citizens. Helsinki police maintain one of the largest facilities for handling the inebriated in the entire Western world. In keeping with tradition the police have stressed the need to improve preventive measures, such as youth police work (including education in law and traffic safety), providing greater information to the public, and increasing the level of cooperation between the police and the public.

One of the driving forces in the development of a community philosophy in Finland has been the perception of a growing gap between police and the public. The police workload has increased and, under increasing pressure to perform, the police tried to increase effectiveness by seeking more equipment and more advanced technology. As a result, by the beginning of the 1970s, the police had become oriented more toward patrolling in automobiles. The police, who were in contact with the public only in criminal matters, began to be perceived as distant and impersonal. This situation helped lead to the rebirth of COPPS in Finland— a return to the old village police system, with the local police officer living in his or her own district and being considered the village's own officer.[67]

SUMMARY

This chapter discussed COPPS as it has developed internationally. Several common themes or practices are identifiable: the taking of police from their "mechanized fortresses" and putting them into closer contact with the public (together engaging in the use of problem solving methods), decentralizing the organization to areas and neighborhoods, developing a sense of "community," and sharing decision making (empowerment) with the public. We also saw that some venues initiated a pilot project before implementing the concept departmentwide; another common denominator seemed to be the need for sound evaluations of community and problem oriented policing to determine what works.

Finally, this chapter has shown that the community and problem solving approach is not that different in foreign venues than it is in the United States. Perhaps most important, this chapter demonstrated that we are indeed learning from, and sharing with, one another. We are a "global village"; we hope this spirit of scholarly interaction will continue. We should also be mindful, however, that the foreign experience is not necessarily a recipe for Americans to replicate; rather, it can serve as a point of departure in considering what is feasible.[68] These venues offer an opportunity for us to examine issues that might arise as COPPS continues to spread across the United States.

NOTES

1. Mark Kesselman, "Order or Movement? The Literature of Political Development as Ideology," *World Politics*, 26 (1973):139–54.
2. Barry Leighton, "Community Policing: The Canadian Experience" (paper presented at the Third Research and Development Conference, Toronto, Canada), April 10, 1996.
3. *Ibid.*
4. *Ibid.*
5. *Ibid.*
6. *Ibid.*
7. *Ibid.*
8. Vancouver Police Department, application for the Herman Goldstein Award for Excellence in Problem-Oriented Policing, April 1999.
9. *Ibid.*
10. *Ibid.*
11. *Ibid.*
12. Vancouver, B.C., Royal Canadian Mounted Police, *RCMP Community Policing: Strategic Action Plan Update, 1992–1995* (June 1993), p. 2.
13. Greg Saville, personal communication, October 11, 1993.
14. Vancouver, B.C., RCMP, *RCMP Community Policing*, pp. 3–5.
15. Richard J. Terrill, *World Criminal Justice Systems: A Survey*, 4th ed. (Cincinnati: Anderson, 1999), p. 358.
16. Jerome H. Skolnick and David H. Bayley, *Community Policing: Issues and Practices around the World* (Washington, D.C.: National Institute of Justice, 1988).
17. Terrill, *World Criminal Justice Systems*, pp. 355, 365.
18. Ted D. Westermann and James W. Burfeind, *Crime and Justice in Two Societies: Japan and the United States* (Pacific Grove, Calif.: Brooks/Cole, 1991), p. 157.
19. *Ibid.*
20. David H. Bayley, *Forces of Order: Police Behavior in Japan and the United States* (Berkeley, Calif.: University of California Press, 1991), p. 87.
21. Westermann and Burfeind, *Crime and Justice in Two Societies*, p. 159.
22. George L. Kelling, Robert Wasserman, and Hubert Williams, "Police Accountability and Community Policing," *Perspectives on Policing*, no. 7 (November). U.S. Department of Justice. (Washington, D.C.: U.S. Government Printing Office, 1988).
23. "Community Police Activities of Japan." (Tokyo: National Police Agency of Japan, 1992), pp. 2, 9.

24. *Ibid.*, p. 5.
25. David H. Bayley, *A Model of Community Policing: The Singapore Story* (Washington, D.C.: U.S. Department of Justice, National Institute of Justice, 1989), p. 8.
26. Skolnick and Bayley, *Community Policing*, p. 9.
27. Bayley, *Forces of Order*, Ch. 2.
28. W. Ames, *Police and the Community in Japan* (Berkeley, Calif.: University of California Press, 1981), p. 39.
29. New South Wales Bureau of Criminal Statistics, 1996.
30. *Stopbreak*. Queensland Police Service, North Coast Region, application for the Herman Goldstein Award for Excellence in Problem-Oriented Policing, 1999.
31. Criminal Justice Commission, *Toowoomba Beat Policing Pilot Project: Main Evaluation Report* (Brisbane, Australia: Author, 1995), p. ix.
32. *Ibid.*, pp. 46, 48–49.
33. Her Majesty's Stationery Office, "Police Reform: A Police Service for the Twenty-First Century" (June 1993):41.
34. Adrian Leigh, Tim Read, and Nick Tilley, *Brit POP II: Problem-Oriented Policing in Practice* (London: Home Office Police Research Group, 1998), p. 1.
35. *Ibid.*, p. iii.
36. Mollie Weatheritt, "Community Policing: Rhetoric or Reality?" in *Community Policing: Rhetoric or Reality?* eds. Jack R. Greene and Stephen D. Mastrofski (New York: Praeger, 1988), pp. 153–74.
37. *Ibid.*, pp. 155–56.
38. *Ibid.*, p. 161.
39. Quoted in Herman Goldstein, *Problem Oriented Policing* (New York: McGraw-Hill, 1990), p. 54.
40. M. A. Hoare, G. Stewart, and C. M. Purcell, *The Problem Oriented Approach: Four Pilot Studies* (London: Metropolitan Police, Management Services Department, 1984), summary.
41. *Ibid.*, p. 55.
42. Kenneth Newman, *The Principles of Policing and Guidance for Professional Behavior* (London: The Metropolitan Police, 1985), p. 12.
43. Quoted in *ibid.*, p. 165.
44. *Ibid.*, pp. 153–74.
45. *Ibid.*
46. Skolnick and Bayley, *Community Policing*, p. 30.
47. Adrian Leigh, Tim Read, and Nick Tilley, *Problem-Oriented Policing: Brit POP* (London: Home Office Police Research Group, 1996), pp. 4–5.
48. *Ibid.*, pp. 39–40.
49. Cleveland Police, Throston Community Policing Team, *Raby Rebels Youth Project*, application for the Herman Goldstein Award for Excellence in Problem-Oriented Policing, 1998.
50. Arthur G. Sharp, "Putting a Shine on 'Spotlight,'" *Law and Order* (November 1999): 75.
51. *Ibid.*
52. Isle of Man Police Constabulary, *Strategic Plan 2000–2003* (Isle of Man: Author, 2000), pp. 2–3.
53. Ruth Geva, "Community Policing in Israel," *The Police Chief* (December 1998): 77.
54. *Ibid.*
55. *Ibid.*, p. 80.
56. http://hongkongnet/Directory/Facts/Population/population.html (17 September, 2000).
57. Hong Kong Police, *Community Policing in Hong Kong: An Institutional Analysis* (Hong Kong: Author, no date).
58. New Zealand Police, *Corporate Plan, 1994–1995* (no date, author, or location given), p. 7.

59. *Ibid.*, p. 10
60. New Zealand Police, *Strategic Plan, 1993–1998, Reference Version* (no date, author, or location), p. 2.
61. *Ibid.*, pp. 16–17.
62. Norwegian Official Reports, *The Role of the Police in the Society* (Oslo: Universitetforlaget, 1981).
63. Skolnick and Bayley, *Community Policing*, p. 25.
64. *Ibid.*, p. 26.
65. *Ibid.*, pp. 26–27.
66. *Ibid.*, pp. 27–28.
67. *Ibid.*, pp. 29–30.
68. Bayley, *A Model of Community Policing*, p. 29.

LOOKING FORWARD
WHILE LOOKING BACK
The Future

INTRODUCTION

The real role of a police officer is that of a peacekeeper; first and foremost, and
when all else fails, police officers should be viewed as the primary person to
whom one can go if one is in trouble or having problems. This basic premise of
policing runs counter to the old view, held by many, that the police were primarily "law enforcement officers," with an emphasis on *force*. At its root, policing
fundamentally involves and affects the well-being of society. This mandate and
role definition absolutely affects everything the police do; it requires the application of problem solving skills, focuses on crime prevention, and represents a commitment to ensuring that every citizen is treated with dignity and respect.

Policing today, furthermore, is changing as rapidly as when Sir Robert Peel
first put the bobbies on the streets of London in 1829. Indeed, this is an exciting

and challenging time in the history of police service, when officers can look forward to using their creativity, energy, and enthusiasm for the solution of problems. Why should it be otherwise, when we recruit, hire, train, and deploy the best and brightest people into police service that we can find?

This chapter considers COPPS from a variety of angles, from the perspective of the future. First we look at how the police, in some regards, have been enjoying some of their most peaceful times, at least in terms of overall crime rates and federal assistance for their COPPS efforts. Then we look more specifically at those forces that may or will influence COPPS in the future. Included are elements or possible occurrences that are possibly *good* (including how the police will change in form and function), some that could conceivably be *bad* (including the lack of, or poor, implementation of COPPS, crime, demographics, technology, and policing models), and those future outcomes that are decidedly *ugly*. Next we examine the changing nature, role, tools, and work character of the rank-and-file officers—and the challenges they will pose for their superior officers. We conclude the chapter with some relevant questions for COPPS in the future.

Crime and Federal Largesse with COPPS

The crime rate in the United States has fallen for an unprecedented eight consecutive years. At first glance, these would seem to be tranquil times for the police. There has been even more good news in police station houses.

In addition to the drop in crime from 1994 to 2000, the federal Office of Community Oriented Policing Services (COPS), created by the Violent Crime Control and Law Enforcement Act of 1994, spent about $9 billion to help police agencies implement COPPS by adding officers to the beat and providing technical assistance, technology, equipment, and training—while generally promoting community policing across the nation. Specifically, by mid-2000 the COPS office had provided funding to 82 percent of police departments in the United States by awarding more than 30,000 grants to more than 12,000 departments. This included funding more than 105,000 community policing officers and training more than 90,000 officers and citizens.[1]

Funding for the COPS office was renewed by Congress in January 2001 for one more year; $1.3 billion was appropriated for additional officers and to provide new investments in technology.

The Good, Bad, and Ugly

"The cup is half full." "The cup is half empty." Should one be optimistic or pessimistic about the nation's future? One thing is certain: Our society is changing. Chapter 2 examined a number of those changes with people, criminality, and the fear of crime and its effects on neighborhoods—all of which pointed to the challenges that lie ahead for the police.

The following section considers some of those forces that may serve either to "fertilize" or "poison" COPPS efforts—as well as several ways in which society is in a state of flux—with attention to the specific impact those changes will have on COPPS. Those changes could be termed "the good," "the bad," and "the ugly."

Possibly Good . . .

As noted previously, the crime rate in the United States fell for an unprecedented eight consecutive years from 1992–2000, to its lowest point in a generation. Certainly a robust economy and the overall aging of the country (and the failure of the predicted "superpredator" juvenile offender to materialize) contributed in large part to those declines. More and more, however, experts are also pointing to the methods used by police as a substantial cause for the decline in the nation's crime levels—COPPS being prominent among them. It is obviously vital for the country that we stick with what got us here and that COPPS become more deeply ingrained in the fabric of American policing.

Optimists believe that several social forces are favorable to the expansion of COPPS: popularity with citizens, the availability of officers on foot patrol, giving ordinary citizens a say in their local government, empowerment of minority groups, recent federal support for and investment in the concept, a virtual explosion of research into the strategy, and the emergence of a new breed of police executives who are willing to make changes based on empirical evidence rather than relying on tradition.[2] Some futurists also see COPPS undergoing a metamorphosis in the near future, including the following changes:

- Ethics will be woven into everything the police do: hiring processes, FTO programs, and decision-making processes. Emphasis on accountability and integrity within police agencies will increase as policing is elevated to a higher standing, reaching more toward being a true profession—and, concomitantly, the majority of officers will be required to possess college degrees.
- Formal awards ceremonies will concentrate as much (or more) on improving citizens' quality of life as on felony arrests or other high-risk activities.
- Communications will be greatly improved through internal intranets, containing local and agency operational data, phone books, maps, calendars, calls for service, crime data sheets, speeches, newsletters, news releases, and so on.[3]
- Major cities will no longer require policing experience for chief police executives (they may be recruited from private industry). The head of the future police agency will essentially be recognized as a CEO with good business sense coupled with police experience as the trend toward privatization of certain services becomes more prevalent. Knowledge will continue to increase at lightning speed, forcing the CEO to be involved in trend analysis and forecasting in order to keep ahead of the curve.

Advancements in hand-held computer devices will greatly enhance supervisors' management and communications capabilities. (*Courtesy* Reno, Nevada, Police Department)

- The rigid paramilitary style currently effective will become obsolete; it will be replaced by work teams consisting of line officers, community members, and business and corporate people.
- The current squad structure will give way to more productive, creative teams of officers who, having been empowered with more autonomy, will become efficient problem solvers, thus strengthening ties between the police and the citizenry.
- Neighborhoods will more actively participate in the identification, location, and capture of criminals.

The days ahead could be exciting and positive for both the police and the citizenry at large.

Conceivably Bad . . .

It must be remembered, however, that very often "the fleas come with the dog." In other words, both serious and minor problems may accompany the future expansion and application of COPPS across the nation. Following are some of those considerations, including implementation of the concept in general, with possible problems involving crime, demographics, and technology.

Implementing COPPS

Some authors point to what they believe are several unfavorable social forces that militate against the future of COPPS: local governments being pushed toward a more legalistic, crime-control model of policing; a public that is less willing to pay more taxes to address fundamental social problems; and a public policy that does not allow the police to focus on the root causes of crimes, but rather on their symptoms—criminal conduct—through aggressive strategies rather than through COPPS.[4]

Indeed, the landscape of policing is littered with the skeletons of strategies and approaches that died after the departure of a dedicated COPPS chief or sheriff. Although it is hoped that such a fate will not befall COPPS, history has shown that it is a possibility that cannot be ignored. Norman Inkster, Commissioner of the Royal Canadian Mounted Police, believed that

> If we do not welcome new modes of thought and action, we will be powerless to deal with the new age and circumstances that are almost upon us. Police officers will also have to spend more time on the amelioration of human problems than on crime fighting if they are to minimize the cost and pain of social unrest.[5]

COPPS still faces challenges. Many departments continue to struggle with the challenges of implementing COPPS as an organizational philosophy. Two obstacles contribute to this challenge: First, COPPS may be passed off as a fad, or implemented as a series of temporary programs, simply to take advantage of the available federal funding and create a positive public image. Second, police executives may be tempted to turn the tenets of COPPS into dogma, seeking hard and fast rules that conflict with the flexibility and adaptive characteristics essential to the philosophy.[6]

Equally critical to the survival of COPPS is its ability to evolve. COPPS is an outgrowth and reflection of the larger society as a whole, and we need to look only at the rapid transformation of the demographics of the country in general (discussed later) to understand how significant this is. We must continually reevaluate the methods by which we carry out the practice of COPPS.[7]

Many pertinent questions remain. How many police agencies have made a commitment to COPPS? Demonstrated a link between COPPS and improved police performance? Restructured their organizations to support officers who are applying COPPS as a daily practice?[8]

Although much of society has come to realize that the police cannot function independently to address crime and disorder, some segments have not, or have taken the wrong approach. For example, in many jurisdictions officers have been mandated to "partner" as part of their regular duties. Too many agencies have entered into partnerships because they seemed "right." There is, however, more to creating and sustaining effective partnerships; indeed, many partnerships are ineffective. The challenge to leaders, today and in the future, is to develop meaningful and lasting partnerships rather than the superficial ones that exist in many communities.[9]

Furthermore, COPPS calls for police to be empowered, yet many officers may feel uncomfortable exhibiting authority on behalf of their agency, or making sophisticated decisions when attending neighborhood or community meetings. For those officers, the concept of partnership can mean simply attending

PROBLEM ORIENTED POLICING

The Cornerstone of Progressive Policing

POLICE EXECUTIVE RESEARCH FORUM

Training in problem solving has helped officers to better understand the complexities of crime and to address the underlying causes more effectively. (*Courtesy* Police Executive Research Forum)

occasional neighborhood association meetings or visiting neighborhood leaders who live on their beat. Partnerships for the sake of partnership do not endure, and they can work only when the mutual benefits to the parties involved are well defined, understood, and attainable.[10]

Crime

It is also a foregone conclusion—without needing to "look into a crystal ball"— that new criminal types will dot the national landscape in the future: better educated, upscale, older, and increasingly female. Computer crimes will increase dramatically, including cyber-terrorism, identity theft, credit card fraud, consumer fraud, stock market–related fraud, and industrial espionage; these crimes may well become the next national crime-fighting obsession. To meet these challenges, the police must become better educated, adaptable, and equipped. Training will have to be virtually continuous to address complex threats to society.[11]

Chapter 2 discussed the growing rift between the "haves" and "have-nots" fostered in part by the differences between people in terms of access to and knowledge of computer technology. As a result, street crimes and other crimes by the underclass may also increase dramatically, because the underclass believes hope is declining even further. The poor will become poorer, which could contribute to still-alarming levels of youth violence.[12]

Some Dire Demographics

The demographic makeup of the United States itself may pose serious challenges for the police in general and COPPS in particular. For example, single-occupant households represented 17 percent of the total in 1970 and 25 percent in 1997 and are projected to increase to 27 percent in 2010; average household size has been steadily declining from 3.14 in 1970 to 2.64 in 1997. Likewise, the percentage of married couples has gone from 70 percent in 1970 to 53 percent in 1997, with a continued decline predicted.[13]

These figures represent threats to societal stability, because the smaller the household, the less the commitment there is in a population to one another, and the less likely deviance is to be managed at the household level, thus necessitating governmental intervention. Marriage is our most stable family structure; between 1980 and 1997, however, there was a 20 percent increase in the never-married category—the highest rates were among African Americans and Hispanics.[14]

Another destabilizing force is the number of people who in a given year change where they live. The average person moves once every six years. But approximately 17 percent of the population moves each year. Thus, long-term neighborhood stability is the exception rather than the rule. Home ownership— another stability factor—is also of concern, with 72 percent of African Americans and Hispanics and 38 percent of whites unable to afford a modestly priced home. Single females fare even worse—57 percent of single white women, 78 percent of

African American women, and 73 percent of Hispanic women are unable to afford a modestly priced home. Being African American or Hispanic and/or being single is a risk for poverty and criminal victimization.[15]

Technology

As mentioned previously, the rapid expansion in computer technology, although certainly a strong advantage for society overall, bodes ill as well. The first problem lies in adopting computer technologies to policing. Whereas the U.S. Air Force can drop a smart bomb down a smokestack and the army is rapidly moving toward the electronic battlefield, modern day crooks and hackers engage in a variety of cyber crimes, and (even though the technology exists) police are still unable to halt a high-speed chase that threatens the lives of officers and citizens.[16]

Here's another aspect of the police-and-technology problem. From 1995 to 1998 (the last year for which such applications were received), the federal Office of Community Oriented Policing Services poured hundreds of millions of dollars into police agencies by providing grants for equipment.[17] Problems connected with the arrival of new equipment into police station houses have occurred, however. First, many departments lack the in-house computer expertise to install or run the software and equipment. Many police executives believe that they hire people only to be police officers—not to be computer programmers or database experts. But the nature of the policing business is changing; officers with such skills are not only desirable and valuable but are also increasingly and rapidly becoming a necessity as problem solving aids.

In many police agencies, information technology staff are often civilians and are generally kept away from the operational side of the organization. They understand what computers do, but not necessarily how that capability supports the operational needs of the police officer on the street.

The police are already playing "catch-up" to counter passwords, digital compression, steganography, remote storage, audit disabling, anonymous remailers, digital cash, computer penetration and looping, cellular phone and phone card cloning, and a host of other evasive criminal schemes.[18]

Which Policing Model?

Despite the changing environment and population discussed previously, many people remain convinced that the police will not change much and believe in the current policing model—with its so-called war on crime and war on drugs—in which a crime control paradigm assumes that ours is a mean world, that individuals are personally responsible for crime, and that deterrence works. They also believe, in a world with the available technology, the police in the not-too-distant future might be in a position to practice the following:

- In a cashless society, monitoring people's financial transactions would be easier.

Laptop computers and video cameras are advanced technologies that are being installed in patrol vehicles by many agencies. (*Courtesy* Kris Solow, City of Charlotte, North Carolina)

- DNA could be imprinted on our birth certificates and other records.
- Handheld body scanners (like the one in the movie *Total Recall*) will soon be available.
- Organic memory chips could be implanted in police officers' brains.[19]

Surely not many people in our society, which values personal liberty and the right to privacy, would wish to live in such a society.

The alternative model, the peace model, is seen as providing remedies to that of crime control. With its emphasis on restorative justice (a wide range of efforts and programs for making the community—and especially the victim—"whole" after a criminal event), real peace becomes possible when neighbors treat each other as neighbors and practice restitution and reconciliation. The first and best line of defense against crime is to keep it from occurring. Police, citizens, and community organizations must partner to develop and execute a coordinated effort to solve crime-breeding problems.[20]

The Ugly . . .

The bad guys win.

Rebellion of the Rank-and-File,
or, "Revenge of the Grunts"

It would be a tremendous oversight to fail to mention the role of rank-and-file officers among the changes to be witnessed in future police service. For many reasons—including the fact that future generations will have been raised to be at ease and fluent with information technologies, as well as their entering a police service that is much more involved with collective bargaining—future generations of police officers will be vastly different from those of the past.

In the past—particularly under the professional model of policing—while undergoing the academy phase of their training, recruits adopted a new identity and a system of discipline in which they learned to take orders and not to question authority. Indeed, much of the emphasis was on submission to authority. Recruits learned that loyalty to fellow officers, a professional demeanor and bearing, and respect for authority are highly valued qualities. That theme—and the police executive's set of expectations for recruits—must change, however. In the future officers will be hired only if they can critically think, plan, and evaluate. At the same time, chiefs, sheriffs, commanders, and even sergeants will wield less power and control and filter less information; instead, they will move into enhanced roles as coaches, supporters, and resource developers.[21]

People entering police service in the future will not usually possess military experience with its inherent obedience to authority, but they will have higher levels of education and will tend to be more independent and less responsive to traditional authoritarian leadership styles. These recruits will have been exposed to more participative, supportive, and humanistic approaches; they will want more opportunities to provide input into their work and to address the challenges posed by problem solving. The autocratic leader of the past will not work in the future. The watchwords of the new leadership paradigm are *coach, inspire, gain commitment, empower, affirm, flexibility, responsibility, self-management, shared power, autonomous teams,* and *entrepreneurial units.* Therefore, a major need for police leadership will be the surrendering of power to lower-organizational employees (a flattened hierarchy).

Police officers of the future will also function in very different ways and on very different terms than officers of the past. Given existing technologies and what they bode for the future, every officer will function with few time and space constraints, because all officers will be equipped with a pager, cellular phone, and laptop computer with software that includes encryption programs, sophisticated databases, and search engines. These officers will be able to have "real-time" chats with officers from other agencies or in other states or even countries. Every rookie, before going on the streets, will be thoroughly computer literate and able to use crime analysis software.[22]

With such tools, it is easy to envision an officer's home, car, or convenience store becoming his or her workplace. Identification of suspects in the field will take a quantum leap with electronic telecommunication of fingerprints, scanning of retinal patterns, and facial ratio and heat patterns that say positively, "This is the bad guy." Officers will also access maps and data; be able to bring up any call, crime type, or problem by geographic area; and sort this information and compare similar incidents. They will be able to touch their computer keys and ask for the top 10 crimes in their beat area, while receiving instant crime analysis for use in deployment and other operational decisions. All civilians will likewise be trained in computer use.[23]

See Exhibit 15.1 for an example.

Questions for the Future

COPPS has now existed for more than two decades. In the future, will this concept continue to spread and thrive? We believe that it is here to stay. Because it has not yet been embraced by all of the 17,000 police agencies across the United States, however, we close the book with several questions (not given in any order of importance) that, for those agencies, still require answers:

- Will those departments come to believe that they alone cannot control crime, and truly enlist the aid of the community in this endeavor?
- Will those chief executives acquire the innovative drive necessary to change the culture of their departments, implement COPPS, flatten the organizational structure of their departments, and see that officers' work is properly evaluated?
- Will those police executives have the necessary job security to accommodate COPPS? Should at-will employment of chiefs place COPPS at risk?
- Will those departments work with their communities, other city agencies, businesses, elected officials, and the media to sustain COPPS?
- Will police unions work with administrators to effect change needed for COPPS?
- Will police employees who have not yet done so, from top to bottom, sworn and civilian, realize that the traditional "sacred cow," reactive, "widget-counting," pinball-like mode of policing has obviously not been successful and cannot work in the future?
- Can those police departments, from top to bottom, become more customer oriented and value oriented?
- Will those police executives and supervisors develop the necessary policies and support mechanisms to support COPPS, including recruitment, selection, training, performance appraisals, and reward and promotional systems?
- Will those police executives and supervisors begin viewing the patrol officer as a problem solving specialist? Will they give street officers enough free time and latitude to engage in proactive policing?

Exhibit 15.1   Twenty-First Century Police Department: Naperville, Illinois

Over the past decade, companies in the manufacturing, entertainment, and defense industries have used a tool called "process mapping" to help them describe, analyze, and, ultimately, improve how their organizations operate. Recently, members of the city of Naperville, Illinois, Police Department and 23 other police agencies were invited to attend training in process mapping, which involves the development of three different flowcharts that visually depict the series of activities involved in carrying out one of the organization's major functions:

> The *as-is map* describes the organization as it currently exists. This map is based on interviews and observations of people and is used to diagnose waste, duplication of effort, coordination of problems, or breakdowns in the flow of information.

> The *should-be map* makes short-term changes to reduce waste, remove duplication, and improve coordination and flow of information. This map is based on management analysis of the as-is map and suggestions gathered from field personnel during interviews.

> The *could-be map* describes the ideal process for the future. This map is based on the organization's vision and highlights the long-term changes that are needed to get there.

As an example, Naperville is focusing on "crime solving" as the major function to be mapped and is focusing on one crime type: burglary. Process mapping allows the agency to *increase the clearance rate for crimes* by identifying areas where new work methods or organizational changes might improve police ability to investigate crimes and arrest offenders; and it *makes more widespread and effective use of automation and technology* by identifying areas where work processes can be improved, such as automated case reporting.

Source: City of Naperville, Illinois, Web page, "Twenty-First Century Police Department," 1997, pp. 1–2.

- Will those police departments come to view COPPS as a department- and citywide strategy? Will they invest in technology to support problem oriented policing?
- Will those agencies attempt to bring diversity into their ranks, reflecting the changing demographics and cultural customs of society?

The Society of Police Futurists (www.policefuturists.org) provides valuable information about future trends and technologies. (*Courtesy* Police Futurists International)

SUMMARY

This chapter has examined the future of COPPS. Two questions that were asked in Chapter 2 (in discussing our changing society) might again be posed: Does anyone believe the years ahead are likely to be tranquil? Does anyone think we can afford to "hurtle into the future with our eyes fixed firmly on the rearview mirror"?[24] In truth, we could be moving into some of the most dynamic years in the history of the United States; we must anticipate what is coming and plan for it. But much work remains to be done. Police innovation seldom occurs easily. The most difficult obstacle to change for any police agency is probably that which is within—its own resistance.

Where should today's police agency be amidst exponential social, demographic, and technological changes? A major force of the twenty-first century is technology. If the police are not on the cutting edge, they are already behind the curve. But, remember, technology alone will not get the police to where they need to be in terms of serving communities and field officers better, because it merely provides information and allows us to do things more quickly. In addition, the police agencies need to change their structures, cultures, values, and processes; empower their employees and develop them to be professionals; hire and train for new skills; and decentralize the organization and remove barriers.[25]

Another question, posed by former COPS director Joseph E. Brann, is whether we can ever envision a point at which we no longer talk about "community policing."[26] Will there be a time when COPPS is the orthodoxy of policing—the way business is done—when its principles and practices are so ingrained in our policing organizations that we simply refer to them as *policing*? Many people, both inside and outside police station houses, will rejoice when that day arrives.

NOTES

1. Thomas C. Frazier, "Community Policing Efforts Offer Hope for the Future," *The Police Chief* (August 2000):11.
2. Roy Roberg, John Crank, and Jack Kuykendall, *Police and Society*, 2nd ed. (Los Angeles: Roxbury, 2000), pp. 521–23.
3. Dave Pettinari, "Are We There Yet? The Future of Policing/Sheriffing in Pueblo—Or in Anywhere, America," http://www.policefuturists.org/files/yet.html (13 February 2001).
4. Roberg, Crank, and Kuykendall, *Police and Society*, pp. 522–23.
5. Norman Inkster, "The Essence of Community Policing," *The Police Chief* (March 1992):28.
6. Joseph E. Brann, "Where We've Been . . . Where We're Going: The Evolution of Community Policing," in *Community Oriented Policing and Problem Solving: Now and Beyond* (Sacramento, Calif.: California Department of Justice, Office of the Attorney General, Crime and Violence Prevention Center, July 1999), pp. 11–20.
7. *Ibid.*, p. 20.
8. Sheldon Greenberg, "Future Issues in Policing: Challenges for Leaders," in *Policing Communities: Understanding Crime and Solving Problems*, eds. Ronald W. Glensor, Mark E. Correia, and Kenneth J. Peak (Los Angeles: Roxbury, 2000), pp. 315–21.
9. *Ibid.*, p. 319.
10. *Ibid.*
11. Pettinari, "Are We There Yet?" p. 3.
12. U.S. Department of Justice, Federal Bureau of Investigation, "Law Enforcement Futures Project," p. 4.
13. Police Futurists International, "Visioning Twenty-First Century Crime and Justice." http://www.policefuturists.org/fall99/ 21crime.htm (20 October 2000):1–2.
14. *Ibid.*
15. *Ibid.*
16. Pettinari, "Are We There Yet?" p. 1.
17. Jennifer Nislow, "Big Benefits, Huge Headaches," *Law Enforcement News* (May 15/31, 2000): 1.
18. "Cybergame for the Millennium: Cops 'n Robbers Playin' Hide 'n Seek on the Net," *Police Futurist* 8(1):4.
19. Police Futurists International, p. 4.
20. Gene Stephens, quoted in *ibid.*, p. 5.
21. Pettinari, "Are We There Yet?" p. 2.
22. *Ibid.*
23. *Ibid.*
24. Neil Postman, quoted in David Osborne and Ted Gaebler, *Reinventing Government: How the Entrepreneurial Spirit Is Transforming the Public Sector* (Reading, Mass.: Addison-Wesley, 1992), p. 19.
25. Pettinari, "Are We There Yet?" p. 1.
26. Brann, "Where We've Been . . . Where We're Going," p. 19.

PROBLEM SOLVING
CASE STUDIES

Although many examples of COPPS initiatives are dispersed throughout the text, here we provide six case studies specifically concerning the police application of problem solving techniques. All of the venues discussed followed the S.A.R.A. process of problem solving, discussed in Chapter 4 and other chapters. They are as follows:

    I. Casual Labor Problems in California
   II. Crises with Canoe Races in La Crosse
  III. On Broadway, Green Bay Style
  IV. Tracking Truancy in Baltimore
   V. Park Problems in Texas
  VI. School Truancy in San Diego

I. CASUAL LABOR PROBLEMS IN CALIFORNIA

Some residents of Glendale, California, a community of 200,000, had experienced a 25-year problem with day-laborers, or "casual-laborers"—people who solicit temporary employment in residential and commercial areas. Traffic problems, littering, and the use of nearby alleys, parks, lots, and streets as rest rooms were some of the common problems. Two officers met with home and business owners to hear their complaints; the officers also met frequently with the laborers to learn of their problems and obtain their cooperation.

    Many of the laborers, officers learned, were recent immigrants from Central or South America or Mexico; with limited formal education and English-language and work skills, they had few other options for earning a living. Officers agreed that a hiring center could resolve many of the complaints from both sides. An advisory board was created, composed of police, Home Depot (many laborers already gathered near a store to seek work), city officials, residents, Catholic Charities, the Salvation Army, and redevelopment representatives. Home Depot agreed to provide building materials and to fund a staff position for five years; Catholic Charities agreed to administer the site; and officers received two grants totaling nearly $100,000 to fund part of the construction. The city enacted an antisolicitation ordinance to steer casual laborers to the center—which also offered English-language, computer, and immigration law classes.

The number of incidents involving the laborers and police, fire, and other city services decreased substantially, residents are no longer subjected to their strong neighborhood presence, and the laborers no longer use open areas as rest rooms. Employers also benefit from the center, which divides workers by specialties (painting, plumbing, and so forth).[1]

II. Crises with Canoe Races in La Crosse

During the mid-1980s the village of Coon Valley, Wisconsin, began hosting an annual canoe race down a Mississippi River tributary. The spring event attracted students from area colleges and from around the country. Following the races, crowds up to 8,000 people would gather in the nearby town of La Crosse, with its 51,000 residents and another 15,000 college students. During the late 1980s and early 1990s, the crowds had become unruly, injuring police officers with thrown objects, vandalizing and burning police vehicles, and causing firefighters to turn their hoses on crowds to clear the streets. As many as 150 arrests were made each year, often by officers clad in riot gear.

In the mid-1990s the police created a problem solving team, which began by holding several meetings with stakeholders, surveying the college population, and reviewing relevant news articles and police reports. They learned that most problem people in the crowds were not college students and that the worst problems began at tavern closing time.

Prior to the 1993 and 1994 events, police sent letters to local media to solicit their help in presenting a positive image of the event; officers also appeared on television, exhorting students to maintain a positive image for their university. The Tavern League was persuaded to pay for free bus transportation during the event, which helped relieve downtown traffic and drunk driving problems. An alcohol-free college dance was held, and uniformed and plainclothes officers videotaped the event, inhibiting disorderly conduct. The city's public works crew conducted a special cleanup, removing bottles and other debris that might be used to injure others; tavern operators were urged to serve alcohol in plastic cups. Downtown parking was modified, eliminating traffic problems and freeing officers for crowd duties.

In 1994 police made only 14 arrests during the event; there was a "100 percent reduction in confrontation," and neither police nor firefighters had to use force to control the crowds.[2]

III. ON BROADWAY, GREEN BAY STYLE

The city of Green Bay, Wisconsin's Broadway Street had 18 problem taverns operating in a three-block business district, which, during the past 40 years, had witnessed many shootings, stabbings, and other violent crimes; Broadway Street became known as the "Wild West." Officers assigned to the district as problem solvers observed a disproportionate demand for police and rescue services in the area, an unusually high concentration of public-disorder crimes (battery, disorderly conduct, theft, vandalism, prostitution, public urination, and drug activity), as well as visibly intoxicated people engaging in a variety of inappropriate behaviors.

Approximately 20 individuals, mostly intoxicated people and those with mental illnesses, were involved in most of the area's complaints, and most victims of serious crimes were patrons of the problem taverns. A city committee often approved and renewed liquor licenses without question; even convicted drug dealers were granted bartender licenses. No liquor license had been revoked since the 1970s. The environment also contributed to problems, with several taverns having dark alcoves and doorways facing alleys, permitting criminals easy access to the taverns and drug dealers with a means of ducking into the taverns and melting into the crowd. Poor landscaping and dense undergrowth also provided places for intoxicated persons to hide and live on the streets.

The Green Bay Police Department (GBPD) targeted a core group of individuals who accounted for most of the problems in the area. Officers provided liquor store and tavern owners a list of people who were habitually drunk, asking the business people to refuse to sell liquor to these people. (The American Civil Liberties Union challenged this approach as targeting some individuals to be denied legal goods and services, but the policy was defended on the grounds that it was based on a Wisconsin statute prohibiting distribution of alcohol to "known habitual drunkards"; this "no-serve" practice turned out to be one of the most successful programs implemented in the area.)

Officers also issued citations and made arrests for ordinance violations in the area and modified the environment, trimming shrubs, changing building accesses, improving lighting, and eliminating litter and bedding generated by transients. An educational campaign was launched, informing the public about how it could influence who was issued liquor licenses. City ordinances were created dealing with bar owners, including a point system whereby points were assessed against the liquor license on conviction of an alcohol-related offense (12 points over a designated period of time resulted in tavern closure).

During the ensuing four years, five problem taverns were closed and the area experienced an infusion of new business activity—$8 million in public and private investments, 410 new jobs, and 33 new businesses. The area also experienced a 58 percent reduction in calls for service in the same period, along with a 70 percent decrease in rescue calls and a 69 percent reduction in disturbance calls. There was some displacement of some problem taverns and habitually intoxicated persons to other parts of the city where enforcement was not so stringent; this displacement, however, had a side effect: Other neighborhoods asked for, and received, COPPS efforts in their areas as well.[3]

IV. Tracking Truancy in Baltimore

In 1998 community and business leaders and police managers identified juvenile crime and delinquent acts as a major cause of social disorder in Baltimore, Maryland's southeastern police district. Thirty percent of the students were absent at one school—Canton Middle School, an urban school with a racially mixed population of 746 students, where chronically absent students (defined as absent 30 days or more per school year) represented 35.6 percent of the total student body. Juveniles experienced victimization at rates disproportionate to their numbers at the school, and during school hours, many problems concerning graffiti, loitering, petty theft, joyriding, and daytime burglaries were traced to these truant juveniles. Historically, when truant juveniles were taken into custody, they were released to a parent or guardian, and no subsequent sanctions were applied. Research indicates that children make important formative life decisions at the middle school age, and that poor school attendance is a primary barrier to student achievement. Therefore, Canton was selected for the police department's model intervention strategy. A letter, prepared on police department letterhead and personally delivered by a uniformed officer, notified parents of the 50 most truant children of a mandatory meeting with police, school, and social service agency officials.

The police gave parents notice that they were responsible for their children's attendance at school and provided suggestions on how the parents could obtain assistance in that endeavor. The parents were also told that if they did not fulfill their obligations, they would be required to appear in court. Twenty-eight of the 50 targeted students drastically improved their attendance after this meeting. The remaining 22 families were summoned before a judge, who admonished the parents and informed them that they had but one more chance to improve their children's attendance. When 10 children still remained truant, their families were prosecuted and convicted for "Failing to Send Child to School." One parent was incarcerated for a weekend, and the others were given combined probation and community service.

A designated truancy officer visited at-risk students at their homes to ensure that they were attending school and to let them know that the police department was monitoring their delinquent behavior. The results of this intervention are promising: Canton's chronic absenteeism dropped from 35.6 percent of the student body to about 12 percent. Indeed, for the first time, the school's overall attendance rate was higher than 90 percent—the highest rate of any school in Baltimore. Daytime crime and loitering were also reduced, students began participating in school activities at high rates, and the police developed a mentoring program as part of the ongoing police–school partnership.[4]

V. Park Problems in Texas

Blue Hole Park in Georgetown, Texas, is located about 20 minutes north of Austin, along the San Gabriel River. A picturesque park, it is surrounded by limestone cliffs and oak trees. In the mid-1990s, however, the park became the site of much crime and disorder, with the police frequently sent there to deal with problems involving assaults, disorderly conduct, drownings, drug offenses, fights, indecent exposure, drunkenness, and robberies. Many visitors—including soldiers from a large nearby army base—had little interest in the park's future, leaving their trash and debris around the park as well.

Three officers anaylzed the problems by meeting with a nearby neighborhood group and reviewing police reports. Several concerns were identified: Park users, often intoxicated, jumped off the 30-foot-high cliffs into the river, resulting in injuries and drownings. There was no parking area, and up to 200 pedestrians mingled with vehicle traffic along the roadway. For immediate control, officers began enforcing laws in the park. Then, learning that the land on which the cliffs were located was privately owned, trespassing laws were enforced. A traffic control plan was initiated, and a local rock quarry donated enough large boulders—260 tons of them—to create a barrier along the riverbank, better defining the roadway and restricting parking. Military authorities, apprised of the situation, warned soldiers against causing problems at the park. Brush and trash were removed. People stopped jumping from the cliffs, and traffic became orderly and safe. Only about 10 calls for service were made to the police during the ensuing year, and there were few medical or fire calls.[5]

VI. School Truancy in San Diego

Much has been written about COPPS initiatives in San Diego. One of the SDPD's most recent successful efforts involved serious school truancy problems. An undercover police officer at one high school overheard students openly discussing skipping classes in order to buy, sell, and use illegal drugs. Two officers were assigned to the problem and began by speaking with more than 40 school administrators, justice system officials, and social service providers. Everyone believed that the problem was even worse than officially recognized; because school funding was tied to attendance rates, school administrators had a disincentive to document the problem accurately.

Problem analysis revealed that 60 percent of thefts, 43 percent of burglaries, and 29 percent of robberies in the school's vicinity where juveniles were suspects occurred during school hours, as did 59 percent of juvenile victimizations. Officers first took the unusual step of surveying truants—25 of the most chronic ones—and learned that 73 percent admitted having committed crimes other than truancy. Their motivations for skipping school were also determined (boredom, being too far behind in schoolwork, dislike for teachers, and tiredness). Officers also learned when the students were most likely to skip during the school day, where they hung out, and different measures that would deter them from skipping school (most citing tighter controls, including juvenile hall and police enforcement).

A Juvenile Enforcement Team (JET) was launched, which quickly compiled a listing of the 65 most chronic truants. The schools were contacted each day to learn which of those students were absent. Each day, an hour before school started, JET officers visited an average of five children they believed needed extra attention—even obtaining written parental consent to come into the children's homes and encourage them to get out of bed. Some chronically absent children wanted to attend school but were not permitted to because of medical conditions such as lice. Others came from families that did not speak or understand English, thus parents could not comprehend school correspondence regarding their children's absences. A legal gap was also found to exist between the state's statutes concerning chronic truancy and the municipal ordinance for daytime loitering. Daytime loiterers were sent to traffic court, whereas chronic truants were referred to a school attendance review board, which might take up to six months before a student's case would be heard. A new ordinance was drafted to bridge this gap. A retired National Football League head coach was recruited to establish a mentoring program.

Before the team began increasing enforcement of truancy violations, the average chronically absent students missed 43 percent of school days; after the program, this rate dropped to 18 percent.[6]

NOTES

1. Rana Sampson and Michael S. Scott, *Tackling Crime and Other Public Safety Problems: Case Studies in Problem Solving* (Washington, D.C.: U.S. Department of Justice, Office of Community Policing Services, 2000), pp. 125–26.
2. *Ibid.*, pp. 89–91.
3. "Street Sweeping, Broadway Style: Revitalizing a Business District from the Inside Out." In U.S. Department of Justice, National Institute of Justice, *Best Practices in Problem-Oriented Policing: Winners of the 1999 Herman Goldstein Award for Excellence in Problem-Oriented Policing* (Washington, D.C.: Author, November 1999), pp. 1–7.
4. "Reducing Chronic Truancy and Daytime Delinquency." In U.S. Department of Justice, National Institute of Justice, *Best Practices in Problem-Oriented Policing: Winners of the 1999 Herman Goldstein Award for Excellence in Problem-Oriented Policing* (Washington, D.C.: Author, November 1999), pp. 8–11.
5. Sampson and Scott, *Tackling Crime and Other Public Safety Problems,* pp. 135–37.
6. "Truancy Control Project: Juvenile Enforcement Team Officers Help Remove Attendance Barriers." In U.S. Department of Justice, National Institute of Justice, *Best Practices in Problem-Oriented Policing: Winners of the 1999 Herman Goldstein Award for Excellence in Problem-Oriented Policing* (Washington, D.C.: Author, November 1999), pp. 27–30.

A Community Survey in Fort Collins, Colorado

Following is the Community Service Survey formerly used by the Fort Collins, Colorado, Police Department (FCPD) and adopted by many other police agencies. Respondents may complete the survey via the Internet, clicking on their responses.

For items 3 and 4, which ask how safe the city and the respondent's neighborhood are, possible responses are "no response," "very safe," "above average safety," "average safety," "below average safety," and "very unsafe."

For item 5, which asks how often certain activities or crimes occur in the respondent's neighborhood, possible responses are "no response," "never," "rarely," "sometimes," "often," and "constantly."

For items 6, 7, and 8, dealing with rate of satisfaction with the FCPD in different types of contact, possible responses are "no response," "very satisfied," "somewhat satisfied," "satisfied," "somewhat unsatisfied," and "very unsatisfied."

For item 9, asking whether respondents would support different types of police responses to nonemergency type calls, possible responses are "no response," "yes, this is acceptable," and "no, this is not acceptable."

Item 10 asks respondents to indicate whether they agree or disagree with several statements concerning police activities and programs; possible responses are "no response," "strongly agree," "somewhat agree," "agree," "somewhat disagree," and "strongly disagree."

For item 11, regarding the importance to the community of various police department programs, possible responses are "no response," "very important," "important," "somewhat important," "not very important," and "unimportant."

Fort Collins
POLICE

Community Service Survey

Dear Members of the Fort Collins Community:

We at Fort Collins Police Services are interested in your thoughts and ideas! We know our citizens are concerned about crime and safety in their neighborhoods. We also know that the citizens of this community have some excellent ideas about how to deal with these important issues. We are asking for your assistance in identifying problems to which you believe we should be responding differently. In addition, we are interested in your opinion of our current performance. Please assist us by completing the following survey. It should only take about 20 minutes to complete. Thank you for your help!

Sincerely,

Dennis Harrison, Chief of Police

A printed version of this survey is also available if you would prefer. If you'd like us to mail one to you, or if you would like to speak to someone about the survey you may call Officer Bud Bredehoft at (970) 221-6830, or send him e-mail at lbredehoft@ci.fort-collins.co.us.

Your Neighborhood

Please complete this survey based upon where you live in the City of Fort Collins. You may answer all of the questions, or as many as you'd like.

1. Where do you live in Fort Collins?

Use the map and select the area number which includes the area in which you live: (The areas extend beyond the map along the streets indicated by the thick black area boundary lines)

No Response ▾

1a. I do not live in Fort Collins, but I work or attend school in area:

No Response ▾

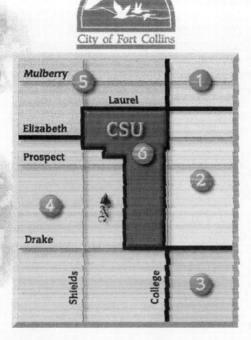

2. What is your age group?

No Response ▾

3. How safe of a place to live is Fort Collins?

No Response ▾

4. How safe of a place to live is your neighborhood?

No Response ▼

5. Let us know how often the following activities or crimes occur in your neighborhood:

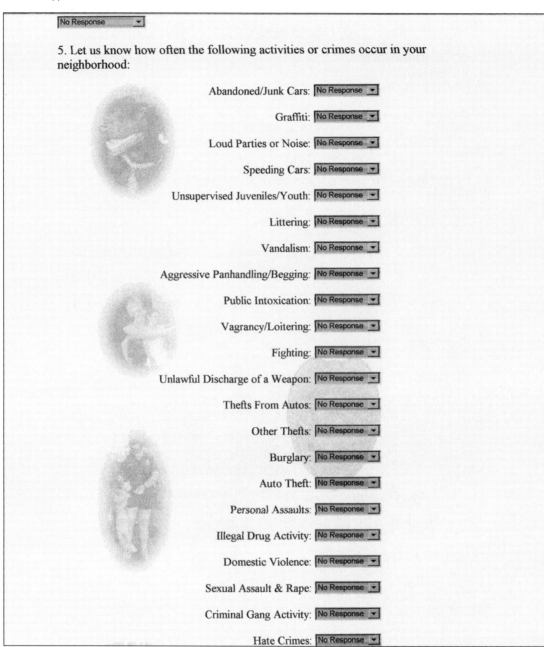

Abandoned/Junk Cars: No Response ▼

Graffiti: No Response ▼

Loud Parties or Noise: No Response ▼

Speeding Cars: No Response ▼

Unsupervised Juveniles/Youth: No Response ▼

Littering: No Response ▼

Vandalism: No Response ▼

Aggressive Panhandling/Begging: No Response ▼

Public Intoxication: No Response ▼

Vagrancy/Loitering: No Response ▼

Fighting: No Response ▼

Unlawful Discharge of a Weapon: No Response ▼

Thefts From Autos: No Response ▼

Other Thefts: No Response ▼

Burglary: No Response ▼

Auto Theft: No Response ▼

Personal Assaults: No Response ▼

Illegal Drug Activity: No Response ▼

Domestic Violence: No Response ▼

Sexual Assault & Rape: No Response ▼

Criminal Gang Activity: No Response ▼

Hate Crimes: No Response ▼

Additional comments:

Contact with the Police

6. Rate your level of satisfaction with the Fort Collins Police in the following areas:

How often an officer patrols your neighborhood: No Response ▼

General police service in your neighborhood: No Response ▼

7. If you personally had contact with Fort Collins Police Services within the past 12 months, rate the level of service you received based upon the following type(s) of contact you had:

Called 911 for emergency assistance: No Response ▼

Called for a non-emergency reason: No Response ▼

Dealt with a police officer in person: No Response ▼

Spoke on the phone with an officer: No Response ▼

Received a traffic citation: No Response ▼

Was stopped by the police but not cited: No Response ▼

Contacted a Police Services employee who was not a police officer: No Response ▼

Other personal contacts not listed above:

What could we have done to improve your contact(s) with Police Services?

Service Expectations

8. Rate your level of satisfaction with the Fort Collins Police in the following areas:

Providing quick response to emergency situations: No Response ▼

Controlling crime in your neighborhood: No Response ▼

Helping with neighborhood nuisance problems: `No Response ▼`

Providing crime prevention advice: `No Response ▼`

Understanding community concerns: `No Response ▼`

Providing fair and equal treatment to all: `No Response ▼`

Handling citizen complaints against police officers: `No Response ▼`

9. Calls for service which are not emergencies can often be handled by alternative, non-traditional methods. Please indicate whether or not the following options would be acceptable to you:

The officer schedules an appointment to meet you at a later time:
`No Response ▼`

The report is handled over the telephone:
`No Response ▼`

You fill out a report form and mail it to the Police Department:
`No Response ▼`

You fill out a report and fax it to the Police Department:
`No Response ▼`

The report is made in person at the Police facility:
`No Response ▼`

`Additional comments:`

Community Involvement

10. Please indicate how strongly you agree or disagree with the following statements:

Police officers should spend more time making personal contacts with neighborhood residents and businesses instead of only responding to incidents as they occur:
`No Response ▼`

Police officers should be assigned to a neighborhood on a long-term basis:
`No Response ▼`

I would like to see officers more involved in community programs such as school activities and scouting:

> [No Response ▼]

I feel comfortable contacting the Police Department to make suggestions or complaints against its employees:

> [No Response ▼]

Making communities safer and more livable is a responsibility that should be shared by both the police and community residents:

> [No Response ▼]

I would like to be informed of community policing activities in my neighborhood:

> [No Response ▼]

The police should receive cultural training to better serve our minority communities:

> [No Response ▼]

11. Please indicate the importance to the community of the following Police Department programs:

Neighborhood Watch Programs:

> [No Response ▼]

Citizen Patrol:

> [No Response ▼]

Gang Prevention:

> [No Response ▼]

Bicycle Patrol:

> [No Response ▼]

Citizen's Academy:

> [No Response ▼]

Motorcycle Traffic Patrol:

> [No Response ▼]

Neighborhood Police Sub-Stations:

> [No Response ▼]

Drug Abuse Resistance Education for kids (D.A.R.E):

> [No Response ▼]

School Resource Officer Program:

> [No Response ▼]

Loud Party/Disturbance Enforcement:

No Response ▼

Downtown Cruising Diversion:

No Response ▼

Specialized Drunk Driving Enforcement:

No Response ▼

Abandoned Vehicle Enforcement:

No Response ▼

Underage Drinking/Liquor Enforcement:

No Response ▼

Foot Patrol in Business Areas:

No Response ▼

Camera Radar Enforcement Program:

No Response ▼

Automated Traffic Enforcement via Intersection Cameras:

No Response ▼

```
What community programs would you like to see
implemented in Fort Collins?
```

```
Any other comments?
```

```
   Clear all fields              Submit the form
```

When you are finished, click on
the submit button once please.

If you would like to speak to someone about this survey you may call Officer Bud Bredehoft at
(970) 221-6830, or send him e-mail at lbredehoft@ci.fort-collins.co.us.

Thank you very much for your time!

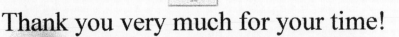

Fort Collins, Colorado Police Services
http://www.ci.fort-collins.co.us/C_SAFETY/C_POLICE/

City of Fort Collins Website Information

--Click on text in graphic below for action indicated--

Search City Website   City Service Locator

Contact Information

Department Home   City Switchboard   Mail Department   Mail Webmaster

Search City Website | Copyright Information | City Service Locator
Department Home | City Switchboard | Mail Department | Mail Webmaster

[RETURN TO TOP OF PAGE]

Source: Reproduced by permission of the Fort Collins, Colorado, Police Department.

A STRATEGIC PLAN SURVEY IN PORTLAND, OREGON

As part of the review and updating process of its community policing strategic plan for 1998–2000, the Portland Police Bureau solicits citizen input concerning how goals are to be achieved. Citizens may complete the survey via the Internet or using conventional means.

Following is the bureau's two-page "Community Policing Strategic Plan Suggestions" survey instrument on the Internet.

Community Policing
Strategic Plan Suggestions

The Portland Police Bureau is asking for your ideas in order to create a working draft of the 1998-2000 Strategic Plan. You do not need to be an expert on past strategic plans to provide valuable information; a good idea of what public safety efforts are working and what still needs attention is all that is needed. Thank you for your assistance on this project.

First Name _____

Last Name _____

Organization _____

Address _____

City _____

State _____

Zip _____

Phone _____

E-mail _____

These comments (check one):

☐ are my personal opinion
☐ reflect the views of my organization or unit

1. In the last two years, what activities or programs have substantially contributed to reducing crime and the fear of crime in Portland? Give examples of ones that stand out.

> [blank box]

2. What activities or strategies are particularly important to work on in the next two years? These can be existing efforts that should continue, new ones that should be implemented or existing efforts that need more attention.

> [blank box]

Use the "Submit" button to send us your comments.

> Submit

If you wish to respond in greater detail by mail, please attach this page as a cover sheet.

Return replies to:

Strategic Plan
Portland Police Bureau
1111 S.W. 2nd Ave., Room 1552
Portland, OR 97204

Fax: 823-0289

Interoffice: B119/R1552

INDEX

A

Abilities, evaluation of, 333–36
Abington, Virginia, COPPS initiative in, 365–66
Academy training, 170, 221–22
Accelerators of crime, 41–42
Access control, 139, 141
    natural, 133
Access to police service, equal, 331
Accountability of police, 313
    in Britain, 392
    geographic accountability, 357
    in Japan, 380
Administration, COPPS and, 167–70
Administrative crime analysis, 103
Adopt-a-School/Adopt-an-Officer, 131
Affirmative action programs, 251
African Americans. *See also* Minority groups; Police-minority relations
    arrest rate, 255
    changing laws and civil unrest and, 250–52
    culture of, 262–63
    disparity in case processing for, 257–58
    race riots and, 250–51
Alcohol, as crime accelerator, 41, 42
Alcoholics Anonymous, 286
Alcohol-related crimes, 286–88, 423
    case study of COPPS approach to, 423

Alternative Policing Strategy, Chicago (CAPS), 344
Amendment to Civil Rights Act (1972), 250
American approaches to COPPS, 348–73
    in large communities, 348–57
    in medium-sized communities, 357–65
    in small communities, 365–69
American Bar Foundation, 17
American Civil Liberties Union, 423
    Police Practices Project, 253
Analysis by officers, evaluating, 333
Analysis stage of S.A.R.A., 92–96
Angotti, Joseph, 46
Anti-Defamation League, 268
Antiwar movement, 16
Applicants, screening, 208–9
Arlington, Texas, dealing with cruising in, 299
Arlington County, Virginia, 168
    citizens' police academies in, 243
    COPPS initiative in, 357
Arrests, 17, 97, 147
    discriminatory patterns of, 255
    for drug abuse violations, 277
    proactive, 148
Arroyo Grande, California, COPPS initiative in, 366–67
Asian Americans, cultural customs of, 262
Assessment stage of S.A.R.A., 97–99

Assessment variables, 335
Aurora, Colorado, partnerships in, 61
Austin, Texas, COPPS initiative in, 348–49
Australia, community strategy in, 382–90
    "Stopbreak" response in Queensland,
        382–84
Authority
    cultural differences relating to, 271
    developing new forms of limited, 98
Automobile, preventive patrol by, 13. *See also*
        Patrol cars
Awareness of officers, evaluating, 333

B

Baby boomers, 30, 32, 33
Baby boomlet generation, 33
Baby busters (Gen-X), 33
Baldwin, James, 258–59
Baltimore, Maryland
    COPPS implementation in, 178, 185
    tracking truancy in, 424
Barriers to COPPS, identifying, 239–40
Barrow, Alaska, alcohol problems in, 289
Battered women, 290
Battered women's shelters, 149
Bayley, David, 322, 379
Beat profile, 117
Beliefs, debilitating, 194–96
Bennett, Arnold, 306
Beveridge, William, 51
Bias-motivated crimes, 268, 269–70
"Big brother" nature of community policing,
        concern with, 310
Big Brothers/Big Sisters of America, 148
Binge drinkers, 286, 289
Bittner, Egon, 17
Blacks. *See* African Americans
Blackwood's Magazine, 3
Block Watch. *See* Neighborhood Watch
Body position, cultural differences regarding,
        263
"Bombshell" technique, avoiding, 193
Boot camps, correctional, 148
Boston, Massachusetts
    crime reduction in, 40, 149, 150–53
    gangs in, 280–81
    Police Department, 128
        training in, 221–22, 223
Braiden, Chris, 87, 317
Brann, Joseph E., 419–20
Bratton, William, 169, 201
Bribery, 268–70
Bridgeport, Connecticut, crime prevention in,
        134
Bristol, Virginia, corrections initiative in, 73
British Columbia, COPPS initiative in, 376–77,
        379
Broken Arrow, Oklahoma, 212–13
"Broken windows" theory, 126

Brown, Lee P., 83–84, 206
Brown v. *Board of Education of Topeka*, 250
Budgeting, rewarding failure through, 68–69
Buerger, Michael E., 218
Bureaucracy of policing, 196–97
Bureau of Justice Studies, 217
Business, borrowing ideas from, 69
Business leaders, COPPS education for, 242

C

California, casual labor problems in, 421–22
California Department of Justice, 102
Calls for service
    analysis of data, 110–16
    controlling, 330
Camden, New Jersey, 211
Campbell, John, 294
Canada, National Crime Prevention Council
    in, 144
Canadian COPPS, 375–79
    Royal Canadian Mounted Police, 376, 378
    in Vancouver, 376–77, 379
CAPS (Chicago Alternative Policing Strategy),
        344
Carroll, Lewis, 157
Case processing, racial disparities in, 257–58
Case studies, training with, 236–37
Causal relationship, 343
CD-ROM training, 227
Challenges for police, 47–48
Challenge to Change, 293
Champaign, Illinois, addressing prostitution
        in, 298
Change from within police departments, need
        for, 317–18. *See also* Culture in agency,
            changing
Charlotte, North Carolina, school safety pro-
        gram in, 292
Charlotte-Mecklenburg, North Carolina
    false alarms in, 301
    Police Department problem solving training,
        246
Chekhov, Anton, 276
Chelsea, Massachusetts, conflict intervention
        in, 265–66
Chicago, evaluation of COPPS in, 344
Chicago Alternative Policing Strategy (CAPS),
        350–52
Chicago Area Project (CAP), 124–25
Chicago Police Department, 108
    COPPS initiative in, 349–52
    crime prevention by, 133
Chief executive(s)
    as change agent, 199–200
    COPPS and, 167–69
    in future, 409–10
    new leadership style required of, 197
    as risk takers and boat rockers, 199–200
Child custody problems, addressing, 354

Chinese culture, 263
CIAF approach to mentally ill, 285
Citizen involvement, 21, 22
Citizens
  crime control role of, 13
  responsibilities of, 53–54
Citizen satisfaction, COPPS effect on, 331
Citizens' police academy, 243, 267
City employee police academy training, 244
Civil disorders
  riots, 6–7, 250–51
  wave of (1840–1870s), 6–7
Civil law, control through, 99
Civil Rights Act of 1964, 250
Civil rights movement, 16
Civil service systems, 10
Civil society, 53
Clarke, Ronald V., 126, 138
Clearwater, Florida, dealing with homeless in,
  285–86
Cleveland Police, Great Britain, problem youth
  and, 395
Clienthood, individualism vs., 52–53
Closed circuit television (CCTV) cameras, 146
Coach, sergeant as, 237–39
Cochran, Barbara, 46
Cohen, L.E., 125
Coining, 270
Collaboration
  collaborative approach of COPPS, 99–103
  guide to, 100–101
Collaborative problem solving, 233
Colleges, COPPS initiatives of, 370–71
Columbia, South Carolina, Police Department
  performance evaluation, 337
Columbine High School massacre (1999), 290
Command structure, decentralized, 330
"Common wisdom" of policing, new, 17
Communication
  cultural differences in, 262–63
  in future, 409, 410
  nonverbal, 263, 271
  by officers, evaluating, 333
Communitarianism, 53–54
  crime prevention and, 129–30
Community(ies)
  concern over assumption of, 307–9
  crime prevention and, 128–30, 150
  "mental state" of, 340
  mobilization of, 98, 147
Community crime control movement, 17
Community Crime Patrol, 131
Community engagement, 232–33
Community members, COPPS education for, 242
Community needs assessment, 161–62
Community oriented government, 51–79
  communitarianism, 53–54
  illustration of, 73–76
  need for shift in basic model of governance,
    77–78
  partnerships, building, 55–59, 82, 329

examples of, 60–62
  in future, 412–13
  total quality management and, 59–66
  volunteerism, 54–55, 56–57
Community oriented policing and problem
  solving (COPPS), 21, 80–121
  application of
    to domestic violence, 288–90
    to drug violations, 277–79, 280
    to gangs, 279–82
  baccalaureate degree in, 228
  basic principles of, 99, 104–5
  collaborative approach of, 99–103
  concerns and criticisms about, 306–21
    responses to issues, 308–9, 310–12, 315,
      316–18, 319
  crime prevention and, 129, 130–33
  cruising and, 297–99, 300
  definition and illustration of, 99–103
  false alarms and, 299
  implementation of. *See* Implementation of
    COPPS
  Internet, use of, 229–30
  leading and supervising, 416
  minorities and, 259–64
  in Mount Pleasant, South Carolina, 164
  planning of, 157, 158–65
    issues in, 163–65
    needs assessment, 161–62
    participants in, 160–61
    planning document, 162–65
    strategic, 158–62
  problem analysis and, 101–3
  prostitution, dealing with, 296–97
  rental properties and neighborhood disorder
    and, 292–96
  social ecology of, 167
  software for, 117–18, 119
  special populations and, 282–88
  technology of, 416–17
  training for. *See* Training for COPPS
  ways to undermine, 184, 186–87
Community participation, 21, 23
Community Patrol Officer Program (CPOP),
  21
Community policing, 81–84
  basic principles of, 81–82
  "big brother" nature of, concern with, 310
  building partnerships, 82
  contemporary activities of local agencies,
    118
  examples of programs, 82
  in Great Britain, 390–95
  with meetings, 148
  officer's work day in, 86
  paradox of, 308
  police-community relations (PCR) programs
    vs., 82
  problem oriented policing (POP) and, 84
  rural, 369–70
  traditional policing vs., 82–84, 85

Community Policing Consortium, 225, 226, 329
Community problem solving era, 21–24
  reasons for emergence of, 23–24
Community Problem Solving Policing Data-Base Management System (DBMS), 355–56
Community surveys, 66, 74, 117
  to evaluate performance, 344–45
    methods and issues, 338–40
    purpose of, 338
  in Fort Collins, Colorado, 427–35
Competition from private security companies, 17
CompStat meetings, 320
CompStat program, 108, 328
Computer-aided dispatch (CAD) system, 107, 110, 116, 354, 355
Computer-assisted training, 223
Computer crime, 43, 413
Computer-generated crime maps, 107–8
Computerized data, 311
Computer software, 117–18, 119
Computer technology in future, 414, 419
Concord, California, Police Department, 56
Conducting Community Surveys: A Practical Guide for Law Enforcement Agencies, 338–39
Conflict
  civil disorder wave of 1840s to 1870s, 6–7
  in police-minority relations, 250–53
Conflict Intervention Unit (CIU), 266
Constables in Great Britain, role of, 392–93
Constitutional rights, equity of, 331
Control, professionalism and emphasis on, 12–13
Controllers, 95
Conyers, John, 254
Cooperation, interdepartmental, 352–53
Coordination of officers, evaluating, 335
COPPS. *See* Community oriented policing and problem solving (COPPS)
COPS, 24, 118, 219, 222, 225, 226, 319, 321, 327, 408, 414
Cops and Cons program, 131
Corcoran, California, citizen police academy in, 267
Cordner, Gary, 320, 321
Correctional boot camps, 148
Corrections, community, 72–73
Corruption, 7–8
Counseling services in Japanese police stations, 380
Courts, community-focused, 71–72
Co-workers' attitudes, survey on, 342
CPTED. *See* Crime prevention through environmental design (CPTED)
Crack cocaine, 279. *See also* Drugs
Crime(s)
  accelerators of, 41–42
  changing nature of, 34–44

COPPS' effect on, 331
cost of, 35–37
decline in, 34–41
demographics and, 413–14
fear of, 16, 44–46
increase in late 1960s, 15–16
property, 47–48
public perception of, 338
"typical" accounts of, 36–37
Crime analysis, 103–17
Crime commissions, 11–12
Crime control efforts, 331. *See also* Crime prevention
  citizens' role in, 13
  evaluation of, 331
Crime control model of policing, 414–15
Crime fighter image, 11
Crime mapping, 107–10, 116
Crime Mapping Research Center (CMRC), 108, 109, 110
Crime potential forecasts, 107
Crime prevention, 122–56
  benefits of, 127
    diffusion of, 145–46
  brief history of, 123–26
  community involvement in, 128–30, 150
  COPPS and, 129, 130–33
  definition of, 122
  displacement of crime and, 144–46
  effective, 146–47
  through environmental design (CPTED), 133–36, 232, 300–301, 352
    situational crime prevention matrix for, 140, 141–42
    successful case studies of, 137–38
  evaluation of, 146–49, 328
  implementation of programs, 143–44
  ineffective, 147–48
  Japanese community-based, 380
  programs with potential, 148–49
  for safe schools, 292
  shifting emphasis toward, 126–28
  situational, 126, 136–43
  successful cities and their methods of, 149–53
Crime Prevention Coalition of America, 122
Crime Prevention Month Celebration, 131
Crime rate
  decrease from 1992–2000, 409
  federal largesse with COPPS and, 408
Crime series/pattern detection, 106
Crime type displacement, 145
Criminal justice system
  crime prevention and, 152–53
  influences on, 17
  minorities and, 253–58
  more discriminate use of, 98
  organizations in need of attention, 66–69
  partners in, 69–73
  systematic approach to, 69–70

Criminologist, street officer as street-level, 103–7
Cruising, 297–99, 300
Cultural differences, awareness of, 260–64
  perplexing scenarios involving, 268–72
  situational crime prevention and, 142
Cultural diversity training, 233–34
Culture in agency, changing, 189–215. *See also* Organizational change
  case studies of, 210–13
  old management style, changing, 196–97
  rank-and-file and customers, organizational role of, 208–10
  recruitment of women and minorities, 264–65
  resistance to, potential for, 197–98
Curfews for youth, 39
Customer orientation of TQM, 62, 64
Customer-oriented government, illustration of, 74–75
Customs Service's Strategic Problem Solving (SPS) initiative, 369
CyberAngels, 43

D

Dallas, Texas, Police Department, citizenship facilitators in, 267–68
Data
  computerized, 311
  survey, 343
Deadbeat parents, using volunteers to track, 56
Deadly force, excessive use of, 256
Death sentences, 260
Debilitating beliefs, 194–96
Decentralization, 7, 8
  decay in rule of law and, 309
  efficiency and, 330
  in Japan, 380
  in Reno, Nevada, 361
  of services in COPPS, 172
  total quality management (TQM) and, 64
Defense, community, 71
Defensible space, 125, 126
Defensive architecture, 135
Deflecting offenders, 139, 141
Delaware State Police Rural Community Policing Unit, 369–70
Delinquency, crime prevention programs to reduce, 150–51
Delray Beach, Florida, COPPS strategies against drug dealing in, 279
Delta, British Columbia, policing video arcades in, 299–301
Deming, W. Edwards, 62, 64, 209
Democratic National Convention in Chicago (1968), 15
Demographics
  changes in, 30–34
  crime trends and, 413–14

generational divide, 33–34
De Montaigne, Michel, 374
Denmark, COPPS in, 402–3
Denver, Colorado, crime reduction methods in, 149, 150–53
Departmental rank structure, in-depth analysis of, 170
Dependent variable, 343
Design, environmental. *See under* Crime prevention
Detectives, COPPS and, 172
Deterioration of neighborhood, impact of, 47
  dealing with, 292–96
"Devil's advocate" position toward COPPS, 306–23
  concerns and criticisms, 306–21
Dickens, Charles, 29
Diffusion of benefits of crime prevention, 145–46
"Digital divide," 34, 35
DiIulio, John J., 307
Discretion, use of, 16, 18, 22
  concern over increased, 313–14
  professionalism and, 11
Discrimination, 8
  in arrest and traffic citation patterns, 255
  reverse, 251
  systematic, study of, 257–58
Displacement of crime, 144–46
Disraeli, B., 249
Distribution of police services/resources, equal, 331
Diverse police department, developing, 264–65
Diversity, community, 249. *See also* Police-minority relations
  as obstacle to COPPS, 182
Diversity training, 233–34
Domestic violence, 288–90
Domestic Violence/Sexual Assault Prevention, 132
Door-to-door surveys, 340
"Driving while black or brown" (DWBB), 253–54
Drucker, Peter F., 77
Drug house activity, chronic, 294
Drugs
  as crime accelerator, 41, 42
  substance abuse programs, 151
  violations, 277–79, 280
DuBois, W.E.B., 250
Dynamic Community Policing System (DCPS), 117

E

Echo boomers (Generation Y), 33
Eck, John E., 87, 88, 90, 101, 145, 184, 187
Effective behavior, defining, 334
Effectiveness, police, 18, 20
  assessing COPPS effectiveness, 328, 329

Effectiveness *(cont.)*
  evaluating overall, 97–99
  myths about measures of, 21
Efficiency, police, 18
  assessing COPPS efficiency, 328, 329–30
  professionalism and emphasis on, 12–13
Effort needed to commit crime, increasing,
      138–39, 141
80/20 Rule, 105
Einstein, Albert, 80, 324
Elderly, the, 30, 32–33
  effects of victimization of, 33
Elected officials, COPPS and, 174–75, 243–44
Elitism, perception of, 165
Elmhurst, Illinois, COPPS initiative in, 367
Emerson, Ralph Waldo, 189
Empowerment, strategies for, 177, 179, 181–82
England. *See* Great Britain, community initia-
      tives in
Entry and exit screening, 139, 141
Environmental design. *See under* Crime pre-
      vention
Environmental scanning, 161–62
Equal access to police service, 331
Equal Employment Opportunity Commission,
      250
Equity in COPPS, assessing, 330–31
Ethics, 409
Etzioni, Amitai, 53
Eugene, Oregon, COPPS initiative in, 357–59
Evaluation
  of crime prevention, 146–49, 328
  processes of, 167
Evaluation measures, 331
Evaluation of COPPS, 324–47
  case studies of, 343–45
  concern over adequacy of, 318–19
  criteria for, 328–31
    effectiveness, 328, 329
    efficiency, 328, 329–30
    equity, 330–31
    old vs. new, 328–29
  by outside evaluator, 327–28
  officer performance, 331–33
  purpose of, 334
  questions addressed by, 326
  rating scale for, 335–36
  reasons for, 326–27
  required for funding, 326
  revising police performance evaluation sys-
      tems, 334
  skills, knowledge, and abilities, 333–36
  surveys for, 336–42
    analyzing data, 343
    community surveys, 338–40, 344–45
    neighborhood, 340–41
    officers, 341–42
Evolution of policing, 1–28
  civil disorders of 1840s to 1870s, 6–7
  community problem solving era, 21–24
  New York model, 4–7
    Peel's early contributions, 2–3
    professional crime fighter model, 12–17
    professionalism, emergence of, 8–9
    reform movement toward, 12
    rewriting police agency history, 24–25
    technology and, 414
    training and overview of, 232
Excessive force, 255–56
Excuses for crime, removing, 140, 142
External relations, COPPS and, 173–75

F

Facial expression, cultural differences in, 263
Facilitator(s)
  of crime, controlling, 139, 141
  shift in management style from controller to,
      167
Fad, concern over COPPS being, 314–15
Failure, rewarding, 68–69
False advertising, 321
False alarms, 299
Family-based crime prevention, 150
Fantino, Julian, 144
Father absence, 30
Fear of crime, 16, 44–46
Federal agencies, COPPS initiatives of, 369
Federal Bureau of Investigation (FBI), 11, 63
Federal Communications Commission, 302
Federal funding, 320–22, 408
Federal Quality Institute, 63
Federal Trade Commission, 43
Felson, Marcus, 125, 136
Fielding, Henry, 2
Fielding, John, 2
Field interrogations, 148
  of minorities, 255
Field operations, COPPS, 171–73
Field tactics, police, 254–57
Field training officer (FTO) program, 170, 222,
      224
Finances, COPPS and, 167
Finland, community policing in, 403
Firearms expertise, 13
First-line supervisors
  as coach and manager, 237–39
  COPPS and, 169
  organizational change and, 201–4
  problem-oriented, 203
Fisher-Stewart, Gayle, 260
Foot Beat/Walk and Talk, 132
Foot patrol, 6, 8, 13, 21, 84
  in Britain, 390
Force, excessive, 255–56
Foreign venues, COPPS in, 374–406
  Australia, 382–90
  Canada, 375–79
  Great Britain, 390–95
  Hong Kong, 398–400
  Isle of Man, 396–97

Israel, 398
Japan, 379–82
Scandinavian countries, 402–3
Scotland, 395–96
Formal surveillance, 139, 141
Fort Collins, Colorado, Community Service
Survey of, 427–35
Fort Lauderdale, Florida
COPPS initiative in, 352
partnerships in Broward Sheriff's Office, 60
Fort Wayne, Indiana, community-oriented
government in, 76
Fort Worth, Texas, crime reduction methods
in, 149, 150–53
Fresno, California, COPPS initiative in,
352–53, 354
Friedmann, Robert, 318
Funding, federal, 320–22, 408
evaluations required for, 326
Future of COPPS, 407–20
demographics and, 413–14
forces influencing, 408–15
implementation, 411–13
learning from the past and, 411
possible changes in, 409–11
questions for the future, 417–18
rank-and-file officers and, 416–17
Fyfe, James, 87
Fynn, Ed, 168

G

Gaebler, Ted, 67–68
Gainesville, Florida, crime prevention through
environmental design in, 137
Gallup Organization, 360–61
Gangs, 279–82
applying COPPS approach to, 279–82
gang offender monitoring, 148
graffiti and, 281–82, 283
identifying harms from, 93
Gatekeepers, lieutenants as, 200–201
Geller, William A., 198
Generalist approach, 171
Generation Y (echo boomers), 33
Gen-X (baby busters), 33
Geographic accountability, 357
Georgetown, Texas, park crime and disorder
in, 424–25
Ghetto, view of police in, 258–59
Gimmick, concern over COPPS being,
314–15
Goal setting, 165
by officers, evaluating, 333
Goldstein, Herman, 22, 69, 81, 84–86, 87, 99,
127–28, 189, 198–99, 202, 292–94, 314,
316
"Gonin-gumi," Japanese tradition of, 380
Governance, need for shift in basic model of,
77–78

Government agencies, other, 98
COPPS education for, 242
problem solving with, 77–78
Gradual vs. radical change, 191–92
Graffiti, 94–95, 281–82, 283
Graft, 313
Grand Rapids, Michigan, COPPS initiative
in, 359
Graying of America, 32–33
Great Britain, community initiatives in,
390–95
problem oriented policing, 390–91
Green Bay, Wisconsin, case study of problem
solving in, 423
Gresham, Oregon, COPPS initiative in, 368
Grinc, Randolph M., 166
Group dynamics, 191
Guardians, 95–96
Gun buyback programs, 147
Guns
as crime accelerator, 41–42
school violence and, 290–92, 293
supply of and demand for, among gangs,
280–81

H

Harassment of minorities by police, 255
Harlem, New York, 71
Harms, identifying, 93
Hartford, Connecticut, crime reduction meth-
ods in, 149, 150–53
Harvard University Police Department
(HUPD), 371
Hate Crime Prevention program, 132
Hate crimes, responding to, 268, 269–70
Hate Crime Statistics Act (1990), 268
Hayward, California, Police Department
COPPS initiative in, 359–60
cultural changes in, 211–12
Herman Goldstein Award for Excellence in Prob-
lem-Oriented Policing awards, 225, 354
Herocleous, Loizos, 158, 160
High technology, new crimes of, 43
Hill, Steven J., 254
Hispanics. *See* Latino/Hispanics
Hobbes, Thomas, 45–46
Holmes, Oliver Wendell, 1
Home detention with electronic monitoring,
148
Homeless, the, 283, 284–86
training to deal with, 285
Homeless Outreach program, 132
Home ownership, trends in, 413–14
Home Safety and Security Surveys, 132
Hong Kong, COPPS in, 398–400
Honolulu Police Department, 193
Hoover, J. Edgar, 11
Hot spots, 117

Housing disorder problems, 292–96
Human resources, COPPS and, 170–71
Huntington Beach, California, 366

I

ICAM, 108
ICCP, 128
Iceberg Rule, 105
Illinois State Police, 109
Immigrants, serving, 266–68
Immigration, influence of, 31–32
Impact measures, 331
Implementation of COPPS, 162–87
  in Baltimore, Maryland, 178, 185
  challenges of, 166
  components of, 167–75, 176
  crime prevention programs, 143–44
  departmentwide vs. experimental district,
    165–67
  external relations, 173–75
  field operations, 171–73
  in future, 411–13
  human resources, 170–71
  leadership and administration, 167–70
  obstacles to, 182–84
Incarceration rates, 44
Incident-driven policing, problem oriented
    policing vs., 86, 87
Independent variable, 343
Indianapolis, Indiana, 327
Individualism vs. clienthood, 52–53
Inducements to crime, removing, 139, 142
Inferences from sample to population, 343
Informal methods outside criminal justice
    system, 17, 18
Informal surveillance, 139, 141
Information
  conveying, 98
  means for imparting new, 220–27
Information Access Guide, 230
Information Collection for Automated Mapping
    (ICAM), 108
Information systems, 167
Information technologies
  haves and have-nots in, 34, 35
  staff, 414
Initiative of officers, evaluating, 335
Inkster, Norman, 411
Innovation. *See* Organizational change;
    Implementation of COPPS
Innovative Neighborhood Oriented Policing
    (INOP), 166, 364–65
In-service training, 170, 222–23
Instrumentation, performance evaluation, 334
Intellectual capacity required by COPPS, con-
    cern about, 315–17
Interactive training, 227–28
Interdepartmental cooperation, 352–53
Internal communication in TQM, 65

International Association of Chiefs of Police
    (IACP), 9, 225
  Crime Prevention Committee, 128
International Centre for Crime Prevention
    (ICCP), 128
International Problem-Oriented Policing
    Conference, 225
Internet, use of, 229–30
Internet crimes, 43. *See also* Computer crime
Intraagency surveys, 341
Isle of Man, COPPS in, 396–97
Israel, COPPS in, 398

J

Jackson Heights, New York, 266–67
Jacksonville, Florida, reduction of crime
    in, 40
Jail populations, impact of, 43–44
James, Jesse, 7
Japan, community oriented policing in, 379–82
  community-based crime prevention, 380
  decentralization of command, 380
  increased accountability to public, 380
  koban, 380–82
  reorientation of patrol activities, 380
Jobs, changes in types of, 34, 35
Job satisfaction, 330, 341
Johnson, Lyndon, 15
Journalism, tabloid, 46
Judgment of officers, evaluating, 333
Justice, restorative, 72, 415
Justice Department, 24
  hate-crime training curriculum, 268
Juvenile crime. *See also* Gangs
  debate over, 38–41
  school-based crime prevention, 150–51
  school violence and, 290–92, 293
  truancy, 424, 425–26
Juveniles
  as victims, 42
  youth population, increase in, 38

K

Kansas City Preventive Patrol Experiment,
    18
Kelling, George, 12, 126, 169, 201
Kennedy, David, 194, 210
Kennedy, John F., 15
Kennedy, Robert F., 15
Kerner Commission, 253
Keystone Cops image, 8
King, Martin Luther, Jr., 15
Klite, Paul, 46
Knowledge, evaluation of, 333–36
Knoxville, Tennessee
  crime prevention through environmental
    design in, 137

Police Department, SCOPE and, 293

Koban, 380–82

Kobun-oyabun (student-mentor relationship), Japanese, 380

L

Labor markets and crime risk factors, 151–52

Labor relations, COPPS and, 171

La Crosse, Wisconsin, case study of problem solving in, 422

Landlords, role of, 294–96

Landscaping, crime prevention and, 135

Language barriers, 262–63

Lapeer County, Michigan, 290

Large communities, American approaches to COPPS in, 348–57

Largo, Florida, addressing domestic violence in, 291

Las Cruces, New Mexico, 72

Las Vegas, community drug court initiatives in, 72

Latino/Hispanics

culture of, 262, 263

disparity in case processing for, 257–58

Law-abiding citizens, failure to protect, 257

Law enforcement agencies, police organizations as, 10

Law Enforcement Assistance Network (LEAN), 119

Law Enforcement Management and Administrative Statistics report, 118

Lawrence, Massachusetts

customer-oriented government in, 75

evaluation of COPPS in, 344–45

Laycock, Gloria, 327–28

Leadership. *See also* Chief executive(s)

of COPPS, 167–70

improving quality of, 416

new style of, 197

as obstacle to COPPS, 182

organizational change and, 199–207

in problem oriented policing (POP) environment, 238

quality, principles of, 67

in Seattle Police Department, 238

in St. Petersburg Police Department, 239

training for COPPS and, 237

LEAN, 119

Learning. *See also* Training; Training for COPPS

on-demand, 227

from the past, 411

Leicestershire, Great Britain, COPPS in, 393

LEMAS survey, 118

Lewin, Kurt, 191–92

Lieutenants, as "gatekeepers," 200–201

Likert scale, 341

Lincoln, Nebraska, COPPS initiative in, 360–61

Line officer. *See* Patrol (rank-and-file) officers

London Metropolitan Police, 390–91, 393

London Times, 3

Long-term commitment in TQM, 64–65

Los Angeles

Police Department, dealing with gangs in, 281

volunteer programs in, 56–57

M

McEwen, Tom, 204

Machismo, 271

McKay, 124

McNally, D.D., 198

Macon, Illinois, 72

Madison, Wisconsin, Police Department

community surveys in, 66

"Principles of Quality Leadership" development by, 67

Maeterlinck, Maurice, 407

Mail surveys, 339–40

Management, strategic, 167

Management style

bureaucratic, 196–97

changing old, 196–97, 416

participative, 23, 191–92

Manager, sergeant as, 237–39

Managers (third party), 96

Mapping, crime, 107–10, 116

Maricopa County, Arizona

corrections initiative in, 72–73

volunteerism in, 56

Marriage, trends in, 413

Maryland, COPPS initiatives in, 372

Mason, Ohio, customer-oriented government in, 74–75

Massachusetts Criminal Justice Training Council, 344

Massage parlors, 297

Master patrol officers, 210

Mead, Margaret, 191

"Means over ends" syndrome, 69

Measurement. *See* Evaluation of COPPS

Measurement in TQM, 65

Media, COPPS and, 173, 244–45

Mediation, 98

gang intervention using, 281

Medium-sized communities, American approaches to COPPS in, 357–65

Meetings, neighborhood, 339

Megan's Law, 72

Mentally ill persons, training in CIAF approach to, 285

"Mental state" of community, 340

Mentoring, community-based, 148

Merseyside, Great Britain, COPPS initiatives in, 394

Method displacement, 145

Metropolitan Police, London, COPPS initiatives in, 390–91, 393

Metropolitan Police Act (England), 2–3

Michigan State University, National Institute on Police and Community Relations (NIPCR) at, 14, 15
Middle managers
COPPS and, 169
organizational change and, 200–201
resistance to change, 198
training for COPPS and, 237
Miller, Henry, 348
Minority groups. *See also* Police-minority relations
access to information technologies, 35
COPPS and, 259–64
involvement with American criminal justice system, 253–58
perception of treatment of, 16
in policing, 264–65
population growth among, 30
systematic discrimination against, study of, 257–58
terms used for, 263–64
Mission statement, 163, 167, 177, 178, 378
Mobile police-boxes in Japan, 381
Mobilization of community, 98, 147
Modeling behaviors, COPPS and, 170
Montgomery County, Maryland, 175–78
Moore, Mark, 12, 194
Moose, Charles A., 341
Morrew, Mark, 210
Mount Pleasant, South Carolina, 164
Multicultural society, training strategy for policing in, 233–34
Municipal Crime Reduction Working Group (MCRWG), 149–53
Myers, Richard, 249
Myths about measures of police effectiveness, 20

N

Naperville, Illinois, Police Department, 418
Nassau County, New York, policing prostitution in, 297
National Academy of Sciences, 252
National Advisory Commission on Civil Disorders, 15
National Advisory Commission on Criminal Justice Standards and Goals, 15
National Advisory Commission on the Causes and Prevention of Violence, 15
National Conference of Christians and Jews (NCCJ), 14
National Crime Prevention Council (NCPC) of Washington, D.C., 149
National Crime Victim Survey (NCVS), 37
National Institute of Justice, 89, 108, 110, 166, 173, 292, 319, 327, 361
National Institute on Police and Community Relations (NIPCR) at Michigan State University, 14, 15
National Night Out, 132

National Police Chiefs Union, 9
National Prison Association, 8, 12
National Problem Oriented Policing Conference, 356
Native American culture, 263, 264
Natural access control, 133
Naturalization, program helping with, 267–68
Natural surveillance, 133, 135, 139, 141
Needs assessment
community, 161–62
for training, 219–20
"Negotiated" policing, 317
Negotiation teams, 98
Neighborhood Advisory Groups (NAGs), 361–62
Neighborhood Defender Service (NDS), 71
Neighborhood disorder problems, 292–96
fear of crime and, 45
impact of deterioration on, 47
police role in, 292–94
Neighborhood District Attorney (NDA), 70–71
Neighborhood meetings, 339
Neighborhood Policing Restructuring Project, 356
Neighborhood surveys, 340–41
Neighborhood Watch, 125, 143, 147, 278, 356, 392
New approach, time for, 20
Newman, Kenneth, 390–91
Newman, Oscar, 125, 126
New Orleans, Louisiana, mobile crisis service in, 284
Newport News, Virginia, Police Department, problem solving model designed by, 89–99
Newsletters, police, 148
New vision statement, 167
New York City
crime reduction in, 40, 149, 150–53
Police Department (NYPD), 21, 40, 107
CompStat program, 108
zero-tolerance movement in, 319–21
policing prostitution in, 296
New York model, 4–7
New Zealand, COPPS in, 400–401
Nicolosi, Dick, 1
Nila, Michael J., 321
911 calls, 206
nonemergency, 302
Noncausal relationship, 343
Nonverbal communication, 263, 271
Northumbria, Great Britain, COPPS initiatives in, 393
Norway, community initiatives in, 402

O

Objectives, setting COPPS, 165
Offer, Chris, 318

Office of Community Oriented Policing Services (COPS), 24, 118, 219, 222, 225, 226, 319, 321, 327, 408, 414
Office of Community Policing Services, 302
Office of Juvenile Justice and Delinquency Prevention, 41
Office of Strategic Problem Solving, 369
Officer performance evaluations, 331–33
Officer surveys, 341–42
Olson, Robert K., 260, 262
On-demand learning, 227
On-line training, 227
Ontario Provincial Police (OPP), 377
Operation Weed and *Seed*, 332–33
Opportunity for crime, 125
    situational crime prevention and, 138
Orange County, Florida, COPPS initiative in, 368–69
Organizational change, 190–91
    case studies of, 210–13
    first-line supervisors and, 201–4
    leadership and, 199–207
    middle managers and, 200–201
    ownership and, 209–10
    ownership as prescription for, 209–10
    planned, 191–94
    prevailing police culture and, 194–97
    recruitment and, 208–10
    resistance to, 190–91
    time constraints and, 198–99
Organizational structure
    flattening of, 416
    of future, 410
Organizational values as obstacle to COPPS, 182
Osborne, David, 67–68
Outcome measures, 331
Ownership, organizational change and, 209–10

P

Parnas, Raymond I., 17
Participative management, 23, 191–92
Partnerships with community, 55–59, 82, 329
    examples of, 60–62
    in future, 412–13
Patrol activities in Japan, reorientation of, 380
Patrol cars, 11, 13
    two-person vs. one-person, 16
Patrol (rank-and-file) officers
    high status for, 210
    master, 210
    organization role of, 208–10
    ownership and, 209–10
    as problem solver, 88, 208–9
    support for, 172–73
    surrendering power in future to, 416–17
    temperament of, concern about, 315–17
Paulding County, Georgia, 76
Peace model of policing, 415

Peel, Robert, 2–3, 4, 16, 68, 81, 122, 128, 322, 407
"Peel's Principles" of policing, 3, 4
Perception
    of COPPS, survey on, 342
    of crime, public, 338
PERF, 16, 89, 110, 225, 230, 238, 356
Performance criteria, 334
Performance evaluation systems. *See* Evaluation of COPPS
Permanent officer assignment, 361
Perpetrator displacement, 145
Personalization of service, 21
Philadelphia, services to immigrants in, 266–67
Phoenix, Arizona, volunteer programs in, 56–57
Physical disorder, fear of, 45
Physical environment alteration, to reduce opportunities for problems, 98
Physical force, excessive use of, 255–56
Planned change, 191–94
    "bombshell" technique, avoiding, 193
    of organizational values, 193–94
    radical vs. gradual, 191–92
Planning, 157–65
    issues in, 163–65
    needs assessment and, 161–62
    by officers, evaluating, 333
    participants in, 160–61
    planning document, 162–65
    strategic, 158–62
Plea bargaining, 257
Police
    proper role for
        constables in Great Britain, 392–93
        debate over, 309–11
        Scandinavian theory of, 402
    public perceptions of, 252–53
    view of public, 252–53
Police-community relations, 8, 13–15
    community policing vs. programs of, 82
Police Executive Research Forum (PERF), 16, 89, 110, 225, 230, 238, 356
Police field tactics, police-minority tensions and, 254–57
Police Foundation, 16
Police-minority relations, 249–75
    balancing crime strategies and democratic principles, 260, 261–62
    changing laws and civil unrest, 250–52
    complicating factors and possible solutions, 258–59
    confronting issues in, 259–60
    COPPS and, 259–64
    hate crimes, responding to, 268, 269–70
    history of conflict in, 250–53
    perplexing scenarios in, 268–72
    sources of tension in, 253–57
    successful initiatives, 265–68
Police performance evaluation systems, revising, 334

Police reports, 110
Police studies, 11–12
Policewomen's movement, 12
Policies and procedures, analysis of existing, 169–70
Policing a Free Society (Goldstein), 84
Policing for prevention, 152
Policing models, 414–15
Political era, 7–8
Political leadership as obstacle to COPPS, 182
Political machines, 5
Political neutrality of police, issue of, 311–12
Political support for COPPS, 173–75
Politicians, COPPS education for, 243–44
POPNet, 230
POP TRACK, 119
Population (survey), inferences from sample to, 343
Portland, Oregon
   alcohol-related crime in, 286–88
   cruising in, dealing with, 299
   drug dealing in, COPPS strategies against, 280
   landlord training in, 294–96
   partnerships in, 60
   strategic plan survey in, 436–38
Pound, Ron, 198
Presentence investigation (PSI) indicators of recidivism, 257
President's Commission on Campus Unrest, 15
President's Commission on Law Enforcement and the Administration of Justice, 15–16, 255
President's Information Technology Advisory Committee, 35
Prevention. *See* Crime prevention
Preventive patrol, 21
Prison populations, impact of, 43–44
Pritchett, Price, 198
Private policing, 17
Private services, connecting with, 98
Proactive action, survey on, 342
Proactive arrests, 148
Problem
   determining extent of, 92
   identification of, 90–92, 117
Problem analysis, COPPS and, 101–3
Problem analysis triangle, 93–95, 96
Problem-Oriented Policing (Goldstein), 84
Problem oriented policing (POP), 84–99
   basic principles of, 86–88
   defining "problem," 90
   early beginnings of, 84–86
   in Great Britain, 390–91
   leadership and supervision in POP environment, 238
   problem solving model for, 89–99
   view of line officer in, 88
Problem Resolution Team (PRT) in Lincoln, Nebraska, 360
Problem solving, 235–37. *See also* Community oriented government

in British Columbia, 379
   case studies in, 421–26
   collaborative, 233
   communitarianism and, 53–54
   implementing, 166
   methods of, 205–6
   with other government agencies, 77–78
   partnerships for, 57–59
   by patrol officer, 88, 208–9
   recapturing officers' time for, 204–7
   risk taking and, 180
   strategies, 183–84
   training in, 235–36
Problem solving case studies, 421–26
Problem solving exercises, 236–37
Problem solving model. *See* S.A.R.A. problem solving model
Problem solving tracking and resource system (POP TRACK), 119
Process measures, 331
Professionalism
   bureaucracy of policing and, 197
   emergence of, 8–9
   fundamental ambiguities of notion of, 10
   problems with, 15–17
   professional crime fighter model, 12–17
Prohibition, 11
Promotion systems, 170
Property, crimes against, 47–48
Property identification, 139, 142
Prosecution, community, 70–71
Prostitution, 296–97
Public expectations, survey on, 342
Public housing, policing problems in, 292–96
Public information officer (PIO), 244–45
Public opinion surveys, 338
Public perception of crime, 338
Public safety, concern over COPPS and maintenance of, 309–10
Public service, 12

Q

Quality leadership, principles of, 67
Quality of life
   assessing improved, 329, 330
   property crimes and, 47–48
Quality Service Audit in Lincoln, Nebraska, 360–61
Queensland, Australia, 382–90
Questionnaire, survey, 339–40

R

Race riots, 250–51
Racial profiling, 253–54
Racism. *See also* Minority groups; Police-minority relations
   justice system and, 253–58
   racial profiling and, 253–54

Radelet, Louis, 13–15
Radical vs. gradual change, 191–92
Rainbow Coalition, 252
RAND Corporation, studies on racism, 255, 257–58
Rank-and-file officers. *See* Patrol (rank-and-file) officers
Rating scales, 334
  for evaluating COPPS, 335–36
Rational choice theory, 125, 136
Recidivism, presentence investigation (PSI) indicators of, 257
Recruit academy, 221–22
Recruitment, 208–12
  of minorities, 264–65
  organizational change and, 208–10
Reform
  in late 1800s and early 1900s, 9–12
  from 1940s through 1960s, 12–13
  as reaction to partisan politics, 8
Reform movement, 9–12
Regional community policing institutes (RCPIs), 24, 226–27
Regional Community Policing Training Institute at Wichita State University, 219
Regulation of conditions contributing to problems, 98
Reiss, Albert, 17, 47
Reno, Nevada
  community surveys in, 66
  Police Department
    COPPS initiative in, 361–62, 363
    field training officer program, 222
Rental properties, neighborhood disorder and, 292–96
Repeat call analysis, 110–16
Representative sample, 343
Research on police work, 17–20
Resistance to change, 190–91
Resistance to COPPS, potential for, 197–98
Response, police
  delay in, 254–55
  response time to calls, 18, 206
Response options in S.A.R.A., 96–97, 98–99
Response time, 18, 206
Responsibilities of citizens, 53–54
Restorative justice, 72, 415
Reverse discrimination, 251
Rewards and recognition, TQM and, 65
Rewards of crime, reducing, 139, 142
Richmond, Virginia
  city employee police academy training in, 244
  corrections initiative in, 73
  crime prevention through environmental design in, 137–38
Riots, 6–7, 250–51
Risks associated with crime, increasing, 139, 141
Risk takers, chief executives as, 199–200
Rochester, New York, 129

Rockland County, New York, diversity training in, 234
Role of police, survey on, 341
Roll-call training, 223–24
Routine activity theory, 125
Royal Canadian Mounted Police, 376, 378
Rule of law, concern over COPPS impact on, 309
Rural community policing, 369–70

S

S.A.R.A. problem solving process, 90–99, 317, 319, 326
  analysis, 92–96
  assessment, 97–99
  response, 96–97, 98–99
  scanning, 90–92
  training in, 235–37, 238
  use of, 292, 364
Sabotage, 198
Sacramento, California, neighborhood services in, 174, 175
Sadd, Susan, 166
Safe Haven, 132
St. Petersburg, Florida, 327
  Police Department, COPPS in, 239, 355–56
  reaching out to mentally ill in, 285
St. Louis, Missouri, COPPS initiative in, 353–55
St. Louis County Police Department, 75–76
Salinas, California, Police Department, 109
Salvation Army Intervention Program, 286
Sample, inferences from, 343
San Antonio, Texas, COPPS in, 350
San Antonio Fear Free Environment (SAFFE), 350
San Diego, California
  COPPS initiative in, 356–57
    homeless-related crimes and, 287
  crime rate in, 40–41, 320–21
  crime reduction methods in, 149, 150–53
  Police Department, 40
  school truancy in, 425–26
San Mateo, California, gang violence in, 281
Santa Ana, California, control of cruising in, 300
Santa Barbara, California
  apartment complex crime in, 294, 295
  citizens' police academies in, 243
Santa Clara, California, Police Department, 199
Savannah, Georgia
  COPPS initiative in, 362–63
    training program, 245–46
  field training officer program, 224
Scandinavian countries, COPPS in, 402–3
Scanning in S.A.R.A., 90–92
"Scared Straight" programs, 148
School-based crime prevention, 150–51

School truancy problems, case studies of, 424, 425–26
School violence, 290–92, 293
Scientific theory of administration, 10–11
SCOPE, 293
Scotland, COPPS in, 395–96
Seattle, Washington, Police Department
 leadership, 238
 Strategic Planning document, 163
"Seeding" strategies, 332
Sentences, 258
Sergeant, role of, 201–2, 237–39
Shaw, 124–25
Shock probation or parole, 148
Single-parent homes, 30
Situational crime prevention, 126, 136–43
Situational Crime Prevention (Clarke), 138
Skills, COPPS, 333–36
Skolnick, Jerome, 17, 253, 379
Small communities, American approaches to
 COPPS in, 365–69
"Small wins," seeking, 93
Social control, making use of existing forms of,
 98
"Social disorganization," 124
Social problems, 276–305
 alcohol-related crime, 286–88, 423
 cruising, 297–99, 300
 domestic violence, 288–90
 drug violations, 277–79, 280
 false alarms, 299
 gangs, 279–82, 283
 housing and neighborhood disorder problems,
  292–96
 incurable, concern over COPPS effectiveness
  against, 312–13
 prostitution, 296–97
 special populations, 282–88
 teen hangouts in video arcades, 299–301
Social service organizations, COPPS education
 for, 242–43
Social services of police, 7, 8–9
Social workers, police as, 8–9, 12
Societal stability, demographic trends and, 413
Society of Police Futurists, 419
Software for COPPS, 117–18, 119
Southeast Asian immigrants
 culture of, 263
 outreach programs to, 266–67
Southeastern Community Oriented Policing
 Education Institute (SCOPE), 293
Southern Christian Leadership Conference, 252
Sparrow, Malcolm K., 194, 210
Spatial displacement, 145
Specialist approach, 171
Specialized training, 225–27
Special populations, 282–88
Spelman, William, 87, 88, 90, 95, 106
Split sentences, 148
Spokane, Washington, COPPS initiative in,
 363–64

Squad structure of future, 410
State police, COPPS initiatives of, 369–70
Statewide level COPPS, 372
Statistics on crime rate, 87
Stephens, Darrel, 89
Storefront police offices, 148
Strategic crime analysis, 103
Strategic management, 167
Strategic partnerships, 57
Strategic planning, 158–62
 basic elements, 158–60
 environmental scanning and, 161–62
 evaluation and, 326
 planning cycle, 160–61
Strategic plan survey, 436–38
Strategic thinking, 158
Strategies, selecting COPPS, 165
Street-level criminology, 103
Street officer. *See* Patrol (rank-and-file) officers
Studies of police work, 17–20
Substance abuse programs, 151
"Suicide by cop," 283
Supervision
 intensive, on parole or probation, 148
 in problem oriented policing (POP) environment, 238
Supervisors. *See* First-line supervisors
Support personnel, COPPS training for,
 240–41
Surrey Constabulary, Great Britain, COPPS in,
 393
Surveillance
 formal, 139, 141
 informal, 139, 141
 natural, 133, 135, 139, 141
Surveys
 to assess training needs, 219, 220
 community, 66, 74, 117, 338–40, 344–45,
  427–35
 of COPPS training nationally, 217
 for crime analysis, 117
 for evaluating COPPS, 336–42
 goals of, 339
 LEMAS, 118
 neighborhood, 340–41
 officer, 341–42
 strategic plan, 436–38
Suspect-crime correlations, 106
Suspect profiles, 107
Swanger, Guy, 198
Swanson, Charles R., 192
Sweden, policing in, 402
Systematic discrimination against minorities,
 study of, 257–58
Systematic underenforcement of law, 257

T

Tabloid journalism, effect of, 46
Tactical crime analysis, 103

Tailor-made strategies, formulating, 96–97
Tampa, Florida, partnerships in, 61
Target displacement, 145
Target hardening, 135, 139, 141
Target profiles, 106–7
Target removal, 139, 142
Taylor, Frederick, 10
Taylor, Robert W., 192
Team policing, 21, 23, 317
Teamwork in TQM, 65
Technology(ies)
    computer crime and, 43, 413
    future of policing business and, 414, 419
    information, 34, 35, 414
    training, 227–28, 229–30
Telephone surveys, 339–40
Tempe, Arizona
    crime prevention through environmental
        design in, 133–35
    Neighborhood Assistance Office in, 174–75
    Police Department
        community survey by, 117
        COPPS initiative, 364–65
        Crime Analysis Unit, 110, 111–15
Temperament of officers, concern about,
    315–17
Temporal displacement, 145
Territo, Leonard, 192
Territorial reinforcement, 133
Thames Valley, Great Britain, COPPS initia-
    tives in, 393
Third parties, role in problem solving, 95–96
311 call system, 302
Thurston County, Washington, 72
Timelines, setting, 165
Time management by officers, evaluating, 333
Together for a Safer Campus, 132
Tongans, culture of, 263
Toowoomba, Australia, pilot COPPS project in,
    385–90
Topeka, Kansas, dealing with cruising in, 299
Total quality management (TQM), 59–66, 167,
    344
    definition and rationalization, 59–64
    illustration of, 75
    principal elements of, 64–66
Tourist Oriented Police Service (TOPS) pro-
    gram, 368–69
Traffic citations, discriminatory patterns of,
    253–54
Traffic Stop Statistics Study Act, 254
Training, 170
    to deal with the homeless, 285
    landlord, 294–96
    TQM and, 65
Training for COPPS, 216–48
    academy, 170, 221–22
    assessing needs for, 219–20
    categories of, 220–27
    challenge of, 217–19
    components, 228–32

computer-assisted, 223
diversity training, 233–34
field training officer (FTO) program, 170,
    222, 224
in-service, 222–23
objectives of, 228–32
other considerations in, 240–45
in problem solving, 235–37
processes needed, 219
purpose of, 228
roll-call, 223–24
sample training programs, 245–46
specialized, 225–27
survey of national, 217
Training technologies, 227–28, 229–30
Truancy, case studies on, 424, 425–26
Tumin, Zachary, 277
Turn Off the Violence initiative, 132
Twain, Mark, 216
Two-way radios, impact of, 11

U

Underclass, street crimes in future and, 413
Underenforcement of law, systematic, 257
Uniform Crime Reports, 244
Unions, police, 12
    COPPS and, 171
    rise of militant unionism, 16
United States, changes occurring in, 30–48
    demographics and jobs, 30–34
    fear of crime, 44–46
    graying of America, 32–33
    juvenile crime debate, 38–41
    nature of crime, changing, 34–44
    new "common wisdom" of policing, 17–18
U.S. Holocaust Memorial Museum, 267
Universities, COPPS initiatives of, 370–71
University of Maryland Department of Crimi-
    nology and Criminal Justice, crime pre-
    vention evaluations by, 146–49
University of Nevada, Reno, 228
University of Tennessee's Institute for Public
    Service, 293

V

Values in policing, changing, 193–94
Values statement, 165, 167
Vancouver, Canada, COPPS initiative in,
    376–77, 379
Variables, 343
Vaughn, Jerald R., 207
Verbal abuse, 255
Video arcades, 299–301
Violence
    civil disorder wave of 1840s to 1870s, 6–7
    decline in, 34–38
    domestic, 288–90

Violence *(cont.)*
  gang, 279–82
  school, 290–92, 293
  youth. *See* Youth violence
Violent Crime Control and Law Enforcement
    Act of 1994, 24, 408
Visalia, California, Police Department, 75
Vision statement, 163, 177
Vollmer, August, 9–10, 322
Voltaire, 80
Volunteerism, 54–55
  examples of, 56–57

W

Walker, Samuel, 21, 251–52, 308
Washington, D.C., Metropolitan Police Depart-
    ment, 267
Washington State Institute for Community
    Oriented Policing (WSICOP), 364
Web sites, use of, 129
Weed and Seed initiative, 132
"Weeding" strategies, 332
Weick, Karl, 93
Westley, William, 17, 252–53
West Mercia, policing in, 391
West Yorkshire, Great Britain, COPPS in, 393
"We-versus-them" attitude, 143

Wichita State University, Regional Community
    Policing Training Institute at, 219
Wickersham Commission (1931), 11
Williams, Willie, 233
Wilson, James Q., 17, 126, 200, 253, 307
Wilson, O.W., 11–12
Women
  domestic violence and, 288–90
  policewomen's movement, 12
Work activities, survey on, 342
Workload during shift, 204, 205
Work teams of future, 410

Y

Youth gangs. *See* Gangs
Youth population, increase in, 38
Youth violence
  gangs, 279–82, 283
  homicides, 280–81
  juvenile crime debate, 38–41
  multistate program to prevent, 293
  school violence, 290–92, 293

Z

Zero-tolerance movement, 319–21, 328